# OOH-AAH
## The Bob Booker Story

## Greville Waterman

BENNION KEARNY

Published by Bennion Kearny Limited
6 Woodside
Churnet View Road
Oakamoor
ST10 3AE

www.BennionKearny.com

Back Cover photograph courtesy of Paul Vernon

# ABOUT GREVILLE WATERMAN

I have been a Brentford supporter for around 50 years and have written a few books about the club before I decided to become a bit more ambitious, and thankfully Bob Booker agreed when I asked him if he would like me to write his biography.

I owned a sponsorship consultancy for many years, worked in London and New York, and now teach Autogenic Therapy, a Mind/Body relaxation technique that helps people who are suffering from anxiety, stress and mild depression (please visit www.howtobeatstress.co.uk).

I am a Trustee of a couple of organisations and am constantly looking for fresh challenges that will ideally stretch, challenge and entertain me. I have just been introduced to gardening and am starting to dabble.

I am married to the beautiful portrait artist, Miriam, whose creativity and talent take my breath away and we both take massive pride and joy in the accomplishments of our two children Nick and Rebecca. I dedicate this book to the three of them, as well as to the memory of my parents and Mim's beloved Grandmother.

This book is published by Bennion Kearny and my thanks and eternal gratitude go to James Lumsden-Cook who has now put up with me and my angst for three books.

# CHAPTERS

# FOREWORD

I knew of Bob Booker because of his reputation as a footballer in our area. In fact, Bob and I lived in the next but one street from one another. I had always looked up to him from a very young age, not just because he was so much taller than me (in fact he was so tall the council saved money by getting Bob to change the light bulbs in the street lamps) but mainly because he was such a gentleman and an exceptional footballer.

I didn't realise just how good he was until I was asked to play alongside him in a midweek reserve match for Brentford against Southend Utd. I knew then that this man was destined to have a career in our glorious game. I played as a winger with Bob doing his thing in the middle. We combined well together, and I scored a goal and was signed for the rest of the season, and that is when the Booker/Walsh relationship properly took off.

We enjoyed so many laughs and great times, and although my path has gone in a different direction, our friendship has lasted the test of time. We've spent riotous holidays together, and I couldn't think of a nicer person to spend my time with.

In fact, he is the epitome of the quintessential professional – aside from his feet. I've never in my life seen such big feet! And he's so skinny too! If he had holes up his back, he'd make a good flute. With his feet at ten to two and his skinny torso, it looked like some labourer had abandoned his pickaxe. Anyway, I digress.

Back in the day, we had proper personalities, not like now where footballers are more interested in looking at themselves on the jumbotrons and making sure that their hair is perfectly groomed.

Bill Dodgin was our manager at Brentford and he encouraged us to go out of our way to play positively, and above all, entertain the crowd and enjoy ourselves.

Bob always used to ask me to do either my Worzel Gummidge or Norman Wisdom impression. Now that may seem normal as a passing comment in the pub, but this was when we were marking up at corners!

Our coach, Tommy Baldwin, used to ask what we found so funny during the game, and we'd tell him that I was on the post doing my Norman Wisdom shouting, "Mark him Mr. Grimsdale, mark him."

# FOREWORD

Tommy would just look at us and say nothing because he thought we were joking!

I loved playing at Fratton Park and I remember coming home on the coach after getting whacked 5-0 by Pompey in a reserve match in 1979, and despite losing by that whopping score, I played out of my skin and had a cracker of a game. In fact, I should have got a medal after the shift I put in.

Anyway, some of the boys were playing cards and I decided to do some entertaining, and I was going down well. Just then Bill Dodgin decided to come and sit next to me, "Bradley," he said as he settled in, "Well played, you were our only shining light tonight." "Thanks Bill." He then continued, "Do you know why you are at this club?" I said, "Is it because I'm a hard worker and I'm willing to learn from the best?" He replied, "No, it is because you keep the lads' morale up." He got up, leaving me speechless and went back to the front of the bus!

That was one of the proudest moments in my footballing career, and, don't forget I'd been a youth player at Watford, played for Barnet alongside the great Jimmy Greaves, and also had a short spell at Almeria in the Spanish second division. In fact, my career was so short I only had time to put on one boot.

Anyway, my proudest moment at Brentford was sitting in the stand at Griffin Park with Paul Walker and watching the triumphant return to the club of Bob Booker after he'd been on loan to Barnet. We were playing Hull City and we beat them 7-2, and the great Bobby B notched a hat trick. Paul Walker and I were so overcome by emotion and excitement. We hugged and kissed each other so much during the game that we almost got engaged.

That was it! That was the defining moment in the career of the legend that is the Great OOH-AAH BOB BOOKAH! Afterwards, in the players' lounge, Bob said, "Walshy, I felt great out there and I could have scored another hat trick." I replied, "You might have done so had it not been for those bloody great big feet of yours, now get them in." Which of course, being the gentleman he is, he duly did, although he couldn't get anywhere near the bar because of those huge feet of his.

I really hope you love this book, as it's a true story of a true gent.

Lots of love.

**Bradley Walsh (size 8½)**

# PREFACE

We were away in Majorca last year when I received an e-mail from someone asking if they could write a book about me. At first, I thought it was a joke, but quickly realised it was for real.

The person concerned was lifelong Brentford fan, Greville Waterman. We met up and decided to go for it. I can't thank Greville enough for all his hard work, patience and skill, especially in having to listen to me and my stories for hours on end, and somehow turning everything into readable prose! It has been a long journey and this project would never have happened without him and we have become firm friends.

I am very flattered that Greville thought there was enough interesting stuff about me to fill a book, and I am grateful to you too for wanting to read it. I lost my dad a few years ago, but I know that he would have been so proud, as he was my biggest fan, and he would say to me, "You've done real good, boy."

I wish he was still alive to read it, sitting on our terrace in Majorca, where he spent so many happy hours with us.

I want to dedicate this book to my dad, all my family and close buddies, but more than anything, to my wonderful wife, Nicky, who is my soulmate and has made my life complete.

**Bob Booker**

# INTRODUCTION

Like so many boys before and after me, I spent much of my childhood dreaming of becoming a professional footballer. Sadly, my unrealistic hopes of football fame and fortune received a firm reality check and turned to dust one disastrous and unforgettable autumn's day, way back in 1972.

I was a decent enough young goalkeeper who had played at a reasonable level for Corinthian Casuals, and also had trials for the Great Britain Maccabi Games team. But I was small and a bit frail and, truth be told, a bit too keen on self-preservation. That autumn day I was totally unprepared and unable to cope with the strength and physicality of the Scotland international striker Hugh Curran, who turned my trial at Oxford United into a personal nightmare.

He bashed me around unceremoniously throughout the entire interminable morning, and then thumped 20-yard howitzers past me that I barely saw. I was actually grateful that I hadn't got a touch to them as they whistled past me like Napoleonic cannonballs. Many years after the event I can still picture his vast frame looming over me as he yet again shook off my feeble challenge to head the ball into the net.

In truth, he did me a great favour by totally disabusing me of any misconception that I could compete at this level.

I learned the hard way about the gaping chasm in ability, speed of thought and fitness between a talented amateur and a seasoned professional. That day taught me total respect – and awe, for the 27,938 footballers who were talented enough to have played in post-war English League and Cup football by the end of the 2016/17 season.

I would have given almost anything to even join the ranks of the 2,146 who played only once, or who made a brief and fleeting appearance as a substitute. But it wasn't to be.

This book is my attempt to pay tribute to – and recognise the achievements of – one of the magnificent 27,938: a man who, unlike me and the millions of others who have shared my thwarted ambition, never even dreamed of becoming a professional footballer as a child, so implausible and unrealistic a journey did it appear to him.

# INTRODUCTION

Despite never imagining where his future would lie, Bob Booker enjoyed a professional football career spanning almost five decades, playing 379 times for Brentford and Sheffield United. He was one of only 4,243 footballers to play over 300 games since 1945, before enjoying a long and successful spell in coaching and management with Brighton & Hove Albion where, unusually, he worked for six different managers.

His has been a rollercoaster career. Bob has shared the triumph of promotion at all three clubs, and the despair of relegation. He worked hard, gave his all, played wherever he was asked without complaint, wore every shirt apart from the goalkeeper's, and was rewarded by playing or coaching in all four divisions of the Football League. He also captained his Sheffield United team in their glory days, rising from the Third Division to the First in consecutive seasons.

As a player, he enjoyed many good days when his team won and he played well, and endured just as many terrible ones when he was substituted or dropped, boos ringing down from the terraces. He also knew the misery of suffering long-term, serious and chronic injuries that threatened to end his career prematurely. He eventually had to deal with the stress, disappointment and nagging reality of coping with the fact that he could no longer play the game he loved, and having to decide what to do with the rest of his life.

Where Bob differs from so many others who have had long and successful careers in the game is that it is impossible to find anyone – manager, coach, director, scout, physio, player, journalist or fan – who has a bad word to say about him. Indeed, he is still revered at all three clubs he was associated with. He remains a particular hero at Sheffield United, for reasons we will discover.

In truth, it is not difficult to explain why, as Bob always played with a smile on his face. He never forgot that it was a privilege for him to be a professional footballer. He was, according to a former teammate, Gary Phillips, "As fit as a butcher's dog." Bob always gave everything to the team, sacrificing his own ambitions for the common good; he chased lost causes, never moaned or gave up, and always showed total commitment. Sheffield legend Derek Dooley summed him up perfectly when he described Bob as, "One of those players with the capacity to make marvellous use of modest talents."

Fans could identify with him because he played the way that they surely would have done had they ever been good enough to be given the opportunity.

Everyone who has ever met or had dealings with Bob likes, admires and respects him. He has time for everybody, and never fails to acknowledge just how fortunate he has been.

So how did an apprentice upholsterer from Watford reach these heights in the game as footballer, coach and assistant manager, and why, as Sheffield United author and historian John Garrett recalls, is Bob Booker, "Remembered with awe and a smile?"

Let's join him on his remarkable journey and find out.

Greville and Bob

# CHAPTER 1
# IN THE BEGINNING

It is all too easy to ignore Watford, or dismiss it as a London feeder overspill, as you drive north up the M1 motorway from the capital. But that would be a mistake; Watford is a bustling and vibrant town, home to over 90,000 people, with a long and proud history.

In the 1920s, Watford was the biggest printing centre in the world: Odhams Press dominated. In the first two post-war decades, Watford was also the home of leading British designer furniture manufacturer, Hille. We will return to these two businesses.

Sport has played an important part in the town's history and Watford now boasts a Premier League football team. But for many years after the Second World War they were perennial lower league strugglers playing in a ramshackle stadium, before the glorious Graham Taylor and Elton John era started the club on its eventual rise to its current giddy heights.

Geri Halliwell, Vinnie Jones, Henry Wood, Terry Scott, Gareth Southgate and Bradley Walsh were born there, two of whom briefly played parts in Bob Booker's story.

Garston is a busy suburb of Watford, an eclectic mix of drab estates, leafy avenues and one of the first drive-thru McDonald's in the country. John Albert Booker and his wife, Brenda Grace, moved there with her parents, having met as teenagers in Alton, Hampshire, when John was serving as a wartime military policeman. Much against her father's wishes, Brenda had moved to Alton, joining the Women's Land Army after being bombed out of Portsmouth.

For nearly 70 years, John and Brenda made a home at 5, Queenswood Crescent in Garston, one of the first houses built on a new estate surrounded by open fields. They formed a tight and close-knit team, with John the reliable, calm, good-natured and selfless backbone of the relationship. After leaving the army, he joined Odhams, working for a time as a printer. But his real gift was with his hands, doing almost anything well. Self-employment gave John happiness, learning the basic skills of plumbing, painting and decorating and car maintenance.

Everyone living on the estate knew him: he was in great demand with his neighbours whenever a household task needed doing.

Brenda worked as a waitress in Watford, firstly at The Bodinia and then Clements restaurant, then part-time in a sweet shop on their estate. A gifted cook, she made wonderful homemade cakes and bread pudding, providing an important additional source of income for her son in later life.

Their first child, Tina, was born in 1955. On the 25th of January 1958, the family was completed when a son, Bob, was born.

Customarily for the time, the proud, expectant father had been kicked out of the family home to await the birth. The arrival of a child was definitely women's work; men were neither needed nor welcomed, so John was sent away to watch a local football match. But his timing was slightly awry, leaving the game only to find the midwife at the top of the stairs on his return home. "Mr. Booker, your wife is just about to have her baby," she said. "Do you want to see the birth?"

"Yes I'd love to," he replied, after some thought. But just as he put his foot on the bottom stair, Brenda let out a roar akin to that of a wounded buffalo, causing John to decide on discretion as the greater part of valour. Having listened patiently to the football results downstairs, he headed up the stairs soon after his son was born.

Bob's dad was his exemplar, inspiration and frequent companion. Money was tight but the family was loving and supportive, indulging his whims whenever possible. "We had different groups of friends," recalls the youngest member of the household. "Tina had all her girlfriends around, who played Motown music. When my mates came round we played rock and roll, so there was always music playing. It was an open house – my parents made everyone welcome – and my mum would cook them all bacon sandwiches."

Music played a formative part in Bob's teenage, life. He was a fan of glam rock, a fact that perhaps he should have kept to himself. "I liked Gary Glitter, The Sweet and Mott The Hoople, but my favourite was Alice Cooper because of his costumes and, of course, the snakes."

In time, Bob's musical tastes expanded. The Who and Def Leppard – both important in his life – became particular favourites: he has seen Pete Townshend and Co 58 times. "I follow The Who around the world," confesses Bob. "When I went to Sheffield United, I met Def Leppard's vocalist, Joe Elliott. He was a Blade. We hit it off straight away and became good friends, and he gave me a platinum disc of 'Hysteria' for my first wedding present." This caused a problem. "What do you give a rock star in return? I gave him a framed Sheffield United number 4 shirt. He put it up above his bed, so I managed to get it right."

It was a shared love for The Who that led to Bob meeting Tony Bates. "I went into 'Past and Present Records' in Watford one day and bought 'Live at Leeds' by The Who, and I met Tony outside. He asked me what I had in my bag. I said, 'You won't like it' and pulled out the record. He said, 'I like The Who – why don't you come back to my house and we can have some lunch and play the record?' Forty years later we are still best buddies. Tony, his parents, Pat and Pete, Derek Holt and Robert Barlow remain my closest friends to this day."

Sport played an important part in Bob's life from his schooldays, but he never seriously imagined making a career out of it. Running was an obsession. "All I wanted to do was PE. My attention was entirely on sport. I wasn't interested in anything else." A friend, Peter Bonnick, did his maths homework. "But I was good at practical subjects, like woodwork and technical drawing, and I helped Peter with them in return; they were the only subjects I got qualifications in."

Like father, like son.

Bob was a lanky beanpole who had totally outgrown his strength. He was the school cross-country and 800 metres champion. "That was my distance, as it was all about stamina and endurance, and I always had a sprint finish in me." He ran for Hertfordshire, and his claim to fame was qualifying for the AAA Championship Final, where he came third in the 800 metres to Steve Ovett, the eventual 1980 Olympic gold medallist. Bob ran a PB that day of 2:15. "Steve had already had a shower and got changed by the time I finished."

Bob also played football for the school team. The standard was pretty grim, with a bunch of kids playing kick and rush on full-sized pitches far too big for them. Bob, being taller than the rest, proved almost as useful at putting the goal nets up before each match. When playing, his bravery and enthusiasm were never in any doubt. "I played centre-forward right from the beginning, because I was big and quick and not afraid to put my head in where I could get hurt. I got my teeth knocked out at school once when an opponent kicked me. My top teeth went down into my bottom lip and I needed emergency dental care. I had to wear a brace for about three weeks and eat through a straw. Football was fun because I enjoyed running around but I was never serious about it. Making a career out of football was never even a consideration or on the radar."

That might have changed without the power cuts in 1973 that put paid to the first possible opportunity Bob had to impress professional scouts.

"When I was 15, my dad answered an ad in the *Watford Observer* for young players, and I trained for a few weeks at Watford under their coach, Tom Walley. He was a hard man; you shivered in your boots when he spoke and never dared answer him back. We wore our own kit and played five-a-side, but then I got a letter saying that because of the power cuts, they had to stop the sessions. I still never gave professional football a thought, as most of the boys were far better than me."

Renowned football writer Michael Calvin memorably described Tom Walley as having, "The ferocity of an Army PTI, the warmth of an adoptive father and the philosophy of a Jesuit priest." He was an accomplished spotter of young footballing talent, but his scouting instincts were not aroused by a young Bob Booker, who remained undiscovered and unknown.

Bob's parents were heavily involved with his football. John had never played the game, but he drove Bob to games, picked other players up, handed out the kit, collected all the subs, organised end-of-season events and even managed Woodside, one of the junior teams Bob played for. Brenda played the important role of washing the kit. John would encourage Bob from the touchline, but Brenda largely stayed away, disliking crowds and the thought of hearing any criticism of her beloved son. She made one exception for the final of the Freight Rover Trophy when Bob played for Brentford at nearby Wembley Stadium in 1985.

Bob's house was only a short journey from Vicarage Road – home of the Hornets, as Watford are known – and he used to stand on the open terrace in the Vicarage Road Stand with his dad, where he saw a centre-forward who had a huge influence on him. John Booker was no football expert, but he advised his son wisely before his first visit to Vicarage Road, "You're going to watch a real centre-forward today."

Cliff Holton was a massive raw-boned striker who scored an incredible 293 League goals in 570 appearances; a total bettered only by Arthur Rowley, Jimmy Greaves, John Atyeo and John Aldridge since the war. He possessed a thunderous shot with either foot, described as, "almost impossible to exaggerate" by the *Watford Observer's* veteran football correspondent, Oliver Phillips, and could head a ball further than most mere mortals could kick it.

Holton started his career at Arsenal, playing for them in the 1952 FA Cup Final before falling out of favour, losing his place to the immortal (if ageing) Tommy Lawton, and beginning a long and successful trawl of lower division clubs in and around London and the Home Counties. Watford first signed him in 1959 for a record fee of £10,000, their investment rewarded with a club record 48 League and FA Cup goals on the way to promotion from the Fourth Division in 1960. Holton's sudden and unexpected departure the following year, for nearby Northampton Town, was met with disbelief by dismayed and angry Watford fans. A petition ensued, but the powers that be at the club had ridiculously decided that Holton had been taking his eye off the ball and concentrating too hard on his outside business commitments. How many goals did they expect from him? What a mistake by manager Ron Burgess, who had given his board of directors an ultimatum regarding Holton's departure. Holton blew a massive raspberry at his previous manager by scoring a hat trick on his debut for his new club. Watford fell into an immediate decline following his departure.

Fifteen years later, when long-serving chairman Jim Bonser finally stepped down from his position, he belatedly admitted what every Watford fan had long known, "We got rid of the wrong man."

Holton returned for a second spell as a veteran 36-year-old in 1965, when Bob first saw him play at Vicarage Road. In total, Holton managed 105 goals in 166 appearances for the club and scored hat tricks on successive days.

Holton's ability made a deep impression on Bob, who sought to emulate his hero. As well as his battering ram qualities and aerial ability, Holton and Bob also shared something else in common. For all his size, bulk and strength, Cliff Holton was an accomplished cross-country runner and sprinter who Phillips recalls, "Was devastating once he had a full head of steam to outstrip and out-power the opposition centre-half."

Bob is not alone in his admiration for Holton. I well remember his Leyton Orient team laying siege to the Brentford goal in a second round FA Cup tie at a cold, dank and miserable Brisbane Road in January 1967. The near-38-year-old Holton comfortably got the better of his tussle with Brentford's talented centre-half Peter Gelson, who merely bounced off him whenever they came together. The Bees somehow held out for a much-needed replay, aided by a blatant and unpunished handball on the goal line by Alan Hawley. After triumphing at Griffin Park, they obtained a lucrative third round tie at First Division Sunderland, where the mercurial Jim Baxter – his attention for once on the game, rather than his post-match drink – danced around them at will.

Graham Taylor also made a telling comment about Cliff Holton, resonating with those who know Bob Booker, "He was a complete man and I always felt, when I had left his company, that he had given me positive thoughts, and a positive impression."

Bob also has fond memories of yet another Vicarage Road hero from a slightly later era – Barry Endean. This chunky and forceful striker's moment of immortal glory came in February 1970, when an unheralded, unglamorous, limited, but organised Watford team, newly promoted from the Third Division, beat the mighty Liverpool in the sixth round of the FA Cup on a pitted and grassless abomination of a pitch. Endean, unforgettably described as a "water buffalo of a centre-forward" by Calvin, who had a bird's-eye view that day as a ball boy, scored the winner, timing his run perfectly to dive in and meet Ray Lugg's precision cross after the midfielder had nutmegged Peter Wall.

Bob was one of the 34,047 crammed into a disbelieving Vicarage Road, and had taken note of Endean's endeavour and non-stop running.

Endean's football career also had something in common with Bob's. Having started an apprenticeship as a welder in his native north-east, he was playing for a pub team in his local park, when, out of the blue, he was spotted by a Watford scout and whisked down south, to find fleeting fame, if little fortune.

Bob continued to savour football whenever he got the chance. In the mid-70s, Tony Bates was a keen Chelsea supporter who Bob would sometimes accompany to Stamford Bridge. He shudders, even today, at the memory of being chased onto the platform at Euston Station by a group of seven or eight Chelsea skinhead girls wearing Doc Marten boots and Crombies. They were forced into an undignified and cowardly scramble onto the train home in the nick of time, narrowly dodging disaster.

Bob sometimes drove up with his dad to watch Don Revie's Leeds United, a team in their pomp at this time. He purrs with admiration at the memory of their iconic 7-0 win over Southampton at Elland Road in March 1972, and the cries of "Olé, Olé" as Leeds put together 39 consecutive passes, whilst toying with their hapless opponents. "It's almost cruel," winced Barry Davies on *Match of the Day* that night, but Bob was mesmerised by what he had seen.

Allan Clarke was a particular hero. Bob used to imitate his simple but classic raised arm goal celebration. Their paths would cross years later in 1984, when Bob acted as designated driver for his Brentford teammate,

Alan Whitehead, who had been given permission to travel north, to discuss a potential loan move with Scunthorpe United, then managed by the former Leeds legend. "I sat in reception as Alan went in for talks, and all of a sudden he came out and said, 'Allan Clarke wants to see you.' 'Me? Why?' 'He wants to see if you're interested in coming here.' So I went in and said, 'I can't believe I am here talking to my boyhood hero.' He said, 'Do you fancy coming up and joining us too?' I said, 'I am under contract, and really shouldn't even be talking to you, but I will have a think about it.' I was sorely tempted by the chance to play for one of my heroes, but I had second thoughts and escaped back to London, leaving Alan behind. At least one of us signed for Scunthorpe that day."

Leaving school at 16, Bob was forced to look for work – ideally something physical where he could use his hands. He tried his luck locally at Hille, a famous and well-established furniture factory, next door to where his sister Tina was working at Barclays Bank. He asked about an apprenticeship as a cabinetmaker but there was nothing going. A job in the upholstery department sufficed until a vacancy as a cabinetmaker became available. After a couple of months, he was offered an apprenticeship as an upholsterer and decided to stay where he was. Bob completed his apprenticeship after four back-breaking but happy years, the experience standing him in good stead for his eventual career.

"George Bishop, the foreman, was a hard taskmaster. I was terrified of him. He had this presence, and was old-school, and certainly cracked the whip. He was hard but fair, and I wanted to do well and prove myself to him. I swept up, made the tea, carried the furniture and did the washing up. I looked after the other workers and made sure that they never ran out of equipment or material, which they were grateful for as they were on piecework. I enjoyed it and they were all very friendly to me. It was great preparation for the discipline and teamwork required to become a professional footballer. I started on £60 per week, and gave £20 to my mum, so the money wasn't bad."

Cannily, Bob would also sell his mum's homemade cakes and bread pudding to his fellow workers, so there was generally plenty of money left over to buy records or a new pair of football boots. There was always time for football; with Bates, Bob started to play on Sundays for The Beaver pub team. "I enjoyed it and used to run off my Saturday night beers. I didn't really stand out but I managed to score a few goals."

Another pub team, Rangers, signed Bob, but he wasn't there for long. Holt, a friend of Bates, asked Bob to play for his team, Bedmond – a village a couple of miles away, close to Kings Langley.

This was the big time. Bedmond played in the Herts County League on a fenced-off private pitch, and even (occasionally) had hot water in the showers. Kit was provided and left in a steaming pile in the middle of the dressing room, with every player paying weekly subs to cover the laundry costs. The pitch was surrounded by houses, which were protected by a massive net stretched behind one of the goals. Bob clearly remembers hitting that net far more often than the ones fixed to the goalposts.

The manager, Dave Bromley, was a local landscape gardener and celebrated hard man who saw something in the keen young striker, putting him straight into the first team. Bob's new teammates included a young Vinnie Jones, who was developing in the youth team at the time, and Derek French, an experienced midfielder or winger who was later Bob's physio at Sheffield United, as well as the most talented player in the team. "Bob was a good athlete for his size," says French. "Technically very talented, with a good touch on the ball. He worked hard and he could score goals. I set up most of them for him though, so it really should have been me that made it and not him."

Bob settled in quickly, scoring 15 times in his first full season. He received his first brief mentions in the local press, but making a living out of football was a laughable idea, totally beyond his comprehension.

Bromley thought differently. He approached one of his gardening clients – renowned playwright Willis Hall, of Worzel Gummidge fame, who just happened to be a director of Brentford FC – to tell him about this "tall, young lad who could be a bit useful." Bromley asked Hall to fix up a trial for Bob and Brentford manager Bill Dodgin, sight unseen, agreed.

Upon hearing the good news, Bob's first reaction was, "Where's Brentford, and will I be able to get time off?" Thankfully, Bishop gave him the day off, and Bob was invited to play in a London Midweek League game at Griffin Park on 13th March 1978 against Brighton & Hove Albion – a match that would change his life irrevocably.

Bromley accompanied Bob to a near-deserted Griffin Park. The newcomer apprehensively entered the home dressing room, remembering to knock first. He was greeted with the customary indifference afforded to faceless trialists who come and go with monotonous regularity.

Professional footballers are a cynical bunch, as former Charlton winger Garry Nelson's seminal account of a footballer's life, *Left Foot Forward*, sums up. Of their attitude towards trialists and their predominantly transitory nature, he wrote, "A batch of trialists in. Temporarily. Here because of a motley collection of reasons, virtually none of them has any more chance of sticking than would be the first half-dozen you picked at random, men, women and children, from a bus queue."

The first thing Bob noticed was that the shirts were on hangers – the kit wasn't piled in a heap, and he was even given a towel. To his surprise, there were two faces that he recognised: young midfielder Paul Walker, who he had watched score two goals and miss a penalty when starring at Wembley for England schoolboys against Scotland, and the veteran former Chelsea striker, Tommy Baldwin, quietly seeing out his career at Griffin Park while assisting Dodgin with some coaching. Bob had watched him play on his visits with Bates to Stamford Bridge, and was awestruck to be sharing a dressing room with a former top-level player.

Bob was told to just enjoy himself, and, ideally, put himself about. His nerves were jangling and he was shaking in his boots (lovingly cleaned and dubbined as always). He followed his instructions to the letter, ran around like a headless chicken, gave away a number of free kicks and scored twice as Brentford Reserves lost 3-2 to a Brighton side inspired by goalscoring legend Peter Ward.

Baldwin was impressed by what he had seen, sensing that the gawky young striker had potential, "He was a big lad, enthusiastic, good in the air and he could also play a bit. I thought that he would be ideal for us and, when he filled out, he would be a threat for anyone."

Bromley was also excited. "He had a fine game, and looked better than Peter Ward," he reports. Hyperbole, perhaps, but Bromley had proven to be a good judge of a player. Bob was really grateful to him, "My path into professional football was all down to Dave Bromley. I will never forget the way he believed in me, and got me into the game. He was a giant of a man, who I revered, and I think he would have made an excellent manager in the pro game, but it's all about being in the right place at the right time. And that's exactly what happened to me."

Bill Dodgin had watched the game and later spoke to Bob in his tiny and cramped office, "Well done – I will have a chat with your manager," he told him. "I like what we have seen. Are you working?" Bob said that he was working as an upholsterer. "That's fine," responded Dodgin. "We'd like to see some more of you. Can you get some time off to train with us?" Bishop was amenable, and Bob trained for three days the following week, playing another reserve game against Southend.

Higher# IN THE BEGINNING

His priority, though was to finish his apprenticeship. Football would have to wait a little while longer.

# CHAPTER 2
# THE BEES

Bob was on his way to Brentford, for so many years one of London's lesser lights. He desperately wanted to impress at a club founded in 1889 as an offshoot of Brentford Rowing Club, with football – rather than rugby – only narrowly being selected as its sport of choice. From these inauspicious beginnings, the Bees struggled to make an impact or even survive, facing massive competition to establish themselves within the densely-packed London football scene.

Brentford became known as "The Bees" shortly after Joe Gettins, a student at nearby Borough Road College, started to play for the club. He brought along some of his college friends to watch him play, who chanted Borough Road's rallying call of "Buck up B's." The local press soon started using the name, but misheard "B's" for "Bees." and the latter name has been used ever since.

When the Football League expanded to form a Third Division in 1920, Brentford found themselves playing at a much higher level – elected to the Football League from the Southern League. The next few years saw them struggle to maintain their position. Money was tight and success even rarer. Things finally changed for the better in May 1926 with the astute appointment of Harry Curtis as secretary/manager. His arrival transformed the club's fortunes; within 10 years this legendary, inspirational former referee had masterminded a meteoric rise from the depths of the Third Division to the giddy heights of the top flight. The club's Griffin Park stadium was expanded into a near-40,000 capacity modern arena.

In the years before the Second World War, disbelieving and ecstatic fans packed out Griffin Park, watching their team challenge for the First Division title, become one of the top teams in London, reach the sixth round of the FA Cup and defeat Arsenal five times in eight matches.

Unfortunately, the club fatally overreached itself when, for once, the directors invested heavily in players. The summer of 1939 proved a calamitous time to embark on a spending spree. By the time football resumed after the war, the players had grown old together. Brentford were swiftly relegated, never to return.

# THE BEES

The club stabilised in Division Two before relegation in 1954 saw the beginning of a near-decade of austerity during which, particularly under the astute management of Malcolm MacDonald, the club relied upon a conveyor belt of local youngsters and cheap imports from junior football in MacDonald's native Scotland. Transfer fees were a rarity. Despite the lack of investment, he twice almost led his team back into the Second Division, falling just short. With the end of the maximum wage and money in short supply, a weakened and depleted squad dropped into the bottom division in 1962.

New chairman Jack Dunnett then spent huge sums in the transfer market in an attempt to secure promotion back into the Third and Second Divisions; a narrow miss on Division Two in 1965 was followed by an unexpected and appalling turnaround, with the Bees back in the bottom division in 1966.

The club's profligacy proved to be the economics of the madhouse, and it was a policy that came within a whisker of destroying the club in 1967. Scenting blood, local rivals QPR, a club on the rise but hamstrung by poor facilities at Loftus Road, mounted an abortive takeover bid.

A fierce rivalry had burned for years between Brentford and QPR, but ill-feeling and antipathy hit fever pitch in early 1967, at a time when Brentford were languishing in Division Four and losing money hand over fist. An effervescent Rodney Marsh-inspired QPR team was scoring 103 goals on its way to winning the Division Three and League Cup double. News broke totally out of the blue that plans were afoot for QPR to take over Brentford and move to Griffin Park, with the Bees disappearing into oblivion.

The deal was announced, with QPR's Alec Stock to be overall manager and Billy Gray and Dodgin the coaches. The *Daily Mail* headlined, "Fans call it a sell-out." The *Daily Mirror*, "Goodbye, Brentford."

Concerted protests halted proceedings. Ron Blindell's syndicate finally took over the club. On 23rd February 1967, Dunnett, who had welcomed and encouraged the whole appalling idea, resigned. The club was saved, owing a huge debt of gratitude to the efforts of so many unsung heroes among their supporters, determined to ensure their club's survival. Austerity, though, was the rule for the next few years – a huge debt had to be repaid, forcing Brentford to operate with a skeleton playing squad.

Disaster had narrowly been averted but the club was holed beneath the water line. The next few years saw budgets slashed and squad numbers reduced. Attendances plummeted; sponsorship, hospitality and merchandising revenues were unheard of (and non-existent). Brentford relied totally on the income generated from gate money, director loans and the begging bowl.

Multitasker supreme Jimmy Sirrel took on the unique role of manager, coach, trainer and scout, selecting from a squad of 13 players. There were no reserve or junior teams.

Stringent economies ensured that the overall debt was slowly whittled down, and, with the side struggling for results and reeling from the body blow of losing to non-league Guildford City in the FA Cup, £12,000 was scraped together to bring in Ron Fenton and Allan Mansley – a sum recouped when John Docherty was sold to Reading. The priority was simply survival, with results on the field of far less importance.

1968/69 saw Mansley emerge as Brentford's own George Best, with bigger clubs beginning to take notice of him. A large fee was in the offing before opponents, outclassed by his pace and effervescence, slowed him down the only way they could – by kicking him. He was never the same player again.

Brentford entered the new decade still boasting a squad of only 14 players. Short in numbers, they remained long in character, loyalty, grit and determination through characters including Jackie Graham, Chic Brodie, Gordon Phillips, Alan Hawley, Bobby Ross and Peter Gelson.

Under a talented manager in Frank Blunstone, things slowly improved on the pitch, with the club narrowly missing promotion in 1970 before a wonderful run to the fifth round of the FA Cup the following year and a return to the Third Division in 1972.

£12,000 was invested in the elegant Roger Cross – he of the white boots, long throw and venomous shot – who more than justified his fee, eventually being sold for £30,000, to Fulham, who were happy to pick off Brentford's best players. In turn, despite scoring freely throughout a massively successful loan spell, the directors were content to allow Alex Dawson to return to Brighton when personal terms could not be agreed with the burly striker – a myopic decision in the extreme.

Stewart Houston was well known to Blunstone from their time together at Chelsea, and the £15,000 invested in him – an enormous sum that was only raised with difficulty, after much discussion – was entirely justified when he moved from striker to full back, attracting the attention of Manchester United for a club record £50,000 fee in December 1973. Houston went on to play for Scotland.

# THE BEES

Brentford also hit the jackpot when the board decided, for once, to back Blunstone's judgement by paying an initial £750 – chicken feed even by Brentford's standards – on a tall striker playing for Wimbledon in the Southern League. John O'Mara took time to settle down and initially looked awkward, clumsy and ungainly, but was transformed by his own hard work and Blunstone's coaching ability.

His power, ability to hang in the air and subtle skills on the ground led to a 27-goal season marked by promotion. But just as the Bees were finding their feet in the new division, O'Mara was ludicrously sold to rivals Blackburn Rovers for a paltry £50,000, much to the dismay of the manager and supporters. His cut-price replacement, Stan Webb, proved a misfit.

With relegation looming, the board finally relented and paid around £25,000 to bring back Cross and sign tricky winger Barry Salvage – but it was too little too late. The Bees fell straight back to the bottom division, almost being forced to seek re-election the following season.

A letter published in the *Middlesex Chronicle* aptly summed up supporters' views about the club's parsimony, "Since the 1967 episode I am afraid the club has become very small-minded. Admittedly that was necessary for a couple of years or so, but timidity of this sort prompts me to believe that promotion last year was an unwelcome accident, which has now been rectified."

The nadir was reached on 27th October 1973 with a 4-1 thrashing at Scunthorpe, conceding four times in the opening 17 minutes. It was 36 years to the month since Brentford thrashed Charlton 5-2 to go top of Division One for the first time. The club was now the first to have headed up the top division and propped everyone else up at the bottom of Division Four.

The chequebook was firmly locked away under austerity measures again in the mid-70's, until new manager John Docherty arrested the rot, lavishing a club record £25,000 in March 1976 on Andy McCulloch, an injury-ravaged striker from Oxford United suffering from bad knees.

It took almost a year to get him properly fit, but McCulloch eventually proved a talismanic signing, forming a deadly 58-goal Little and Large partnership with Steve Phillips. McCulloch was eventually sold for a club record fee of £60,000 to Jack Charlton's resurgent Sheffield Wednesday team – a figure far too low for a player of his ability.

Bill Dodgin arrived in 1976. The son of a former Brentford manager, he reversed the decline through his ability to identify and sign skilful players and keep them happy and motivated, building a team that won promotion in 1977/78 through exuberant and entertaining attacking football.

He had a real eye for a player, building his team for a song. Goal machine Steve Phillips cost £5,000 from Northampton, playmaker Dave Carlton a mere £3,000 from the same club, stalwarts Paul Shrubb and Doug Allder were free transfers, and only Len Bond (£8,000), Barry Tucker (£10,000) and Pat Kruse (£20,000 – a club record fee for a defender) cost real money.

The sale of Gordon Sweetzer for £30,000 to Cambridge United, midway through the promotion season, went a long way towards balancing the books. Bob was now training with a club on the up and on the verge of sealing their promotion from Division Four – but one that was always looking for a bargain.

Would he be good enough to earn a contract and eventually make the grade?

# CHAPTER 3
# A NEW WORLD

George Bishop might have given Bob permission to train at Brentford from time to time for the remainder of the 1977/78 season, but he still ensured his employee put in enough hours to complete his apprenticeship, which remained Bob's absolute priority.

Bob's next problem was getting to Brentford's training ground, which was situated close to Heathrow Airport.

Riding his motorbike down the M1 was an option, but it would stick out like a sore thumb amongst the slick and modern motors that he was certain would be found gracing the players' car park. Fortunately, one of the first team players lived in nearby Stevenage, so Bill Dodgin arranged for him to collect Bob and take him to and from training, launching a lifelong friendship with Pat Kruse.

Kruse was a talented central defender who made up for his relative lack of height with exceptionally-timed leaps, enabling him to dominate lower league centre-forwards. He is best known for scoring the quickest own goal of all time, after eight seconds, while playing for Torquay United against Cambridge United in January 1977.

Every book should contain at least one scoop. Kruse can exclusively reveal what really happened that day. "It wasn't eight seconds, it was only six," he insists. "The pitch was frozen. Cambridge's Ian Seddon punted the ball forward from the kick-off. Two forwards chased it and I thought I would flick it back to our goalkeeper, Terry Lee. Unfortunately, I didn't notice that he had come out to the edge of the area. He went to call for the ball, but he had a speech impediment and I could not hear him. And then, to cap everything, he slipped over on the icy pitch, and the ball bounced over him into the empty net."

Despite this total fiasco, Kruse joined the Bees a couple of months later – immediately after playing against them. I clearly remember how calm and impressive he was that afternoon, despite his immediate opponent, Gordon Sweetzer, scoring a hat trick for Brentford. Kruse went on to become a firm favourite during more than 200 appearances for the Bees.

# A NEW WORLD

Bob was terribly nervous on his first day. It reminded him of going to a new school for the first time. His mum gave him a hug, told him to "be careful" and sent him on his way with his kitbag and sparkling football boots, as well as a sandwich for his lunch – as if it was just a day's work at Hille.

Kruse drew up outside, his arrival announced by a trademark squeal of brakes. Bob's first concern was quite simply getting there alive. Kruse drove like a maniac, with little concern for speed limits or the dictates of the Highway Code. The first thoughts about becoming a driving instructor, Bob's profession today, might have become ingrained in his subconscious on such journeys when dual controls would certainly have come in handy.

Kruse did his best to put Bob at ease by telling him what he had let himself in for. He described the training regime, which at that stage of the season was more about keeping fitness levels ticking over, concentrating upon ball skills and the small-sided games which were favoured by manager Dodgin.

He warned Bob about the banter he would face, but the newbie felt factory life had prepared him for verbal jostling. Kruse smiled knowingly, promising to look after Bob.

Thankfully for Bob's lurching stomach, they arrived at the training ground to find battered and decrepit Escorts, Marinas and Vauxhall Vivas where those imagined gleaming Maseratis, Ferraris and Bentleys might have been. Perhaps that motorbike was an option after all.

As they parked up, Bob's legs were shaking, their owner eager to make a good impression. Everything went surprisingly well, with Bob training at the club as often as he could, helped by Hille's transition to a three-day week, allowing him to train at Brentford on the other two days. But his Saturday duties with Bedmond meant he never got to watch the Bees play as they clinched promotion, escaping the Fourth Division alongside his local club, Watford.

Bob still attracted no interest despite his goals for Bedmond. He was still to earn a penny from football. What changed was his attitude. He realised he would need to become more disciplined and professional in his off-field behaviour; he never stopped his visits to regular haunt The Rolls-Royce Social Club with his mates, but he stayed at home far more often and cut back on social drinking.

"My real friends understood what I was doing, and recognised that I had to start looking after myself because I was becoming serious about football," he says. "They were all really supportive of me, but I did begin to experience some jealousy from some of the locals, which I found hard to deal with."

To his delight, Bob had done enough to be invited to pre-season training with Brentford in July 1978, striving to make an impression in the two days he could spare each week.

Pre-season was brutally tough but fulfilling. "Given how hard we trained, two days were more than enough. Bill Dodgin, Tommy Baldwin and the trainer/physio, Eddie Lyons, would regularly take us to Richmond Park for eight-mile runs, which I loved and invariably won, given my background in athletics." This resulted in some of the more experienced professionals threatening to debag this unknown upstart if he did not set a slower pace at the head of the field; finally, an impact at the club – even if it wasn't for his football skills.

Once the hard running was over, the worst was yet to come. The players were forced to sprint to the summit of Pork Chop Hill, a sheer 300-yard climb with pure shale near the top. Most players keeled over, but Bob just gritted his teeth. He was determined to become the fittest player – if not the best footballer – in the squad.

Any scepticism about Bob's description of Pork Chop Hill is allayed in another autobiography, by Leroy Rosenior, who admits that he used to lie awake at night worrying about the following day's hill run, "It took you past this pond and up this steep hill," he says. "Mosquitoes were everywhere under the July sun. The first time I did it, I was so eager to impress I raced off, sprinting around the park and up the hill, sprinting home and collapsing at the line." Only then was he told by one of the Fulham coaches, Terry Mancini, that he had to complete the circuit ten times.

This was Bob's first opportunity to work with Dodgin, who had joined the club in September 1976 when it was at a low ebb. A successful centre-half with Fulham and Arsenal, he found his true vocation as a gifted and enlightened coach at both Millwall and QPR, where he formed a brilliantly effective partnership with Alec Stock, taking an unheralded team from obscurity to the heights of the First Division.

Dodgin became manager at Loftus Road in 1968, also having spells at Fulham and Northampton Town. His record as a coach and manager recorded a highly impressive five promotions in 11 seasons. It was regarded as a real coup when Brentford Chairman Dan Tana appointed him to succeed John Docherty.

# A NEW WORLD

Taking over at Griffin Park meant something particularly special for Dodgin, whose father – also Bill – had managed the club between 1953 and 1957.

Dodgin was popular with players, renowned for introducing an exciting blend of open, attacking football wherever he worked, and treated players like adults, encouraging them to express themselves on the ball rather than worry about the opposition.

Tommy Baldwin, who had previously worked under the likes of Tommy Docherty at Chelsea and Manchester United, became an instant disciple of the Dodgin philosophy of football.

"I didn't know him before I joined Brentford, but I think he was a great manager – one of the best," he reckons. "He just knew so much about football. He could talk to people so that they listened and took on board whatever he said to them, and he had a really simple philosophy about the game. He said you should knock the ball forward and just get it back, knock it out wide and keep turning their defence. You can play two balls back but not three; the third ball must go forward. He talked so much sense about football."

Once the season got into full swing, training concentrated on building and developing the players' ball skills rather than mindless running.

"We played five-a-side and didn't run too far, just a series of short, sharp sprints," explains Baldwin. "We used the football all the time in training, and in those days that was unusual. We were really professional, with good players and an excellent team spirit."

Golf was perhaps almost as great a love for Dodgin as football; Bob remembers him and Baldwin regularly practising their golf swings, chipping a few balls on the training ground as the players went through their paces.

Dodgin recognised Baldwin's ability, eventually making him player/coach. "I like you about the place," he told him. "Footballers get better by watching other footballers and I want them to learn by watching you, and for you to give them the benefit of your experience."

Dodgin knew when to relax, and most Wednesdays would see a team lunch where the entire squad would sit down together and chew the fat over a plate of pasta and a glass or several of wine. Sometimes he invited players' wives and girlfriends to attend, building team spirit and morale.

Winger Doug Allder remembers how the unflappable Dodgin would deal with a bad performance. "A couple of games when we'd been struggling, we came in at half time expecting to get a rocket. He said, 'Sit down,' so we all did, and he stood there with his notepad open in front of him, before calmly asking us, 'Who wants to play golf and who would prefer a game of squash on Monday?' That was it, and we went out for the second half relaxed and with confidence restored."

Bob struggled to deal with the physical and mental challenges posed during the rigours of pre-season training. The fitness elements were fine, but he had never been coached before, and was still developing his control and ability to bring his teammates into the game. Certain that he stood out like a sore thumb with his lack of technique, he remained a trialist, playing without a salary and desperately trying to hang on.

"You had to look after yourself or you would fall by the wayside," he warns. "Pat Kruse kept his word and looked after me. I was not bullied but he was quite right, football banter was totally different from the workplace wisecracking that I was used to. Nothing was off limits. It was so much more cruel, ruthless, and cutting, with lots of girlfriend and mum jokes. If you couldn't take it, you were finished. I was still a small fish in a big pond. I was not shy but I had respect for my teammates and did not want to answer them back, which made it difficult for me."

Bob was amazed at the technical ability of so many of the players, having never previously mixed with professionals. He tried his best to watch them carefully and learn, and was pleasantly surprised by the advice most of the squad offered him. Some of the more experienced players, such as John Fraser, Shrubb, Allder and Kruse, gave him a lot of help, possibly because they regarded Bob as little threat to their places. Dubious driving aside, Kruse took Bob under his wing and became his sounding board.

As a forward, Bob took particular note of the strengths and weaknesses of the Brentford strikers he so wished to emulate, noting McCulloch's aerial presence and leadership skills, as well as Kruse's precise leaps – a talent that McCulloch also shared.

Brentford's leading scorer was the enigmatic Steve Phillips: small, gifted, surly, chippy and as hard as nails. Bob realised that, given their different physiques, they could never be similar players, but he could still take something from his coolness and single-mindedness in front of goal.

"Steve didn't really take too much notice of me, but gave me the odd tip. If you're small, you really have to be special to succeed, and he always managed to find time and space in the crowded six-yard box. He had that devilment about him and would stand up to the bigger players. He was a natural goalscorer, and he and Andy McCulloch formed a brilliant partnership."

McCulloch also has fond memories of the young Bob Booker, "He was eager and willing to learn, and he worked so hard in training. I was delighted to help him. He made it purely on his endeavour, and he fought his way through adversity."

What really helped Bob settle down and win increasing acceptance was, in fact, the main point of difference between him and the Brentford squad. His fellow players, almost without exception, had come into the game as apprentices, and had never held down any another job. They knew little about the world beyond football.

Bob would regale them with stories about the realities of clocking on and off, working in a factory from eight in the morning until five in the afternoon. Alongside reserve goalkeeper Trevor Porter, who was a part-timer and ran his own window cleaning business, he was regarded as a real professional oddity.

Dodgin's foreman was the skipper, Jackie Graham, who was short in stature but a giant in everything he did. "He was the life and soul of the dressing room and played a real captain's role," recalled Bob. "He would have stood out in the modern game like a Billy Bremner or Johnny Giles. He was a leader. He could pass and tackle and set a massive personal example. Bill built the team around him and we were terrified of letting him down."

As for the manager, Dodgin simply described Jackie Graham as "half the team."

Bob also recognised just how special Dodgin was. "I hadn't heard of him before I joined the club, and when I first met him I thought 'What a gentle giant.' He was a big man, very proud, and a perfect gentleman. He was quietly spoken, had a fantastic calmness about him, and I had total admiration for him. He had this presence. He was not a bawler or a shouter, but when he did raise his voice you certainly knew why. He was always constructive and you listened to every word he said. He just wanted you to relax and enjoy your football. He concentrated on what we should be doing rather than the opposition."

"Tommy Baldwin was the perfect foil for Bill and they worked well together, with Tommy taking most of the training. In those days, we didn't have any of the support staff, such as warm-up coaches, dieticians, analysts and masseurs who are taken for granted today, and Tommy did a lot of the work."

"Bill would watch from the sidelines and encourage now and again, and, if he felt the need, he would step in and make some observations about the session. Tommy got us doing fitness and ball work, then small-sided games, which players always love. Bill would take a little bit of shadow play with the starting line-up, but for no longer than 15 or 20 minutes – footballers are not renowned for their long attention spans."

"Bill was a great believer in letting players express themselves and, in my time at Brentford, the players really liked his style. Even when I wasn't in the team I totally respected him and his decisions. I was young and in awe of him but he had given me the chance to become a professional footballer and I owed him everything. I just hope that I made him feel proud of me."

Just as Bob was impressed with Dodgin and Baldwin, he began to make an impression upon them with his effort and obvious improvement. To his surprise, he was picked to play in a pre-season friendly away to Isthmian League Chesham United.

This was the biggest game that he had ever played in, partnering Phillips up front in a 0-0 draw. Bob can remember little about the match, apart from the lushness of the turf, on what was a beautiful pitch at The Meadow.

Luckily, Richard Becher's report in the *Evening Mail*, offering a fairly harsh verdict on a raw youngster making his debut, can refresh the memory, "Big gangling striker Bob Booker, who was quite impressive in a couple of reserve games at the end of last season, missed a few openings which he should have turned into goals." This was Bob's first experience of criticism in the press. It certainly wouldn't be his last.

Playing for Brentford, even in a mixed squad of first-teamers and young hopefuls, gave Bob a massive boost, making him think, for the first time, that he was perhaps not totally out of his depth at this level. His perseverance was finally beginning to pay dividends.

Brentford struggled to adapt to a higher level of football once the season began, scoring a meagre eight goals on the way to winning only three of their first 11 games. Meanwhile, Bob stopped playing for Bedmond and managed the odd game for Brentford reserves, concentrating on the apprenticeship he completed in early October.

His wages at Hille immediately went up to between £150 and £200 per week – good money in those days, especially on piecework. In an idea the PFA would be unlikely to support for the underperforming footballers of today, the size of his salary was dependent on how much work he completed.

Dodgin had asked Bob to tell him when his apprenticeship came to an end. As soon as Bob gave him the good news, the manager summoned him to his office for a chat, leaving his visitor concerned that he would be told not to come to training anymore. The alternative would be… surely not?

Dodgin came straight to the point. "Congratulations," he told Bob. "We have had a good look at you and have liked what we have seen. You have a chance of making it as a professional footballer." A one-year contract was on offer for £60 per week, including a bonus of between £8 and £30 according to the club's standing in the league table and Bob's place in the first team. The signing on fee was £250.

Bob was totally flabbergasted, staring back at his manager, unable to formulate a reply. "It was all a bit of a blur. I was on my own without my dad there to advise me. Negotiation was out of the question and eventually the words 'Where do I sign?' came out."

Bob blurted out the news as soon as he got home. His mum was less delighted than his dad when she learned that Bob had exchanged a guaranteed salary of up to £200 per week for less than a third of that from Brentford. And even that derisory figure might disappear in a year's time.

Bob signed the next day; the money really did not matter. He had proved to himself that he was good enough to come from total obscurity and earn a professional contract.

The previous few months had been gruelling, but he had beaten the odds, which had been stacked against him, and survived the initial boot camp. However proud and delighted he was, he could not rest on his laurels, needing to work hard to improve enough to justify a contract extension over the coming months.

Bob visited Hille to resign, where Bishop wished him all the best and told him he would keep his tools safe for him, "just in case."

Bob's first day as a professional footballer was Friday the 13th October 1978, but the week contained even more surprises for him. Dodgin came up to him. "You are travelling with the first team to Watford tomorrow," he said. "We have had some injuries, and you might even be involved. Get a good night's sleep and meet us there on Saturday at 1.30pm." Such was the way of football in those less regimented days. Today, Bob would probably have been told to travel from his Watford home to Brentford's training ground, catching the coach back to Watford with his teammates, and returning to the training ground after the game – particularly if they had lost – rather than walking the short journey home from Vicarage Road.

Club suits didn't exist in those days. Bob's mum took him shopping to M&S on the Friday afternoon, choosing a suit, shirt and tie so that he would at least look the part. He spent the evening telephoning his disbelieving mates, telling them to be on the terraces the following afternoon.

This was not just any other match. Apart from being a local derby, Watford saw relative neighbours Brentford as their fiercest rivals, and were determined to fully regain bragging rights after the Bees did the double over the Hornets in the latter part of the 1976/77 season, when Dodgin's efforts were already beginning to pay off with the help of talented youngsters.

Inspirational skipper Graham's pre-match words in the tunnel remain a closely-guarded secret 40 years on from the 23rd of March 1977, but they undoubtedly had a galvanising effect. Brentford came out of the starting blocks like scalded cats. A three-goal onslaught in the opening 15 minutes hardly flattered them on a cruise to victory.

The return at Vicarage Road, shortly afterwards, on Easter Saturday, was a totally different affair as the home team laid siege to the Brentford goal. But the ball quite simply refused to go in, aided and abetted by an incredible goalkeeping display by Paul Priddy, who stopped everything, including two penalty kicks from Dennis Bond and Alan Mayes. The Bees stole victory with a header from McCulloch.

This was not an afternoon to tarry long after the final whistle and celebrate victory. It was with a huge sigh of relief when I finally reached the sanctuary of my car, already pointed in the direction of London for a quick getaway.

Just eight games later, Dodgin harshly rewarded Priddy's match-winning performance with a free transfer. More tellingly, Brentford have yet to celebrate another victory over Watford since, despite 16 attempts. The Hornets have certainly taken full revenge on their hapless neighbours.

It would be hard to imagine a tougher and more important match, and Bob's burgeoning career was almost over before it began when he struggled to persuade a jobsworth commissionaire that he really was a player, despite his unfamiliar smart attire. After finally being allowed into the ground, he remembers inspecting the pitch at 1.40pm alongside Graham, desperately trying to hide his nerves. He had no idea that he was playing until he returned to the dressing room and heard his name read out.

Dodgin came round and gave Bob a few quiet words of encouragement to help calm him. He went out to face probably the best team in the league, determined that he would not show himself up.

Just picture the scene: it is 2.15pm on Saturday 14th October 1978 in the home dressing room at Vicarage Road and the Brentford team sheet has just been handed to Watford manager Graham Taylor.

"That's good news, Dougie Allder isn't playing for them," the conversation might have gone. "Who's this Booker fellow wearing the number 6 shirt? Where does he play? Has anyone heard of him? Who cares anyway – let them worry about us."

Despite wearing an unfamiliarly numbered shirt, Bob was partnering McCulloch in a dual spearhead, starting the match brightly by putting in the first shot, blocked by Alan Garner as home goalkeeper Andy Rankin hesitated.

Seven minutes later, he came even closer, passing to Phillips whose shot came back off the post.

Normal service was resumed in the second half as a Watford team on course for promotion slowly took control. Goals from former Brentford Junior Ross Jenkins, a tall beanpole of a striker who was so often a thorn in the side of his former club, and emerging star Luther Blissett, gave them a 2-0 win.

Watford defender Ian Bolton – soon to play a prominent role in Bob's story – was booked for kicking out at Bees goalkeeper Len Bond, and police were forced to move in to quell fighting on the terraces between rival fans.

There were 15,180 people at the game – around 15,000 more than the number who had ever watched a match involving Bob. The 90 minutes at Vicarage Road flew past for him. While he had done his best and put himself about, in his heart of hearts he knew that he was still totally raw and patently unready for this level of the game.

What a week it had been; completing his apprenticeship, receiving an offer of a professional football contract (seeing his salary more than halved for the privilege), leaving his old job, buying his first suit, making his Football League debut at the club nearest to his home and meeting (and being kicked by) an opponent who was eventually to become his brother-in-law. What more could happen to him?

Bob was soon to become related to Bolton, a tough, rugged Watford central defender who, firstly with Sam Ellis and then Garner and Steve Sims, formed a seemingly impassable barrier for over six years in front of Rankin or Steve Sherwood in goal.

Bolton was part of the Taylor revolution which took Watford from the Fourth Division to the First in a mere five seasons. Highly recommended to Elton John by the likes of Don Revie and Brentford chairman Dan Tana, Taylor had led Lincoln City to promotion in 1976, and narrowly beat Bobby Moore to the job.

"I was his second signing straight after Sam Ellis," recalls Bolton. "Years afterwards, Taylor told me he wanted to sign the two meanest and ugliest defenders he could find."

Bolton formed a partnership with Garner after Ellis retired, then played alongside Steve Sims, who was signed as his replacement. "Graham had a way of playing that was drastically misunderstood," he points out, pinpointing the credit for Watford's success.

"He realised that we could not play the big clubs at their own game, so he developed a system that was all about the team. It was a little bit like how Iceland played against England (at Euro 2016). It doesn't matter about possession − it is what you do with the ball that counts."

"It bores me senseless to watch some of the top teams today where there is barely a shot at goal in anger. Can you call that entertainment given the money you have to pay for a ticket? It was all about pressure and keeping the game simple and trying to get the ball into the opposition goal and out of ours. We were all about pressurising teams in their own half and winning that crucial second ball, and when we took over possession 30 yards outside our opponent's penalty area, it was all about shots and crosses, and providing the ammunition for Luther Blissett and Ross Jenkins."

Taylor was one of the first managers to use statistics. Every Monday he would review the previous game with all the players and ask pertinent questions. Nigel Callaghan would be asked how many crosses he had got in. "Four, Boss." "No, it was two – how can we score goals if you don't provide any service?"

Then it would be Blissett's turn to face his manager's scrutiny. "How many shots on goal did you have, Luther?" "Four." "Just two – and if you only shoot twice you can only score two goals. Keep shooting."

The midfield were asked how many second balls they had won, with a constant pressure to improve and succeed. Every player had to do his job and contribute to the team ethos.

Watford would steamroller teams, and Brentford were not alone in being unable to live with them, left way behind in their wake. In many ways they resembled Dave Bassett's all-conquering Sheffield United team of the late 80s and early 90s, in which Bob was to play a key role.

Despite living in the same town, Bolton had never heard of Bob when he first encountered him. "We knew it was his debut and I did my best to put him off with a few well-chosen words," he admits. "I kicked him from pillar to post and had him in my pocket all afternoon, as I have constantly reminded him." Welcome to the Football League!

The next time Bolton came across Bob was when he signed for Brentford in late 1983, after he realised that he was no longer first choice at Vicarage Road.

"Brentford offered me a two-and-a-half year contract, which was very attractive to me at that stage of my career. It was time for a change, and I decided to go there and try and get them out of relegation trouble."

Bob and Bolton soon started carpooling, quickly becoming firm friends. They played snooker in Watford, and Bolton describes his introduction to Tina Booker, with whom he has a daughter, and a granddaughter and 30 years of marriage to celebrate, as "a massive favour."

"In hindsight, from a career point of view, going to Brentford was the worst decision I ever made, because the fire had gone out," he concedes. "I went for the right reasons and the supporters must have felt let down by how badly I played. But if I hadn't have gone there, I would not have met Bob or Tina."

# CHAPTER 4
# SCORING A HAT TRICK – THE WORST THING I EVER DID

It is worth restating just how unusual Bob's achievement was – and the scale of his rise. A few short months after playing barely a couple of levels beyond parks football, with never a thought of rising any higher in the football pyramid, he had joined the ranks of the few to have made a coveted Football League appearance. The question now was – where would he progress from here?

Bob retained his place for the game at Rotherham three days later. Reality kicked in: two tough and experienced defenders, John Flynn and Paul Stancliffe (Stancliffe was later a teammate at Bramall Lane) easily snuffed out his threat in a narrow 1-0 defeat.

Dodgin had seen enough, confirming what Bob already knew; he was nowhere near ready to play regularly at this level.

The Bees had lost three of their last four games, scoring only once. The bottom of the league beckoned. Chairman Dan Tana appreciated that their hard-won Division Three status was already at risk, and allowed Dodgin to spend £58,000 – an unheard of sum – on two players. Defender Jim McNichol, who became the club's record signing, for £33,000 from Luton Town and, more relevantly for Bob, striker Dean Smith who arrived from Leicester City for £25,000.

Recognising the gift of a potentially valuable asset who had arrived totally unexpectedly, Brentford decided to reward Bedmond for Bob's progress. Dave Bromley was delighted at the prospect of the windfall, eagerly anticipating the arrival of the cheque. How this volatile character reacted when a parcel eventually arrived at the club containing a set of Bukta tracksuit tops remains unrecorded – although they were, at least, Bedmond-branded.

What was good enough for Brentford was good enough for Fulham. In 1999, their owner, Mohamed Al-Fayed, sent non-league Rushall

Olympic a similar payment of 30 tracksuits as a gesture of thanks after they signed Zat Knight, who eventually played for England and earned them a fee of £3.5 million when he moved to Aston Villa. It is not known if Fulham included the trousers too.

Several of Bob's detractors are adamant that the club drastically overpaid Bedmond for his services, but he is one of their best ever bargains, playing more than 300 times for the Bees in return for what could only have been an outlay of around £50 worth of kit.

Bob had no issues with being dropped. "I had appeared from nowhere and knew that I simply had to train hard and wait for my next opportunity, so I just buckled down. I did not cause any problems off the pitch as I never knew when the call might come. My priority was to keep learning and improving, and do enough to earn a new contract at the end of the season. This was my living now. I had to impress in training to ensure they kept me on."

With no desire to return to the factory bench, he disappeared into the background for the rest of the season, only making one further substitute appearance, replacing Jackie Graham and almost creating a late winner for Pat Kruse in a goalless draw with Exeter City at Griffin Park. This was the first time that most Bees supporters had seen him, and the general view was of a decent prospect for the future – raw, but certainly with something about him.

Bob travelled a few times with the first team, helping Eddie Lyons with the skips and laying out the kit. Otherwise, he scored four times in a regular run of games for the reserves, continuing to learn his trade. There was a real scare against Portsmouth at Fratton Park, however, when Bob felt a blow to the back of his head while challenging for a high ball, causing him to catch his chewing gum in his throat and swallow his tongue. Lyons noticed that Bob was rapidly turning a funny colour and dashed onto the pitch to save the day. No more chewing gum during matches.

Like Bob, the actor and comedian Bradley Walsh also came from Garston, where he worked as an apprentice engineer at Rolls-Royce. A midfielder or striker who modelled his game on his idol, Manchester United legend Denis Law, Walsh became a firm friend and drinking partner of Bob's, who had first come across him in local football.

Walsh possessed footballing ability and was very clever on the ball, but was far better doing impressions of famous personalities than impersonating an international footballer.

He started off entertaining his workmates with wickedly accurate impressions of Norman Wisdom, John Wayne and Bruce Forsyth, soon building up a reputation by winning a series of local talent shows.

Bob did his bit for his friend by recommending him to Dodgin. Walsh impressed on trial, playing on and off for Brentford for a couple of seasons as a non-contract player without really threatening to break through to the first team.

Dodgin loved having him around, taking Walsh on the coach to away games to entertain the players and ensure that they were relaxed and in good humour before kick off.

His party piece was to stand in front of opposition goalkeepers and defenders at corner kicks and distract them by reducing them to hysterics with his non-stop patter and brilliant impressions. But eventually the penny dropped; despite loving his time at Griffin Park, he would be far more successful as an entertainer than as a footballer, and he departed to find fame and fortune in the entertainment world. Would he have swapped a little part of his well-deserved success for the opportunity to have played just once in the Football League?

*

Bob still lived at home, switching his motorbike for a Ford Cortina, allowing him to share the driving to training. In future seasons, Bob would sometimes travel in with goalkeeper Dave McKellar and defenders Pat Kruse and Jim McNichol. McKellar's chain-smoking caused a few problems, but Bob believed it was good to have the keeper and his two central defenders spending so much time together every day, helping them bond and develop a closer relationship on the pitch.

After their early flirtation with relegation, the team settled down. A run of five wins in six matches helping them finish in a comfortable tenth place in Division Three – a solid achievement in their first season back at a higher level.

Bob could look back with great satisfaction at his first season in professional football. To his delight – and no little surprise – Dodgin rewarded him for his efforts by renewing his contract for another year and giving him a £10 pay rise, taking him up to the giddy heights of £70 per week – still far less than half what he had been earning at Hille.

*

Hopes were high for the 1979/80 season, but they were immediately dashed when joint top scorer McCulloch, who had been tapped up by

# SCORING A HAT TRICK

Sheffield Wednesday's Assistant Manager Ian St John while lying on a stretcher in the Brentford dressing room after being carried off the pitch, decided to leave the club.

Jack Charlton made an opening bid of £60,000 – a derisory offer for such a proven and successful striker, and one simply intended to test the water. Charlton was flabbergasted when the Brentford board snapped his hand off and accepted his first offer in an illustration of the myopic, penny-pinching way in which the club was run in those days.

McCulloch was a hard act to follow. His departure left a huge void. It opened the door slightly for Bob, who had learned so much from his mentor's approach, largely basing his game on his rugged, forceful style.

Dodgin had other ideas and declared his intention to change the way the team played. "Over the past couple of seasons, if we have been in trouble we have knocked a long ball up to Andy," he admitted. "He is such an honest, whole-hearted player that he would chase and frequently win it for us. But that will have to change." The aim was to play out of trouble, keep possession and play more fluent football.

Dodgin was frustrated in his attempts to sign a small, skilful striker in Keith Fear from Plymouth Argyle. Surprisingly, he settled for a total unknown in Lee Holmes, a part-time player from Haringey Borough, who continued to work as a civil engineer.

There were several similarities between Booker and Holmes. Holmes had also been playing at a low level when he was recommended to Brentford by a friend, playing a couple of reserve games as a trialist at the back end of the 1978/79 season, while continuing to train the odd day here and there at the club. As had been the case with Bob a year earlier, he was expecting to be told at any time that his services would no longer be required.

Tommy Baldwin saw something in the six-foot tall, powerfully-built Holmes, thinking that he could make a ready-made and cheap replacement for McCulloch. Dodgin was also convinced and, characteristically, signed Lee in a wine bar near Embankment Station. Borough asked Brentford for some compensation for a player who signed on a free transfer, but Holmes does not know if they received any. Perhaps Brentford were fresh out of tracksuit tops.

At almost 24 years old, Holmes had long since given up any hope of becoming a professional footballer, earning around £80 per week as a newly-qualified civil engineer. Given his work commitments, Dodgin offered him the same again to train twice each week.

In essence, he was being paid more than Bob for working less than half the week at the club; further evidence of how Bob was regarded by the club at the time.

Holmes "had no expectations of getting into the first team," but soon became first choice. Dodgin instructed him to change the way he played. "I used to wander wide and also drop back and support the midfield, but he told me to stay in the middle and remain in the last third of the pitch," recalls the hard-working striker, who struggled to cope with the higher standard of football, scoring six goals that season.

He is best remembered for dashing off on the back of a motorbike while wearing a tracksuit over his dirty and sweaty football kit immediately after a home victory against Southend United. Roaring across London to Barking, Holmes changed into a suit in a pub car park in time for his wedding ceremony, arranged long before he signed for the Bees.

Holmes had made Dodgin aware from the outset that he needed his wedding day off. His manager reassured him that he would be nowhere near the first team at that point. Months later, knowing that he would be playing on the day in question, Holmes looked into hiring a helicopter or even arranging a police escort across town. Neither option was practical, but Dodgin promised to substitute him if the opportunity arose. Brentford's two very late goals meant he was forced to play the entire 90 minutes. In the end, Holmes had a friend sit on the bench with a spare crash helmet, allowing him to somehow reach Barking in time for the 5.30pm ceremony. His efforts were rewarded by a marriage to Janet that lasted more than 35 years.

Dean Smith had scored eight goals in his first season at the club but had often flattered to deceive. A clever footballer who found space in crowded penalty areas, he often seemed to drift out of games, and his languid style did not meet with universal approval, earning him a reputation as a luxury player.

To further complicate matters, Dodgin also signed another Holmes – Billy, this time - for £10,000 from Hereford United, playing a few times up front without impressing.

Lee Holmes played alongside the fading and faltering Steve Phillips, whose golden touch in front of goal had deserted him. He only scored a dozen goals all season as well as achieving the rare feat of missing four penalty kicks. Holmes does not have fond memories of him. "He was selfish and did not help me or make me feel wanted, but once I gave him stick in return he backed off," he says. "Even though I did not like him, he would always have been in my team as he was a natural goalscorer."

So where did this leave Bob? Out in the cold is the answer. He was ignored for the two pre-season friendlies against Football League opposition in Wrexham and Charlton Athletic, starting off the new season where the old one had ended – in the reserves.

Holmes watched him in training and was impressed with him. "He was a better player than me and was harshly dealt with. He was lower down the pecking order. Like myself, he seemed to lack confidence. We could both have desperately done with a boost, particularly as the Griffin Park crowd was not slow to make us both aware of our shortcomings. I was often regaled with cries of 'Fuck off back to Haringey' as I warmed up down the touchline."

Holmes remained until the end of the season, when new manager Fred Callaghan insisted on him signing a full-time contract, offering the princely sum of £100 per week. Lee responded by telling him that he could double that wage working as a civil engineer and non-league footballer. "It made no sense to sign," he says. "I had just got married and had a mortgage to pay, so that was the end of my time at Brentford. I would not bow down to a bully. I made the correct decision. I wasn't good enough to play at a higher level, and I later won two FA Trophy winners' medals at Wembley for Enfield and Wealdstone. I am still working as a civil engineer all these years on."

Bob felt frustrated. None of the strikers were scoring regularly but the team was getting results, losing only four of their first 18 matches to become one of the early pacesetters.

A modern player in his position might have gone squealing to his agent, who would have demanded more respect for his client before planting destabilising stories across the media and asking for a transfer.

Leaving aside the fact that Bob never had an agent at any point during his career, relying initially upon his father to advise him on contractual issues, such actions would have been entirely alien to his nature. He simply got his head down and concentrated on trying to work himself back into favour.

Despite all his efforts, he failed to score in his first three Midweek League matches. But his perseverance was rewarded towards the end of September. Barry Fry, the Barnet manager, had been impressed with his attitude and ability when he watched Bob play for the reserves, and asked Dodgin if he could sign the striker on loan.

At one time, Fry seemed to have the football world at his feet. Having starred for England Schoolboys, signed for Manchester United and become a Busby Babe, he failed to buckle down. His young roommate, Eamon Dunphy, paints a vivid picture of how he allowed himself to be led astray by the "Country bumpkin from Bedford... who breezed around the place as if he owned it."

Dunphy put his finger on the root cause of such behaviour. Football was "A way of life that induced boredom in people with too much time to kill. After a couple of hours' training each morning, professional footballers faced long, empty days with very little to do. The sensible, mature and married went home. But for the unattached, or those of even a slightly wayward disposition, there were many temptations. For the truly feckless or those with hyperactive tendencies, temptation lurked in the form of gambling, women and drink."

Fry's proclivity for late nights, dancing, gambling and getting into numerous other scrapes did not go down well with Matt Busby, and he drifted away from Old Trafford with his potential unfulfilled. Injury brought his playing career to an end shortly afterwards, following brief spells at Bolton, Luton and Leyton Orient.

The mercurial Fry resolved to make his name as a manager, taking charge at Barnet in December 1978 after spells at Stevenage Borough, Dunstable, Hillingdon Borough and Bedford Town.

Barnet were playing two levels below Brentford, as founder members of the new Alliance Premier League. As usual, they were struggling to survive and living a hand-to-mouth existence. Rumour has it that the players' wages were being paid out of the takings from the fruit machines in the clubhouse.

Results on the pitch were poor. The players were finding it hard to come to terms with the departure of Jimmy Greaves, a positive influence in midfield who could still score the odd goal. Discussions were held with former Chelsea icons Peter Osgood and Ian Hutchinson, but Fry pulled the plug on the deals, and later in the season rejected the chance to sign a young striker who had just begun to make a reputation for himself – Kerry Dixon. Instead, he signed Elwyn Roberts for a club record £4,000, and then Martin (Norman) Conquest, both of whom struggled to score regularly.

Fry saw Bob as a potential solution to his team's goal drought, selling the youngster on the move by convincing him of the benefits of playing regular first team football at a decent level of the game, testing himself against gnarled, veteran non-league central defenders.

The deal was soon agreed. As Barnet were part-time, training twice a week, Bob would continue to play for Brentford reserves, training with his parent club whenever his Barnet commitments allowed.

Bob found Fry to be brash, loud and full of enthusiasm and hyperbole. He initially felt that his new manager had stacked extra pressure on him by overselling him and hyping him to the Barnet fans.

"He will improve our side no end," gushed Fry to the local newspaper. "He is tall, good in the air and very mobile. I just hope he can get on the end of our crosses."

"It was the first time there had ever been any real pressure on me to perform," explained Bob, "and I really felt the weight of expectation, as I had been brought in to do a job by Barnet. But once I had settled down, I thrived on the extra responsibility and trust that had been placed in me."

Dodgin thought that the experience of two months at Barnet would "do him good," but was adamant that this was only a temporary move. Fry, conversely, was hopeful that he might be able to sign Bob on a permanent basis. "Bob's chances in the first team have become limited since Brentford bought Billy Holmes and another striker," explained Fry in a newspaper article. "He will still be tied to Brentford but if, after a couple of months, they decided to let him go, we will obviously have to pay some sort of fee for him."

Luckily, Bob never read this at the time. As far as he was concerned, leaving Brentford was never on his agenda.

Bob enjoyed the experience of playing for Fry, who had his own inimitable management style that polarised opinion (Kruse and Joe Allon, for example, couldn't stand him). "What a contrast there was between him and Bill Dodgin," observes Bob. "Barry was an explosive character who bawled and shouted and threw cups of tea around the dressing room. Some of what he said made sense, but most went in one ear and came straight out of the other. Like Dave Bassett, he was a great motivator, and he was totally unpredictable. Sometimes he would slaughter you and on other occasions he would put an arm round you and make you feel ten feet tall. He was one of the most enthusiastic men I ever met, and he has not changed to this day. I wanted to do my best for him."

Bob made a good start and became an instant hit with his new fans when he scored on his debut in a 2-0 Alliance Premier League Cup win over Bath City. Bob's first ever goal in senior football finally got him off the mark, but it was hardly a classic, as John Pollard reported, "He shrugged off a challenge from player-manager Bob Boyd and fired goalwards. The ball struck defender Tony Ricketts and sailed beyond the reach of goalkeeper Bennett." Keith Pike was even more descriptive, "Chasing after Oliver's long pass, Booker seemed to hold back Bath player-manager Bob Boyd before turning and shooting in one movement. Bennett appeared to have the shot covered, but was left completely stranded when the ball struck Ricketts on the arm and deflected slowly into the opposite corner."

Thankfully, there was no Dubious Goals Panel in the Alliance Premier League at the time. The goal was credited to Bob – the first of many.

Fry was delighted with his new capture. "He did very well," he beamed. "He gave us something we haven't had up front. He is very mobile and challenges well. He gave the attack a new dimension."

Bob continued to impress, scoring four times in 15 games for Barnet in the league and various cups. He became a favourite of supporters and teammates alike, playing at Vicarage Road again as Barnet dumped a strong Watford side out of the Herts Senior Cup with a late goal from Lou Adams, created by Bob.

Flourishing from regular first team football, Bob greatly enjoyed his Barnet spell, feeling much fitter. His game had matured and greatly improved. He was particularly impressed with Steve Brinkman, who possessed massive ability but died tragically young after a series of heart attacks. He also enjoyed playing at Underhill, where the slope made it easier for him to jump for crosses. The Barnet players were similarly delighted with him; long-serving defender Kevin Millett remembers how astonished the Barnet players were when Fry succeeded in obtaining a striker of Bob's calibre.

"Playing against tougher opponents helped me grow up and toughened me up," says Bob, summing up his stay. "I had to give as good as I got. Barnet provided a wonderful education for me and I have a lot to thank Barry Fry for. In retrospect, I should ideally have gone somewhere like Barnet before I went to Brentford. But that didn't happen, and I was thrown into the deep end at Griffin Park."

Fry also has fond memories of Bob and the impact he made at Barnet. "I remember Bob very well. His contribution on and off the field for

Barnet in his 15 games was immense. He was great in the dressing room and would do anything in the community for the club, even though he was only on loan. Hopefully his short spell with me at Barnet helped his development and made him a better player when he returned to his parent club."

Dodgin had kept an eye on Bob's progress at Barnet. As results deteriorated and injuries started to bite, he had no option but to recall the loanee. Holmes had bruised his ribs at Carlisle soon after scoring with a brave low header, so Bob was thrown straight back into first team action. More than a year after he last played in the Third Division, on the 8th of December 1979, Bob's life changed irrevocably when he scored a hat trick in a 7-2 thrashing of a struggling Hull City team. His three goals came in the space of just 24 minutes as Brentford notched up their biggest victory since the record 9-0 obliteration of Wrexham in October 1963.

"It was a misty, dark and drizzly day," Bob says of a day he might well remember. "Things started well when I made the second goal by flicking the ball to Steve Phillips, who scored easily. For my first goal, after 35 minutes, I turned away from Gordon Nisbet, went down the right and, as the centre-half slid out towards me and the keeper started to come off his line, I side-footed it towards goal. I didn't hit the ball particularly cleanly, but it went under the keeper and nestled in the corner of the net for my first ever goal in the Football League – something nobody could ever take away from me."

The second goal came after a free kick from Alan Glover was half-cleared and fell to Bob, who poked it home. His hat trick was completed with a volley from Keith Fear's right-wing cross in the 59th minute.

Long-term Dodgin target Keith Fear, signed on loan from Plymouth, was the inspiration that day, pulling all the strings in a free role. He also scored a brilliant goal from out on the wing after a pass from Bob. Phillips scored twice and Bob was tickled pink to beat him to the hat trick. Kruse scored the seventh. Three goals and two assists in his first game of the season – not a bad way to announce your return to the team and mark your full home debut.

The match ball from that day, signed by Bob and his teammates, takes pride of place in the Brentford trophy cabinet, raising the incredible sum of £1,000 at a Sportsman's Dinner at the club.

"I couldn't believe it went for so much, but the guy who bought it said, 'I want you to have it back,' so I gave it to the club. Hopefully one day it will be on display at their new stadium in Lionel Road."

Dodgin was delighted with Bob's performance. "I thought the experience at Barnet would do him good. He is far sharper and has improved his control of the ball. I brought him in to give us some hustle and bustle, and to take the weight off Steve Phillips, and he certainly did that."

In recognition of his achievement, Dodgin also raised Bob's salary by a massive £10, to £80 per week.

Bob knew things could never be the same again after his wonderful achievement. "This was the most exciting day of my life, and it was sheer magic. I was still totally unknown, and very few Brentford fans knew who I was. You could feel the buzz from the crowd, and there were nearly 7,000 people there. But my achievement was a double-edged sword as the hat trick put so much pressure on me; the supporters now expected me to score in every game I played, and unfortunately things went downhill for me."

Much the same had happened to another callow young striker. Andy Woon had burst into prominence by scoring three goals on his full Brentford debut in a 5-0 hammering of Port Vale in early 1973, after arriving unheralded from Bognor Regis the previous October. He hung around for a couple more seasons but, not unexpectedly, failed to meet rising expectations. When you score three times on your debut there is really only one way left to go; his promise unfulfilled, he drifted back into non-league football with Maidstone United. Would the same fate befall Bob?

Bob kept his place for four of the next five games, scoring at Bury, but he could not repeat the form he had displayed against Hull and was dropped. "If it had not been for all the injuries, I would probably have been left out earlier," he reflects sadly. "The crowd certainly didn't help – they quickly got on my back."

Being booed has an effect, and a team suddenly bereft of confidence sank like a stone towards the bottom four after losing six of its next seven games. What did Tommy Baldwin think went wrong? "The luck just ran out, and we never really replaced Andy McCulloch," he felt.

Dodgin did not panic, changing little and persisting with his tried and tested approach. He felt that the tide would surely turn, but it didn't. The rot had well and truly set in. In late February, Bob returned as a half-time substitute at home to Blackpool. After the "young, lanky striker" headed home the equaliser, he made the winner for Danny Salman, which brought about the first victory since Hull, 11 matches earlier. The win proved to be a false dawn; the Bees waited nine more games to record their next win.

Dodgin's last shake of the dice was signing tiny striker Tony Funnell for a club record £56,000 from Gillingham – a Phillips clone who started slowly and didn't improve matters. Six games and four defeats later, Dodgin was given a leave of absence and never returned – poor reward for such a devoted and talented servant to the club, who less than a year previously had loyally turned down the chance to join Chelsea as assistant manager; in retrospect a poor, misguided decision on his part.

Brentford chairman Dan Tana was loath to pull the trigger on Dodgin, "The time around his departure was very difficult. With only a handful of games to go it looked as if Brentford would get relegated, and something had to be done to avoid the drop back to Division Four. The supporters had been demonstrating in the forecourt at Griffin Park. I'd spoken up on behalf of the manager, telling people I thought he was good enough to keep us up. Bill and I spoke about the situation and, until the 6-1 thrashing at Colchester followed by the home defeat to Rotherham, he'd told me not to worry. He had every faith in being able to turn the situation around."

"But after the Rotherham game, Bill came over to my house and we analysed the whole situation. On further reflection, he was no longer convinced that the team would escape the drop. So we came to a mutual agreement that he would step aside. I didn't sack him – Bill was a very good man."

Dodgin was replaced by his former coach, Fred Callaghan, the antithesis to Dodgin. Booker thought that he was "A tough nut – a bit of a character, who worked the players hard."

The days of long liquid lunches and golf outings were a thing of the past as training increased in intensity. Three wins in the last seven matches ensured that the Bees finished two places and a couple of points clear of relegation. Ironically, it was the misfit, Funnell, who finally came good, scoring the winner in the final game of the season against Millwall to ensure Brentford's survival.

This was Bob's first experience of seeing his manager leave. For the first time, he realised just how insecure football was as a profession, and how much his future depended on him staying in his manager's good books.

"I feel very blessed to have played under, and worked with, so many managers. They all had different ways of going about their business. I didn't always agree with them, but I respected them all and that is the one thing that you need from players. Managers have to earn it, and if they don't get it, they will always have problems. Having said that, there are a few that don't care what their players think of them... they believe it's their way or the highway, but luckily I never came across one of them."

"Managers live on results – it's as simple as that. When they're winning they are top dog, but when the team struggles, it's not the players that get sacked. It's cut-throat stuff. Results will make or break them and determine how long they keep their job."

"Losing Bill was tough to take. It was sad to see him go. He had been a father figure to me and given me my opportunity. He believed in me. I felt insecure and concerned about what might happen to me. I knew that I had to prove myself once again."

"It dawned on me that, as players, we are all commodities, pieces of a jigsaw and part of a machine all geared up to get results. The atmosphere changes around a football club when a new gaffer arrives; players start running around and putting themselves about, hoping to impress. I suppose it's human nature. Players that are out of the team and not part of the previous manager's plans are generally pleased to see a new manager come in. It's a chance for them to impress. And the ones that were in the team need to up their game as well. That is why, on lots of occasions when a new gaffer comes in, there is an immediate – if short-lived – change of fortune."

"When Dodgin left, I was in and out of the team. Trying to get used to a new manager was scary. I had gradually gained in confidence and tried to convince myself that I was a good player. I might think that, but would the new gaffer agree with me?" Without the security of a long-term contract, Bob could have been released or transfer-listed quickly. He resolved, as usual, to give everything – hoping Callaghan would see enough in his ability and potential.

"I had heard of Fred from his time at Fulham – he was a fresh face and voice. Working with him was a new experience for me, but we responded to him. He did not change things too much at first, apart from training us harder and longer."

# SCORING A HAT TRICK

The team needed goals, and Bob was brought back into the team for a must-win match at Gillingham. He responded by scoring the winner with a brilliant left-foot curler from the edge of the area – his best goal to date, and one that boosted his confidence and ensured he gained his manager's trust.

The 1979/1980 season had been a rollercoaster for Bob. He had started it totally out of favour, proven himself during his loan spell under Fry, returned with a bang with that unforgettable hat trick against Hull, drifted out of contention again, then ended the season with a crucial winning goal at Gillingham. All in all, he had scored six goals in nine appearances, plus three more as a substitute, making him equal third top-scorer in a team that escaped relegation by the skin of its teeth. In barely a dozen Football League matches, he had already experienced so many ups and downs in his burgeoning career.

# CHAPTER 5
# FACING THE BOO BOYS

Bob's time at Brentford often saw him booed unmercifully. He was a Marmite figure throughout his time at Griffin Park; most supporters loved him, seeing a lot of themselves in his effort, non-stop energy, determination to win, team ethos and no little skill; others rejected him on sight as being unfit to wear the shirt. Still more damned him with faint praise, patronising and denigrating him for the very versatility that made him such a valuable member of the squad.

They made no allowance for his late arrival to the game. Unlike most of his fellow professionals, he had undergone no apprenticeship. Certain fans failed to credit his willingness to sacrifice himself for the good of the team and do his utmost, without complaint, in whatever position he was asked. He was the first Brentford player to wear every shirt from 2-11, feeling proud to have done so. Surely he deserved appreciation and recognition, rather than a cacophony of jeers, insults and derision?

It is worth pointing out that there have been many examples of Brentford players who the fans loved to hate or hated to love; players who came in for regular and vituperative abuse. Stan Webb, Barry Lloyd, Lee Frost, Keith Bowen, Booker's brother-in-law Ian Bolton, Tom Finney, George Torrance, Steve Butler, Ian Holloway, Wayne Turner, Dean Martin, Leon Townley, Mark McCammon, Paul Brooker and Calum Willock easily spring to mind.

A Brentford programme from 1955 even contains an appeal from the manager, Bill Dodgin (Senior), for the supporters to show more patience and understanding towards a certain young player just making his way in the first team.

How does it feel as a footballer to be booed, barracked and abused from the terraces, particularly by your own so-called supporters? Does it inspire you to greater heights in order to try to stuff the critical words back down the throats from whence they came, or do you retreat into your shell and play less expansively, more cautiously, trying to eliminate risk from your game? Do you become determined not to make another mistake that could bring about even more criticism?

Joey Barton was typically forthright in his views on this subject, "External support is vital. I know this will sound cheesy, but when you know your fans are rooting for you, when you hear the low rumble of a supportive chant at a key moment, it does lift you."

The main problems Bob faced were of pressure and unfulfilled expectations. "I have received lots of criticism throughout my career and if you are not careful it can destroy you," he warns. "You begin to ask, 'Do I really deserve to be slaughtered when I am doing my best?' As a player, you need the manager to believe in you. When things got really bad, Fred Callaghan would only play me away from home so that I could get some respite from the boo-boys. I played far better away from home because the pressure was off me and the fans really got behind us. I felt supported and encouraged by them and I once won an award as away player of the year. It showed what I could do when I knew that the fans were on my side and gave me their unconditional support."

"The problems started very soon after the hat trick against Hull, which was both the best and the worst thing that could have happened to me. At first, there were a few murmurings of disapproval and grumbling whenever I made an error, which soon developed into constant abuse. 'Get off Booker, you can't even trap the ball, you're rubbish,' was typical of the insults I had to put up with. Things got so bad I could even hear people laughing at me, which was utterly soul-destroying. Given the size of our crowds, I could clearly hear every comment aimed at me."

"The harder I tried, the worse it got. Nothing would go right for me. The ball would bounce off me. I would miss open goals. A simple five-yard pass became a real challenge. The crowd would boo longer and louder and I would go into my shell. It got to a stage where I froze whenever the ball was passed to me. I really did not want it anywhere near me. I hated the fact that my family, sitting in the stand, could hear every comment. It made me feel angry and embarrassed. It even affected my home life. I shut myself away and became a bit of a recluse."

"As a player, you have to learn to adapt. But it isn't pleasant or easy. Fans don't care if you came from non-league or, in my case, local Saturday football; no allowances are made for your inexperience. Immediately after my hat trick I was floating on air and I felt no fear. But my balloon was pricked very soon afterwards and then playing football got a lot harder. The pressure of needing to win games, play well, keep your place in the team and earn another contract can be overwhelming. Supporters' expectations are massive, which is only fair – it is an old adage that they pay their money and are entitled to say what they like. But I wish they would consider the effect that their words can have."

Bob had no delusions of grandeur. He knew that he had to find a similar strength of will and purpose if he was to cope with the constant barracking and criticism he was facing. "There is no solution apart from keeping your head down, trying your best to ignore the taunts, and just getting on with your game until things turn around. If you don't keep believing in yourself and grow a thick skin then you're dead in the water. I knew I wasn't really ready for this level of the game, but I had given up my job with good money and a trade behind me and I felt honoured to be a professional footballer, so I wasn't going to give up or just let it drift away. It was really hard at times, but I am proud to say that I did not crumble. The experience I gained from working in the real world at Hille really helped me cope."

A single goal can help. "It is hard to describe exactly how it feels when your confidence is high, but you seem to do everything instinctively and it all comes off for you. You take shots quicker than normal, you take one touch instead of two; if you're playing in defence your timing of tackles is better and you win all your headers. In midfield, every pass you make is right on the money."

Bob's dad helped him through the difficult times, bolstering his son's confidence when they were driving home after matches. He would act as a sounding board and encourage Bob to maintain his self-belief, but inwardly he was also hurting. Bob's old friends in Garston were supportive, doing their utmost to keep his spirits up.

Is Bob's reaction to booing the norm? Richard Poole played for the club as a young homegrown 16-year-old during the early and mid-70s. It was an era when Brentford were not blessed with a plethora of talent and, with budgets stretched, generally had to make do with whatever combination of players they could scrape together. Performances were inconsistent to say the least, veering from one extreme to the other, with the fans not slow to express their wrath and disapproval at some of the substandard fare they were forced to endure.

"I felt really sorry for my teammate, Stan Webb, as he was onto an absolute hiding to nothing from the moment he signed for us," says Poole. "His move turned out to be a poisoned chalice because he had the near-impossible task of replacing a living legend in John O'Mara. The fans were furious at the lack of ambition shown by the club by selling O'Mara just after we had won promotion; they saw poor Stan simply as a cheap replacement, and took their frustration out on him. I thought he was a good influence around the club and really not a bad player at all. He had scored goals regularly in the Second Division at both his previous clubs, and, given half a chance, I am sure that he could have done the same for the Bees."

"I remember he would stay behind with us apprentices for extra training in the afternoon and give us some advice, but maybe he was too nice a person, which can be a bad failing for a footballer. He was strong and could certainly mix it, but the constant barrage of criticism affected him. His performances suffered and he lost confidence. Given more time and a more sympathetic response from the Brentford supporters, he would have done much better at the club. I am sure that he must have been delighted, and seen it as suitable revenge, when he scored a crucial goal against us after he had moved to Darlington."

Poole received some harsh criticism from Brentford fans when he returned in a reserve game for Watford shortly after his departure. His parents watched on, suffering. "It was so bad that some of my new teammates asked me what was going on. The supporters who were giving me such a hard time lived really close to my family, and that was very upsetting. Generally, you do hear all the comments from the crowd, good and bad – particularly when there are not too many supporters in the ground. It certainly has an impact on your game."

"When I first came into the side as a youngster, my concentration was totally on the game – to such an extent that I really only heard the crowd noise when there was a break in play. I remember an important home game against Colchester United, with Griffin Park full to the brim. I was waiting for a corner kick to be played into the penalty area and I heard a voice behind the goal shouting 'Come on Richard!' It really got through to me, inspired me and made me feel ten feet tall."

"As for being booed by away fans, that simply meant that I must be doing my job properly and getting something right."

Poole scored a memorable goal at home to Bradford City. "I saw everyone standing up and applauding and, for me, it was like there were thousands and thousands of fans cheering me on and supporting me. Even now, over 40 years later, I get goose pimples just thinking about that magic and unforgettable moment. When you are a local boy and you are cheered on, it gives you such a boost; conversely, I can still remember that horrible reserve match for Watford against Brentford when I was booed, and it really affected my game."

The similarity between Poole and Bob's words about the effect of barracking on a player's game and psyche is striking. Bob was not alone in his reaction and attitude to his treatment by some home supporters. Despite all the difficulties he faced, there were still good days for Bob. Many Brentford fans deeply appreciated his efforts, as this wonderful letter from John Baynton, written the day after the hat trick against Hull City and carefully preserved in Bob's scrapbook, demonstrates:

*Dear Bob,*

*This is just a quick letter to say how much I and my friends enjoyed and appreciated your performance against Hull last Saturday. You worked so hard chasing and challenging for the ball that you thoroughly deserved your hat-trick and we are absolutely delighted for you. In particular, your first effort showed tremendous skill and control.*

*I hope to see you in the first team again on Saturday and feel sure that if you work as hard as you did the other day you will keep your place in the team – a big striker is just what Brentford need at present. I'm not expecting you to score goals necessarily but it would be nice!*

*Anyway, the very best of luck to you and thanks for a memorable match.*

*Yours sincerely,*

*John Baynton*

# CHAPTER 6
# MAKING MY WAY

Fred Callaghan was chairman Dan Tana's selection to replace Bill Dodgin, a hard act to follow who had deserved better treatment. With recent history at the club, Callaghan was an obvious and easy choice.

A long-serving, dependable and popular full-back for Fulham, playing nearly 300 games for the Cottagers before injury forced him into retirement at the end of the 1973/74 season, Callaghan soon moved into coaching, enjoying a successful spell with Enfield before switching to Griffin Park in February 1977 to assist Dodgin. His initial stay coincided with an outstanding run of results and performances as the team soared up the table. At the end of the campaign he left to become manager at Woking, rejoining Brentford when the call came from Tana with the Bees in dire peril of relegation.

Callaghan was what Andre Villas-Boas recently referred to, at a football conference in Amsterdam, as a "bipolar" managerial appointment – the total antithesis to his predecessor. A blunt and tough taskmaster, he soon set out to show everyone who was boss and put his own stamp on things. His way or the highway. Bob and the rest of the players soon discovered that their new manager had a totally different approach to the far more easy-going and laid-back Dodgin. The new regime and change in style paid instant dividends as Callaghan revitalised a faltering Brentford, inspiring his new team to three wins and two draws in their final seven games. Relegation was narrowly averted on the last day of the season – comparable to Martin Allen's appointment in place of Wally Downes in 2004, at a time when the Bees looked doomed, prior to "The Great Escape."

Callaghan's first move, in the summer of 1980, was to bring in former Chelsea legend, Ron Harris, as his player-coach and club captain. Harris received instant respect thanks to his fearsome reputation, bringing about a huge improvement in the team's defensive record. The Bees had leaked 73 goals the previous season, but conceded only 49 in 1980/81.

The combination of Callaghan and Harris was initially successful. Bob realised how important it was for a manager to dovetail well and share the load with his assistant. "The manager must know he can totally trust and rely on you," he outlines. "Your working relationship has to be watertight. You might not socialise, but the workplace is where it counts. When managers move from club to club it's quite normal for the assistant to follow him. In my case, it was to be a little different."

Bob was starstruck by the new arrival. "Ron 'Chopper' Harris was one of the hardest players you could ever meet. Fred was vocal and animated and Ron was very quiet and kept himself to himself, but they worked extremely well together and we respected both of them. Ron was still playing, so it was a real bonus to have his knowledge and top-level experience on the pitch. He was a Chelsea legend." Bob and Tony Bates used to watch Harris in his prime at Stamford Bridge. "When Tony found out he was my coach, I knew the question would come up about getting his autograph. I put it off as long as I could, but did eventually ask Ron, who gave me a real old-fashioned look that curdled my blood. He obviously thought that I was trying to make fun of him, so I ensured that he signed one of his photos 'To Tony.' What a leader – he was such a quiet man, but he didn't need to open his mouth. He played in a lot of the games as a sweeper and was a huge influence in helping to tighten up our defence. His pre-game ritual was to stand in a hot bath filled shin-high to warm up his feet. He disdained shin pads, wore the longest aluminium studs in the world and was a total no-nonsense footballer."

"One thing you didn't do was take liberties with Chopper Harris," continues Bob. "The younger professionals and apprentices would compete in a no-holds-barred five-a-side game on a concrete car park behind the home end at Griffin Park. Chopper always joined in, and this was a real baptism of fire. There was a corrugated iron fence surrounding the car park. Ron didn't hold back; he played hard and not always fair." Harris wanted to toughen everyone up by showing no mercy. "I managed to hold my own, but some of the apprentices were quite often left squealing on the floor or felt the full force of Chopper smashing them into the fence. It was survival of the fittest for about an hour – make or break, a good grounding for any young player. Ron could take it too, and he would never let you know when he was hurt."

Callaghan demolished much of what Dodgin had carefully built. He instigated a mini clear-out, transfer listing and eventually seeing off established and experienced players such as Len Bond, Jackie Graham, Dean Smith, Steve Phillips, John Fraser and David Carlton. Lee Holmes, too, was soon on his way following his refusal to sign full-time terms. "He wanted a change of faces and voices, and to build his own team."

Callaghan wanted his own men *in situ* – ideally hungry, young players with everything to prove. Ably assisted by his best ever signing, scout *extraordinaire* John Griffin, from Fulham, he recruited some of the finest prospects seen at the club for many years. David Crown, Terry Hurlock and Gary Roberts were all inspired bargain buys from non-league clubs in the days when it was still possible to steal a march on your competition through a combination of hard work, excellent contacts and a good eye, identifying players who were not yet on their radar. In Griffin, Brentford were fortunate to have the services of one of the best in the business.

Mark Hill and Barry Silkman were less successful purchases, but David McKellar, signed for £25,000 from Derby County, proved a calm, safe and consistent replacement for Bond. He was a massive improvement over another youngster, Paul McCullough, who had singularly failed to impress after some eccentric displays in goal. "A scruffy bastard who didn't look like a professional footballer," says Bob. "He was too brave for his own good and the fans called him 'The Kamikaze Kid,' but he was far too prone to errors. He wasn't fit enough and the moment I saw him in the car park stuffing his face with a burger immediately before a game at Charlton, I feared the worst."

Many years later, in late 1992, midfielder Grant Chalmers was dragged out of the club bar at the last minute to sit on the bench after Chris Hughton had injured himself in the warm-up against Derby. The substitute had to be substituted after suffering from the effects of a now-unwanted pre-match pie.

Silkman was a real showman: bare chest, medallion and perm. One day, he and Bob competed in a Crossbar Challenge from the halfway line – no competition, really, as Silkman succeeded with three of his five attempts, whereas Bob's efforts could have been choreographed by Sir Barnes Wallis, of Dam Busters fame. But for all his effervescence and talent, Silkman was inconsistent and temperamental, drifting away to local rivals QPR before finding fame and fortune as an agent.

There was also a reprieve for midfielder Paul Walker, who sparkled for half a season, looking as if he was finally going to fulfil his vast promise and even signing a new four-year contract before again falling out of the reckoning. Bob was not alone in feeling that he never made the most of his ability. Callaghan and Harris thought Walker should have reached the top, but he was too undisciplined. His squat body shape always saw him struggle with his weight, never looking after himself properly – a criminal waste of a huge talent.

Bob signed a one-year extension to his contract in the close season, sending his salary to the giddy heights of £90 per week. Slowly but surely his value was being recognised by the club.

Obviously flush with cash, he made the momentous decision to leave home, buying a small flat conveniently situated just across the road from his parents, who paid his deposit and, in the best tradition of single sons, allowed Bob to bring his washing home every week.

Unlike the previous season, no new strikers arrived. Bob was given the chance to stake his claim. He started well, scoring against Yeovil and Wimbledon in pre-season and particularly enjoying a 3-0 win over a strong Chelsea team in the memorial match for the legendary *Middlesex Chronicle* journalist George Sands, who had reported on 1,126 consecutive Brentford matches before his death.

Bob initially partnered Tony Funnell up front ("He got on the end of my flicks"), with the speedy David Crown on the left wing making an instant impression after his arrival from Walthamstow Avenue. "He was skilful and could cause mayhem. He was also very inconsistent and sometimes he disappeared from the action."

News spread far slower in those days – long before the internet, wall-to-wall digital television and radio, and social media. I well remember coming in from playing cricket late one Saturday evening in August 1980 and switching on my television set to see, to my amazement, Brentford featuring on ITV's *The Big Match* – capturing an impressive and totally unexpected 3-2 win at Walsall.

Was this really Brentford wearing an unfamiliar sky blue away kit? Who was this fearsome long-haired, bearded figure marauding around the midfield, leaving bodies prostrate in his wake, his earrings flashing in the late summer sunshine like a Norse God?

Terry Hurlock later joined Stan Bowles and Chris Kamara to form one of Brentford's finest ever midfields. Hurlock was a Griffin discovery who had been released by West Ham, but the 21-year-old rapidly made a reputation for himself at Leytonstone & Ilford, before the Bees pounced where others hesitated, paying a derisory £10,000 for him.

Bob was perplexed at first sight. "We met him for the first time in the dressing room at Walsall, and nobody knew who he was. We had heard that he was a tough nut who had had some problems with the law. He was wearing jeans and flip-flops with no socks, the scruffiest hair that I had ever seen, a beard and those earrings."

If the players were bemused by Hurlock's appearance and manner, things changed as soon as he stepped out onto the pitch. "He was awesome and far better than any of us. He could tackle and pass, although he needed to get a bit fitter. He had had a tough life and was real old-school. He had a group of hard-looking mates who were a good influence on him and helped keep him out of trouble. He knew he had to change now he was in the public eye. We became good friends and I made him laugh, which was fortunate for me, as you really didn't want to get on the wrong side of Terry Hurlock. He was a loveable rogue who relished a good time. He had a short fuse – you couldn't remove that from him or he wouldn't have been half the player." And what a player he was. "He could do the lot – pass, tackle for fun, score, and get around the pitch. He was a leader, one that would die for his team. He reminded me of Bryan Robson and, in my opinion, he was just as good."

Hurlock quickly settled into league football, rapidly became the best player in the team and was soon being scouted by higher-level clubs, who dithered over his off-the-field reputation. He stayed at the club for five years – far too long given his talent – before being sold to Reading for a club record £92,500. He later achieved cult status at Millwall, a marriage made in heaven, winning an England B cap. He also starred at Glasgow Rangers and Southampton before his career was ended at the age of 37, ironically in a friendly match against Brentford, when he broke his leg in a challenge with another hard man, Martin Grainger – the biter bit.

The best description of him was by his teammate Francis Joseph, who likened him to "A caveman carrying a sledgehammer." He was The Incredible Hulk, an impassable barrier who could play the game as well as intimidate.

With Griffin's help, Callaghan brought in some exceptionally talented players. Gary Roberts, another non-league bargain for £6,000 from Wembley, competed with Crown for the left-wing spot. Known as "Gasping" because he was always on the lookout for a beer, Roberts's talent was appreciated by Bob. "He did it off the cuff and could beat players at will. He didn't like a tackle but he had two great feet and always chipped in with goals." His career was sadly curtailed by injury.

Bob started the 1980/81 season well. The fans were slightly more tolerant of him, recognising his non-stop effort, but the goals soon dried up. Shortly after spearheading a recovery from a two-goal deficit at Millwall, he was dropped.

Opposition players hated The Den. Eamon Dunphy perfectly sums up what they had waiting in store for them. "Having wound their way through a maze of narrow streets off the Old Kent Road, visiting teams would draw up outside what looked like a derelict factory. Grey was the primary colour. What wasn't grey needed a coat of paint. The pitch was tight – and bumpy. The visitors' dressing room was dark and narrow, as welcoming as a British Rail loo. Only good teams and brave players survived their introduction to the Lions' Den. Even then, some of them changed their minds when the game kicked off. At that stage, visiting players discovered that the fans were as hostile as the *décor*. Even small Millwall crowds made a fearsome noise, which chilled the bones of many a northern hard man who'd come to London believing southerners were soft. This was the wrong part of London."

It is not unsurprising that Brentford's two goal scorers against Millwall were the indomitable Booker and Hurlock. Bob headed past John Jackson, before setting up Hurlock, who drilled in the equaliser. Bob remembers sliding into the advertising hoardings after he made the mistake of scoring right in front of the home fans. His celebrations were cut short by a veritable hail of spittle and he beat a hasty retreat.

Callaghan paid tribute to Bob's "100 per cent honesty" but dropped him, favouring new signing Gary Johnson, who arrived from Chelsea, together with former Bees loanee Lee Frost, for a combined £30,000. They formed a new strike duo which, for all Johnson's good touch and clever football brain, proved to be singularly lacking in punch, physicality and cutting edge, scoring only eight goals between them in 37 matches. Johnson was not blessed with pace and Harris remembered him as "The one fellow that I could beat in a sprint – and at my age I could not beat too many." Frost, so impressive in his previous stay at the club, was an abject failure and suffered badly at the hands and mouths of an impatient home crowd. "He had a lot of ability," says Harris, "but was never keen enough or the bravest of players."

Bob played 19 of the opening 23 league games but realised that he was still extremely raw. Happy to be earning a living from a profession he had now grown to love, he returned to the reserves, getting his head down, learning, and resuming his partnership with Funnell.

With Tommy Baldwin leaving with Dodgin, no coaches remained with any experience of playing up front, while the other forwards at the club were also young and callow. They were largely left to fend for themselves and learn from their own mistakes.

Bob might not have been so phlegmatic had he realised that, in December 1980, Callaghan had placed him on the transfer list with a £5,000 price on his head, alongside, Funnell, Willie Graham and Iori Jenkins. Bob had no inkling of this – the first he knew of it was when I showed him a faded local newspaper clipping. He responded with amazement; his manager had taken neither the time nor trouble to inform him, and he remained in blithe ignorance – the way of manager/player communication in the bad old days.

Nobody, not even Barry Fry, came in for him, and the season meandered on. In a remarkable achievement, the Bees kept six consecutive clean sheets, scoring just four times in those six games, all against Walsall. No wonder the fans, who had so little to shout about, were getting restless.

The season was drifting to its conclusion with the Bees safely in mid-table when Callaghan finally lost patience with the patently underperforming Frost, who was unceremoniously dropped and was never seen in league football again. Bob was restored to the first team alongside Johnson, responding with four goals in the final six games of the season as Brentford went undefeated and scored nine times; impressive when they only scored 52 goals in their 46 league games.

Bob scored "a beauty" from 15 yards, at Oxford United, according to local journalist Dean Bartram, who also described him as possessing "Latent skill in the (Derby County hitman) Roger Davies mould." His goal helped win a point in his first game back, impressing his manager with his work rate.

Bob also played well at home to high-flying Chesterfield, who were beaten 3-2 thanks to a quite incredible and unforgettable 30-yard own goal from their defender John Ridley, who, harassed by the ever-willing Bob, panicked and magnificently curled the ball way beyond the reach of his helpless goalkeeper, John Turner. As the ball crept across the line, the crowd gasped in astonishment – then burst into hysterical laughter. Bartram was rapidly becoming a fan of Bob, describing him as "Undoubtedly the most improved player on Brentford's books" as his fine form continued with a headed assist for Johnson to score.

Next up were Sheffield United, caught up in a relegation dogfight and desperate for points. Brentford trailed early on before battering their visitors, who were saved by a stupendous goalkeeping display by Steve Conroy. He appeared unbeatable but Bob broke their hearts with a late near-post flicked header from a Roberts corner; a goal which essentially helped to relegate his future team, going down by a single point.

Bob scored in each of the next two games: the clincher in a comfortable 2-0 win at doomed Colchester United, with a confident finish from the edge of the box, and then a perfectly timed diving header from a Kruse cross which helped defeat champions Rotherham United. He also played a key role in the winner when his shot was cleared off the line by a defender's hand before Hurlock smashed in the rebound.

Bob's form was sufficient for his manager to take him off the transfer list, apparently without informing his player again. Bob remained totally unaware of the situation – footballer as chattel. The season ended with a dull goalless draw at Swindon Town, but Bob was joint top-scorer alongside Crown and Funnell, notching eight goals.

Brentford finished in a healthy ninth place and Bob was included on an end of season tour of Yugoslavia, experiencing foreign conditions for the first time, including the serving of a whole pig on a spit during a visit to Dan Tana's luxurious house on an island off the town of Split.

Bob had started the season well before faltering. Had another manager come in with the £5,000 fee set by Callaghan (or nearest offer) he could well have been on his way out of Griffin Park. But as always, he persisted, worked hard and, when opportunity came again, took it. He ended up back in his manager's good books and established in the team.

Thirty matches started in all competitions and equal top scorer – not bad for an unheralded lad from Garston.

# CHAPTER 7
# JACK OF ALL TRADES

The following season saw a major change for Bob. Typically for Brentford, the squad lacked depth and was thin in numbers. When injuries began to bite, Fred Callaghan was often left short of options. Only one substitute was allowed in those days, and Callaghan and Ron Harris, recognised their overwhelming need for a versatile player capable of covering several positions, deputising whenever and wherever the need arose.

There was obviously no money available to bring in an experienced utility player or increase the size of the squad, so they were forced to look for a suitable candidate from within. Bob was their unanimous choice, although few other options existed, particularly as Fred felt that Bob was never going to score regularly enough to remain his first-choice central striker.

Bob had many positive qualities for Callaghan and Harris to work with; tall, fit and extremely strong in the tackle, he had some pace, could run all day, was no mug on the ball and excellent in the air.

Callaghan thought Bob would be better and more effective playing the way he was facing rather than with his back to goal, benefiting from more time on the ball. His positive attitude, as well as his open-mindedness and eagerness to learn new skills and develop his game, was vital. The more valuable he proved to be, the more likely he would be to earn a new contract – a not unimportant consideration for a young footballer still seeking to establish himself and make his way in the game.

Callaghan has only warm and positive memories of Bob at this phase of his career. "He was a terrific lad and a useful footballer who could play anywhere." He is not trying to damn him with faint praise when reminiscing that Bob, "could do a bit of everything. He always gave you 100%. I felt he was at his best in midfield, where he was a bundle of energy. He was also excellent in both penalty areas."

Paul Shrubb and Paul Walker had started the season in midfield, with Bob up front alongside Gary Roberts. But after a surprising, fortunate win at Fulham on the opening day of the season (a penalty and a perfectly-taken Roger Brown own goal), results tailed off. Bob only managed one goal, at Portsmouth. He loved playing at Fratton Park, always seeming to score there – perhaps a tribute to his dad, who had attended school with Pompey legend Jimmy Dickinson.

Not before time, Callaghan changed things around in September. New striker Keith Bowen arrived from Northampton, with Bob asked to move to midfield, where he soon settled, continuing to play regularly for the rest of his career. Bowen had a famous father, Dave, the former Northampton, Arsenal and Wales wing-half. He had scored consistently at Northampton, but for all his effort, the Third Division was a step too far. Bob felt for him. "Like me, he struggled with the crowd – they were quick to express their disapproval. Keith wasn't a strong character or very forceful in the dressing room. He could not handle the higher level after proving himself in the Fourth Division."

Harris, on the other hand, felt that Bob had all the attributes necessary to become an exceptional centre-half, a position he really enjoyed playing in. Harris particularly recalls a Milk Cup tie at Blackburn in 1982 when Bob performed like Roy of the Rovers, inspiring the Bees to a creditable 0-0 draw and aggregate victory over their higher division opponents. Local journalist Sean Gilligan's match report said Bob operated "as a left-back, a midfielder or as an extra attacker, when the need arose."

From time to time, Bob even appeared ahead of the normal first-choice centre-half, Alan Whitehead – an expensive buy from Bury who never really made the position his own, nor justified his huge, tribunal-fixed £78,000 club record fee. New chairman Martin Lange's first act on joining the board was to help pay this enormous, unforeseen sum, writing a personal cheque for £65,000 to help resolve yet another Brentford financial crisis.

Whitehead's arrival saw the end for stalwart Pat Kruse, inspiring this tortuous pun from Gilligan, "The nuclear warhead has replaced the Kruse missile as Brentford's secret weapon at set pieces." Whitehead was, in fact, known to the other players as "Large Head," for obvious reasons. He was not alone in receiving a nickname based on his physical characteristics, as the Fulham goalkeeper of the time, Gerry Peyton, was also known as "Bombhead." Leroy Rosenior credited Peyton with the "Biggest-sized head in football." Perhaps the two should have had a competition.

Circumstances dictated Bob's initial move even further backwards. Playing as a central defender in a tight and keenly contested local derby in January 1982 against a rampant Fulham team who would win promotion that year, Bob stepped in when Whitehead limped off with a twisted ankle, leaving Bees fans fearing the worst. A man inspired, Bob totally snuffed out the threat of Dean Coney, Fulham's highly-rated young striker, earning apt press plaudits as a "hero" and "little short of a revelation" in his "emergency role with a display of perception and skill that made him by far the Bees most influential player." Callaghan also praised the display of a player who had filled in at full-back and midfield, but never centre-back. Brentford supporters regarded him in a totally different light after that performance, impressed by the unexpected quality he had shown in an entirely new position.

Bob would still play up front from time to time; his prowess there played an important part in Brentford's run to the Freight Rover Trophy Final in 1985. But from 1981 until he left the club seven years later, he became established as the squad's utility player, playing any position without complaint and with unfailing consistency. Without this versatility, Bob's career would arguably not have lasted nearly as long or been quite as successful.

Contrast his positive attitude and love of the game with the powerful, sad and haunting words expressed by former player Curtis Woodhouse in his recent autobiography. "Once I became a pro, I felt it was over," he wrote. "I loved the journey; I hated the destination. The more money I earned the more I hated football. It did not represent anything good and became a bigger burden. It's not the industry everyone cracks it up to be. Deep down, a lot of players will detest what they do – and that's understandable. When it becomes a job, everything changes; there are different responsibilities; there is the pressure of making the team, of being suspended, of getting injured, of being part of a billion-dollar industry with a lot on the line for a lot of people. Don't misconstrue my meaning – there are far worse jobs out there – but the day after I quit I woke up and a huge weight had lifted."

Bob had never faced the gruelling challenge of competing, in a survival of the fittest, with so many other young hopefuls, all seeking to make their way into the game from their early teens. That is, perhaps, why he never lost his love and enthusiasm for playing football, an attitude which also rubbed off on his teammates. The immortal Alfredo Di Stéfano once said that to deserve to wear the Real Madrid badge, "You have to soak the jersey in sweat." Bob followed this advice and played every game as if it would be his last.

Bob felt that playing in other positions gave him a different perspective on the game, re-energised by the fresh challenges he faced.

"Up until 1981, I had always played centre-forward, where you tend to be in the spotlight, particularly if you are scoring goals. You see your name in the papers, everybody loves you and you might even get a goal bonus in your wages – not that Brentford ever gave me one. But in my case, having not previously played higher than park football, I often struggled for form, and I was relieved when I was given the chance to play in other positions."

He favoured midfield. "You are always involved in the action. I loved the physical side of the game, and my fitness and enthusiasm meant that I could get around the pitch. I could stick my foot in, there was space for me to play, it was the perfect position for me. Most importantly, the pressure was off. I no longer felt that I was expected to score a goal every time I played. I learned how to play there by watching some of the country's best players like Graeme Souness, Bryan Robson, Gordon Strachan and Paul Gascoigne. They all seemed to know what they were going to do with the ball before they took possession of it. I did my best to observe them, and I just hoped that some of their magic would rub off on me. Never for one moment did I ever imagine that I would end up playing against them all."

"Players like Gazza are very few and far between. He was a total genius who excited and electrified everyone who was privileged enough to watch him play. Our paths did cross a few times; once at White Hart Lane he totally dominated the game and all I could do was hold my hands up and acknowledge that he was on another planet to me. Later, that same season, I did a bit better against him at Bramall Lane and took home the man of the match champagne. It was such a privilege to play against him."

"I also replaced Alan Whitehead from time to time at centre-half, and I slotted into the role fairly smoothly. I loved playing there, especially at Sheffield United where I was pitting my wits against players like Ian Rush, Ian Wright and Mark Hughes. I felt great if I didn't let them score. That was an amazing feeling which I was fortunate enough to experience on occasion."

"Playing at centre-half, you see the whole game from a completely different perspective. Everything is in front of you, unless you're chasing Wright or Rush – then, of course, all you see is their backside as they leave you trailing in their wake, something that happened to me far too often. But having played as a striker, you can hopefully read and anticipate what a centre-forward is going to do and identify what his strengths are. Does he like going short or does he prefer getting tight to you or even running in the channels? Your own experience as a striker also makes it far easier to defend set pieces – you know the sort of runs that forwards are most likely to make, and can mark up accordingly."

Bob recognises how much his versatility added to his game and his career. "Being ready, willing and able to play anywhere was the making of me, and filled me with pride and confidence. All I ever wanted was to be given a first team shirt, irrespective of what number was printed on the back of it."

"I can only explain it as 'getting used,' but in a nice way. If a full-back got injured I would play there, the same when a midfielder was injured, suspended or fell out of favour. It got me the title of 'Mr Versatility.' My job was easy and straightforward – win the ball and ideally give it to another player wearing a red and white striped shirt. I always tried to find Stan Bowles and then it was job done. I could take a breather while he dwelt on the ball and performed his magic."

Bob wore every shirt number apart from goalkeeper, winning Brentford's player of the year in 1983. "This was one of the proudest moments in my career, particularly as we boasted the likes of Stan Bowles, Terry Hurlock, Chris Kamara and Francis Joseph in the team, and I managed to beat them all to this fantastic prize. Not bad for the upholsterer from the factory, even if I say so myself. At that time, little did I know that a few years down the line, when I became a coach, it really made my job so much easier knowing and understanding the needs and requirements of every position, gained from my own playing experience."

Sometimes, unfortunately, things did not go quite so well for Bob when he covered a key player's absence. Gary Roberts missed an FA Cup defeat in a replay at Colchester where the Bees subsided to a listless 1-0 defeat, and Bob came in for some criticism in the local press. "Gary Roberts's out of touch replacement Bob Booker proved to be little more than a pale parody of the missing winger," ran one report. Tough words, particularly when he came closest to equalising from an effort which hit the crossbar.

Well-respected and long-established scout John Griffin smiles when asked about Bob – a common reaction from anybody when they are discussing him – and remarked that he thought Bob had been an honest player whose versatility was his greatest asset to his team. "You could play him anywhere and he always gave you total commitment, and a seven out of ten performance."

John then went on to give Bob perhaps the most fulsome tribute I have ever heard about him, "Every club needs a Bob Booker, and the day we make Bob Booker the 11th man in our squad we will have a very good side indeed." Such a positive verdict from a scout of Griffin's calibre and experience should not be disregarded or taken lightly. Bob was deeply touched when told about John's words.

I also thought about Bob when I read Lincoln City manager Danny Cowley's recent description of one of his players, Lee Angol, as "An iPhone 7, because he can do a bit of everything."

Ironically enough, as soon as Bob had begun to play regularly in midfield, Brentford managed to strengthen the position – and not just with anybody. Two special players arrived at Griffin Park at the end of October 1981 – Chris Kamara and the immortal Stan Bowles.

Kamara came from Portsmouth in a straight swap for David Crown, who had become expendable given how quickly Roberts had developed. "I was a better crosser and dribbler than him," recalls Roberts, "whereas David was quick and direct." Meanwhile, Callaghan and Lange took a huge gamble on Bowles, who had been seemingly drifting towards oblivion at Leyton Orient. Bob was stunned when the club managed to sign him.

The term "genius" is thrown around with gay abandon, often applied to the merely very good rather than the rare one-offs and special ones. But nobody could ever quibble or complain at Stan being so described. In a wonderful career spanning the best part of 20 years, he played nearly 600 games – testimony to the fact that he was not just a luxury player who picked his games, but a lover of the game and a tough competitor.

Immaturity, massive competition for places and some dodgy off-field connections cost Bowles the opportunity of early stardom at Manchester City, but he rehabilitated himself in the nether regions of the Football League at Crewe and Carlisle. While other teams dithered, Gordon Jago took the gamble and signed him for Queens Park Rangers in September 1972 for what turned out to be a bargain £110,000. Rodney Marsh had long been the idol of all QPR fans, who had bemoaned his transfer to Manchester City, of all places, but Bowles proved the perfect replacement, becoming an instant hero at Loftus Road and giving the hallowed number ten shirt a worthy new owner.

Bowles spent seven productive years in his pomp at QPR, but his ability, consistency and excellent goal-scoring record failed to convince successive England managers of his temperament, playing only five times for his country – a terrible waste of talent and an indictment of the cautious and puritanical establishment running the game at the time, incapable of coping with free spirits like Bowles. He joined fellow mavericks such as Frank Worthington, Alan Hudson, Charlie George, Peter Osgood and Tony Currie in being treated with suspicion, never fulfilling their undoubted ability at international level.

At QPR, Bowles was neither the first nor last player to fall out with the mercurial Tommy Docherty, who sold him to Nottingham Forest in December 1979. Out of the frying pan, into the fire: he also fell foul of Brian Clough, ruling himself out of playing in the 1980 European Cup Final. His career looked like it was drifting towards its conclusion when his next move, to Leyton Orient, left him treading water. But a revitalised talent enjoyed one last hurrah when he joined Brentford in October 1981 for what proved to be a giveaway £25,000 fee.

Lange and Callaghan had taken a chance, but it proved to be an inspirational move for the club as Bowles rediscovered his enthusiasm for the game, invigorating players and supporters alike with his sparkling presence and twinkling feet. Despite his advancing years, he provided marvellous value for money, playing nearly 100 games for the Bees, scoring 17 times and assisting on countless others. He has gone down in Brentford legend by forming the final leg in what became perhaps their finest midfield trio since the Tony Harper, Ron Greenwood and Jimmy Hill partnership from shortly after the end of the Second World War.

The new arrivals impressed Bob straightaway. Kamara was a tireless box-to-box runner and, according to Bob, "The first one on the training pitch and the last man off – a real leader." He provided goals, heading ability and had the energy to get into the box to finish off his chances. I can still see him celebrating wildly and provocatively in front of the Swindon fans after scoring from a 20-yard looping header in a 3-0 win against his former team; he just laughed off the abuse and vitriol his behaviour generated. Brentford were unstoppable that night and totally dominated a team that usually beat them.

Bowles was just Bowles. Callaghan was astute enough to give him the freedom to roam at will. He did little running, confining himself to the left side of midfield, but he didn't really need to – his teammates did it for him. He simply conserved his energy, sprayed the ball around and cut helpless opposition defences wide open with his rapier-like passes.

Hurlock was the perfect foil for Bowles and Kamara, a passionate, aggressive presence who took no prisoners. Together, the three of them formed an unbeatable combination.

The fans adored Bowles and a season's best attendance of nearly 7,000 crammed in to see him make his debut at home to Burnley. Three days later, he pulled all the strings as the Bees destroyed Swindon, maintaining his consistency for the next 18 months. He scored regularly: six times in 1981/82, plus a remarkable 11 goals the following season when he played over 50 times and laid on goals aplenty for the rampaging forward line of Tony Mahoney, Francis Joseph and Roberts, although sometimes he was too clever for them to read his intentions. Stan could do seemingly anything on the pitch; the complete master of the ball, with a left foot that was like a wand.

Bob couldn't believe his luck playing alongside such a legend. "You would never see Stan on a match day until about 20 minutes before kick-off, as he had generally come directly from the betting shop," he remembers with awe. "He didn't muck about in training, but never ran around too much either. He never wore shin pads, but that was OK as nobody could ever get close enough to kick him. He inspired us. You could not help but learn from watching him."

Young full-back Terry Rowe also benefited from playing alongside Bowles. "He was a model professional," he says. "It was an honour for me to play in the same team. He was forever offering me encouragement and advice."

Watching Brentford take penalties has understandably always been a source of great stress to fans over the years. I have never known whether to focus my attention on the goal or fix it on a point five feet over the crossbar, where the ball was more likely to appear once it had been struck. Yet with Bowles, I never worried. He scored 11 out of 12 times from the penalty spot, languidly strolling up and sending the goalkeeper and the crowd behind the goal one way, before stroking the ball effortlessly into the other corner of the net. I still cannot believe that he actually missed one kick. In fact, I remain sceptical, as no photograph seems to exist of that rare occurrence, alleged to have taken place one Friday night at Wrexham in 1983. Bob was never in any doubt about Bowles's prowess from the spot, "I never bothered watching him take any penalty kicks as the outcome was a foregone conclusion. As soon as the referee blew his whistle I would simply start walking back to the centre circle for the restart."

# OOH-AAH: THE BOB BOOKER STORY

Not content with that, Bowles produced his party piece of scoring directly from a corner against Swindon. He was naturally deadly from long-range free kicks, as Wimbledon's Dave Beasant could attest. Bowles was a star you simply could not take your eyes away from. He also mucked in and was just one of the lads. There were no airs and graces and he always played to win, giving everything he had rather than merely going through the motions and playing only when the mood took him.

Bowles provided full value, lighting up Griffin Park with his genius and ever-present cheeky smile. The fact that he had been a hero at Brentford's massive rivals, QPR, was soon forgiven and forgotten. He provided such pleasure to untold millions of fans with his skill, *joie de vivre* and overall approach to life, remaining fondly remembered by everyone associated with the club. We all salute him and send him and his family our best wishes and gratitude for the pleasure he gave us.

The Brentford team was beginning to gel early in 1982, although they were more dangerous on the counter attack, with a far better record away from home, where they won 11 times, than at Griffin Park. At home, they struggled to break teams down, feeling pressured by an impatient crowd quick to find fault whenever things went wrong. A run of nine wins in 14 games threatened a late charge for promotion, but their hopes were dashed when Wimbledon, desperate for points in their ultimately unsuccessful effort to avoid relegation, recovered from a two-goal deficit to win by the odd goal in five. The victors that day were inspired by the pace and clinical finishing of a young, unknown striker called Francis Joseph, who ran the Bees ragged and had a promising future.

Aside from Bowles, the other highlight for Bob was playing against 35-year-old George Best in a friendly match against the touring San Jose Earthquakes. Bob scored the final goal in an 8-2 rout as well as tripping Best up – "The only way to stop him."

Finishing in eighth place was an excellent achievement, but goals were still in short supply. Nonetheless, the Bees went into the following season in good heart, knowing they were only a couple of strikers short of having a team capable of mounting a serious promotion challenge. They had now discovered a player in Bob who could fill in almost anywhere on the pitch, reliably putting in committed, wholehearted performances.

73

# CHAPTER 8
# A LOST OPPORTUNITY

Almost 35 years on, the 1982/83 season still seems to have panned out confusingly, eventually ending like a damp squib after promising so much for so long. Everything seemed set fair for the Bees to celebrate a triumphant return to the Second Division after nearly 30 years in the nether regions of the Football League. But things fizzled out – it's Brentford, innit?

In Fred Callaghan's third full season in charge, he had finally succeeded in building a team in his own image. Most importantly, he had managed to fill the yawning chasm up front. Goals rained in from all over the field; after a meagre 52 and 56 league goals in the two previous seasons, Brentford ended top scorers in the league with 88 goals, breaking the hundred-goal barrier with 107 in all competitive matches.

Four players reached double figures in the League: Francis Joseph, Gary Roberts, Chris Kamara and Stan Bowles, with Tony Mahoney close behind on nine and Keith Cassells on seven. Bob Booker, who wore the number nine shirt only once all season, chipped in with six goals.

The increase in goals scored was more than matched by those conceded, with the number rising from 49 and 47 to a leaky and totally unacceptable 77, the fourth-worst in the division.

With 165 goals in their 46 league matches, the Bees were certainly the team to watch for excitement, even if supporters had to avert their eyes at times from some of the unfolding defensive chaos and madness.

Callaghan's Midas touch returned with the signings of new strikers Mahoney and Joseph, apparently completing the final pieces of the jigsaw. Mahoney came from the scrap heap at Fulham, where he had previously flattered to deceive, and jumped at the chance when Callaghan offered him a three-month trial. A regular first team spot and a manager who believed in him transformed Mahoney, who provided the strength, hold-up play, aerial ability and goal threat that had been missing since Bob's displays towards the end of the 1980/81 season.

Joseph had begun his career at Wealdstone and Hillingdon Borough, where his manager, Allen Batsford – previously in charge at Wimbledon when they rose to the Football League – told him, "If you're still playing for me this time next season, I will kill you – you're going to be a professional." Fortunately for his life expectancy, Wimbledon recognised his potential, and he thrived under Dario Gradi and Dave Bassett.

Joseph made quite an impression on Brentford fans that night in April 1982, singlehandedly changing the course of the game with lightning pace, explosive shooting and the two-goal burst to earn his team an unlikely win over a Brentford side still chasing promotion. "I often think that night was the making of me as a footballer," he acknowledges.

After Wimbledon's relegation, his departure from Plough Lane was inevitable, although he rejected an offer from Millwall. "I knew that if I had a couple of bad games there'd be a good chance that I'd be found hanging from a lamp-post outside The Den," he suggested. He never regretted his bargain £40,000 move to the Bees.

Joseph could not believe the number of chances that were created for him at his new club, predominantly by the best midfield in the division in Hurlock, Kamara and Bowles, "The service to the front players was so good – it was a striker's dream. The service at Wimbledon was also good but at Brentford there was a lot more imagination and creativity."

Joseph finished with an impressive tally of 26 goals, but the number of chances he spurned made him rue his failure to score at least 60 times and break Dixie Dean's goalscoring record of 1927/28.

Joseph's partnership with Mahoney was a potent combination of pure pace, strength, bravery and finishing ability. Using his speed to get down the channels, he also proved a composed and deadly marksman.

The two complemented each other perfectly, but there was a healthy rivalry and tension. They spurred each other on. "We didn't always see eye to eye. We'd congratulate each other whenever we scored, but if either of us missed a chance and the other one was in a better position, boy did we bicker. If he scored then it made me try even harder to get one myself, and I'm sure it was the same in reverse."

Roberts, too, welcomed their arrival, "We had never had sufficient punch, pace, or physicality up front, but they were exactly what we had been missing," he feels. "Now we finally had some cutting edge, with Tony being the perfect foil for Francis."

The 1982/83 team was so nearly an exceptional one, demonstrated by the fully-deserved victory over First Division Swansea in the Milk Cup, where Roberts scored a memorable goal in the first game at Griffin Park, going outside Gary Stanley at pace before hammering the goal home via the underside of the bar. He then opened the scoring after just 20 seconds in the replay at the Vetch Field, inspiring the Bees to a famous victory in what goalkeeper Paddy Roche described as "The best performance by a Brentford side in my time at Griffin Park."

Most Brentford supporters feel that Callaghan's squad was totally lopsided, incorporating the best strikeforce and midfield in the league, backed up by one of the worst defences and goalkeeper. Almost as fast as Joseph, Mahoney and Roberts scored at one end, the likes of Roche, Graham Wilkins and Alan Whitehead threw them in at the other.

Joseph considers that verdict harsh. "I don't think it was as simple as that. More than anything, I think we missed Danis Salman's pace at full-back." Roberts agrees that the team's defence was its Achilles heel, and that the loss of Salman's ability to read the game and speed of body, thought and mind was crucial.

Joseph was frustrated and dissatisfied with the team's final league position, "I think that side was so close to achieving big things for the club. It was a real missed opportunity. Finishing ninth wasn't good enough, because we had the potential to win promotion. People can point to all kinds of excuses, but we still should have gone up. In my view no Brentford side since has matched the skill of that squad."

Terry Rowe was similarly bemused, "We really should have gone up. The team contained players who were a cut above the rest, and we regularly played the opposition off the field. But we lacked a killer instinct and lost a number of games we should really have won."

The team was often a joy to watch, playing sophisticated passing football combined with real punch up front, at its best rivalling Brentford's current Championship squad. But the injury bug bit hard with too many changes and too much instability in defence. The reliable Barry Tucker was never properly replaced at left-back, where Wilkins struggled after playing nearly 150 first team games for Chelsea, never coming to terms with the differing demands of the Third Division.

Dave McKellar had also fallen out with his manager after two years of exemplary consistency in goal, apparently refusing to play. Eccentric former Chelsea goalkeeper Petar Borota decided to play in Portugal instead of Brentford – one wonders if he regretted his decision – forcing Callaghan to make a last-minute move just before the start of the season, rescuing Paddy Roche from the dole queue.

# A LOST OPPORTUNITY

Young reserve striker Keith Tonge remembers Roche's unexpected arrival at the club. "We were at Butlins in Bognor Regis as part of our pre-season training. One morning, we saw Paddy Roche walk out of Ron Harris's bedroom, which ensured that they both received a lot of stick from the squad, who had just been reminded by the manager about the ban on overnight guests. He'd signed the previous day and must have arrived overnight. We all remembered him from his Manchester United days, and some of the players, in particular the ace wind-up merchant Gary Roberts, didn't waste any time in reminding him about some of his televised mistakes. Paddy was a really nice man and he just laughed at all the abuse and ribbing he received."

The two keepers could not have been more different in style. McKellar – calm, composed and utterly reliable. Roche – mercurial, frenetic and acrobatic, like a cat on a hot tin roof, matching moments of brilliance with far too many daft errors that almost beggared belief. He played a major part in the victory at Swansea City, pulling off a series of elastic reflex saves from Bob Latchford, and an incredible penalty save preserved the lead against Portsmouth on Good Friday, greeted by a fusillade of golf balls from the furious and frustrated Pompey fans behind his goal. Then, characteristically and ineptly, he fumbled a soft effort to gift them a late equaliser. The defenders all had total confidence in McKellar; the same never appeared to be the case with Roche, who was prone to losing concentration and was inconsistent and unreliable.

The soft defensive underbelly, coupled with the tragic loss of rejuvenated striker Mahoney in December with a leg horribly broken in three places in a cup replay with Swindon, sabotaged Brentford's realistic promotion push. I can still hear the terrible crack after his accidental collision with an opponent, and Mahoney was never the same player again, losing his pace, confidence and mobility upon returning the following year: yet another highly promising player whose potential was unfulfilled for reasons totally beyond his control.

The Bees went into freefall, losing eight of their next 12 matches. In truth, they never really recovered in the second half of the season, with new arrival Cassells – Mahoney's intended replacement – understandably taking time to settle in.

The Bees did not travel well all season and won only four away games, including a remarkable 7-1 thrashing of Exeter City when Cassells, Joseph and Kamara each scored twice and spent the final 20 minutes competing with each other in a fruitless bid to notch a hat trick, screaming in vain at Roberts to cross the ball rather than go for glory.

Bob cemented his place in the team, starting 31 games and coming on as a substitute in eight more, wearing the number 2, 3, 4, 5, 6, 8, 9 and 12 shirts, proving yet again that he could fill in wherever was necessary.

Roberts might well be outwardly flippant and a born joker, but he is also a keen and astute observer of the game and players, evidenced by his long and successful spell as manager at Cambridge City. Gary gives a frank and in-depth verdict on Bob's strengths and weaknesses.

"Bob Booker did what Bob does; he was never able to make one position his own when given his chance, but he had a valuable part to play in his role as our super sub. He had good desire and was a totally honest player whose touch and technique were average, but he more than made up for his shortcomings with his desire – he gave everything he had, his enthusiasm was infectious and he provided us with the versatility and physicality we needed. I would call him a jack-of-all-trades, and perhaps his versatility hindered him and prevented him from becoming an automatic starter. I think he was at his best at centre-half with the game coming onto him. He extracted the utmost from his ability, which was a testament to him, particularly when he joined Sheffield United. He did so well there, at a far higher level of the game than he had experienced at Brentford."

I think Pep Guardiola's recent evocative description of versatile footballers like Philipp Lahm – calling them "Swiss Army Knife players" – is far kinder and more apt.

Joseph is in a unique position to comment on Bob's performances at both clubs, having already been at Bramall Lane when Bob joined Sheffield United in 1988. He has a lot of time for his former teammate. "Everyone got on with Bob – he's an unbelievably nice bloke. He was a very accomplished player, too. The fans didn't always see or appreciate quite how good he really was. Bob had been at Brentford for a fair few years and, in my opinion, his move away from Griffin Park was the making of him as a player. I wouldn't say that he had been at Brentford for too long, but sometimes a move away and a new start elsewhere can give a long-serving player a huge boost in confidence and energy. Bob became a hero at Sheffield United."

Bob mainly played in defence in 1982/83, as the first-choice back four of Salman, Whitehead, McNichol and Wilkins never played together all season, with at least one of them always on the injured or suspended list.

He scored a crucial last-minute equaliser in September at Brisbane Road, when his long-range effort took a deflection and arched in a gentle parabola over the straining Mervyn Day. He repeated the feat the following month when a ten-man Brentford team recovered from a 4-1 deficit to draw at Doncaster Rovers in an astonishing game.

Playing in midfield instead of Hurlock, Bob scored at Bramall Lane – an excellent volley this time as the Bees won – and remembers how impressed he was with the size of the stadium and the fervour of the home fans. Orient also suffered at the hands of Bob in their return match at Griffin Park, when he scored twice in a 5-2 win.

Brentford's Milk Cup run ended in the Fourth Road at First Division Nottingham Forest, where Bob conceded a penalty for tripping Stephen Hodge. A look of horror and disgust crosses his face when he recalls the glorious chance he missed to equalise, blazing his close-range shot high and not so handsomely over the bar.

Local journalist Sean Gilligan spoke for most Brentford supporters when he recognised Bob's progress and his value to the team. "Bob Booker is probably Brentford's most consistent player this season," he wrote. "Ironically, he was once the target for the Griffin Park fans when he played up front, despite a good scoring record. He deserves great credit for weathering the storm, and he is now a crowd favourite."

Quite how much of a favourite became clear when Bob was named the Brentford supporters' player of the year for 1982/83, despite a season in which the likes of Bowles, Hurlock, Kamara, Roberts, Joseph and Mahoney had all sparkled. Yet it was the un-flamboyant, unspectacular journeyman who beat them all to this coveted award.

This recognition of his efforts by the fans was the apogee of Bob's career and his proudest moment to date. "It was hard at the time of the barracking," he reflected at the time. "But I have put that behind me and I am willing to play anywhere. The fans like to see someone who tries his best and gives 100%, and that's what I try to do." His parents were present at the player of the year dinner, taking great pride in their son's achievement.

Roberts paid tribute to Bob and his reversal of the fans' perception of him, "He had a real empathy with the fans at Brentford, sometimes even a love-hate relationship. But I think that they finally appreciated just what he brought to the team."

So the season ended in deserved triumph for Bob, but it had been a massive opportunity squandered for the club. A combination of ill luck and underperformance saw Callaghan's chances of glory disappear.

# CHAPTER 9
# MONEY TALKS

As the 1983/84 season began, Bob was entering his fifth full season of league football and, at 25 years of age, was surely coming into his prime. He had now made over 100 appearances for the Bees, coming off his best ever season, culminating in his player of the year award. As an established and valuable member of the first team, the Brentford fans were finally beginning to accept and appreciate him.

One would have expected the club to reward his achievements, leaving him luxuriating in the security and comfort zone provided by a lucrative long-term contract. The truth was somewhat different.

Playing contracts nowadays, particularly at the top end of the game, tend to be long and complex documents containing a myriad of tailored bonus clauses ranging from the weird to the incredible. Paul Gascoigne apparently demanded that he lived close to a fishing lake, and Stefan Schwarz's contract banned him from space travel. Neil Ruddock's contained a weight clause whereby he would be fined if he failed to keep his weight within acceptable bounds and proved unable to get into the outsize pair of shorts provided to him by Crystal Palace.

Salaries can include a basic annual figure plus a confusing combination of signing-on fees, loyalty and image rights payments and moving allowances, as well as goals, assists, clean sheets and appearance bonuses.

Free cars and accommodation are often provided, with some top foreign players rumoured to have their income tax paid. Nice work if you can get it. Squads also share bonuses based on league and cup achievements.

A recent survey highlighted that, buttressed by the massive new television deals in force until 2019, top earners in the Premier League receive upwards of £250,000 per week, with an average top-flight player being paid in the region of £49,000 per week. In the Championship, the average wage is around £6,000 per week, reducing to £1,400 in Division One and £750 in Division Two. Remember, though, that these averages are bumped up by those players at the top of the food chain in each division, with many earning very little indeed. Indeed, recently I heard of some youngsters at a southern Division Two team who were only earning around £100 per week, despite being first team regulars.

Thirty years ago, before the influx of foreign investment, satellite television and sponsorship money, players earned far less, with a much more even playing field. The average top-level player received around £25,000 per year (250% of an average worker's wages), reducing dramatically to around £11,200 and £8,300 per annum respectively in Divisions Three and Four. Lower division footballers were earning roughly the same as the man in the street or unskilled workers.

Bob is a hoarder by nature. A folder containing a bundle of papers turned out to be the original copies of all his playing contracts. They provide fascinating if somewhat painful reading.

Mark Lawrenson summed up the difference between now and how things were done in his and Bob's era, "When I was playing, a contract was probably no more than five pages long," he said. "Nowadays they are more like a John Grisham novel."

Bob's contracts were no different: short, sharp and to the point. Their very lack of length and detail highlighted the unequal balance of power that existed between footballers and their clubs – serfs and their masters.

As a Third Division footballer, Bob and thousands like him were considered interchangeable and disposable assets with a limited value and shelf life, easily replaceable by somebody just as good or even better. Very often, players were informed of their release by letter – or, worst of all, through a local newspaper headline.

Take it or leave it was the prevailing attitude; contract negotiations were practically non-existent, and the entire renewal process generally took less than ten minutes. "The approach from the club was 'Here's your new contract, sign here and shut the door after you,'" says Bob. "We were never made to feel valued or important."

In his autobiography, *The Rocky Road*, Eamon Dunphy pithily summed up the concept of footballers as chattels, as well as their uncertain future. "Despite the hours, pay and the illusory glamour, we were basically slaves. You couldn't leave the club until the bosses decided they didn't need you anymore. A bad injury could end your career. There was no pension. The only certainty was that some time in your early to mid-30's you would be disposed of. Parting would be swift and brutal. Just as most men were reaching their prime in their chosen walks of life, you would be finished. If you lived in a club house – a tied cottage, as many players did – you and your family could end up on the street, with just your scrapbook and memories of 'The best years' of your life."

Bob survived on a series of one-year contracts during his first spell at Brentford, never even bothering to ask for an extended one. He knew that such a suggestion would have been received with total incredulity and laughed out of court. He handled what little negotiation took place on his own, with occasional input from his dad. Any self-respecting agent would have run a mile, starving to death on what little commission he would have earned from Bob.

Some players openly boasted of how much they earned, but the Brentford squad kept how much – or little – they received close to their chests. From what he was able to discover from the odd unguarded comment, Bob reckons he was never close to being one of the top earners during his first spell at the club.

"Potential new signings could negotiate from a position of strength, as the club would do whatever it could to meet their salary demands. I, on the other hand, was penalised for being a loyal and long-serving player who had started on peanuts and been grateful for it. I had no leverage and was taken for granted."

How much did Bob earn throughout his career? We already know he was on piecework when he completed his apprenticeship at Hille in 1978, earning between £150 to 200 per week, or between £7,800 to £10,400 per annum – exceptionally good money for the time, and well in excess of the then-average UK annual salary of £5,440.25.

Becoming a professional footballer and a supposed public entertainer, Bob had taken a phenomenal cut in his salary, earning far, far less than he had been as an upholsterer – way under the national average wage.

In 1986, eight years after he first became a professional footballer, Bob caught up with where he had been at Hille and broke the £200 per week barrier as a well-established player. He would have been far better off, financially, remaining as an upholsterer.

Bob's weekly salary rose as follows throughout his career:

**1978/79:** £60 per week, plus £250 signing bonus.

**1979/80 (July 1979):** £70 per week.

**1979/80 (December 1979):** £80 per week.

**1980/81:** £90 per week, plus £10 per week extra when playing in Football League and FA Cup matches, and £10 per week towards travelling expenses during the playing season.

**1981/82:** £100 per week, plus £10 per week extra when playing in Football League and FA Cup matches, and £15 per week towards travelling expenses during the playing season.

**1982/83:** £120 per week, plus £10 per week extra when playing in Football League and FA Cup matches, and £20 per week towards travelling expenses during the playing season.

**1983/84:** £140 per week, plus £10 per week extra when playing in Football League and FA Cup matches, and £20 per week towards travelling expenses during the playing season.

**1984/85:** £170 per week, plus £10 per week extra when playing in Football League and FA Cup matches, and £25 per week towards travelling expenses during the playing season.

In addition, Bob picked up a handy £60 bonus for reaching the final of the Freight Rover Trophy, which would have risen to £70 had the Bees won.

**1985/86:** £170 per week, plus £10 per week extra when playing in Football League and FA Cup matches, and £25 per week towards travelling expenses during the playing season.

**1986/87:** £225 per week, plus £25 per week extra when playing in Football League and FA Cup matches, however the £25 per week travelling expenses allowance was discontinued.

**1987/88:** £225 per week, plus £25 per week extra when playing in Football League and FA Cup matches.

**1988/89:** £225 per week, plus £55 per match extra when playing in Football League and FA Cup matches. Bonuses had also risen to between £25-£65 for a draw, and £50-130 for a win, according to the club's league position.

Bob's move to Sheffield United in November 1988 deprived him of a share of the £150 FA Cup bonus, paid to each qualifying player in recognition of Brentford's tremendous run to the 6th round of the competition. Bob hoped he would receive a salary that reflected his experience as well as the status of his new team, when he moved at the age of 30 to a far bigger and better-financed club than Brentford in Sheffield United. He was not to be disappointed. The first difference he saw was the offer of a contract taking him to the end of the 1989/90 season – his first ever such contract, rising from £225 to an unprecedented £350 per week.

United also demonstrated a sense of ambition that was sadly lacking at Griffin Park, offering a two-way contract that automatically increased his weekly salary from £350 to £375 should the Blades be promoted to the Second Division for the 1989/90 season, as proved the case.

The signing-on fee, £12,500, represented unheard of riches, paid in four equal instalments of £3,125 between December 1988 and the end of June 1990. He would receive an appearance fee of £30 per match in the Third Division, or £50 in the Second Division.

A promotion bonus of £2,000 was on offer for reaching the Second Division, as long as he played a minimum of 15 matches.

Far too late in his career, when his days as a striker were long behind him, he was finally offered a bonus of £50 for every goal he scored, as well as £25 for every game in which United kept a clean sheet.

Moving north from his home in Watford, Bob was given a travel and accommodation allowance of up to £100 per week for a 25-week period, plus up to £1,000 towards his removal, legal and estate agency costs.

No wonder Bob thought that he had died and gone to heaven; he even worried that perhaps there had been some mistake and the figures were wrong. He could not sign it quickly enough before they could change their mind. He was finally being properly rewarded for his labour. The size and structure of his new contract also clearly demonstrated that you were only treated fairly when you moved to a new club.

Bob's consistency, and the prospect of a second consecutive promotion – to the unforseen heights of the First Division – saw him receive a new contract in December 1989, six months before his existing agreement was due to expire. His salary of £375 per week rose with immediate effect to £425, increasing to £500 when Sheffield United reached the top division for the 1990/91 season.

Bob's next signing-on fee, of £14,000 in four payments, came between 1989 and 1991. Appearance fees for the First Division also rose from £50 to £75 per match, with a £2,000 bonus on offer for achieving promotion to the First Division. Bob's goal bonus hit £100, with a clean sheet bonus of £50.

All these increases meant Bob had more than doubled his salary from the highest point of his Brentford days, reaping the reward for his talent, longevity and enthusiasm. A further extension in February 1991, until the end of the 1991/92 season, included another signing–on fee, of £10,500, payable in three tranches between June 1991 and June 1992. Rent allowance and fees were also provided.

Bob was called in to see Derek Dooley, a true Sheffield legend, once a marauding and fearless centre-forward for Sheffield Wednesday and now United's managing director. He lost his leg when gangrene set in after it was broken in an on-pitch collision, and was loved and admired by Wednesday and United fans alike for his bravery and integrity. He gave Bob the good news about his contract extension and Bob left the room after a brief conversation, having agreed to the terms on offer. Soon afterwards, there was a knock on the door and Bob reappeared. Dooley was used to players haggling endlessly over their contracts, and here surely was yet another ungrateful malcontent who had returned in order to try it on with him. "There's no more money in the pot, lad, so don't bother trying," Dooley riposted in a pre-emptive strike. "No, no," replied Bob. "I've just come back to thank you, and to let you know that I will give the club everything I have both on and off the field." Dooley was reduced to total silence. Bob's behaviour, attitude and manners brought a tear to his eye.

After three years at Bramall Lane, Bob rejoined Brentford in November 1991, returning as a hero with recent top-level experience. Brentford took over the last few months of his existing contract, extending it by a further two seasons. At the age of 33, Bob received a two-and-a-half year contract from the Bees.

His salary stayed at a whopping £500 per week throughout the agreement, with a huge signing-on fee of £36,300 between 1991 and 1993, as well as relocation fees. By the end of his career, Bob was receiving a salary around 25% above the average national annual wage, which in 1993 was £20,818.

Had he not received the unexpected opportunity to move to Sheffield United at a time when it seemed that the best part of his career was well behind him, Bob would have earned little more than a manual worker – a poor return for a professional sportsman and entertainer.

Bob was also offered a testimonial by Brentford – the 24th such award since the war – and followed in the footsteps of the likes of Ken Coote, Tom Higginson, Peter Gelson, Gordon Phillips, Alan Hawley, Alan Nelmes, Jackie Graham, Danis Salman and Stan Bowles.

The bigger the star, the more likely he is to receive a hugely lucrative testimonial which he really does not need. Niall Quinn, Jamie Carragher and Wayne Rooney have recognised this anomaly and generously given all the proceeds to charity, with Rooney donating a massive £1.2million to children's charities. Footballers at the sharp end of the game cannot afford to make such a gesture, as a testimonial, like a cricketer's benefit, is seen as a way for supporters to give something back, with the player eventually receiving a much-needed tax-free boost to what, as we have already seen in Bob's case, is often not a massive salary.

Some Brentford players did better than others, but in relative terms what they received from their testimonials was chickenfeed. Coote, the club's record appearance holder across 514 games, was rewarded with a crowd of 7,400 for his match in 1965 against West Ham, managed by his former teammate Ron Greenwood, earning £1,100 – around £19,000 today. Higginson's testimonial netted £1,850 in 1969, or over £27,000 today. Gelson was granted two testimonials, in 1970 and 1975, ending up with the equivalent of about £38,000, a fair reward for the loyalty he showed the club. Defender Nelmes did almost as well in 1978, with 7,400 fans watching him sign off with a trademark own goal in an 8-2 thrashing administered by Chelsea. But he was laughing all the way to the bank with his £7,193, or over £37,000 today.

Bob's testimonial did not prove to be anywhere near as successful, mainly because, unusually, he was playing for United throughout his testimonial year, preventing him from co-ordinating any potentially lucrative money-spinning social activities around the Brentford area.

His manager at United, Dave Bassett, urged Bob to transfer his testimonial to Sheffield, where his new-found popularity and infinitely greater number of supporters would undoubtedly have resulted in a far more substantial reward. Characteristically, Bob refused, wanting to keep faith with the fans who, it has to be said, had initially given him an extremely hard time, but who had (over the years) grown to appreciate what he brought to the Brentford team. "Maybe I could have made a lot more money from my testimonial," he says. "I certainly could have done with it, but I am still happy with the decision I made."

Bob did not organise any race nights or dinners, simply concentrating on his testimonial match, on 11th May 1990 at Griffin Park, pitting Brentford against a United team newly promoted to the First Division. Coachloads of United supporters travelled to London to boost an extremely disappointing crowd of 1,531. Bob played for both teams in a light-hearted match which was won 4-2 by Brentford, with Bob scoring the customary last-gasp penalty kick gifted to him, carefully slotting past a less than vigilant Vinnie Jones, guarding the United net as a guest player.

Everyone had a great time, which was Bob's priority, including the follicly-challenged Brentford midfielder Wayne Turner, who turned out wearing a comical hairpiece. But Bob's ailing coffers received little boost from the proceeds of such a poorly attended game, raising only around £4,500 in total. Bob's overwhelming objective – rewarding the Brentford fans to whom he felt he owed so much – had been achieved.

Bob was proud to get onto the property ladder with the two-bedroom maisonette near his parents, paying £27,000 – seemingly a small fortune at the time. As a talented builder and decorator, his dad did the work for nothing, but it was difficult to make ends meet. "For the first time in my life, at the age of 22, I had to fend for myself," says Bob. "I found it really hard and a real shock to the system. I was only being paid £90 per week, and suddenly I had to pay for my mortgage, utilities, food and petrol." At least his mum saved him any laundry bills. "I didn't have much money to spare each week, but the bank of mum and dad came in very useful, and they were always there for me. I collected bits of furniture from all over the place and called in favours from friends and family. I had sadly lost my nan prior to getting the flat, and I still carry a note she gave me telling me to buy something for the flat with the £5 that was attached. God bless her. She had always taken a massive interest in my career, and I hope that she is very proud of me."

Bob also acquired his first really serious girlfriend in 1984 – so serious that he married her in 1991. "I met Christine Schmid in a pub. She lived nearby, in Abbots Langley, and came from a large and close-knit Irish family. She had four brothers, who I knew from local football, and four sisters, so I knew that I had to be on my best behaviour. You didn't mess with them. She had been dating a Watford player, Richard Jobson, but they broke up soon after she met me."

Football always came first for Bob, and Christine had to fit in with his match schedule and training regime. "I saw a lot of her, but I was very disciplined. Each Friday at 10pm, she knew it would be time for me to take her home. The flat looked great and dad had done a fantastic job in the kitchen fitting it out in the Brentford colours of red and white. That, of course, was also why I decided to join Sheffield United, as my kitchen would still be properly colour co-ordinated."

Bob was constantly overdrawn. "But luckily my sister worked in a bank and gave me a lot of excellent financial advice. That being said, I did blow the odd £50 in the local snooker hall with Ian Bolton, and he was obviously a terrible influence on me. My other extravagance was music, and most of what little spare cash I had went on buying the latest LPs, particularly anything by The Who. I would still go out with my friends, but only early in the week and on Saturday nights. I would generally spend around £5 on a few drinks and an obligatory kebab on a night out." The glamorous life of a footballer in the 80s! Bob never received any dietary advice from Brentford, who would probably have been horrified if they had known about his calorific input, but those were less scientific times when a footballer was left to his own devices.

Most footballers now spend the summer months resting and recuperating from the rigours of the previous season, usually on some exotic foreign beach. "Out of season, I worked for a good friend, Russell Hansard, who ran a builders' yard," says Bob. "I asked if they needed any help, and Russell and his dad, Colin, employed me through the summer, which helped me financially and allowed me to keep in shape. I don't think many footballers would have done that, but I had worked long days at the furniture factory prior to becoming a footballer, so I had a real work ethic. It was an easy adjustment for me to make."

"It was backbreaking work, humping bags of cement, and Russell and I used to time how quickly we could finish our tasks. I loved it. What a buzz – one of us would be standing on the lorry, the other would hoist the hot bag of cement onto his shoulder and get it into the cement shed as quickly as possible, and then come back for the next one." The pair got it down to 45 minutes. "My shoulder would be on fire, but it was great fun and healthy work outside in the sunshine. It is something I will always remember with joy." Brentford's management knew nothing of his moonlighting, nor his occasional deliveries in a little tipper truck.

"I still have nightmares about one of my early deliveries. I'm still not sure if some of the lads stitched me up or whether it was my own carelessness and stupidity. I dropped off a yard of sand, which is a fair amount. Feeling pleased with myself, I knocked on the door to collect the money. A very polite lady answered and asked me what I wanted. I said, 'The money for the sand, please.' There was a blank look on her face and she replied, 'What sand? I haven't ordered any.' What an idiot I was." It had been delivered to the wrong house. "I now had to shovel a yard of sand back onto the truck, which took me about an hour-and-a-half. When I finally got back to the yard the lads were in hysterics. I had some great times there and I'll be forever grateful to Russell and Colin for helping me out."

The money Bob earned from his summer exertions gave him a much-needed financial boost, helping him pay some of his outstanding bills.

His relationship with Chris was progressing nicely. "I was very close to her family, and at the end of every season, when the training kit at Brentford was being replaced, I would ask the kitman for any spares for her brothers. They loved them. They were all in the landscape gardening trade, so quite often you would see Brentford tops, sweatshirts and tracksuits popping up all over Watford. Christine worked in the accounts department for a scaffolding company called Alan Drews, so she had a steady income." The flat had greatly increased in value, allowing them to move to a nearby two-bedroom terrace.

"I sold the flat for £46,000, which left me with a profit of £19,000 after I paid off the mortgage, and I put it towards the £93,000 cost of the new house. That seemed a really massive sum to me, particularly given how little I was being paid. Now we had two incomes between us it was just about doable, although we were generally overdrawn. Dad helped me do it up and we made it into a beautiful house."

Bruno the Rottweiler – "A fantastic dog who we adored" – spent ten happy years as the latest addition before suffering a tumour. Overseas holidays were rare given their financial constraints, although Bob and Chris went to Cyprus and stayed in a Menorca timeshare thanks to her sister.

Bob also developed another lasting hobby. His old friends Bill, Tony, his dad, Pete (better known as Parker due to his uncanny resemblance to the character in *Thunderbirds*) and Derek loved bird-watching. Bob soon caught the bug, becoming equally keen and committed. Whenever they could, Bob and his mates would spend weekends away, camping in the open air, sleeping under the stars, enjoying long walks, relaxed pub meals and the odd sight of their favourite species. They clubbed together to buy an old banger for £80, in which they would drive to Minsmere, a nature reserve in Suffolk. "We pitched our tent outside The Lion Inn in Theberton, and we still go there over 30 years on."

The majesty and peace of the barn owl makes it Bob's favourite bird, and he loves watching them feast on mice and voles in meadows on late summer evenings. "Bird-watching took my mind off the pressures of football and helped me relax and escape from the demands of fans, particularly after I arrived at the madhouse that was Sheffield."

"Life was simple and good. I enjoyed DIY and spending time with Chris's family. Her mum, Helen, was a great cook, and every Sunday the whole clan would gather together for a gargantuan meal."

"Brentford would train between 10-1, so I would leave home at 8.45am. By this time, I carpooled with Gary Phillips, Wayne Turner and Gary Blissett, who was always late. Once I left him at Rickmansworth roundabout to teach him a lesson. It cost him a fine when he eventually turned up really late for training, mouthing imprecations at me."

"We combined running in Richmond Park, sprints and doggies, with lots of small-sided games, which just emphasised how poor most players' touch on the ball was. Gary Roberts, Andy Sinton and Robbie Cooke were the main exceptions to the rule."

"We would always end up with an optional shooting practice where the ball ended up more often than not on the railway line, which backed onto the training ground, rather than in the back of Gary Phillips's net. Footballs were expensive and if you bashed one over the fence you had to go and fetch it and take great care to avoid the live rail – but thankfully we didn't lose anybody."

"Steve Perryman was the most tactically astute of all the Brentford managers I played for, and he was the first to introduce pattern of play sessions where he would set us up and use shadow play. We would stand still and he would then reposition us to ensure that the whole team knew how to respond to all the situations that we would experience in games. Nobody took any liberties, and everyone took things seriously. The tackling was fierce and nobody held back. Gary Roberts always did his best to avoid any physical contact, and Jamie Murray and Terry Hurlock were the ones to stay away from."

Every Friday, the worst player of the week in training would be awarded the yellow jersey. Woe betide any player who kept missing the goal in finishing sessions: baring their backside and touching their toes while the rest of the squad took pot shots from the penalty spot was the punishment for that indiscretion. Brentford's horrendous record from penalty kicks may not have made that the worst forfeit in the world.

After training on Tuesdays, the squad would repair to a local café for a fry-up or pasta. "Some would then go for a drink in the afternoon, but generally I would go out walking with the dog and rest up. Every Friday we would be given a brown envelope with our wages in it, and it wasn't until late in my career that our money would be paid directly into our bank account and we would be paid monthly, rather than weekly."

"We travelled by coach to most away games, and when we went up north I would be picked up at Toddington Services on the M1 along with the likes of McNichol, McKellar, Carlton, Tucker and Phillips. If we had a journey of more than three hours, we would stay overnight, generally in a pretty basic three-star hotel on the outskirts of our final destination – the cheaper the better. Over the years, I shared a room with Pat Kruse, Terry Hurlock and Terry Evans, and we had some great fun – even if, quite sensibly, the minibar had been emptied before our arrival." No drinking was allowed on Fridays, but a card school often developed after their roast dinner. "Hurlock, Kamara and Bowles were the keenest players, but the stakes were very small, and nobody won or lost much money. We were all in bed by 11pm, and on Saturday we would all go for a walk after breakfast before the manager held a team talk. Bill Dodgin never really mentioned the opposition, but, as the game became more sophisticated, we would be given more information on our opponents and their strengths and weaknesses. We would have a light lunch of scrambled eggs, boiled chicken, toast and fruit, and on the journey home the coach would always stop for pre-ordered fish and chips. We would have a few beers if the gaffer gave permission, which didn't happen too often if we had lost."

"For home games we would arrive at Griffin Park at 1.30pm, when the team would be announced, unless the manager had told us the previous day if we were playing. There would be a short team meeting, and we would stretch and warm up on the pitch at 2.30pm. Wives, partners and guests would join us in the Players' Bar after the game. The more established players brought their wives and kids and made it a family day out. Most of the women dressed up smartly, and I do remember that Andy McCulloch and Pat Kruse had particularly pretty wives."

Things changed when Bob signed for United. "Chris didn't move up with me as I wasn't sure how long I would last. She did not want to give up her job. We needed the money and she was also very close to her family. We agreed that she would come up after I'd settled in. Looking back, the whole situation was a bit strange, but I was totally committed to making a success of the move and establishing myself in Sheffield, and this solution, tough though it was, worked best for us both."

Leaving home for the first time and moving alone to a new city in the north of England was a challenge, but Bob had to go where the work was to continue his career. The life of a journeyman footballer was neither a secure nor a luxurious one, and Bob and Chris had to be extremely flexible and make serious sacrifices in order to get by.

One thing was for sure, Bob would have to keep working after he retired from football.

# CHAPTER 10
# WHAT A LETDOWN

The 1983-84 season was a total anti-climax with very little to write home about.

Stan Bowles had finally begun to feel his age and retired at the end of the previous season, and his massive influence was greatly missed. How do you replace the irreplaceable? With great difficulty, particularly when money is tight. Fred Callaghan made a catastrophic mistake in his recruitment, as his replacement for Bowles, Terry Bullivant from Charlton, made little impact. He was the total antithesis to Bowles: a tough-tackling ball-winner by nature, contributing little apart from unnecessary aggression and three red cards throughout his unimpressive three-season stay. The team's creative spark was lost. "A poor replacement," was Bob's damning verdict on him.

Keith Cassells was different in style to the still-injured, sorely missed Tony Mahoney – another round peg in a square hole. He worked hard, ran tirelessly and scored a reasonable nine goals, but Brentford had lost the power provided by Mahoney, missing a focal point upfront. This had a serious knock-on effect on Francis Joseph, whose league goal tally declined by a quarter. Eighteen goals was still a respectable total, but far fewer than was hoped for or expected. Generally, he was left to forage on his own. The reliable Gary Roberts, as always, got into double figures, but nobody emerged to fill the gap.

The midfield did not take up the slack, with the Hurlock-Kamara-Bowles axis, responsible for a crucial 24 goals the previous season, replaced by a new midfield comprising Hurlock, Kamara and a combination of Bullivant, Booker, new signing Tom Finney and Bowles, who returned for a brief final hurrah in December. Their goal tally declined to a paltry 14.

From being the league's top-scoring team the previous season, the Bees tally dropped to 69 goals, 19 less than the year before. The defence remained as porous as ever, conceding 79 times – two more than in 1982/83 and the fourth-worst record in the league.

Unsurprisingly, Brentford struggled desperately against relegation for the entire season, playing dull, uninspiring football. The fans responded accordingly, average attendances at Griffin Park falling dramatically from a respectable 6,184 to a worrying 4,735.

Injuries struck hard, with Bob suffering a badly pulled hamstring, "I missed a lot of football with it. Hamstring injuries are always difficult to assess, as you are champing at the bit to play again and convince yourself that you are OK, but sometimes you end up coming back too soon, and run the risk of it going again." Hurlock and Kamara also missed 22 matches between them. Callaghan was also never able to field an established back four due to a series of injuries to his defenders.

He made two major signings in goalkeeper Trevor Swinburne – no real improvement over Roche – and Ian Bolton, whose arrival from Watford was regarded as a major coup. He took over the captaincy but, as Gary Roberts remarked with his customary lack of sentimentality, "He was a total disaster – we could all see from the first training session that his legs had gone."

In the amusing and highly engaging book by former Notts County defender David McVay, *Steak… Diana Ross. Diary of a Football Nobody*, the former teammate of Bolton at Meadow Lane commented, "In the shower room, Ian Bolton assesses his day. Smoke from his third filter tip of the morning (two before training) shrouds the giant concrete communal bath. By 1pm he has consumed several bacon butties at the café on the corner of the ground and is well on his way to his second ten-pack of Rothmans." Maybe that explains the precipitous end of his career at Brentford, at the age of just 30.

Paul Roberts, a no-nonsense, tough-tackling defender, arrived from Millwall, remaining best remembered for almost literally putting his head in the lion's mouth by provocatively celebrating Francis Joseph's winning goal at his old club in front of the home fans, one of whom jumped over the barrier and assaulted him.

The Milk Cup provided a welcome respite from the torments of the league with Brentford receiving a plum draw of a two-leg tie against Liverpool. Almost 18,000 fans – a figure that will never be equalled – packed Griffin Park in the largest crowd since Burnley's FA Cup replay visit in 1965, witnessing the Bees put on a brave display that was poorly rewarded by an undeserved 4-1 defeat. Roberts – always one to rise to the big occasion – scored a clinical equaliser, but hopes of an upset disappeared when Danis Salman's long-range effort screamed past Bruce

Grobbelaar but clanged against the post, bouncing to safety. Bob came off the bench, but played from the start in the second leg at Anfield, where the Bees chased shadows and conceded another four goals without reply.

Relishing the chance to pit his wits against Liverpool, Bob was in awe of the opposition. "They had so much more ability than us and their brains worked far quicker. If we took three touches, they took two; if we took two, then they only needed one. They knew, instinctively, exactly where they were going to pass the ball before they got it, whereas we had to think, take a touch and have a look. Fred and Ron told us to get in their faces, shut them down and try to upset them, but they just picked us off. Deep down we knew exactly what was going to happen – and it did."

The players no longer seemed to respond to Callaghan's approach. Ron Harris left suddenly without explanation, and the nadir was reached with a spineless 6-0 thrashing at Southend, themselves a poor team who would go down at the end of the season. An astonishing 12-minute horror show in the FA Cup at Gillingham followed, conceding four goals to squander a seemingly comfortable 3-1 lead.

The writing was on the wall for Callaghan. Roberts suggested that his undoing was his failure to bring in suitable defensive replacements. Bob recognised the inevitability of a change against a backdrop of a poor squad lacking quality. "Results declined, confidence waned, everyone played badly, players lost faith in the manager and it came as no surprise when he was sacked," is his sad summation of what occurred.

Callaghan's brusque manner did not help his cause and Martin Lange fired him in February 1984. When he was interviewed for *The Big Brentford Book of the 80s*, Lange admitted to some misgivings over his decision. "I thought Fred was a good man and a decent manager. He had some faults but was a terrific judge of a player and knew the lower leagues well. Fred was a good first manager for me and it took a lot of soul-searching when I decided it was time for him to go. I do sometimes look back and wonder if I should have given him a little bit longer, but his departure was down to my inexperience and I was getting a lot of flak from the fans and took the easy way out."

Harris is completely honest and open about what went wrong. "We lost the dressing room, results started to go badly, things never worked out and I left before Fred. You don't have to mollycoddle the players but after some defeats Fred made them all come in on the Sunday. Some had a long way to travel and started moaning and groaning." Lange took note, coupled with a series of demonstrations against the manager in the Braemar Road forecourt.

As of 25th June 2017, there have been 55 managerial casualties among the 92 Premier League and EFL clubs since the beginning of the 2016/17 season. Headless chickens Leyton Orient disposed of four managers, Wigan three, and 13 other teams made two changes. Poor Russell Slade also suffered the ignominy of being sacked by two crisis clubs in Charlton Athletic and Coventry City.

At the start of the 1992/93 season, the first year of the Premier League, the average tenure of a top division manager was 3.24 years, or 1,184 days. The latest figures suggest that they now last for 2.28 years, but removing the longest-serving manager, Arsène Wenger, from the calculations reduces the figure to a mere 1.29 years. The life expectancy of a Football League manager is even more tenuous, with an average of just eight months in the bear pit that is the Championship. On average, it takes a sacked manager 18 months to get a new job, and 58% of first time sacked managers never receive a second opportunity to get it right. A tough, competitive and high-pressure job.

Despite Lange's misgivings, nearly four years was long enough for a fair assessment to be made of Callaghan's work. Bob has concerns over the lack of patience and time afforded to football managers. "A manager lives and dies by results, but when I was playing he would get at least two or three seasons in which to build a team and put his own stamp on a club," he says. "It is totally different in today's society, which demands instant success and gratification. Three defeats and the fans are unsettled and start muttering. Six, and they are baying for the manager's head."

Brentford were in dire straits, just as when Callaghan took over the reins in 1980. Once again, relegation beckoned. A new saviour was needed to ensure that the club's Third Division status was maintained.

Callaghan's replacement was Arsenal legend Frank McLintock, who had previously endured an unsuccessful spell in charge at Leicester City and more recently coached at Queens Park Rangers. According to Lange, he was the only candidate seriously considered for the position, arriving with a ringing endorsement from former Arsenal manager Bertie Mee.

The appointment was initially successful; McLintock managed to keep Brentford's head above water, with the team finishing one place and three points clear of relegation. Survival went down to the wire, but safety was almost assured when the Bees beat their nearest rival Scunthorpe by three clear goals in the final week of the season.

McLintock and his assistant, John Docherty, relied upon a series of short-term deals for experienced players in order to plug the gaps – as always, there was little money to play with. Bill Roffey, Bobby Fisher ("a Lionel Ritchie lookalike") and Nigel Gray all impressed. But perhaps the most important move McLintock made – with 12 games to go – was restoring the now fully fit Booker to partner Joseph up front. In his first regular outings at centre-forward since 1981, Bob repeated his previous tally with four goals. The striking partnership scored nine times as Brentford did just enough to escape the drop.

McLintock is quick to recognise Bob's contribution to the team's survival. "I always thought that Bob was very talented, and was at his best playing at centre-forward. He was mobile, if not overly quick, but he gave us enthusiasm, height and presence, and provided us with a target to aim for. Perhaps he was just a little bit too nice. He was such a lovely, friendly lad and a real gentleman. He wasn't very aggressive and, given his height and strength, he might have bullied defenders a bit more."

McLintock and Docherty, who played the hard-talking bad cop role to perfection, had managed to arrest the slide, obtaining some breathing space for the ailing club. Could they now inspire the team to kick on over the following season?

# CHAPTER 11
# WEMBLEY WOE

The career of a lower division footballer is one that can hardly be described as glamorous, rarely emerging from obscurity into the glare of the national spotlight. Personal glory comes a distant second to their main priority of ensuring they keep their job, feed their family and remain gainfully employed for as long as possible. Local personalities and heroes at best, most of their headlines and coverage come from the pages of the local rather than national media. Apart from the short-lived publicity gained from being a part of the odd FA Cup giant killing, they generally live their lives in partial obscurity well below the parapet.

Bob Booker was no exception to this rule, his career and accomplishments barely touching national consciousness. The one exception was his three-goal feat as a young unknown against Hull City, a feat so unusual that it merited a brief mention that evening on *Match of the Day*. But for the most part he was just another journeyman footballer, practically unknown outside West London and the Watford area at a time when Third or Fourth Division football was rarely on television.

Bob had never played in a live televised match and only flitted (briefly) across the screen on two occasions: ITV's highlights of Brentford's 2-2 draw against Sheffield Wednesday in January 1980 and the team's exciting win at Walsall that August.

Wembley Stadium was seen as an unattainable pipedream for footballers playing outside the top two divisions, with lower division teams almost never appearing there. Leyton Orient staged a couple of Third Division South matches there in 1930 while their Lea Bridge Stadium was being refurbished, and, bizarrely, non-league Ealing AFC played at Wembley eight times in 1930/31.

No Third Division team has ever reached a Wembley FA Cup Final, although Plymouth Argyle and Chesterfield came closest, losing narrowly to Watford and Middlesbrough respectively in the semi-finals in 1984 and 1997.

The Football League Cup is an entirely different matter, with Fourth Division Rochdale losing in a two-legged final to Norwich City in 1962 –

the first time a club from the bottom division had reached the final of a major cup competition, but not one staged at Wembley.

Wembley hosted the League Cup Final for the first time in 1967 and, since then, Queens Park Rangers and Swindon Town from the third tier have won there; in 1967, with former Brentford winger Mark Lazarus scoring the winner, and 1969. Far more recently, Bradford City became the first fourth-tier club ever to reach a major Wembley cup final in 2013, losing heavily to Swansea City.

Two years before their introduction, the Football League promotion playoffs were still a figment of Martin Lange's imagination in 1985. Moving to Wembley in 1990, there is a deep irony that the man who largely invented them was the chairman of a club which has suffered more than almost any other team from their torments. Brentford currently hold a 100% failure record in their eight Sisyphean playoff attempts, from 1991 to 2015.

In 1984/85, Bob and his teammates were offered another unexpected route to Wembley when the Associate Members' Cup, a year-old competition open only to the 48 third and fourth tier clubs, gained a sponsor, a new name in The Freight Rover Trophy, and the reward and lure of a Wembley cup final; something Brentford had not experienced since 1942, when they beat Portsmouth in the London War Cup.

With the teams split into Northern and Southern groups, there were five rounds to overcome before the final. Brentford were one of the few teams to take this much-derided competition seriously, fielding strong teams from the outset – perhaps reflecting their lack of depth. Frank McLintock put pressure on his players to show maximum effort. "I really wanted us to progress as far as possible in this tournament. I was still new to the management game and I thought that a run in the competition would help build up our confidence."

Reading were beaten comfortably over two legs. A late Robbie Cooke goal brought victory over a poor Cambridge United team in a drab and soulless game that hardly grabbed the attention of the Griffin Park faithful. Just 2,003 supporters were in attendance; I preferred a candlelit birthday dinner with a girlfriend in Little Venice to the frigid Royal Oak terracing.

The Bees stood only three rounds from Wembley and potential glory. Cometh the hour, cometh the man – Bob was the hero in the Area Quarter Final when his two goals, one of them a perfectly placed lob ("Just like David Beckham," according to the goalscorer) ensured victory at Swansea.

Bob noticed a perceptible change in attitude from the players at this point. "At first, these were just another set of fixtures that we could have done without. But as we progressed, things changed. There was the carrot of Wembley, and we began to see the twin towers in the distance for the first time after we had won at Swansea."

The draw for the Semi-Final could not have been worse; an away tie at AFC Bournemouth, higher than Brentford in the league table. The Bees, however, gave everything, winning by the odd goal in five after a titanic struggle. Robbie Cooke's marksmanship and a superb last-gasp save by new goalkeeper Gary Phillips stood out.

An exceptional purchase from Cambridge United, Cooke replaced Joseph, who fractured his right shin early in the season against Wigan. Despite several sad, fruitless and short-lived comeback attempts, he never regained full fitness, much to Bob's sadness. "Losing Francis was a massive shock and a terrible blow for us. We really relied upon him for our goals. He tried to come back a few times, but he was never the same as he had lost his greatest asset, which was his pace. Afterwards he always seemed to run with a bit of a limp." His career never recovered.

Striker Rowan Alexander, signed earlier in the season from St Mirren for £25,000, found the move to English football difficult, scoring after 90 seconds of his debut at Leicester but never really convincing after that. Easily knocked off the ball and lacking a good touch, his one saving grace was a massive standing leap, enabling him to hang and beat much taller men in the air. It earned him the nickname "Skippy." "He was all I could afford and he was a gamble that, unfortunately, didn't pay off," admitted his manager.

Cooke, on the other hand, handsomely paid back his £20,000 transfer fee many times over, scoring 64 times in all for Brentford before being sold to Millwall for a profit three years later. Initially arriving on loan, he was quick and "A little ferret," according to Bob. A penalty area predator who finished clinically, he formed an excellent partnership with Bob. Gary Roberts remembers him as being "Sharp with a little bit of nastiness too."

Phillips was a larger than life goalkeeper who was the life and soul of the party. Arriving for a bargain £4,000 from Barnet, the loud, brash character quickly replaced Swinburne. "A total nutcase who would attempt to kiss directors on the coach home after games," remembers Bob, describing the suits as "rather bemused" by Phillips's affections. "He was an eccentric loose cannon who loved the social scene and always struggled with his weight and fitness, but he was a strong character, brave, decisive and a great shot stopper who was never totally reliable. But overall he did really well for us."

Cup fever finally hit West London; the biggest crowd of the season, 8,214, packed Griffin Park to see Brentford play Newport County in the Area Final. For once, the Bees did not freeze. "We battered them," remembers Bob with a smile, having set up two of Roberts's four goals in a 6-0 thrashing, three of which came in a joyful three minutes and 15-second spell either side of halftime. Roberts's dad decided to go down for a drink just before half-time, returning a few minutes after play resumed to learn all about his son's three goals. The victory was celebrated with an exuberant pitch invasion. Brentford were awarded two penalty kicks: one scored and the other missed by Keith Cassells. "I never took penalties," comes the withering reply when Roberts ponders the chance he had to score six. "To me they weren't proper goals." Try telling that to the likes of Cooke.

Brentford's Wembley opponents for what was dubbed "The Family Final," were Wigan Athletic, a bogey team for the Bees despite finishing just below them that season. Craggy, no-nonsense and tough, Colin Methven and Steve Walsh presented a formidable barrier at the back. The terrifying Graham Barrow – their own version of Terry Hurlock – rampaged around the midfield.

Bob shudders when recalling his tussles with him. "Barrow had a well-earned reputation for upsetting people. He was thick-skinned and could take most of the verbal stuff, and the physical side of the game was never a problem to him. He also had the biggest nose I had ever seen, which was always the preferred topic amongst players trying to wind him up. This would upset him and put him off his game. It really was his Achilles' heel. I'm no George Clooney by any stretch of the imagination, but Barrow was certainly no oil painting either. I always did my best to tease and try to distract him, and take his mind off trying to beat me up."

Gary Bennett was also a battering ram of a centre-forward, giving defenders no respite. Tony Kelly, called "The little fat kid in midfield" by McLintock, was a real livewire with an eye for a pass. Several talented local youngsters in the squad, such as Warren Aspinall, David Lowe, Kevin Langley, Paul Jewell and Mike Newell, would play at a higher level in the coming years. They were tough opposition but beatable by a well-prepared, on their game Brentford team which went into the final in excellent form after 13 games without defeat.

Brentford had one final league match to play after the annihilation of Newport, drawing 1-1 with Millwall on 19th May, followed by a long and seemingly interminable gap of 13 days to fill before the Freight Rover Final took place on 1st June.

After an exhausting and nonsensical 61 games in nine months – only in England are footballers outside the Premier League expected to perform like packhorses and play 46 league games, as well as in a variety of cup competitions – perhaps Brentford would keep things ticking over with a few gentle training sessions intended to ensure that their bodies and minds were as fresh and focused as possible for what would certainly be the biggest game of their careers for most of the team.

That is not what transpired. Figuring that the season would be finished by mid-May, the players had booked a post-season holiday in Corfu, intended as a players-only celebration and bonding session for everybody to let their hair down and totally unwind.

In 1985, attitudes towards diet, fitness, "refuelling," nutrition and exercise, even for professional sportsmen, were totally different to those held today.

Lange now made the truly horrendous decision to use the trip to reward the players' achievement in reaching Wembley, agreeing to pay for it. The management team accompanied the squad on this ill-advised and ill-fated trip, filled with "training runs and work-outs" according to the local newspaper, to keep the team fit before the massive challenge that lay ahead.

There is no doubt that "work-outs" took place in Corfu. The majority seemed to be held in bars and restaurants.

There are several accounts of the trip. Piecing together exactly what happened takes great difficulty, hampered by the rather muddled and indistinct memories of some of the squad, whose stories differ in some of the finer details, if not the basic facts.

Roberts is absolutely certain that the preparation for the final "was awful. We should have managed the period before the game much better. The worst decision we made was to go to Corfu. The trip had already been planned as an end of season holiday for the players. We were about to play the most important game of our lives – it should not have gone ahead. There was nowhere to train out there and we had to beg Club Med to allow us to use a small patch of grass. What made matters even worse was that our flight home was delayed and we got back a couple of days before the game, under-prepared, sleep-deprived and only just in time for our designated training day at Wembley."

McLintock has very few memories of the trip, suggesting they had all returned the week before the big match. Bob queries whether going to Corfu was a good idea, describing it as "A massive own goal." His prime memory is of Joseph, who was still on the injured list, turning up for what passed as a training session wearing a sombrero and crocodile shoes.

Phillips adds a crucial detail, recalling that Joseph, who admittedly would never be fit enough to play at Wembley, carried a glass of rum and coke at the time. He also remembers full-back Jamie Murray turned up late for another evening training session, dressed in a trilby hat and Gucci shoes.

"We were back in London four or five days before the match," explains Phillips. "It has to be said that we certainly looked good at Wembley. We were all boasting terrific suntans. It was a terrible mistake going to Corfu. We were red-hot favourites and thoroughly expected to win, but Wigan had some really good players and were far better than us on the day. We played really poorly."

One story suggests Phillips almost missed the Wembley final when he required stitches in his hand after cutting it badly falling on a hard surface after diving to catch a pineapple. In his wisdom, very late one evening, he decided to set up his defensive wall and practise defending free kicks outside a Corfu bar, as one does.

Terry Hurlock also thinks that they got back a week before the game. "Looking back, it wasn't a very clever thing to do for the club to send us all away," he concedes. "We all came back knackered."

The events in Corfu, when nobody cancelled the trip or succeeded in keeping the players under control, speak volumes for the lack of discipline, demonstrating how footballers thought and behaved at the time. It could surely never happen today. Perhaps the biggest day in the club's post-war history was soured and ruined by crass stupidity and unprofessionalism. The players never stopped to think how disappointed and let down their supporters, who were looking forward to their big day out at Wembley, would feel about their total non-performance on a day which turned out to be an anti-climax and damp squib.

"A number of people thought it was the fact that the players had been away on an end of season break which had proved detrimental," argued Lange. "I personally don't agree with this." He offered no other reason or excuse.

Whatever happened, Brentford froze at Wembley against a Wigan team playing as if they had been sent to boot camp and fed raw meat in the build-up. A boiling hot day seemed to sap the energy from Brentford legs. Wigan, attacking remorselessly from the first whistle, prevented a listless Brentford team getting anywhere near them. They defended poorly, and were punished when 18-year-old defender Keith Millen made his first costly error since his recent arrival in the first team, misjudging a long punt forward which striker Mike Newell blatantly controlled with his hand before scoring.

Many years later, Tom Bune, the referee on that ill-fated day, admitted to me there was more than a suspicion of handball by Newell. He was well behind the play as Wigan broke forward quickly, but part of his decision to allow the goal apparently rested upon the lack of obvious and concerted protests from the Brentford team. Being polite, restrained and well-behaved in football gets you nowhere, as subsequent Brentford teams have found to their cost.

Worse was to come. Soon before half-time, Brentford carelessly gave the ball away from their own throw-in near the corner flag. Kelly scored from the lay-back.

In an excellent crowd of 39,897, more than 25,000 Brentford fans helped their team rouse themselves from their torpor, albeit temporarily, after the break. Cooke scored the best goal of the game with a sharp turn and an instant volley into the roof of the net, but three minutes later the Bees self-destructed again, conceding a soft third goal by David Lowe following a corner. Despite a late and fruitless flurry, the match, as a contest, was over.

Bob was particularly disappointed. For the first and last time, his entire family had come to watch him play. He desperately wanted to put on a show for them. He received little service, feeling devastated as the game passed him by. Midfielder Terry Bullivant replaced him to no real effect on the hour, Brentford's challenge fizzling out in the Wembley sunshine.

The Wigan hordes celebrated wildly, the Brentford supporters slunk away, sad and disappointed by their team's non-performance on the big occasion. Their fury would have grown had they known of the events in Corfu in the previous days. At least Bob received a medal, keeping it as a proud symbol of his appearance at Wembley Stadium. As some form of consolation, Brentford received a branded Sherpa Van, also earning around £70,000 in their share of the gate receipts.

McLintock made no effort to hide his frustration. "We never really got started. Some players froze but it is difficult to say why, because Wembley affects different players in different ways. It has never been a happy hunting ground for me."

Corfu had more to do with it than Wembley. "We let ourselves and our supporters down," says Bob.

# CHAPTER 12
# TREADING WATER

Being part of a team that played at Wembley Stadium was probably the highlight of Bob's Brentford career. The rest of the average 1984/85 season was totally overshadowed by the magnificent cup run, eclipsing a carbon copy of what was to transpire with monotonous regularity throughout the remainder of Bob's initial spell at the club: mid-table mediocrity and a series of humdrum and forgettable performances.

The Bees never mounted a serious promotion push nor looked in any real relegation danger – a "never" team, as Bob described them, that always had the potential but never really achieved anything.

In Bob's final four full seasons at the club, 1984/85 to 1987/88, Brentford finished in 13th, 10th, 11th and 12th places – "bog standard," in Bob's inimitable words. While the supporters were relieved not to suffer the trauma of a relegation dogfight, as had been the case in 1980 and 1984, they voted with their feet over the poor quality of the football, a lack of sustained entertainment, and little perceived ambition. The average attendance figures at Griffin Park over those four drab seasons tell their own sad story: a high of 5,234 plunged to a pathetic 3,918 in 1986/87.

The club trod water throughout this period. Only in 1988/89, the season in which Bob left the club, did Steve Perryman, who had succeeded Frank McLintock as manager in early 1987, bring in quality recruits such as Neil Smillie, Richard Cadette, Tony Parks and Simon Ratcliffe, adding to shrewd earlier purchases in Keith Jones and Gary Blissett. The side finally gelled and narrowly missed the playoffs, reaching the sixth round of the FA Cup and exiting gloriously to Liverpool, having deservedly beaten the likes of Manchester City and Blackburn Rovers. Speculating to accumulate resulted in rewards.

Bob played a full part in 1984/85, scoring nine times – his best ever season's tally – partly thanks to a successful striking partnership with Robbie Cooke. They were particularly potent against Bradford City, scoring four times between them, including a Cooke hat trick. Even then, the Bees somehow found a way to lose.

McLintock faced a near-impossible task to bring about any sustained improvement and build upon the impetus of the Wembley appearance, managing with one hand behind his back in 1985/86, bereft of the services of four key members of his Wembley squad. Keith Cassells and Chris Kamara were dissatisfied with the terms offered to them, and departed for Mansfield and Swindon at the start of the season, for a combined total of £31,000. Both were sadly missed.

Gary Roberts fractured his ankle in a clash with Graham Roberts in a pre-season friendly against Spurs, "I wasn't sent for a scan and was told it was a ligament problem," he laments. "Arthritis set in which ended my career." Another huge loss. However much he exasperated teammates and supporters, Roberts was an unpredictable talent who possessed a spark of inspiration and ingenuity, providing a regular source of goals and assists from the left wing.

No Brentford supporter could possibly begrudge Terry Hurlock his move after more than five years at the club, where he had been well looked after and supported off the pitch by chairman Martin Lange. No doubt things were helped by his home in Braemar Road, less than a minute's walk from Griffin Park. The only surprise was his exit, in February 1986, to another Third Division team in eventual champions Reading, paying a club record fee. Perhaps higher-ranked teams had been scared off by his off-field shenanigans; he remained a massive on-field influence.

Lange attempted to minimise the potential impact of his departure. "In the final analysis we are getting £95,000 for a 28-year-old," he asserted. "We have had the best years of his career, so it seemed to make sense." Not perhaps his most perspicacious comment. Terry was in fact still only 27 when he left Brentford, and played regularly for another decade for the likes of Millwall, Glasgow Rangers and Southampton, as well as earning three England B caps.

Francis Joseph's initial comeback attempt ended in disaster, forcing another operation to insert a pin in his leg. He barely played all season.

Massive gaps were left by arguably the best players in the squad, leaving McLintock reliant on inexperienced youngsters such as Keith Millen, who was rapidly developing into an excellent defender, Terry Evans, Tony Lynch and Roger Joseph.

Winger Ian Holloway made an excellent initial impression on loan from Wimbledon, showing natural ability combined with massive energy. Bob rated him very highly. "Ian was a colossus – one of the fittest players I have ever seen," he assesses. "He could run for England, and probably faster than me." Holloway struggled with the debilitating effects of glandular fever when he eventually signed for the club on a permanent basis for a not insubstantial £28,000 fee. McLintock remembers, "Ian had real problems at the time, and never performed for me. He would keep coming into my office and apologising. He worked so hard in training and had no energy left for the weekend. In retrospect I should have stopped him training for two days each week and he might have had something left in the tank for Saturday."

McLintock was frustrated at having to make bricks without straw. During the previous season he even resorted to buying two players out of the army – a gamble that did not pay off.

"Steve Butler came from the army with George Torrance. He eventually developed into a regular lower league goal scorer, but unfortunately long after he had left Brentford. I am afraid that he was absolutely bloody useless for us, but I knew that it would probably take him a couple of years to get used to the pace of the full-time game. I was pleased to see that, in time, he settled down and did well. He was out of his depth and it was all far too much, too soon for him, although he worked hard and tried his best."

A tight rein was kept on the chequebook, but McLintock was allowed to make one major signing, which turned out to be an overwhelming success. Andy Sinton had been a stand-out member of a young and struggling Cambridge United team that had plummeted down the divisions. John Docherty had given him his initial opportunity, and the 19-year-old followed his former manager, "who recognised my potential," to Griffin Park for a bargain £25,000 in December 1986.

He already knew two other former Cambridge players in Jamie Murray and Cooke, making an instant impression by scoring a last-minute winner on his debut against Bury. Brentford's customary penalty taker, the clinical Cooke, allowed him to take a penalty, which he coolly converted. Sinton was quite surprised by the unexpected gesture, "I had been taking them for Cambridge since I was 17 but I didn't expect Robbie to pass up the chance to score himself. He said, 'Go on, take it, you're playing so well there's no way you will miss it' – and thankfully I didn't."

Originally from Newcastle but used to digs in Cambridge, Sinton took time to adjust to the hustle and bustle of London. Initially, he lodged with Murray, then moved in temporarily with Bob's parents, who "were lovely and really looked after me."

Roberts played his last game for Brentford during Sinton's debut, noticing the youngster's potential, "He was bright and bubbly in training, but not yet the finished article."

Sinton recalls his development at Griffin Park. "This was a step up for me, and I learned a lot from the players around me, who were a great bunch. I started out in centre-midfield until Steve Perryman moved me out to the left wing, where I could come in on my right foot." Sinton soon started attracting interest from higher-level clubs. After rejecting the opportunity to join Oxford United, he finally moved to Queens Park Rangers for a much-needed record fee of £350,000 as soon as Brentford's FA Cup run had ended in March 1989, going on to enjoy an exceptional career that culminated in him playing for the likes of Sheffield Wednesday and Spurs, and winning 12 England caps. Brentford also received another sell-on windfall of £235,000 when he moved from Loftus Road to Sheffield Wednesday, collecting a total return of £585,000 – not bad for an initial investment of just £25,000.

Sinton has extremely fond memories of his time at Brentford, remaining grateful for the help he received from Docherty, McLintock and Perryman. Bob also recognised his talent – "He gave us a different dimension," he felt, sensing that Sinton was destined to play at the highest level.

As usual, Bob filled in everywhere, ending the season in Hurlock's vacant midfield role and captaining the side for the first time in a 2-1 win at Newport County. "It was a massive honour that meant a lot to me. I relished the extra responsibility and tried my best to set an example and lead and inspire my teammates." He was a near ever-present in the side, playing 44 league games (his highest ever total for the club) as consistently as ever, helping plug the gaps from losing so many leading players.

Sinton was a big admirer of Bob and his contribution. "Bob was a lovely, hardworking guy and a very useful footballer who was good around the dressing room," he says. "I was delighted he went on to do so well. I can't say a bad word about him – I really enjoyed playing with him at Brentford."

# CHAPTER 13
# INJURY STRIKES

Bob's career had been on a largely upward curve since his return from Barnet. He suffered the odd dip in form and fortune but remained a regular, if not automatic choice, for all three managers he played for following his loan spell. By the beginning of the 1986/87 season, he was a seasoned, established professional with over 250 first team appearances and the supporters had finally – perhaps even grudgingly – come to recognise and acknowledge his qualities, eventually paying him the ultimate compliment by giving him his own song.

"Bob was not having a good game and went up for a header and was nowhere near the ball," recalls Bees fan Richard Merritt. "This prompted someone standing in the Royal Oak to shout, 'Booker, you're lost in a desert!' This comment raised a few chuckles, and the man standing next to him immediately started to sing the Egyptian Sand Dance tune. The chant was born: Dada da da da dada dada dada da – BOOKER!"

Profiling Bob in their *Timeless Bees* book, Graham Haynes and Frank Coumbe noted of the Booker anthem, "The extended, pronounced 'oo' in his name became something of a catchphrase, this originating from when he first played at Wigan Athletic and was referred to in this way over the PA system."

Bob's eventual acceptance, grudging respect and, finally, admiration (if not love, exactly) from such a demanding set of fans may have owed much to the kind of reasons Joey Barton offered when explaining his reception from Newcastle United fans. "I made a connection with the fans because I stood for something beyond my footballing ability," he wrote. "My values were their values. I played, and knew what pulling on the shirt meant." These words could just as easily be applied to Bob.

At first glance, there is much to be said for a footballer's life; getting paid (inordinately well at the top level) to kick a ball around and keep yourself fit, lots of free time, the adulation of adoring fans. The truth, of course, is different and far more prosaic, particularly at the lower end of football's totem pole. There is the unrelenting grind and pressure of having to prove yourself every week, knowing that your contract is running down, devoid of any guarantee that you will receive a new deal or find an alternative employer.

You might be replaced when a new manager comes in; someone with ideas and plans which exclude you. There is the stress of having to find something new to do when your footballing career ends at an age when your contemporaries are already well-established in their jobs. There is the challenge of having to live carefully and moderate your eating, drinking and socialising, the relentless pressure of facing the opprobrium of loud-mouthed fans quick to find fault and criticise, generally holding totally unreasonable and unrealistic expectations of you. Social media is yet another outlet for so-called fans to vent their bile and spleen without much chance or fear of retaliation.

But the greatest fear for any footballer is the prospect of his career ending suddenly and prematurely through injury. According to the Professional Footballers' Association, the average length of a post-war player's football career is only eight years. Footballers are a thousand times more likely than the average worker to have to quit their career through injury, and it is estimated that half of all footballers retire prematurely through chronic or acute injuries.

Andrew Ward and John Williams provided a vivid and disturbing description in their magnificent book, *Football Nation*.

"Injuries are a footballer's biggest frustration. Injuries are a nightmare beyond personal control. You can recover from bad form, you can solve a loss of confidence, but there is nothing you can do about injury. Disability brings anxiety, guilt, anger, uncertainty, embarrassment and sometimes depression. All you can do is accept a place on the sidelines, learn patience and develop your strength of character. But there is nothing like playing. If the team is doing well you want to be part of it. If the team is doing badly you think you could make the difference. But you can do nothing. You are injured."

For Bob, who had previously only had the odd hamstring and ankle problem, disaster struck in an otherwise totally forgettable Littlewoods Cup tie at Griffin Park on 2nd September 1986. He had started the season in his now customary midfield spot in the first team, experiencing the team's usual slow and indifferent start, gaining just a point from the opening two league games and suffering a narrow one-goal defeat in the first leg of the Littlewoods Cup tie at Southend United's Roots Hall.

On an unseasonably misty and drizzly evening, an eerie Griffin Park was nearly deserted, with only 2,632 of the most committed fans in attendance.

They were rewarded with an exciting match, the visitors proceeding to the next round of the competition with a narrow 3-2 victory. After his exploits at The Den in January 1984, former Bee Paul Roberts, now plying his trade at Southend, again fell foul of his former supporters – Brentford's this time – when he was grabbed around the neck by a supporter as he was about to take a throw in. What was it about him that caused fans to react in such a way?

In the 40th minute, Bob's world got turned upside down. It was something he found hard to accept. "One moment I was happy, content and established, doing something that I loved. Then it all changed. In a split second, I went from being a fit young man to a cripple."

"I can still remember what happened as if it was yesterday. Everything seemed to take place in slow motion. It was just a typical, harmless midfield challenge with Southend's Danny O'Shea, where we both slid in for the ball on the greasy surface. I knocked the ball away and he carried on and caught my knee front on, and I just felt this terrible crunch as he caught me with his studs. It wasn't a high tackle on his part. I just felt this numbness – at first I thought I'd broken my leg, as I could not feel anything at all. My left knee was bent back and the knee ligaments had snapped."

"I was lying on the floor but struggled to my feet, which was a daft thing to do. As I stood up and put my weight on my leg everything below my knee just flopped and I collapsed onto the grass. The top of my shin and my knee felt terribly painful. There were no cuts or bones sticking out or swelling at that time, but I just knew when I looked down at my leg that it was really serious."

"I remember the nagging thought flashing through my mind, 'That's it, that's my lot, I'm finished as a footballer.' Danny O'Shea was really concerned about me as I had come off far worse than him, and he was leaning over me asking, 'Are you OK?' I was eventually stretchered off in agony – there was no oxygen in those days. I don't blame Danny in the slightest, as it was simply two committed players going for a 50-50 ball. It was a total accident and I really appreciated it when he rang me up in hospital and apologised after I had had my operation."

"I was feeling really sick, shocked and distressed." Ron Woolnough, the physio, reinforced how bad he thought things were, predicting a 'really serious' knee ligament injury ahead of the scan the following day. "Frank McLintock did his best to calm me down, telling me not to worry and that I would get sorted. Incredibly, I was simply strapped up, given some painkillers and a set of crutches and driven home by my dad that night, rather than taken straight to hospital. Next day, the scan confirmed my worst fears. I had snapped the anterior cruciate ligament in my left knee. This was probably the worst injury you could get at the time, far more serious than a broken leg. The ACL supports the knee, but it had totally snapped as I over-extended in the challenge."

"Thankfully, I had an operation within three days, and Ron Woolnough ensured that one of the top orthopaedic surgeons in the country, Professor Paul Aichroth, operated on me at The Wellington Hospital in St John's Wood." The institution has been described as the Rolls-Royce of hospitals. "Dad drove me there and his Vauxhall Viva looked totally out of place in the underground car park next to all the flash motors owned by their better-heeled patients. I cannot thank Ron enough – I would never have played again had he not got me to the surgeon quickly enough for him to repair the damage."

"The operation took two hours, and Professor Aichroth opened up the inside of my knee joint. He then drilled through the side of the knee and joined what was left of the ligament with some carbon fibre, onto my hamstring, which was then threaded through my knee and ended up acting as my cruciate ligament, with three metal pins on the other side to hold it into position."

"I woke up afterwards still thinking that it was the end of my career. I knew that it was extremely rare for a footballer to come back and play again after such a serious injury. I stayed in hospital for ten days with my leg in a full plaster cast, feeling sorry for myself."

Ron Woolnough offered good news, bad news and a dose of total realism during a visit shortly after the operation. The damage had been repaired, but the battle to return, if Bob pursued it, would be long and hard. "Chris and my family came to see me, and my teammate Terry Evans was a more than welcome visitor – he had recently recovered from a similar injury. He totally understood what I was thinking, as well as the torment and uncertainty I was going through. He and I became great friends, and I was so grateful to him as he helped me get through a really tough time."

"Eventually I went home, which is where the problems really started. I was still on crutches, and we had steep stairs, which I couldn't manage. I moved into my sister's house just down the road, where there was a downstairs toilet, and stayed there for a couple of weeks." A black Labrador puppy, Benson, provided welcome company during days which

Bob says "dragged on interminably." Two months later, the cast came off. "I could hardly believe how thin, wasted and withered away my leg was. It seemed more like an arm or even a twig than a leg. It was soul-destroying for me. I was so depressed and demoralised just looking at it that I cried my eyes out. I was totally convinced that I would never regain any semblance of fitness."

"I really wasn't aware just how tough the rehabilitation process would be. Today, it would be a far easier process, and I would not wish what I had to go through on anybody. Ron Woolnough couldn't do enough for me. He even organised a local physio to come to my house a couple of times each week to help me practice straightening my leg, which was an excruciatingly painful process. I felt totally divorced and cut off from Brentford – my club which I had served loyally and, quite frankly, for not much financial reward for the past eight years. There was very little contact from either the directors or management. Frank McLintock did ring me a couple of times, but as an injured player I was of no use to him. He had his own problems, given Brentford's mediocre results and performances."

Future Brentford teammate Billy Manuel starkly sums up the feeling of being injured, "You're a piece of meat," he says. "If you're not playing, you're not thought about."

Bob would surely have felt even worse had he read his manager's weird, perhaps unintentionally disparaging comment about him in the local press. "He's such a marvellous club man and has such a good effect on team morale," he began brightly. "It's good having him around even when his best isn't always good enough." Talk about a backhanded compliment!

Bob feels very conflicted about the way the club treated him. "I have to thank the club for the way they looked after me in terms of organising and paying for my treatment, but pastoral care was unheard of in those days, and nothing was said to reassure me about my future. I was left to twist in the wind, knowing full well that my playing contract would expire long before I was fit enough to start playing again – if indeed I was ever able to do so."

"What brought it home to me even harder was that within a couple of days of my injury – just a couple of days – the club went out and bought a direct replacement for me in Wayne Turner. He was a combative defensive midfielder with First Division experience who cost £35,000 from Coventry City. That certainly did not help my feelings of insecurity and concerns about my future, although I was tickled pink that they'd had to spend that amount of money to replace me. As it happens, Wayne found it hard to settle down at Griffin Park. He also suffered at the hands of the supporters, who never really took to him. That being said, he lived fairly close to me and he was one of only a few players who took the time to come and visit me; something that I really appreciated, which gave me a real boost and helped me keep in touch. I really missed the banter and camaraderie of the dressing room. I was still getting paid but, of course, I now just received my basic wage of £225 per week, and lost my appearance and performance bonuses. It was hard to get by, and I was really grateful that we had Chris's salary too, as without it we would really have struggled."

"I went stir crazy and was pretty tough to live with. Chris bore the brunt of my frustration. The hours and days really dragged. I just sat in the garden, read the paper and saw my friends, who took me out for a drink from time to time and tried hard to raise my spirits. I didn't go to any matches as I was still struggling to get around and did not want to risk doing further damage to myself. I also could not face having to deal with lots of well-meaning supporters asking me how I was, then having to smile and answer positively. In reality, I was racked with fear and self-doubt."

Eventually, Bob progressed from two crutches to one, then a walking stick and, finally, to walking freely. The next stage of his recovery involved going to a nearby rehabilitation centre, Garston Manor that mainly dealt with road accident victims. Bob went there every day for two months in order to regain strength and full use of his leg, finding the experience deeply moving and affecting.

"It was a difficult time both physically and emotionally. I saw some terrible things there, and met some wonderful people, some of whom would never walk or speak again. Seeing them helped me get my own situation into perspective and made me realise just how lucky I was." One patient, Len McCarthy, became a great friend and inspiration. "He had suffered an industrial accident while working on a building site, and I did whatever I could for him. I used to push him around the hydro pool on a lilo and help dry and dress him. I worked hard to build up my core and raised £3,000 for the centre by doing the plank exercise on my elbows and toes for 45 minutes – it was the least that I could do."

Following another examination, Professor Aichroth said Bob would most likely play again. In the New Year, he received permission to start working out in the gym, located in the subterranean gloom under the main stand at Griffin Park. The fit players were all based at the training ground a few miles away, rarely crossing paths with him.

McLintock had not been able to turn things around. A run of eight league games without a win culminated in an appalling performance and abject surrender at Port Vale at the end of January 1987, causing Martin Lange to decide not to renew the manager's contract which expired at the end of the season. McLintock decided to leave immediately, but he should be remembered with gratitude for his achievement in leading the Bees to a Wembley Cup Final. His inability to replace many of his best players under tough financial constraints hampered him. Robbie Cooke and Andy Sinton were exceptions and, in November 1986, McLintock brought in two veterans in the shape of Chelsea's giant central defender Micky Droy and Tottenham Hotspur's Steve Perryman, who became player/assistant manager. They provided experience and composure, but McLintock's signings often failed. Lange says he was, "One of the nicest men you could ever meet. His biggest problem at Brentford was that he found it difficult to adapt to the lower leagues after being involved at the top level of the game throughout his long career."

Lange found "an obvious replacement" in Perryman, who was approaching the end of a magnificent playing career. Appointed player-manager, he brought in his former Spurs teammate, Phil Holder, as his assistant.

Bob was not surprised at the appointment, but worried, as ever, about what it could mean for him. "Steve oozed class as a footballer, and even at his age he was still the best player at the club. He could play anywhere in defence and midfield and rarely gave the ball away. It was great for the young players to have him in the team, and they were in total awe of him. It's always an uncertain time when a new manager comes in, but this was going to be particularly difficult for me – not only was I injured, but my contract was going to expire while I was still out of action."

"I was not even sure if Steve knew who I was. He had never seen me play for the club, was unaware of what I had done for Brentford over the previous eight years and owed me absolutely nothing. Quite naturally, his main priority was the fit playing staff. However, immediately after he had been appointed as manager, he went out of his way to come and meet the injured players. He just said, 'I hope that you can all get fit and play for me. You are not forgotten. Good luck and keep going.' This simple act of kindness and good man management gave me a terrific boost. The way that he had shown some interest and encouraged us to get fit, so that he could then make a decision on whether we were in his plans, impressed me enormously, and made me even more determined to play again."

Bob reinforced his efforts to regain fitness, including building up his quads by carrying apprentices up the terracing steps at Griffin Park – totally backbreaking work. He was beginning to feel the benefits, winning the mental battle he had been fighting and finally spotting light at the end of the tunnel.

"I was still not allowed to kick a ball but, for the first time since I got injured, I began to think, 'maybe, just maybe, I can get back to some sort of fitness and play again.' To my surprise and amazement, Steve Perryman came up to me at the end of the season and offered me another one-year contract, which I signed without even opening or reading it. I was just so grateful for the faith he had shown in me. I have never found out what actually happened but I suspect that Martin Lange might have got involved and told Steve that I was a good club man and worth keeping around because of my attitude and versatility. I certainly didn't cost them that much money!"

# CHAPTER 14
# ON THE SCRAPHEAP

Steve Perryman told the local newspaper why he kept Bob Booker on, confirming the player's suspicions. "I have signed two players in Bob Booker and Terry Evans who I have never seen play, on the advice of chairman Martin Lange, who has given each a contract following their serious injuries," he said.

This gave Bob the task of proving he was fit and good enough to make a contribution to the revamped squad that Perryman was building at Griffin Park.

Brentford had won nine times in the league under Perryman at the back end of the 1986/87 season, finishing in a par-for-the-course 11th place.

Perryman had been allowed one highly significant signing just before the transfer deadline, striker Gary Blissett arriving from Crewe Alexandra for £60,000. The story goes that Brentford were also offered the young (and totally unknown) David Platt as part of the deal, but were unable to afford the fairly small asking fee – another one who got away.

There was a pre-season clear-out of some of the more experienced players: Francis Joseph, Ian Holloway, Paul Maddy, Jamie Murray and Micky Droy were allowed to leave. Despite his age, Droy was a real loss – Keith Millen, in particular, had learned much from him. Fortunately, Terry Evans would develop into an ideal replacement.

New arrivals included the tough and no-nonsense Andy Feeley and the versatile Colin Lee in a dual role as player and youth development officer. In September, another high-quality recruit arrived in midfielder Keith Jones, signed from Chelsea for £40,000. Perryman was being supported in the transfer market in a way his immediate predecessors had not been.

Doubtless aided by his hard summer work in Russell Hansard's builders' yard, Bob had recovered sufficiently from his injury and rehabilitation, progressing far enough to be allowed to join his teammates in pre-season training. But he was still struggling to regain the level of fitness required by a professional footballer.

He was impressed by Perryman's approach to training. "Steve was what I call a purist coach. He had learned how to play the game at Spurs, where players were brought up on passing and movement. Steve allowed us to have some fun, but he demanded high standards; we always knew when it was time to buckle down and work hard, and he improved us technically. Training was fast-paced and based on his pass and move principles."

"Steve used to join in and set the bar high through his own personal example, so you knew exactly what was expected of you. This was not easy for me, as even my best friend would not have described me as the most skilful player in the world. I was certainly no Glenn Hoddle. I could get by and had a decent level of ability but I brought other qualities to the team. Perhaps Steve's biggest problem was in getting used to working with players who were less gifted than him. Just because he could do certain things didn't mean that we could, but he was always looking to get the best out of you and, eventually, the team flourished under him."

Bob made his long-awaited return to football as a late substitute in a 6-2 victory in a friendly match at Truro City on 27th July 1987, nearly 11 months after he had sustained his injury. This huge milestone marked the end of almost a year of pain, insecurity, and despair, rewarding the dedication and skill of Professor Aichroth and Ron Woolnough, as well as his own work ethic and utter determination to do everything within his power to play again.

Bob received a heartfelt round of applause from his teammates as he took to the field at Truro with ten minutes to go, appreciating just how hard it had been for him to fight his way back to something approaching fitness. "It was now more of a mental rather than physical struggle for me. It was really nerve-wracking and I felt so scared. I thought that my leg would go again as soon as I went into a tackle. What I really needed was for an opponent to whack me so I could get it over and done with."

He came through the ordeal feeling exhausted and exhilarated, "After that, I played a full 90 minutes with the reserves against Staines. I now knew that my knee was not going to go again, but it would take me quite a while to get my confidence back. That would be the hardest thing."

The biggest boost was visiting Professor Aichroth for a final time to be signed off. Everything was going to plan, he was told, anticipating first team action by the end of August 1987 – exactly a year after suffering his injury.

Fit to play did not mean match-fit, which would prove to be the biggest frustration for Bob throughout his remaining time at Brentford. He did not play nearly enough football to recover full match fitness during his rehabilitation, always struggling to regain his mobility and former sharpness. He was never able – or more accurately, allowed – to show Perryman his true capabilities. He became a squad player, on the bench at best.

Bob's chance finally came on 12$^{th}$ September 1987, just over a year after his injury; his replacement of Keith Jones, in the dying minutes of a 3-2 victory against Southend United, preceded his first and only start of the season, which was a week later against Blackpool when Gary Blissett was suspended after the first of three red cards he received during a tempestuous season. Bob lasted until half-time of a 2-1 win, limping off with a groin strain – a niggling injury which could have been expected given his lack of football.

It turned out to be a stop-start season. Sometimes he was named in the matchday squad, appearing from the bench 14 times in all competitions, generally for short spells without any real impact. The closest he came to scoring was a header, which forced a save from Brighton keeper John Keeley in an FA Cup defeat at Griffin Park.

He found sitting in the stand frustrating but enlightening, becoming a keen and astute watcher of the game – standing him in good stead for his later coaching career.

Bob strived to stay involved by travelling to as many away games as possible, pulling his weight by helping the kitman, making teas and coffees on the bus for his teammates and even picking up the pre-ordered fish and chips – the customary post-match meal in those less enlightened times!

A regular in the reserves, he played in a variety of positions, scoring four goals while encouraging and supporting the youngsters. He just missed out on another Wembley appearance when a strong Brentford team unexpectedly lost to Wembley FC in the semi-final of the Middlesex Senior Charity Cup, with the final against Hendon due to be played at the national stadium.

Bob understood how his role had changed, accepting and making the best of changing circumstances given his weakened knee.

"I had to adapt my game to the state of my knee, and even though I came through a lot of physical challenges unscathed, I had lost my confidence and did not play sufficient games to get it back," he admits. "My knee felt totally different than before the injury. I could not stretch it fully, and in the back of my mind I was always worrying that it might go again. I still had the engine, drive and enthusiasm to get around the pitch, but turning and twisting took a bit longer and was far more laboured. The real problem was that I did not play enough to get fully match fit."

Loan moves were far less common in the late eighties. It never crossed Bob's mind to ask for one, "I loved the club, but maybe I should have thought more about what was best for me, and tried to go out on loan. Nobody ever came in for me, although there were rumours that Dave Bassett had previously shown some interest in signing me when he was at Wimbledon." Prophetic words.

Perryman and Phil Holder were gradually rebuilding the squad, overseeing a transitional 1987/88 season with a 12<sup>th</sup> place finish. A run of seven wins and one defeat in 11 games between November and January propelled the team towards the top of the table, but normal service was soon resumed, with only three more wins in the final 18 matches once inspirational loanee Graham Rix returned to Arsenal, having made a huge impression during his short stay at the club, "He transformed us. It was just like having another Stan Bowles in the team," says Bob.

Perryman made a naïve and cardinal error in playing loan striker Paul Williams in a meaningless Sherpa Van Trophy tie against Notts County. The prolific striker earned a recall to his parent club, Charlton Athletic, after his hat-trick, rather than, as had seemed likely before the game, signing permanently for the Bees. Yet another one who went on to far better things, including England B and Under-21 recognition and a big-money move to Sheffield Wednesday.

Goals were in short supply at the club: only 53 in 46 league games. Andy Sinton top scored with 11, but Blissett was a major disappointment, coupling nine goals with his appalling disciplinary record.

There were some signs of promise in the form of young attacking full-back Roger Stanislaus and the exciting Allan Cockram, rescued from obscurity after scoring 29 times in 31 games from midfield at St Albans City, having failed to make the grade at Spurs. He was perhaps my last true Brentford hero with his long, enviously flowing hair, sinuous dribbling, ability to place a pass on a sixpence and goals from spectacular curling and dipping long-range efforts. Always seeming to play the game with a smile on his face, Cockram was a true crowd-pleaser. I totally ignored and forgave him for his blindingly obvious weaknesses, such as his inability and disinclination to track back, tackle and press.

Bob was a qualified Cockram fan. "Technically he was unbelievable – he had everything. He was two-footed and possessed incredible touch, awareness and vision. But he was a luxury player, you had to give him the ball and at our level he just did not see enough of it. When he didn't have it, he was a total passenger. Steve Perryman loved him but, unfortunately for Allan, his successor, Phil Holder didn't, and wasn't prepared to put up with his shortcomings in defence. Great hair, though."

The realisation that he was no longer considered a first team regular spurred Bob to seriously consider retiring when his contract expired. A friend offered the opportunity to become a partner in a cleaning business. Demoralised at 30 years of age, Bob felt his best days had gone. He wasn't in the manager's plans and felt his time at Brentford had probably run its course. If he helped run the cleaning business and perhaps played part-time for a local non-league team, with a bit of luck he could probably earn far more with two salaries than he could as a full-time footballer.

So much for his plans, though. At the end of the 1987/88 season, Perryman called Bob into his office and praised his hard work and influence. "I can't promise that things will change a lot for you next season," he cautioned. "But I really want you to stay for another year and fill in wherever and whenever necessary. What do you say to that?"

A pregnant, eternal pause is said to have followed. A nonplussed Bob struggled to compute what he thought he had heard. Finally, he managed to blurt out his reply, "Thanks boss, I won't let you down." He went home to tell a delighted Chris that his retirement was on hold; they could definitely afford the mortgage for another year and postpone further conversations and decisions about the immediate future.

The next season was to be the most exciting for many years. Brentford finished in an unprecedented seventh place, falling just four points short of the playoffs when they finally ran out of steam after playing a remarkable, ridiculous, exhausting 63-game season, including that run to the sixth round of the FA Cup.

The greater the budget the better the players a manager can buy; the more talented and experienced the players, the better the team will probably perform. The 1988/89 season clearly demonstrated the truth of this maxim.

Lange and Perryman used the transfer market cleverly and wisely. Brentford continued their stepping-stone status by selling two excellent young players, Roger Joseph and Andy Sinton, to higher-level teams. Full-back Joseph went to Wimbledon for £150,000 – the best player at the club – whilst Sinton went more controversially, joining local rivals QPR for a club record fee (at the worst possible time, just as the promotion race was hotting up). Perryman, however, was allowed to reinvest these funds in the transfer market, taking full advantage of his chairman's largesse by bringing in players of a calibre rarely seen at the club for many years.

In the close season, a near club record fee of £77,500 was invested in Sheffield United's Richard Cadette, whose mazy close control earned him the sobriquet of "The Wriggler." He formed a potent partnership with the revitalised Blissett, producing 32 goals between the pair in all competitions. Goalkeeper Tony Parks arrived from Spurs for £60,000 to replace Gary Phillips, who joined Reading. Tricky winger Neil Smillie was a bargain free transfer from the same club, a sterling servant for five seasons. Maltese international John Buttigieg signed from Sliema Wanderers for £40,000, but was bemused to discover that the Bees would not employ the sweeper system that would have best utilised his silky skills, and soon faded away. In January 1989, £100,000 was found to sign Norwich midfielder Simon Ratcliffe, the first six-figure fee ever paid by the club.

Brentford signed Ratcliffe by fighting off the challenge of Sheffield United, whose manager, Dave Bassett, showed either pragmatism or sour grapes. "I believed him to be worth around £50,000," he said, pulling out of the chase. Cadette disagreed, really rating Ratcliffe, who he thought was the type of midfielder needed by every successful team. "He was horrible and could kick people," he said.

With the influx of so many talented footballers – "Good players who could really play," according to Cadette – Bob was never going to challenge for a starting role. He was part of the squad that travelled to Portugal for the Alliance Cup, but was involved in only one of the four games, barely featuring in pre-season.

The number of substitutes allowed increased to two in 1987, with Bob's versatility ensuring he was often named to sit on the bench. He benefited from Cockram's misfortune when the midfielder injured his ankle and had to miss a month's action. Bob had a run of five consecutive matches in September and early October, taking part in two wins.

Bob's performances were no better than average. He was booked for only the third time in ten years and substituted four times. His most difficult game came against a rampant Sheffield United team, already looking like promotion certainties, who hammered the Bees 4-1 at Griffin Park in September. Bob lasted 78 minutes before Perryman mercifully replaced him. "Bob Booker failed to blunt the Blades's inventive midfield," said the local paper damningly, before peremptorily dismissing him as "ineffective" the following week, when Brentford struggled to beat Gillingham by a single goal.

Bob remembers the Sheffield United game very clearly. "I was still worried about my knee, and my main priority was simply to try and get through games as well as I could, without doing any further damage. Sheffield United brought a lot of fans who made a great deal of noise and created a great atmosphere, and they battered us. They were unstoppable and totally outmuscled us. Their style of play was really simple, straightforward and totally effective. They tackled like demons in midfield, hustled you off the ball, seemed to win every challenge and then just got it wide where two wingers fired in crosses for Brian Deane and Tony Agana, who were a real handful, far too good for Third Division defences to cope with. I couldn't get anywhere near them on the pitch that afternoon as Simon Webster never allowed me any time on the ball. I admired them and I realised straight away that they were a team on the rise with a formula that was going to bring them a lot of success."

"My old mate from Bedmond days, Derek French, was the physio at Sheffield United and still lived near me, so he gave me a lift home after the game. I used the journey to bend his ear. I said, 'You've got a hell of a team there and I'd love to play for you,' but my tongue was firmly in my cheek. I was desperately hanging on at Brentford, a million miles away from being fully match fit. My knee was throbbing as we talked, and the idea that a team on the up like them would ever need me – a half-fit crock with a dodgy left knee – was frankly laughable and ridiculous. A total pipedream on my part."

"Derek was bubbling over with enthusiasm. 'Dave Bassett's got everybody playing out of their skin. It's great up there, we are on a roll and I am sure we will be going up. Oh, by the way, he had you down as their danger man today from set pieces – got that one wrong, didn't he?' That comment put me back in my place and stopped me in my tracks, but little did I know what was going to happen very soon afterwards."

Bob quickly put the conversation out of his mind. When Cockram returned to fitness he fell even further out of the reckoning. He made what turned out to be his final first team appearance for Brentford as a substitute in a drab 2-0 home defeat to Preston North End in October 1988.

Everything changed with a telephone call.

"Derek French called me out of the blue on Sunday 20th November 1988, a date that is totally fixed in my memory, 'How are you doing, Bob?'

he asked. 'Simon Webster broke his leg yesterday at Mansfield and we need to find a replacement straight away. Are you fit, because Dave asked me to give you a call and wants me to sound you out and see if you are interested in coming up for a chat?' 'Well I scored against Orient Reserves on Tuesday so, yes, I suppose so,'" was Bob's less than totally convincing reply. Bassett saw Bob as the permanent replacement for Simon, filling that midfield role by getting up and down the pitch, winning second balls, getting it forward to the strikers quickly, scoring goals and showing strength and aggression. Not too much to ask for.

Bob knew, in that instant, that the Gods had smiled down upon him – his luck had changed massively for the better. Webster's misfortune was horrendous – he was challenging a Mansfield Town striker when a teammate slide-tackled the opposition player and took out Simon in the process, breaking his leg in two places. Derek French described the injury as the worst he had seen in his time at United. Bob had considered himself close to the footballing scrapheap. Such is the way of sport, for as someone is helplessly slithering down a snake, another is gleefully climbing the ladder.

After more than two years in the wilderness, the well-regarded manager of a Sheffield United team on the rise, lying in second place in the league table with promotion well within their grasp, wanted to sign Bob.

It turned out that Bassett and French had talked about possible replacements for Webster, with the physio first mentioning Bob's name. Bassett, who remembered Bob from his time managing Wimbledon, was quickly persuaded that he might fit the bill.

Bob told Derek that he would have to speak to Perryman in the morning, but made it clear that he would walk to Sheffield if he had to. His clapped out Ford Fiesta meant he nearly did, which would not have done his knee much good.

Bob talked to Christine that night. "I was in a state of shock and had totally mixed emotions about the conversation with Derek. I thought my career was on the skids and winding down, and I fully intended to retire at the end of the season. Here, totally unexpectedly, was an opportunity for me to join a team that was rapidly going places, when I was going nowhere."

"I felt excited at the challenge, and had a renewed sense of determination to prove that I was still up to it. It felt so good to be needed again, when I had been a spare part for so long at Brentford. On the one hand, I started to regain some of my confidence immediately, but on the other I felt a sense of abject terror at what lay ahead."

After training, Bob asked Perryman for permission to chat to United. The manager wished him good luck with the opportunity, agreeing not to stand in Bob's way. "He was fantastic to me and I knew I had nothing to lose given that I wasn't in his plans. I simply had to seize this chance, as I knew that I wouldn't get another one."

"My dad drove me up to Bramall Lane on the Tuesday. I still found it hard to take in what was happening to me. I just hoped and prayed that I didn't get up there and discover that it was all a typical Derek French windup; that he'd been playing a practical joke on me."

"I met Harry Bassett soon after I arrived and found out, to my relief, that he was expecting me and still wanted to sign me. I knew of Harry because of his Wimbledon connection and the fact that he lived near me in Bedmond, but we hadn't met before. He explained the role he wanted me to fill and told me he thought that I could slot straight into the team and play in central midfield."

"Just then, Derek Dooley, the managing director, came into the office. I don't think he even knew who I was until Harry introduced us. That was a breath of fresh air, seeing a director let the manager get on with his job, unlike some directors and chairmen in the modern game who think they are the manager. I remembered my dad's advice: when you shake someone's hand, mean it and look him straight in the eye. 'I'm very pleased to meet you, Mr Dooley,' I said. He then left us to it."

"Let's just say that it didn't take very long – about 30 seconds in total – for me to agree terms. I just wanted to say 'Where's the pen?' Somehow I stayed cool and asked if I could have a chat with my dad outside. Harry said, 'No problem, son,' so I went outside the office and back down the tunnel. This was just like the scene out of *Only Fools and Horses* when Del Boy and Rodney became millionaires. I didn't bother to tell dad what I had just been offered – I am not sure if I had really taken in the figures typed on the contract; instead there was a silence before we both screamed 'Yes!' and embraced each other. Then, with a tear in his eye, he said, 'Look, son, you've worked your socks off in the lower divisions all your life. You've earned this opportunity and really deserve it; so go and enjoy it.' We hugged each other and made our way back to the office where I tried, and failed, to look cool."

The prospect of a medical terrified Bob. "Harry must have been a mind reader. He said, 'Don't worry about your knee, Derek French will sort it out,' and he was right."

"I signed the contract that day in case they changed their mind, and went back to Watford in a total daze. I basically came home just for a day. It was manic and my feet never touched the ground. I sorted out arrangements with Chris, who was totally delighted for me, packed a bag and was back in Sheffield on the Thursday for my medical, which thankfully was a formality. I am absolutely certain that I wouldn't have passed one today. Anyway, I was laughing, as I had signed the contract beforehand, so they were stuck with me irrespective of whatever problems the medical highlighted. I then played half a game for the reserves at Huddersfield that evening."

The excellent *Life With The Blades* video saw popular Sheffield broadcaster Dave Kilner given total behind-the-scenes access at Bramall Lane throughout the 1988/89 season. There is a wonderful scene that purports to cover the actual signing of Bob, as he and Bassett are interviewed in the manager's office immediately before allegedly putting pen to paper. The conversation is wooden and a little contrived – both Bob and Dave spout a series of *clichés*. It comes as no surprise to discover from Bob that the interview was in fact staged entirely for the cameras, having taken place some days after the actual signing ceremony had been completed, when Bob was already a Blade.

Bob called Perryman to say that he had signed. "He was delighted for me and wished me well. I never said goodbye to either the players or supporters, but that's the way football is." As David McVay's book, *Steak... Diana Ross 11* confirms, "No long, lingering goodbyes. Grab your boots and off you go."

But Bob didn't even have time to pick up his boots. "I left all my old stuff at the training ground. Life was different at Brentford, I was given one pair of studded match boots and one pair of rubbers each season and after that I had to pay for them myself. I even had to wash my own training kit. As soon as I arrived in Sheffield, I was given as much kit and as many pairs of boots as I wanted. That was the first indication that I was now in the relative big-time."

"I had loved my time at Brentford, but it was time to leave – it was now or never. I had always wanted to play for a bigger club and at a higher level and now – out of the blue – the chance had come. I could not let it slip and I had to grasp it with both hands."

Brentford marked his departure by paying tribute to him in the matchday programme, "One of the most popular players in our 99-year history, Bob Booker, has joined Sheffield United on a free transfer in recognition of his great service to the club. The club will, of course, honour his benefit game which will take place later this season."

Perryman also had his say. "As you all know, Bob Booker has moved on to Sheffield United. It is a good move for him at this stage of his career and perhaps, in a way, it is the end of an era at Brentford. Most supporters will be sorry to see him go and although I have only been associated with him for two years, he has always given me tremendous support and great help. I wish him the best of luck in his future career."

After ten years and over 300 games for Brentford, this marked the end of a major episode in the life of Bob, a proven survivor who achieved much at Griffin Park through effort, energy, determination and hard work – far more, perhaps, than he and anybody else might have imagined. New challenges and massive expectations awaited him at Bramall Lane.

# CHAPTER 15

# THE ONLY THING IN COMMON WAS THE RED AND WHITE STRIPES

Bob's initial impression about his move was that Brentford and Sheffield United had very little in common with each other apart from their red and white striped shirts.

"Going to Sheffield United was a huge move for me. Because it came completely out of the blue, I had very little time to think. Once I had the call, it was all a bit of a whirlwind. I really didn't know what to expect, having been at one club for ten years, and not having anything to compare it with, apart from a very brief loan spell at Barnet, which was an eye-opener in itself given the way in which that club was run."

"On paper, Sheffield United looked like it was a big club with a massive fanbase. Little did I know that their expectations would be so much greater than anything I had ever experienced at Brentford. I was in for a massive shock. I was equally exhilarated and worried about what lay ahead. I was a babe in the wood, with no idea about what to expect."

Bob's first real sight of Bramall Lane took his breath away. "I had played there a few times previously, but generally the players had their heads down and were immersed in a card school when the coach arrived. I had never really taken any notice of the stadium. As I drove in, I took it all in – what I saw stunned me. Everything was so imposing compared to Griffin Park, which was homely in the extreme. The first thing I saw was a massive stand right in front of us with giant letters spelling out 'SHEFFIELD UNITED FOOTBALL CLUB.' That really set the tone. I couldn't believe the size of the car park, and I had the choice of about 200 car parking spaces. Little did I know that in two hours' time I would have my own space – number 26. I just hoped that my new shirt would have a lower number on the back."

"I love Brentford and Griffin Park, always will do, but this was just on another level. There was no car park at Griffin Park – it was a cramped and old-fashioned stadium with massive charm and ambience, dating back to the very early days of the 20ᵗʰ century and situated in the middle of a maze of narrow little streets filled with terraced houses. Whenever we played there, I had to drive slowly around the ground, sometimes several times, and search for a parking space. I always worried someone would think I was a kerb crawler. Quite often I would be forced to park up to 20 minutes away from the stadium, and then sprint to the ground to ensure I arrived in time for kick-off – not the best preparation for a match, but at least I got some sort of a warm-up."

Supporters share Bob's love of Griffin Park and the anticipatory buzz of adrenalin and excitement on turning the corner into Braemar Road, seeing the stadium emerge. Going to Griffin Park is just like being at home: I feel safe and happy there and it has become a major part of my life. I have laughed and cried there, smiled and frowned, cheered and jeered – but never, of course, at Bob. I have made long-lasting friendships. I once vowed never to return, yet found myself steering a path back there a fortnight later. Griffin Park, old, outdated and decrepit though it might be, is seared into my soul, as are all the memories, sweet and sour, of matches long since passed and players – good, bad, indifferent and maybe even great.

Bob had no idea that Bramall Lane was the oldest stadium in the world still hosting professional football matches. "It felt so distinguished and possessed a real sense of tradition and heritage," he continues. "As my dad and I waited to meet Dave Bassett, I remember looking at all the photographs of famous teams and players that were displayed on the walls. I wanted nothing more than to become part of this club. Maybe I too would one day earn the right to see my face there."

"Later on, I was taken for a tour of the ground which would have taken no more than five minutes at Brentford where, there was only a skeleton staff, assisted by a wonderful army of volunteers, but at Bramall Lane it seemed to take forever. We went through some large offices, and there must have been around 20 people all staring at me, probably thinking, 'Who is this bloke, is he a new player?' I found their interest and curiosity somewhat unnerving, as I really wasn't used to so much attention. I was then introduced to the pools office representative, Mick Rooker, who was to become my right-hand man and a great friend. Mick started speaking to me and it was impossible to stem the flood of words that cascaded out of his mouth in a thick northern accent, very few of which I understood. I was just like a nodding dog, agreeing with everything he said, although I did not have the faintest idea what he was talking about. What on earth was he saying – did they speak another language up north?"

"We then headed down the tunnel. The hairs on the back of my neck still stand up when I think about what I saw that day. This historic stadium was really about to become my new home. I tried to act as if it were just another ground – I'd played at so many, including Anfield, but this just seemed different and awe-inspiring. Deep down, my legs were shaking and my stomach was in knots." Welcome to Bramall Lane.

"I kept looking at my dad, who was just as impressed as me. His mouth gaped open with the wonder and scale of it all. To my right was the Kop, which just seemed to go back forever and ever. On the other side of the pitch, there was soon to be a massive new stand with 31 executive boxes spanning the width of it. Little did I suspect, that in years to come, one of the boxes was going to be named after me and my name would be engraved on a brass plaque on the door."

"Everything was on a far bigger scale than at Brentford. I knew that the crowds here were between 11-15,000 – well over double, maybe even triple what I was used to. Yes, I had played in front of nearly 18,000 fans at Griffin Park, but Brentford normally attracted between 4-6,000 spectators at their home games. It was going to be a big step up for me."

"We made our way back down the tunnel and went to the laundry room, where I met the two laundry ladies, Peggy Platt and Mary Coldwell. What was a laundry lady? My mum did my laundry. We had to keep our own training kit clean at Brentford and were given two sets that lasted us the whole season. Here, I was standing in this enormous room, which contained about 40 pigeonholes, all jam-packed with sparkling clean kit, numbered and ready for the players in the morning."

"Before we left Bramall Lane, I gave several press interviews. By the time I came back to Sheffield on the Thursday I was all over the back page of the local paper. There were also thousands of supporters who were not exactly backwards in coming forward and telling you how they felt. I had received a lot of criticism from the Brentford fans, but there were far fewer of them. This was totally different. There were only a couple of weekly newspapers covering the Bees and their circulation was tiny compared to the Sheffield Star. In turn, Brentford were rarely featured in the national press because they were competing for attention with about a dozen other London teams. It was relatively easy to remain below the parapet. My life was about to change, big-time."

Goalkeeper Graham Benstead made the journey in reverse, joining Brentford in July 1990 for £70,000 after spending a couple of years at Bramall Lane. "There was such an aura about Bramall Lane when I arrived, even though we were in a relegation scrap," he says. "It was obvious to me that Sheffield United were, and still are, a massive club. They seemed to be in a different league even to my previous team, Norwich City. The fans were so friendly, knowledgeable and passionate; even now they recognise me and treat me well every time I return to the city. We moved to the Rother Valley, just outside Sheffield, and soon settled down. We were happy living there, and that amazing man, Derek Dooley, took me under his wing and looked after me."

"Like most managers, Dave Bassett was most comfortable with players and staff he had worked with previously. He wanted characters who he knew and could trust – it seemed like he wanted to resurrect 'The Crazy Gang' from his Wimbledon days. Harry had this knack of finding players who could do a job and suit his style of play. He soon got his own boys in, and built up a large southern contingent at the club, with the likes of Derek French, Geoff Taylor, John Gannon, Mark Morris, Simon Tracey, Glyn Hodges, Kevin Gage, Francis Joseph, and of course, Bob Booker. But everybody got on and there were no cliques in the dressing room."

"The facilities were excellent, we were well looked after. There was no goalkeeping coach, so I used to work with Geoff Taylor and then join the rest of the squad for shooting practice and fitness work. Our style of play was simple and very effective; we would overload one side of the pitch with Tony Agana running off Brian Deane, and I would roll the ball out of the area, which was rare in those days. It allowed me to get further distance on my clearances and launch it up the right side, aiming for Deane or Bob, who were both exceptional in the air. We would build from there, pick up the second balls, aim to get it out wide, put in crosses and play as much as possible in the opposition's box. We used to steamroller teams who could not cope with our pace, strength and physicality – but there was also a lot of skill and ability in that squad."

Benno received initial criticism from supporters who were not enamoured with his new-fangled habit of dribbling the ball out of the penalty area before clearing it. "It's obvious that some of our fans don't like to see Graham take the ball out of the area," retorted Bassett, in typically forthright manner. "That's their privilege. But I should like to ask them not to blame him. He's playing under my instructions. He not only gets greater distance, but the ball takes a lower trajectory in flight, and is therefore much easier for our front players to control. If you don't like this tactic, have a go at me. At the moment, he's in an awkward situation. If he dribbles the ball out, he gets a roasting from a few fans, if he doesn't, he will certainly get a roasting from me." That seemed to do the trick, and all was going well until Simon's injury at Mansfield.

"Bob came in straight away so we did not lose any impetus," says Benstead. "He and I also hit it off from the start. We had a lot in common and shared the same sense of humour. After a sticky start, he gradually got more and more popular, particularly as he had a knack of scoring goals from corners. He would stand nonchalantly holding onto the post before the kick was taken, then drift into space and score. He eventually became a talisman and a legend."

"I had a knack of saving penalty kicks. I think I saved four that season, including one from Keith Jones of Brentford. I was always confident I wouldn't be beaten. I never really worked on it, but I used to have a sly look down to my left and go the opposite way. That seemed to work well. It got to the point that I'd be disappointed if I let one in, and I generally went the right way and got a touch to the ones that beat me."

"I lost my place near the end of the season, which came as a real shock to me. I still don't know why, as I thought I had played consistently well. I felt that the manager didn't trust me in the big games, and it's true, I did lack confidence in my own ability. Simon Tracey was waiting in the wings and took over for the run-in. I didn't rant and rave, although I was really disappointed, and I never got my place back. There was no keeper on the bench in those days, so I was never really involved after that."

Bassett does not shed much light on the rationale behind his unexpected decision in his autobiography, commenting enigmatically, "I've never been governed by logic. Instead, I put a great deal of store in my gut feelings – and it was this sort of abdominal nudge which persuaded me, with just six vital games to go, to drop [Benstead], who had been a part of almost every game that season. Many people thought that I was mad, but I felt that it was time to put my faith – and the club's future – in the hands of a young and inexperienced player [Tracey]."

Bassett laughs when told of Benno's continuing confusion. "Graham was a lovely fellow who did a good job for me," he says, happily setting the record straight to give Benstead peace of mind. "He had a great personality, was good in the dressing room and he handled himself really well. Deep down, though, I just felt that Simon was the better goalkeeper. He was a better shot stopper and dealt more positively with crosses. He also had a good temperament for a keeper – he was calm, laid back and never panicked, whereas Graham was a bit more hyper and erratic. It was my job as a manager to replace players with better ones and always pick who I thought was the best player in every position. Sentiment or personal feelings could never come into it." Finally, Graham knows why that tough decision was made.

Graham loved everything about the club and the city. "But when it became clear that I was not going to get my place back, I spoke to Bob and asked him to call Steve Perryman for me and see if there was an opportunity for me at Brentford," he says. "I was a Spurs fan and Steve was my hero. I set the wheels in motion, that's how deals got done in those days before every player had an agent. We went on an end of season tour and I ended up speaking to Perryman in a telephone box in Spain, a conversation that cost me an absolute fortune. We agreed the deal there and then. Harry Bassett said that I could go and talk to them, so I signed as soon as we got back to England."

"There was no comparison between Brentford and Sheffield United in terms of their size and stature and the quality of their facilities. Griffin Park was a homely stadium, not at all like Bramall Lane; it was smaller, far more intimate, there was even a washing line in the physio's room, and the fans were far closer to the action. They were not slow in letting us know how they felt about our performances at times. Everything about Sheffield was on a larger scale. The fans were so passionate, you always kept bumping into them on the streets throughout the week."

"We won the league in 1991/92 mainly because we had Dean Holdsworth, Gary Blissett, Neil Smillie and Marcus Gayle up front, and Terry Evans and Keith Millen winning everything in defence. Bob came back to Brentford halfway through the season, and he worked hard and, as usual, gave 100% whenever he was fit. Our style suited him down to the ground. Let's just say that Phil Holder played the long ball game even more than Dave Bassett. Unfortunately we came straight back down the following season when Bob barely played because of his knee. After we were relegated, Bob retired and Dave Webb replaced Phil Holder as manager. He soon got rid of me and also cleared out most of the squad. He just did things his way, including taking me off at half-time at Rotherham. You certainly didn't argue with him."

Bob did brilliantly during his Sheffield swansong, says Benstead. "He made everyone else play better by sheer force of his personality and personal example. He remains a good friend and an absolute legend at both Brentford and Sheffield United. Like him, I was so fortunate to play for two such wonderful but totally different clubs."

# CHAPTER 16
# THE BLADES

So what had Bob Booker got himself into? Sheffield United meant so much to the city and its supporters, but its magnificent tradition and heritage couldn't prevent the club from languishing in the depths of the Third Division.

Sheffield is a real football city, sustaining two big clubs despite having a population of only around half a million. The DNA of each club is totally different. Wednesday used to be the working class club, United's roots belonged firmly amongst the upper echelons. This has changed over the years; the current perception is that United is the champion of the working classes.

The rivalry between the two clubs is fervent, rabid and deeply held – no half-and-half friendship scarves are visible in Sheffield. United fans celebrated all the harder on 5th May 1990, on promotion to Division One, smug in the knowledge that Wednesday had been simultaneously relegated to Division Two. Local journalist Jonathan Foster did his best to explain the background to the rivalry in *The Independent*. "Sheffield is a uniquely insular city, the least cosmopolitan of all the large cities in Britain, with little apart from football in which jealousy or passion can be invested."

United experienced a yo-yo decade and a half, rising to the heights of sixth place in Division One in 1974/75, missing out on European qualification by a mere point. According to John Garrett, the club historian and a veritable fount of knowledge regarding all things United, says they were down by Christmas the following season. Jimmy Sirrel failed to reverse the decline during three seasons in Division Two, leaving Harry Haslam to preside over another relegation in 1978/79. United fell into the bottom division two years later when Don Givens missed a crucial last-gasp penalty kick against fellow strugglers Walsall, saving the visitors and condemning the club to relegation. The agreed penalty taker, John Matthews, bottled the responsibility.

Garrett suggests the main reason for this calamitous fall – from top to bottom in six tumultuous and tempestuous seasons – was the club overreaching itself in building the huge new main South Stand, sitting on the site of the old cricket wicket at Bramall Lane. In 1972, the decision to concentrate exclusively on football removed the financial drain of cricket on the club's resources, with Yorkshire CCC using Bramall Lane less often as a venue. If progress was to be maintained, the stadium needed to be exclusively a football one.

The new South Stand opened at the beginning of the relegation season of 1975/76, crippling the club financially for the best part of two decades. The squad was in a state of transition following the departure of Tony Currie and the imminent retirement of several popular and reliable club stalwarts such as Len Badger, Billy Dearden, Alan Woodward, Ted Hemsley and Eddie Colquhoun. Replacing their talents was a tough task, United had always been a selling club, learning little from the sales of star strikers Mick Jones and Alan Birchenall on the way to relegation in 1967/68, ending a proud stay of seven years in the top flight.

Promising young players such as Keith Edwards, Imre Varadi, Tony Kenworthy, Gary Hamson and Simon Stainrod were thrown in too early and discarded too soon, understandably proving unable to arrest the slide. Attendances declined, money was scarce (reserved to help pay off loans and interest charges), confidence evaporated and managers came and went, provoking understandable anger and frustration among fans. All in all, a recipe for disaster – even if local folklore insists that the real reason was a curse put on the ground by a departing member of the cricket committee. Whatever the cause, nemesis arrived in May 1981, when a club that had won the FA Cup four times and Division One once in its long and proud history, spending 55 years competing at the top level of the Football League, somehow found itself relegated to the lowest. Things could get little worse.

With only one real direction to go in, new chairman Reg Brealey decided upon a brave and ambitious, if highly risky, policy of speculating to accumulate. The club was around a million pounds in debt, but the decision was nectar to the long-suffering supporters' ears. Ineffectual manager Martin Peters did the decent thing and fell on his sword. Ian Porterfield initially proved an inspired appointment from Rotherham, where he had reinvigorated Sheffield's near-neighbours on a shoestring, leading them to the Third Division Championship. In turn, Andy Daykin was one of the first of the new breed of commercial managers, applying an innovative, lucrative commercial and sponsorship strategy which helped pay for an influx of new players.

These were not the normal combination of has-beens and never-weres, but players of a calibre and cost rarely seen at this level. Tricky winger Colin Morris, a £100,000 bargain signing from Blackpool provided a winning combination of pace, guile and goals from the wing. Keith Waugh cost £90,000 from Peterborough, finally providing the solution to a long-term problem in goal. Keith Edwards made a triumphant return from Hull City to score 35 league goals. United romped to the title by an emphatic five-point margin.

The supporters responded to the change in fortune and approach. Porterfield's decision that United possessed far more potential as a club than Rotherham was fully vindicated, with a crowd of nearly 24,000 at the last home game of a wonderful season.

1982/83 saw the team in mid-table with few signs of progress. But everything came together the following season: Paul Stancliffe arrived from Rotherham to become the team's defensive mainstay and Edwards and Morris scored a prolific 53 league goals between them. Glenn Cockerill excelled in midfield after joining from Lincoln City, helping United to four consecutive victories in April, only to choke on the brink of promotion by losing to rivals Wimbledon and Bolton Wanderers. A subsequent victory over Newport County left the Blades sweating on Hull City's final match, in which they needed a three-goal victory at Burnley to pip United at the post for the final promotion place. An evening of unbearable tension and bitten fingernails saw Hull fall narrowly short. United had returned to Division Two by a single goal.

United found it far harder to cope with the higher level. Fans soon expressed their disapproval at the quality of some of the football played by an underperforming team. Porterfield responded by bringing in vastly experienced players such as Peter Withe, Phil Thompson, Ken McNaught and Ray Lewington – a short-term policy fraught with risk as they had no resale value, with the team cruelly dubbed "Dad's Army." Thanks mainly to the efforts of Edwards and Morris, the Blades rose up the table, but the improvement was temporary and Porterfield's contract was terminated.

On cursory examination, this seemed a more-than-harsh decision. Porterfield had overseen a rise of two divisions in his four-and-a-half seasons in charge, finishing sixth at the end of the 1985/86 season. But his man management was lacking, frustrating supporters with his functional and negative style of football. Their protests were heard and acted upon by a board of directors who had also experienced problems and run-ins with the manager.

Dooley felt that Porterfield "seemed to lose the plot and might have benefited from firmer control. His management style and philosophy seemed to change." He believes that "The writing was on the wall from early in the 1985/86 season, six months before he finally went."

Youth team coach Billy McEwan was the chosen replacement, possessing the advantage of being *in situ* and having worked with all the emerging young players already at the club. An excellent coach with a good eye for spotting talent, he brought in the likes of Peter Duffield, Mark Todd, Chris Wilder and Martin Pike; good, solid professionals who were all picked up for next to nothing to form part of the backbone of Dave Bassett's subsequent squad. But his marquee signing, striker Richard Cadette, whose £130,000 fee from Southend United was part-financed by supporters, proved a damp squib in front of goal.

McEwan was a dour, strict man who was neither a good communicator nor comfortable with the media. The players did not respond well to him. Despite an acceptable 9th place finish in 1986/87, the quality of football was still not to the supporters' liking. The following season proved far more difficult, with results declining and attendances plummeting. McEwan's fate was sealed when, in January 1988, Oldham won 5-0 at Bramall Lane; relegation was beckoning.

Garrett recalls that Lawrie McMenemy, then struggling at soon-to-be relegated Sunderland, was initially regarded as the strongest candidate for what was rapidly turning into a poisoned chalice, presiding over falling gates, supporter dissatisfaction (and, perhaps, unrealistic expectations), internal strife and limited funds to strengthen a patently unbalanced and underperforming squad playing a turgid brand of football.

This somewhat unattractive proposition still drew nearly 50 applications. Who knows what might have happened had fate not intervened. Bassett, understandably, was struggling with the near-impossible challenge of replacing the legendary Graham Taylor at Watford. Results were poor, and Crystal Palace chairman Ron Noades had heard that Bassett was on the verge of the sack, particularly as he had been appointed directly by the chairman, Elton John, without full consultation with his fellow directors. Noades, who knew Reg Brealey, asked Bassett if he was interested in the Sheffield United job. According to Bassett, Noades "felt sure that he could get me the job." Exhausted at pushing water uphill at Vicarage Road, where he felt the dice were loaded against him, Bassett welcomed the prospect of a new challenge. Fans, players and directors alike were resisting all his efforts and not responding to him, although his style of football was similar to that employed by his predecessor. The situation drew parallels with Alex Ferguson's departure from Manchester United; any successor, however talented, was inevitably doomed to failure.

After the fateful call from Noades, Bassett immediately shot to the top of Brealey's list, having previously worked miracles in managing Wimbledon from bottom to top divisions on a minuscule budget. Bassett decided to resign from Watford, meeting Brealey and Derek Dooley at Chewton Glen Hotel in the New Forest just a week after leaving the club. Dooley immediately recognised his quality, and Brealey soon convinced the rest of the board.

Bassett did his due diligence and joined United with his eyes open, well aware that the club had gone through seven managers in the past 15 years, inviting him to "become a contender for one of the fastest-growing obituary lists in the game." Intrigued by the challenge of reviving the fortunes of a "sleeping giant" despite the relegation dogfight lying ahead, he faced the prospect of being given little or no money to replenish and reinvigorate an ailing squad.

His 18-month contract paid half the money he had earned at Watford, and he initially agreed to work with the existing backroom staff. Dooley describes his pay as "peanuts."

A total breath of fresh air and the total antithesis of the uncommunicative McEwan, Bassett soon demonstrated his intention to brush the cobwebs out of a stagnating football club. For all his efforts, he could not keep the club in the Second Division, overseeing a loss to Bristol City in the end of season relegation play-offs. At least he had kept his word to Dooley when he promised to get the club out of the division in his first season.

Bassett immediately offered his resignation, telling Dooley he would walk away without a pay-off. But the club recognised that his approach and personality were a perfect fit for their current predicament, swiftly telling him to bring his family up from London, go back into his office and begin preparations for next season.

Bassett had already started clearing out deadwood, bringing in the players he needed to mount an immediate promotion challenge. His old mate Wally Downes – "Someone I could trust" – arrived from Wimbledon as the first of many. Bassett struck pay dirt when he swapped Martin Kuhl for Watford's Tony Agana and Peter Hetherston alongside a £35,000 cash adjustment (something that deeply impressed Dooley, who was cautious about authorising any expenditure). Hetherston made no impact but Agana was an inspired signing, providing pace, power and goals before being sold to Notts County for £750,000.

Bassett used the close season wisely to rebuild a squad in his own image, capable of playing the high tempo, physical game he favoured. He raised funds by selling the likes of Peter Beagrie, Richard Cadette, Tony Philliskirk, Clive Mendonca and Chris Marsden. His encyclopaedic knowledge of footballers, in particular those in the lower divisions, enabled him to bring in Brian Deane, Francis Joseph, Graham Benstead, Alan Roberts, Martin Dickinson and Ian Bryson for bargain fees.

Deane went on to become a Bramall Lane legend and play for England, fetching a £2.7 million fee from Leeds. He cost a mere £30,000, and was spotted by Bassett on a night when he was watching the Doncaster left-back, Rufus Brevett. A chance encounter with Chesterfield manager Kevin Randall resulted in a positive endorsement of the awkward and gangly young striker, helping persuade him that Deane was a far more valuable asset.

The Bramall Lane revolution continued with a total revamp of the coaching and medical staff. Bassett was wisely allowed to bring in his own team of trusted advisors: Geoff Taylor, Bassett's "right arm," Keith Mincher, and Derek French arrived to assist the manager, acting as his support and sounding board.

In his programme notes for the opening home game of the season, Bassett challenged the fans to stop living in the past, predicting a bright and exciting future. "We cannot afford to keep looking over our shoulders about what used to be," he wrote. "We have a generation of kids supporting us who never saw Currie or Woodward play. They are now looking for new heroes and it is up to us to give them what they want. We have to create a new image and offer you a new heritage without in any way depriving you of the wonderful store of memories you already have."

Cultivating a positive attitude and reviving confidence and flagging spirits in a quiet and depressed dressing room was vital. The "former Wimbledon clowns," French, Joseph, and Downes certainly helped. Downes, in particular, became more of an off-field cheerleader than an on-field influence, having seen his career ended by a broken ankle.

Bassett cannily arranged a pre-season tour of Sweden with four matches against weak lower league opposition. His team scored 32 goals and rediscovered the experience of winning, something all too rare in their recent past. Full-back Chris Wilder recognised the value of his manager's actions. "We had pre-season matches designed to give us confidence and a feeling of unity."

Bassett's revitalised, restructured and rebuilt team, aptly described by Tony Pritchett in the *Sheffield Star* as "Bassett's Bombardiers," took to the Third Division like a duck to water. An emphatic 6-1 hammering of a decent Chester team, with Agana and Deane each scoring hat tricks, emphasised the strength of their promotion challenge. The two strikers formed a perfect partnership, combining power, pace, aerial ability and skill. Supported by Duffield and Joseph, they benefited from some wonderful service from the wingers, Bryson and Roberts. Todd and Webster, meanwhile, dominated the midfield, harrying and chasing, helping the ball on and hoovering up most of the second balls. Paul Stancliffe and Brian Smith were massive barriers in defence.

Bassett's ever-smiling face and exceptional communication skills – he was invariably bright, sharp and funny, understanding the importance of providing regular pithy sound bites to the local media – saw the supporters happily re-engage with their team. Attendances grew rapidly to watch positive, exciting and effervescent football, with plenty of goals and penalty area action.

September saw a full-strength Sheffield United team beat Scarborough 2-1 to win the Yorkshire and Humberside Cup. A minor competition, but Bassett justifiably celebrated his first trophy at the club. "I know this is not a major milestone in the club's history and will scarcely go down in the annals of the game," he reflected, putting his achievements into context, "but, after all, when did United last win a cup anyway? Winning is a habit and one to be encouraged."

Webster's serious injury at Mansfield left a yawning gap in the midfield, but Dave Bassett knew exactly who he wanted to replace him. The rest is history.

# CHAPTER 17
# THE CHALLENGE

It had been over two years since Bob had last played regular first team football for Brentford, taking part in only 25 games in the intervening period. He started seven times, lasting the full 90 minutes on only one occasion, leaving him gasping for breath by the final whistle at Bristol Rovers.

There were obvious and serious question marks about his fitness when he joined Sheffield United. Would his ailing left knee stand up to the physical pressures and demands of first team football? Would he be able to twist, turn and demonstrate the mobility, flexibility and stamina required to play regularly in the Third Division, particularly for Sheffield United, a team that prided itself on a punishing and demanding, high tempo style, requiring its players to maintain exceptional fitness levels?

The mental pressure of a promotion push was something that he had never really experienced at Brentford, who had only rarely threatened to challenge for honours, such hopes invariably proving a flash in the pan.

Could he rise to the challenge of becoming a starter again after such a long period marooned on the periphery of the action?

Nearly 15,000 supporters would bay their disapproval at him if his performances fall short of their expectations. Tony Pritchett's in-depth articles and match reports in the pages of the *Sheffield Star*, allied with supporters criticising and venting their fury on the notorious *Praise or Grumble* post-match show on BBC Radio Sheffield, awaited him.

These were all issues that deeply concerned Bob once he put pen to paper, however, his feet barely touched the ground as he was thrust straight into the promotion maelstrom, quickly dismissing and dashing negative thoughts and fears from his mind.

Derek French, Dave Bassett's ebullient physio who played such a valuable role in keeping the squad fit and in good cheer, had worked with Bassett during Wimbledon's meteoric rise to the First Division. Apart from his short, ill-fated spell at Watford, he had known nothing but success, and was regarded as a lucky charm by his manager, who called him, "The best signing I ever made."

# THE CHALLENGE

Derek and Bob had stayed in touch since they played together for Bedmond, although Derek's passion for jazz funk and Bob's taste for heavy metal precluded many conversations about music.

French has much to say about Bob's state of health at the time he joined the club. "Bob lived near me in Watford and I had seen him privately a few times for rehabilitation sessions when he was recovering from his injury. I knew how serious it had been and, quite understandably, he was very concerned about whether he would be able to play again, as ACL repair work in those days was nowhere near as advanced as it is today."

"Before we signed him, Dave Bassett had asked me about his fitness and whether I thought we would get anything out of him. I told him it would be a bit of a gamble but, knowing Bob as I did, I thought that coming up to Sheffield and having a change of scenery would give him a massive boost. I honestly couldn't guarantee anything. That being said, he was going to be coming on a free transfer, so it was really a low-risk gamble that wouldn't cost us anything if it did not work out."

"If his knee had been totally knackered we would not have been able to sign him, but Harry was only hoping to get a year or, at best, a couple of seasons out of him, so we didn't bother with an in-depth medical examination. We just made sure that he kept himself in decent shape."

"After he signed we worked really hard with him. Every day after training he would come to the gym and do lots of extra work to strengthen his knee. He showed a lot of dedication and determination. He fully understood that he had been given an unexpected last chance to extend his career and be part of a team that was going to win things. The transfer gave Bob a new lease of life as well as a huge mental lift. I think that in his excitement he simply forgot about his knee, ignored the pain and just got on with things. He did not want to miss out."

"Bob kept himself very fit over the three years he was with us. We knew that his knee was always going to deteriorate over time. He started playing every game for us after such a long break from regular action, and was put straight into the firing line, so he initially suffered from a few niggles and hamstring problems, but nothing that was unexpected or out of the ordinary. After a few months, he got himself really fit, mainly thanks to his own hard work, and he was really flying. He looked after himself very well and was never really a drinker. He was determined to enjoy the time he had in Sheffield and threw himself into the local community. He was a total credit to both the club and himself."

Bassett confirmed in his autobiography that he initially saw Bob merely "as a short-term solution." But he wryly amended his opinion. "Did I say short-term?" he asked. "I thought Bob might last six months until Simon Webster recovered, but he did fantastically well. We got far more out of him than I ever thought possible."

United historian John Garrett admits to having vaguely heard of Bob before he arrived, putting him in the minority of fans despite Bob scoring at Bramall Lane for the Bees back in 1982. Derek Dooley, meanwhile, had absolutely no idea who he was when Bassett informed him that he wanted to sign Bob. He was simply grateful that he would not cost anything.

Bob received a new lease of life in Sheffield. The fact that he played so regularly for United for three years, missing only five matches in the 1988/89 season after making his debut in late November, clearly demonstrates the power of mind over matter.

The first that United supporters heard about the move was on Wednesday 23rd November, "BOOKER PRIZE FOR BASSETT" read the *Sheffield Star*, allowing Tony Pritchett to announce that Booker would "reinforce Sheffield United's promotion challenge."

"I have known Bob a long time," Bassett was quoted as saying. "He comes from the same town as Vinnie Jones, but there the similarity ends. I wanted to take him at Wimbledon a few years ago, but I couldn't do the deal. I had my eye on him again this season but until the accident to Webster it wasn't so urgent. I didn't want to sign him just to play in the reserves but now we need an extra man. He can play midfield or up front and I have brought him to go into midfield for us."

"It is unbelievable coming here at this stage of my career," said Bob. "After 10 years-plus at Brentford, to finish my career here is tremendous. I have been blown off my feet today; it is a dream. I am really excited about it."

The first half of Thursday's reserve game at Huddersfield blew out the cobwebs from his recent travelling up and down the motorway, with an eye on making his debut against Bristol City at Bramall Lane on Saturday. Bob's experience allowed him to husband his energy, passing the 45 minutes relatively unscathed. But he could already see the difficulties that lay ahead.

"The Huddersfield game was a real eye-opener. Harry had the reserves playing in exactly the same way as the first team, which was fast moving and high-energy football. I had experienced their system at Griffin Park earlier in the season when I was playing against them, which I found hard enough. Now I needed to adapt very quickly or else I could see problems ahead and I would not last long at the club. In a nutshell, I was nowhere near fit enough to keep up with the pace of the football the Blades were playing."

Matches were coming thick and fast. Still in the FA Cup and the Sherpa Van Trophy, United's Saturday games were generally punctuated by a midweek match. Bob scrutinized his fitness levels, training regime, and preparation. He needed to tailor and adapt his routine in line with his new demands.

"I needed to train hard, but also train smart. To play Harry's game you simply had to run for 90 minutes – there was no escape and no hiding place. I was so relieved that I had only played 45 minutes at Huddersfield after the week that I'd had – that was more than enough and all I wanted to do was to crawl off the pitch, get back to my hotel, and catch up with some much-needed sleep."

There was no respite. "Derek French wanted me in early on the Friday to give me a massage and start me off on my new training regime. I owe him so much for the way he managed my knee, and I couldn't have survived at the club without him. On our way back to the hotel, he gave me the rundown on what I was in for the following day, which would be a typical Friday morning's training session: a warm-up and ball work with Geoff Taylor, before Harry would turn up at some stage and take the rest of the session."

"I wasn't sure what they had in store for me and was pleasantly surprised when Derek said, 'Don't be surprised if Harry throws you straight in on Saturday, there's a real opportunity for you here if you're up to the challenge.' I was as nervous as a kitten before my first training session on the Friday, and felt exactly like I had so many years ago, when Pat Kruse gave me a lift to the Brentford training ground for the first time. I said, 'Come on Bob,' as I prepared to enter the dressing room. 'You're a seasoned pro with over 300 games under your belt, you can do this.' But I still felt like a little boy on his first day at school."

"I needn't have worried because there was a strong southern contingent in the squad. Harry had already brought in a number of his former 'Crazy Gang' members from Wimbledon in Simon Tracey, Francis Joseph, who, of course, I also knew from my Brentford days, and Wally Downes, with John Gannon soon to follow. As soon as I entered the dressing room I heard a voice with a strong northern accent shout out 'Not another Southern softie.' That was my welcome to the northern bunch – in this case Dane Whitehouse, who was born in Sheffield. This broke the ice and for the next ten minutes it was like World War Three, with good-natured abuse flying everywhere between the northerners and southerners!"

There was no rite of passage or initiation ceremony for newcomers in 1988. Bob was not required to stand on a stool or similar and sing a song as the price of his admission into the group, sparing his new teammates his ghastly, tone-deaf rendition of a favourite by The Who, Def Leppard or even, heaven forbid, Alice Cooper.

"I could tell straight away that this was a happy and united dressing room, full of strong characters who were all pulling together and supporting one another in a way that I had never experienced before in my career. Dave Bassett, Geoff Taylor and Derek French ran a close-knit and happy ship where everyone worked and played hard, and laughter was never far away. You can never win anything if your dressing room is divided into cliques with lots of whispering in dark corners, but here, everyone mixed and gelled together."

Bob was immediately made to feel a part of the group, welcomed by the likes of Chris Wilder, who became manager of the Blades in 2016, and fellow midfielder Mark Todd. Bob clearly remembers his first sight of his new skipper, Paul Stancliffe, who had marked him out of the game as a Rotherham defender in his second match for Brentford way back in October 1978. "He walked into the dressing room and spotted me, did a double-take and shouted 'What on earth are you doing here – you're even older than me!' He was right, too, as I was born four months before him. Well, that was music to the ears of the northern contingent, who laughed their collective heads off. While I was still trying and failing to come up with a witty riposte, the ex-Wimbledon crew came to my rescue. 'He might be older than you, Stan, but he's played more games already than you'll ever do, and he can score goals too.'"

No pressure then. Little did they realise that Stancliffe would play 674 times in a 20-year Football League career – nearly double the number Bob managed!

More relaxed and at home after this lively introduction, Bob knew his performances on the pitch would count for more than those in the dressing room.

"Geoff Taylor popped his head around the door to tell us it was time to leave for the training ground. I wondered why he kept his distance and didn't come in, but my unspoken question was answered when his words were met by an immediate fusillade of laundry baskets, kit and football boots. There was no hiding place in this dressing room – you either joined in or fell by the wayside."

"Chrissy Wilder and Mark Todd offered me a lift and, from that moment on, Chris and I became great friends. He was a lot younger than me, but we soon discovered that we had much in common. We came from close-knit families and we were both local boys made good." Born in Stocksbridge, Wilder had been an apprentice at Southampton, but he finally signed for his beloved local club and was ultra-proud to be a Blade. "His mates sat right behind the dugout at Bramall Lane and the main characters of that group were two lads called Witt and Dallas, who also became great friends of mine."

"Chris was the manager of their Sunday morning football team and he often invited me to go along to watch the lads in action. This was a bit weird as on a Saturday they were all at our game singing Sheffield United songs – and, eventually, even my name – but the next morning I was just one of the lads watching them play. We would end up at the local pub after the game having a few beers together. This might not have been ideal preparation for training the next day, but it helped me settle down and become part of the local community. Chris played an important part in my life in Sheffield."

"On the drive to the training ground, Chris and Toddy started teasing me about the match at Griffin Park, 'You were rubbish and got taken off!' The banter was as cutting as anything I remembered at Brentford – that's footballers for you – but it also had a serious side. I soon realised just how important Simon Webster had been to the team and how popular he had become. I realised that I had a large pair of boots to fill."

Webster had overcome a difficult start at the club and the initial disapproval of the fans to become a dominant figure in midfield. Neither spectacular nor eye-catching, but highly effective in terms of winning the ball and passing it to a teammate, he would be a hard act to follow.

Bob knew the other players would be watching and judging him on the training ground, just as he did to every newcomer he had encountered at Brentford. Part of the furniture and a respected senior player at Griffin Park, he now found the roles reversed. All bets were off; it was up to him to prove that he deserved to be there, adding something to a team that had already demonstrated that it would be challenging for honours that season. If he didn't, he knew his stay would be short and retirement would beckon again.

"After the warm-up, the footballs came out. Every dodgy touch of mine was greeted with cries of 'How many games have you played?' The banter flew, but I did OK. By now, Harry had arrived and made his way over. In his strong Cockney accent, he said, 'OK Geoff, that's enough of that rubbish!' Even the manager was throwing insults around and the players were loving it."

"We all caught our breath for a moment while Harry and Geoff had a discussion. I looked behind me and Dane Whitehouse and Simon Tracey were wrestling with each other on the floor, which was apparently a fairly common occurrence." Nobody took any notice.

"As soon as Harry began to speak, the atmosphere changed. The players all gave him their full attention and you could tell he commanded their total respect. Even now, nearly 30 years on, I can clearly remember what he said, 'Right lads, listen up. These players come with me, the rest of you stand on the side. Watch and listen and keep stretching.' Harry then started calling out the team for tomorrow's match and my name was included. I did a double take. Was I really in the starting eleven, could I have misheard him? My stomach lurched and I didn't know whether to feel terrified or exhilarated. After the week I'd had, I really wasn't expecting that, despite the hint that Derek had given me." The team lined up in a 4-4-2 formation, with Bob in midfield. "I was next to my new little Irish mate Toddy, who was a great technical player and way out of my league in terms of ball skill."

"Now came the hard work. I was given a crash course into what was required to play centre-midfield in this Sheffield United team, and I knew that I had to be a quick learner. Harry stood over some footballs just outside our penalty area, in front of our back four. He served them in turn to the centre-halves, and then the full-backs. Each time he shouted out 'Two touches, hit the corners.' As the ball went forward, we all squeezed up the pitch like soldiers in formation, filling in areas where the ball might go. At the top end of the pitch, Deane and Agana knew exactly where and when to run. If they ended up receiving the ball outside the box, they gave it straight to one of the wingers and then sprinted into the penalty area, where they knew the ball would go."

"I was used to picking the ball up from one of the Brentford defenders, turning and then looking either to make another short pass to a midfielder and keep possession, or to hit the ball long towards one of the wingers or central strikers. I would then follow my pass as quickly as I could and attempt to join in with the next phase of play. Harry fired in a set of detailed instructions to me and made it clear that I would have to reprogramme myself." Everything was done differently in terms of the style and pattern of play. "The midfielders were the workhorses of the team."

"He told me that I should never come short for the ball from the defenders as they would be aiming what he called a 'Reacher Ball' to either Deane and Agana, or towards the touchline, ideally level with the opposing penalty area. We were always looking to turn the opposition defence by getting the ball in behind them."

"As soon as the ball was launched forward by a defender, or Benno in goal, my first task was to keep up with the play and then get goal-side of my opposing midfielder and look either to get a knockdown from our strikers or wingers, or pick up the second ball as it was half-cleared. When I got the ball I was instructed not to do any Cruyff turns or anything fancy on the ball, but to play a simple forward pass, ideally to one of the wingers. Once that mission was accomplished, I was not allowed to rest on my laurels, but told to get into the penalty area as quickly as possible in order to support the strikers and get a strike in on goal – not much to ask for. I quickly learned the hard way that every game would consist of a series of lung-busting 70-yard runs up and down the pitch."

"That was only half the task. When the opposition were in possession, I had to squeeze up on them, try to compress the pitch and ideally stop them playing. We needed to win the ball back and start the entire process yet again. Set pieces were crucial to our success, and with my height and strength in the air I was told to make late runs from beyond the far post and ideally meet Brian Deane's near post flick-ons. I was also allocated a strong header of the ball from the opposition and told to mark him at their set pieces – not too much to ask for from an old crock with a dodgy knee."

Stunned by the extent of his workload, Bob cast a furtive glance at his midfield partner, the tiny Mark Todd, wondering whether he had been a six-footer before he joined the club, and was gradually being worn down by the demands of his duties.

"After about 15 minutes of pattern of play work, Harry brought in some of the other squad members who set up as he expected Saturday's opponents, Bristol City, to do. Every possible detail was covered. Finally, we practiced a series of attacking and defensive set plays. By now my head was reeling with information overload and the need to keep concentrating on what I had seen and heard – and this was supposed to be a quick and easy training session."

"What Harry said was just as important as what he did, and he spoke simply and passionately about the importance of getting back on track as we had lost two of our last three league games. He emphasised the need for all of us to remain switched on at set plays and every time the ball was out of play."

"At the end of the session, he finally introduced me to the squad and said to the lads, 'I'm sure you'll make him welcome – even if he is a Southern softie.' He then turned to Geoff Taylor and asked if he wanted to take the lads for a ten-minute game of North v South. This was greeted by cheers from everyone and the next few minutes were total mayhem and carnage as the tackles flew in with barely a thought about there being a game tomorrow. The final whistle blew and luckily everyone was still in one piece."

Bob says the "banter" was "relentless" on their return to the stadium for hot baths. "Wally Downes and Simon Tracey seized an unwary apprentice and threw him into the kit skip, where he was forced to remain for about five minutes, which must have seemed interminable for the poor lad. Thank goodness I had never been an apprentice. I can't imagine anything like that being allowed to happen today."

"After our hot soak, Chrissy Wilder informed me that we were all going down to the social club to have lunch together. Now I began to understand why this team was so successful, as all the players had bonded together to form a tight-knit unit which was physically and mentally strong and full of winners, with everyone supporting each other."

Stancliffe itemised the club fines. "These included being late, wearing dirty boots or the wrong kit, not wearing flip-flops in the dressing room and borrowing someone else's shampoo. The list went on and on, and I knew I had to be focused and on the ball at all times or my improved wages weren't going to last too long."

"After lunch, Chrissy Wilder invited me back to his house, which he shared with Tony Agana." Bob, though, needed to recover from mental and physical exhaustion, returning to his hotel to rest and start preparing for one of the biggest games of his career. "I was at a new club with new players, a new manager – unlike anyone I had ever previously worked for – new fans and new expectations. I'd only been there for a couple of days but I already felt like a Sheffield United player. Now I had to go out and perform like one."

# CHAPTER 18
# GOING UP

Bob slept well the night before his Sheffield United debut, enjoying a leisurely Saturday morning, trying to conserve what little energy he had left. The weight of expectations was reinforced when he picked up the *Sheffield Star* to see the banner headline bearing his name, alongside Tony Pritchett's analysis of his playing style. "Booker is a big aggressive player who has a lot of experience up front as well as in midfield," he wrote.

There was more to read in the dressing room before the match, opening the official programme to see his manager's words in *Dave's Diary*. "The loss of Webster was a particular blow – to the player most of all, of course. I always knew that with his height, strength, enthusiasm, bravery and experience, Webbo could do the job for us in midfield and he has come through a rocky start with the club to be accepted. Indeed the Bramall Lane crowd, which I feel appreciates and loves honesty, has made him one of their favourites. We shall miss him."

"Even before Simon's accident I had my eyes on Bob Booker at Brentford. When I was at Wimbledon I tried to sign him but for some reason the deal couldn't be done and, again this season, I checked on him. Bob is the sort of player I like. He is big, strong and has been around at Brentford for 11 seasons, but there was no point in bringing him into the club to play reserve team football. The Webster incident changed all of that and I am looking to Bob, and to our other newcomer, Steve Thompson, to blend in and do their stuff."

A brief squib about Bob appeared on the *Behind The Scenes* page, welcoming him to the club alongside a very old photograph, showing a much younger Bob with his boyishly handsome face totally unlined, free of all the stresses, worries and concerns of his recent life.

The message was loud and clear. Playing for Sheffield United was a totally different proposition. Bob used the term, "never team," to describe Brentford in the *Flashing Blade* fanzine. Here, a promotion challenge was definitely on the agenda, with a manager and a demanding set of supporters scrutinising his every performance. He knew they would voice their discontent if things went badly. Everyone was counting on him to perform; there would be no hiding place if he failed.

Throaty roars of support echoed from the huge crowd of 11,248, "A big step up from what I had been used to at Brentford." Bristol City were no mugs, starting the day in tenth place in the league table, with an experienced squad containing players of the calibre of ex-Blade Keith Waugh, John Bailey, Carl Shutt and Alan Walsh. Their challenge was easily swept aside by a rampant United team which won 3-0.

Bob nearly scored when he managed to find space in a crowded penalty area. "Waugh brilliantly turned away a great header by new man Booker," reported Pritchett. Playing well within himself, concentrating on simply doing the basics, Bob got through the 90 minutes by following the instructions he had been given the previous day. "It was a fast and furious game but the lads were brilliant, well drilled, and everyone knew their job – except me. The game totally passed me by and I couldn't handle the pace and intensity. The ball always seemed to be flying over my head and when it did occasionally drop near me I just concentrated on doing something simple. The lads helped me through the game and I was shattered afterwards. It was no more than a steady debut, but we won, and that was key, as it proved we could win with me in the side."

Evidently Bob hadn't done too badly, receiving congratulations on his performance from his manager and teammates. "An eye-opening debut for Bob Booker," concluded the local newspaper, "who slotted straight into Simon Webster's job like a ready-made understudy."

Exhilarated and exhausted, Bob knew his career had been reborn, finally finding a team that played to his strengths. Perhaps there could be a seamless transition between Webster and Bob.

A hard-fought 2-2 draw at Swansea saw him make an impact the following weekend. "Booker took possession around the halfway line and his curving ball forward destroyed the centre of the Swansea defence, leaving Agana to run on unchallenged and score," runs the match report. Bob laughs at it. "This goal clearly demonstrated what was drilled into us every week in training. What I did was totally instinctive. I did not have to look up and just played the ball in first time knowing where the strikers would be. If, during training, I trapped the ball, looked up and took an extra touch then Harry would stop the game and make me do 20 press-ups. I knew I wasn't Tony Currie – my job was to play the ball into space, and it was up to the strikers to time their runs. Tony judged it perfectly at Swansea and that helped make me look good."

United reached the Third Round of the FA Cup after winning at Doncaster Rovers. Two days later, a painful reminder of Bob's past saw his nemesis, Graham Barrow, now playing for Chester and as tough and unyielding as ever, cautioned for what was described as an "assault" on Bob in their Sherpa Van Trophy clash. Bob remembers "us both kicking lumps out of each other."

Soon after, Dave Bassett made a rare mistake, playing Bob on the dreaded plastic pitch at Deepdale. "I really shouldn't have played and I was surprised that I was picked," Bob admits. "The pitch was horrendous and the ball bounced around everywhere. I could barely turn or move. My knee was so painful."

Christmas saw the Blades in third place in the table behind Wolves and Port Vale. "Sophisticated Wimbledon, long ball and direct," wrote Pritchett, describing their style. "It provides goals, penalty area excitement and pressure, and the crowd love it." Bob had also passed muster. "Bob Booker went straight into the side and continued the successful run," recorded the newspaper.

Bassett presided over revolution rather than evolution, turning the club upside down. In his first year in charge he had moved out 22 players, signing an identical number. Normally, new players take time to settle down but in this instance he received an instant return. Bassett brought in players who he had either worked with before or were handpicked to fit the system he had introduced.

United were still competing on three fronts at the start of January: Division Three, the FA Cup and the Sherpa Van Trophy, where a narrow defeat at Wrexham helped curtail the likely fixture pile-up that lay ahead. Defeat came at a cost, with Graham Benstead sent off after the final whistle for stupidly and pointlessly berating the hapless referee, Rodger Gifford, after he allowed a late and suspiciously offside looking winner from Kevin Russell. Bob was also dismissed for the first and only time in his career after a clash with Geoff Hunter who was also sent off. "He hit me," Bob later complained. "I did not hit him. I have played this game for ten years and never lifted my hands to a player in my life." No wonder the *Sheffield Star* exclaimed, "UNITED DOWN, OUT AND DISGRACED."

Pressed about what really happened between him and Hunter on that long-forgotten evening at Wrexham, Bob takes a moment to reflect. "On the way off the pitch at half-time, Geoff Hunter started arguing with me, and we ended up pushing our heads together like rutting stags, waiting for a reaction from the other player. Well, there certainly was one from him as he then spat in my face, and that's when I retaliated and tried to headbutt him. Otherwise, I was always in control of my temper throughout my career. That was the only time that literally and figuratively I saw red."

Benstead wrote a letter of apology to Chairman Reg Brealey and the rest of his board, escaping with a one-match ban. He would regret his mistake, opening the door for his rival, Simon Tracey, to make his debut. Bob escaped any club punishment but was suspended for three games, a potentially costly ban given the intensity of the promotion race in which United found themselves. In retrospect, his enforced break did him some good and enabled him to rest and recharge his batteries before returning refreshed to the fray.

Bassett was not "happy with some of the things that have happened but I'm not entirely surprised," he said. "A lot of our players have not been in the situation of challenging for promotion before and have to get used to the pressure."

Given his size and strength, Bob more than knew how to look after himself. "My disciplinary record was only average and I was booked fairly regularly throughout my career, but I don't think I was a dirty player. I played hard and, most of the time, I played fair. If I was tackled or brought down I tried never to let my opponent see that I was hurt. With one notable exception, I would simply get up and jog off and occasionally make the odd sarky comment, like 'Is that all you've got?' The so-called hard men couldn't handle that. The fact they had tried to hurt you and failed and often ended up getting themselves booked, really wound them up. If I felt it necessary, I would stand my ground, but I knew just how far I could go and controlled my aggression, which I feel was a real strength and gave me an advantage. I also tried to get the referee on my side by finding out his first name from the match programme and using it whenever we spoke. It worked every time as it just seemed to help me build a rapport with him; a little bit of banter with the ref could often save you from a booking if you made a bad challenge. This was a trick that I continued to use when I was an assistant manager."

Bob put himself back in his manager's good books by scoring his first goal for the club four days after the Wrexham fiasco, finding space in the penalty area to head the ball firmly beyond Gillingham's Phil Kite.

United comfortably beat Gillingham to end a mini-slump with their first victory in the league for four games. The fans had been fickle, with crowds declining to 9,336 – over 6,000 fewer than had watched the surprise defeat by Chesterfield in the previous home game, 19 days earlier. A concerned Bassett appealed to the supporters to keep the faith. It wasn't quite as simple as that; on a bank holiday, the Chesterfield encounter was an attractive local derby in which the visitors brought far larger support than Gillingham. The Gillingham match was also the first home game of the New Year – a time when attendances are notoriously low given the state of peoples' finances after the holiday period.

Bassett's words had some effect, as there were over 10,000 supporters at every home game for the rest of the season; an improvement, but far less than the 20,000 figure he wanted and expected.

Victory over Colchester saw United reach the Fifth Round of the FA Cup for the first time since 1968, receiving a tough draw away to Norwich City, who were challenging for the First Division title. This was the biggest game of Bob's career to date, relishing the opportunity to test himself against top-level opposition in front of nearly 25,000 fans, including over 5,000 Blades. Benstead, too, had the chance to prove that his former team was wrong to let him go. United played valiantly, Deane, and then Agana, after an excellent through-ball from Bob, scored and terrorised the home defence with their pace and power, before an own goal by Steve Thompson and a dubious penalty led to an unlucky 3-2 defeat. Bob is still bemused at the result. "We battered them and I don't know how we lost," he rues.

Defeat in such a cruel fashion still instilled confidence from the quality of the performance, allowing a squad weakened by suspensions and serious injuries to concentrate all its efforts on winning promotion.

Bassett was concerned that his team was being treated unfairly. "United are being branded as a physical or even dirty team," he claimed. "The club may be suffering because I am the manager. I am concerned at what I believe to be the Wimbledon connection… and that some officials have a belief that all teams that I control must be a problem."

Bob's old friend, Francis Joseph, bowed out with a goal against Gillingham, made for him by Bob's near post flick-on. Gillingham were persuaded to sign him for £5,000; it was excellent man management by Bassett, who felt that Joseph's talent was "beginning to wane." He told Tony Pritchett he had authorised the transfer to help "a good friend down the years" find a new club when otherwise he "would be giving him a free transfer in the summer."

It was an unspoken vote of confidence in his existing strike force of Deane and Agana, who were now supported by the lively John Francis and Peter Duffield. Joseph did not settle at Gillingham, soon drifting out of the Football League. Persistent injuries blunted the impact and stunted the career of a pure goalscorer who had once promised so much.

In a programme interview, Deane revealed just how surprised he was at his impact since his move from Doncaster Rovers. "I didn't expect to score so many goals," he admitted. "But the team's style of play creates so many chances that I'm bound to get a few. I have struck up a good relationship with Tony Agana, both on and off the pitch. Our styles of play seem to blend nicely together and it's a pleasure to play with him."

Agana echoed his sentiments. "I've had terrific help from the other forwards. Brian Deane's flick-ons and lay-offs have allowed me to exploit my pace, while the crosses coming in from Ian Bryson and Alan Roberts have created lots of scoring opportunities. And we mustn't forget the service I have received from John Francis and Peter Duffield when they have played. They have all made my job that much easier."

Deane would finish with 30 goals in all competitions, but Agana just edged in front of him, scoring 31 times – if you count one he scored in the Yorkshire and Humberside Cup Final against Scarborough. Duffield also weighed in with 15 goals, and proved deadly from the penalty spot, scoring from all five of his attempts. No wonder the Blades scored 93 league goals, as well as a further 31 times in the four cup competitions that they entered.

By early in the New Year, it was simply a question of which two of Wolves, Sheffield United and Port Vale would win automatic promotion, escaping the play-off lottery.

United eventually rediscovered their form and consistency, losing only five of their last 25 matches. Blackpool were thrashed 4-1, with Pritchett in raptures over Bob, "He did much to install himself in the fans' regard with his best performance since joining the club," came the verdict. "He played with muscular control throughout."

Moving to centre-half when Stancliffe was injured during the match against Reading, Bob demonstrated his versatility, totally dominating the free-scoring Trevor Senior, or "Tricky Trev" as he was known. Pritchett was becoming an admirer of Bob, recognising what he brought to the team. "Bob Booker did the work of two men on Saturday – and did it well! He proved he can do the central defence job if necessary." Bob was delighted to get the chance to play at the back for the first time. "I loved facing the play and having the ball come onto me. Playing centre-half for Sheffield United was pretty simple – you won the ball and got rid of it straight away without fuss or frills." His second goal for the club, at

Southend, could not prevent a narrow 2-1 defeat in a game where he also moved to right-back after a reshuffle.

United fans were initially unconvinced that he was good enough to play for their club. A massive turning point came on 4th April 1989, when thousands travelled the short distance to Mansfield for a crucial promotion clash, watched by 8,524 fans against a team with nothing to play for except local pride.

To say that the weather was unseasonable is a gross understatement. The heavens opened, with gale force winds and a snowstorm adding to an absolute freeze. Bassett described it as "A wretched night." Stancliffe felt that it was "One of the worst nights I can remember" and David Todd, braving the conditions on behalf of the *Sheffield Star*, called the conditions "Cold, wet and miserable."

A relentless battle ensued. Mansfield were full of confidence after defeating Wolves and Port Vale, taking control and forcing Benstead to keep his side on level terms. Driven back by a combination of the opposition and the appalling conditions, United discovered a new hero.

"It was Bob Booker who emerged as the star of the second half," noted Todd. "The former Brentford man began to dominate midfield with an important tackle here, a simple pass to set things moving there."

"He almost found a way through with a good run and cross from the right and, after a shaky moment when a sloppy backpass almost let in Kent, pressed forward again. Kent went shoulder-to-shoulder with him into the penalty area and although the referee did not give anything immediately, a waving flag from the linesman prompted him to point to the spot. Peter Duffield slotted home his fifth penalty of the season to send the United followers wild."

Benstead narrowly beat Bob to man of the match, but this was the game that saw the Sheffield United supporters finally accept him and take him to their hearts.

Many members of *S24SU* Sheffield United fans' forum recall that wintry night in Mansfield among their favourite memories of Bob. I hope that they do not mind me reproducing their comments about both him and the appalling conditions.

Grecian2000 recalls, "Booker's heroic performance in the most hideous conditions at Mansfield." The aptly named Snowman says, "Anybody who was there at Mansfield in the snow will tell you how that one game showed all that any Blade needed to know about Bob Booker and how he was and is still a Blade. He absolutely epitomised what we were then and hope to become again in spirit, guts, determination and sheer honest work rate."

SUFC Handsworth also saw that game as a milestone for Bob. "Like many Blades fans, I wasn't a fan of Bob Booker until the aforementioned Mansfield game," he says. "That night in dreadful conditions – snow, sleet, rain, freezing temperatures – he was awesome. From then on he never looked back at the Lane. He was a great character who epitomised everything about the Bassett era at our club."

Chris Wilder could see the difference in Bob after his performance. "Bob got himself going and full credit to him. The supporters appreciated his efforts and he went on to be an extremely popular player and a little bit of a cult hero from then on."

Promotion nerves jangled as United lost at home to a mid-table Cardiff team after a poor and nervy performance. Bob missed a glaring chance to equalise. "Perhaps trying to be too careful, Bob Booker side-footed over the bar from around the penalty spot," said the *Sheffield Star*.

Injury kept Bob out of a reunion with his former Brentford teammates. Chasing a play-off place themselves, the Bees earned a deserved 2-2 draw. Bob then played an important role in helping the Blades win a vital point at Craven Cottage where, according to Pritchett, he provided, "Strength and weight in midfield."

The final home game saw Bob injure his hamstring during a 5-1 victory over Swansea City. "I went on a mazy run down the right wing, which was a really daft thing for me to do," he says. "I felt my hamstring go and the injury ended my season. I couldn't play at Wolves where we clinched promotion, but stood on the touchline cheering us on. I really wished that I had been fit enough to have been on the pitch."

United finished in second place with 84 points, just pipping Port Vale on goal difference, and the Blades returned to Division Two in triumph after a season away.

It did not take long for Bob to realise that this United team was easily the best that he had ever played in; jam-packed with talent, well-coached, fit and organised. Everyone knew his job, boosted by an irrepressible team spirit.

Bob enjoys reminiscing about the individuals with whom he shared a dressing room and so much success.

"I could see from the start that we had two unbelievable strikers at this or really any level of the game. Brian Deane was a beanpole and the biggest bargain I have ever seen. Harry really had a knack of picking out a player. He pounced for him when others hesitated and also remembered Tony Agana from his Watford days. They formed a perfect partnership – a real Toshack and Keegan scenario. For a big man, Brian had great ability: he was two-footed and wonderful in the air. He was not a battering ram, and unlike Billy Whitehurst, who came in the following season, he was a bit of a wimp and really didn't like it if a centre-half got stuck in. He went on to play for England and fully deserved to do so."

"Playing with two wingers who crossed the ball non-stop meant that the service to them both was incredible, but they knew how and when to make the right runs, and they could both finish. They were rarely more than 20 yards apart and really complemented each other. Agana had the pace and Deane had a big stride and was much quicker than he looked. Tony was sharp over the first ten yards and ran the channels well. He was all left foot and reminded me of Francis Joseph in his early days at Brentford. Ironically, Jo had been brought in by Harry as first choice. But he couldn't stay fit and that opened the door for Agana."

"We practised crossing in training under Geoff Taylor and all our hard work bore fruit. Alan Roberts was quiet and unassuming, but he was two-footed and his delivery into the penalty area was excellent, although he did not track back as much as he should have done."

Ian Bryson – 'Jock' as he was called – was brought up on his parents' dairy farm in Ayrshire, a £40,000 bargain from Kilmarnock. "He was tough, could run all day and also did his share of defensive work," says Bob. "He was perfect for Harry's system."

"Mark Todd was a small Irish lad who had worked well with Simon Webster before I arrived. He had learned his trade at Manchester United and was technically excellent. He was much more creative than me but he could also put his foot in and win the ball when he had to. We hit it off straight away, and he is still doing a great job at the club heading up the community section."

"Left-back Martin Pike was a bubbly Geordie lad who signed from Fulham. He had a great left foot and took dangerous curling left-footed corners that he generally aimed at Brian Deane at the near post."

"Brian Smith was a quiet man who was a quick and versatile defender, but he broke his leg in April. He had the pace to clear up any balls played over the top and never gave up. We missed him when he was injured."

"Paul Stancliffe was our club captain and undisputed leader. I had known and played against him for years and he set a wonderful example.

He was a no-nonsense defender who headed it and booted it away. He was loud and a good talker who organised the back four and he wasn't slow to challenge anyone who wasn't doing his job."

"Steve Thompson was a very experienced defender who provided experience and calmness when called upon."

"Chris Wilder missed some of the season through injury but was a steady right-back. He was not the quickest of players but he loved getting forward on the overlap. He was a good all-round footballer who read the game well and was a hard tackler who also possessed a nasty streak. He was a local boy, so he really relished our success."

In goal, Bob credits "Benno" with being a good kicker of a dead ball, but "dodgy on back passes." "He was not the bravest, but did a really good job and was brilliant at saving penalties. Simon Tracey came in for him just before the end of the season, which was a surprise at the time, but it clearly demonstrated just how ruthless Harry Bassett could be. Benno had done very little wrong, but managers have to improve the team if they believe they can do so and not show any sentiment. On balance, I think it was the right move as Simon was a better kicker of the ball and shot stopper, and just had a bit more quality all round. The shared Wimbledon connection couldn't have done him any harm either."

"John Gannon came in during the season and eventually took over from Toddy, who was similar to him in style. He was a left-footer who was also great on set pieces and took wonderful curling corners."

"We had a strong bench with two excellent strikers in John Francis and Peter Duffield, who provided cover and fresh legs. Francis was quick and sharp; he came into the professional game late and was trying to make up for lost time. Duffield was a nasty little Geordie, a really great lad who loved scoring goals and never stopped moaning if he did not get the ball or missed a chance. All he wanted to do was score and he would even celebrate his goals in training. He was coolness personified at penalties and the two of them did a great job for us. Another big lad, John Moore, came in late on in the season from Hull City, but did little. I am not sure what Harry saw in him."

"Dane Whitehouse was another young Sheffield boy who was making his way in the game. He played a few matches and you could already see how talented he was. He was certainly one to watch for the future as well as being a livewire in training."

Promotion was a magnificent achievement given the club's straightened circumstances. The celebrations were long, loud, and fully merited, culminating in a week of mayhem in Magaluf. Bob was overcome, understandably struggling to put his emotions into words when interviewed in the *Sheffield Star*, "This is tremendous, I can hardly believe it," he told them. "Eleven years in the game and this is my first promotion. It has been a long wait, but it was worth it. I hope that the next celebration is not another 11 years away." Prophetic words.

Bob still feels proud when he looks back on what was an unforgettable season. "It felt like being on a rollercoaster – I went from being on the verge of retiring to winning my first ever promotion. I managed to regain my confidence, fitness, passion for the game and sense of pride in my own performances, all of which I thought had gone for good. It was a wonderful feeling to be a winner, especially after so many years of going nowhere, and I just wish we had received a medal to mark our achievement. The team was a good, strong unit with so much more to give and I felt so proud and fortunate to be a part of it."

As usual, despite his concerns and misgivings – initially shared by many of the Sheffield United supporters – Bob had been more than equal to the enormous challenge that he faced upon his arrival at Bramall Lane.

After a long and difficult gestation period, the ugly duckling had been transformed into a swan.

# CHAPTER 19
# BECOMING A BLADE

A veteran of supporters' criticism at Brentford, Bob hoped for a clean slate from Sheffield United fans, given his lack of match fitness after his career-threatening injury.

Everything started well; the positive write-up in the *Sheffield Star* and Dave Bassett's welcome to him in the programme, was sealed by a ripple of applause when his name was announced just before kick-off against Bristol City on 26th November 1988.

It didn't last. "There were a few moans and groans even on that first day when I gave the ball away," Bob says. "Things got far worse over the next few matches as I was not playing at all well. I desperately wanted to fit in and not let anyone down, but the harder I tried the worse I played. I was just not contributing enough. My passing was poor, I mistimed a lot of tackles and my heading was weak. I was off the pace and always a split-second too late." Too often, he forgot his instructions and tried to take the ball off the back four, "who correctly ignored me and whacked it up the field, which meant that I had even more ground to make up. I felt just like a dog chasing after a ball and never quite getting there in time to catch up with it."

"The crowds were far larger than I had been used to, and I felt straight away that they were not going to take to me. As the games went on, the abuse got worse. I could hear most of what was said about me and none of it was complimentary. It just seemed like a repeat of what had happened at Brentford, but far more cutting as there were a lot more supporters at Bramall Lane letting me know how they felt about me." Some of the comments from the terraces were particularly cruel, especially the "Bobby Blunders" nickname that many fans delighted in using.

Analysing why things were going so badly, Bob felt it was down to a combination of lack of fitness and confidence levels being low. He found the Bassett way hard to grasp. He worked hard to strengthen his knee. Derek French was always there for him, and he did extra gym sessions every free afternoon. But the unyielding fixture list meant less time for training and recovery, so Bob's main path to fitness was playing games. "I just wish that the fans could have seen me sweating in the gym and realised just how far behind the rest of the squad I was in terms of my match fitness, and yet how desperately keen I was to succeed," he says. "Then they might have cut me some slack."

Brentford fans were pretty much inured to failure, devoid of any great expectations. At Bramall Lane, Bob encountered a bunch of supporters whose life revolved around their club; nothing else mattered, the matches were cathartic expressions of their pent-up frustration. Woe betide any player who did not pull his weight.

Most supporters only take note of what they see on the pitch, rarely seeing footballers as human beings with families, suffering from the same stresses, off-field problems, aches, pains, injuries and illnesses as everyone else. They are expected to behave like automatons, shrugging off all their cares and distractions in search of the perfect performance.

"I don't think Bob Booker was particularly singled out for booing, but many fans were critical of him in that first season, certainly up to the Mansfield game in early April 1989," says Andy McWhirter, a United fan who saw most of Bob's matches during his spell at the club.

"He got quite a bit of stick in the *Flashing Blade* and there was certainly a lot on *Praise or Grumble*, plus you'd hear stuff in the ground and on the way to away games. There was a lot of groaning about his perceived poor play. I think the main problem he had was in replacing Simon Webster, who had been outstanding and as influential as Deane, Agana and Stancliffe." McWhirter says the team was never quite as dominant once Bob replaced him. "If I am entirely honest, Bob's wonderful display in the freezing cold and sleet at Mansfield was pretty much what we'd seen consistently from Webbo in the first part of the season."

Bob was not alone in falling foul of the United supporters, "There have been plenty of other players before, during and after Bob's time at the Lane who also received criticism. Ironically, Webster had received his share the season before, and John Gannon also received massive stick in the early part of the 1989/90 season."

McWhirter feels the booing had a lot to do with the culture of Sheffield as a city. "For me, Sheffield is a gritty, honest northern city and the football fans probably reflect that. Most fans will have a gripe if the team or particular players are playing poorly and not hold anything back. However, if the team and the players are putting in the effort and playing well, those same fans will sing their praises. Is that being fickle or just honest? I'd say the latter. I suppose expectations also play a part as the higher the expectations, the more criticism if things go wrong."

"I don't think it's scapegoating, I just think in Sheffield we tend to tell it as we see it. If a player is playing poorly he'll generally hear about it from the fans. The flip side is, if they play well those same fans will praise them. Webbo and Bob turned it around and became firm fan favourites – Bob spectacularly so."

There are many similarities between the attitude of United and Millwall supporters. Former Lions Assistant Manager Joe Gallen recently remarked in the *Daily Telegraph*, "The Millwall fans can be tough. But they can be great and, once they are on your side, they can be amazing. Once they're against you, they tell you how it is. Personally, I like that a lot." Millwall skipper Tony Craig made it clear what was expected of their players, "If you aren't showing your worth, they will show it. But put your body on the line, show a bit of passion and you'll get that passion back."

Supporter and author Gary Armstrong suggested, "Perhaps Booker got it in the neck because his presence epitomised the actions of a boardroom that had, in previous years, sought something for nothing; seeming to blow any monies earned on projects unknown or not understood. To his credit, Bassett made some remarkable cheap signings and could spot a bargain. The fans took a while to realise this and, initially, probably thought that bargain basement and left-field signings such as Bob were just more examples of the same rubbish they'd been served up over the previous five years."

Perhaps the fans could see that after so many years without real success, Bassett was on the verge of achieving something special at the club. Desperate to regain their former status, Bob's early struggles threatened to jeopardise their potential success.

Bob found it hard to cope with the opprobrium, "The pressure was relentless and the jeers from the terraces really got to me. I thought that it was unfair given my circumstances, but then I started to think rationally about how I had overcome similar problems at Brentford. I could either give in to the booing or fight it. If I allowed myself to get too upset and affected by it, then I knew that I was finished. I was determined to carry on doing what had helped me survive for so long, and I knew that all I could do was to figuratively put blinkers on whenever I played, keep working hard, try to keep my spirits up and show as much desire and determination as I could."

His teammates accepted him from the start, subjecting him to the customary abuse and banter. But Bob felt isolated in Sheffield. "This was the first time I had lived away from home," he says. "It took time to settle down in the north, however friendly and welcoming everybody was. I also had nobody I could talk to about what was going wrong, as you could never show weakness or really open yourself up to your teammates." His dad was his sounding board and "I talked to him a lot on the telephone but it wasn't the same as seeing him all the time. Not having Chris with me was also hard to take. Bruno, my Rottweiler, gave me unconditional love, but he could not really provide me with any practical advice about how to sort myself out. I was unsettled and lonely and it all affected my performances."

"Harry Bassett never criticised me or put me under any additional pressure, and even when the situation deteriorated he kept encouraging and supporting me. 'Keep going, keep trying to do what I have asked you to do,' he repeated. The most important thing was that he picked me every week and I felt that I had his backing and that of the team too."

There was no hiding place off the pitch. Sheffield United was always a major topic of conversation throughout the city. Nothing less than promotion was expected, as the fans and media were quick to let the players know. Sheffield Wednesday fans, who detested everyone and everything associated with their rivals, compounded the problem. There was no respite from Bob's own supporters, who made it clear, often to his face, how unhappy they were with his performances.

Tony Pritchett, the chief sportswriter of the *Sheffield Star* and the Saturday classified paper, the *Green 'Un*, was sympathetic and generous towards Bob in his columns, something that aroused the ire of many fans. "Whoever the fans were critical of, Pritchett would seem to go the other way and rave about them," reckons McWhirter. "Jamie Hoyland was average at best, but if you read Tony Pritchett's match reports you'd have thought we had another Bryan Robson on our hands."

Comments filled the letters column in the newspaper – some erudite and well thought through, but most bemoaning Bob's perceived shortcomings. "Try as he might, Bob Booker is just not good enough," raged one Nigel Matthews. Pritchett reflected that the letters column was the most "interesting and controversial section in the sports pages of our newspapers," and warned, "You should see the ones we don't print."

Many supporters found their voice within the pages of the *Flashing Blade*, a fanzine edited by long-term supporter Matthew Bell which became one of the most widely-read, original, irreverent and best-written fanzines to emerge at the end of the 80s.

Later, Bob Booker was celebrated and immortalised as a folk hero in its pages. Initially, though, he was the subject of several critical, if not mocking, mentions. The *Flashing Blade* named him as joint winner alongside Bobby Robson of "The Luckiest Man Still To Be In Football Award," and he was unchallenged in the "What Do You Expect On A Free From Brentford Award?" Apparently, the *Voice of the Beehive*, a Brentford fanzine, had sarcastically claimed that Bob's move to United had "rocked the world of football to its foundations," naming him in their Brentford All-Time Liability XI – a fact gleefully reported by the *Flashing Blade*.

*Praise or Grumble*, the popular forum on BBC Radio Sheffield, encouraged supporters to phone in straight after every match, emotions still running high, and tell the presenters exactly how they felt about what they had just witnessed. Disgruntled fans were allowed to air their frustrations and vent their spleen. The conversations were blunt and often cathartic, with no feelings spared. Driving home after each match, Bob used to dread listening to the programme, but resisted switching the radio off, feeling a masochistic compulsion to hear the unflattering comments aimed at him, "Who the hell is this Booker bloke... totally useless... can't trap a bag of cement... slow... rubbish... dodgy knee... too old... what is Harry doing?"

"In truth, I took an almost perverse delight in forcing myself to listen to the show, and occasionally I would smile when I heard a lone voice in the wilderness declare, 'Give him some time, he's trying hard... he's passionate about what he does,' but that was very much the exception rather than the rule. I found the general tone of the show to be utterly demoralising. I would drag myself back to my digs with the words of scorn and derision ringing in my ears, drown my sorrows with four cans of John Smith's, wolf down a KFC takeaway, watch a video and stare at the walls worrying about how I was going to get myself out of this mess. Eventually I would drift into a troubled sleep and it would be Groundhog Day as I'd wake up to a headline such as 'BOO BOYS AFTER BOOKER' in the local paper, and the whole process would start again." He nearly reached breaking point. "Maybe I even found some of the criticism motivating. I am sure that it helped make me even more determined to succeed."

Rather than stewing on his own, Bob needed to share his problems, obtaining help and advice from somebody who fully understood the ethos of the club and how the United supporters thought. His choice was an inspired one as he spilt the beans to the irrepressible Mick Rooker, of the club's commercial department who listened carefully to Bob's tale of woe and gave him the following words of wisdom.

"Give 100%, don't hide because Blades will suss you; acknowledge them at the end of the match to tell 'em you're here and you're not scared of being seen."

This was wise counsel – blunt and to the point. Bob followed it to the letter, emerging from his cocoon, raising his head above the parapet, beginning to embrace the city which eventually took him to its heart, embracing him right back.

Matters did not improve overnight. The rumbles of discontent from the terraces and local media continued well into 1989. But slowly and surely, through sheer hard work and bloody mindedness, Bob managed to raise his game.

"I was feeling a bit better by February. I was getting fitter and more able to keep up with the pace of game. It took a while, but I finally got used to the system, which I knew suited me once I was physically able to carry out my role. I was slowly becoming more of a physical presence off the ball and I started doing simple things on it. The fans slowly began to come round and I could tell that they were now undecided about me – which was a real improvement."

"The Mansfield match was played on a really wretched April night with an unseasonal combination of freezing mist, snow, sleet and rain. Something seemed to click that night as I felt for the first time that every supporter was with me. I was right on my game from the start and the supporters – drowned rats all of them – started to sing my name. I won every tackle, second ball and header and the crowning glory was when I drove forward and was brought down in a heap for the penalty that Peter Duffield scored to win us the game. This was a massive turning point – I felt that I had contributed greatly to our winning three crucial promotion points in a tough local derby."

"Unlike most of my teammates, I always wore a short-sleeved shirt, whatever the weather. I think I proved that I was not a Southern softie that night. I remember walking round the pitch after the final whistle and received my first standing ovation at the club. I felt I was finally a Blade – I belonged."

# CHAPTER 20
# TWO IN A ROW

At last, Bob's financial situation had changed for the better. His weekly wage rose to £375 after promotion and his bank account was boosted by a £2,000 promotion bonus. Any summers in Russell Hansard's builders' yard would only be necessary for his fitness now. Not that he needed it; an exhausting season saw him complete 40 games for the first time since 1985/86. His knee had taken a battering thanks to the relentless schedule. Allied to the mental stresses and pressures of the new experience of a promotion challenge, Bob was left totally shattered and desperately requiring a break.

Knowing he had contributed greatly to a job well done, he could forgo the builders' yard in favour of Cyprus with Christine, leaving Bruno in kennels.

Bob's knee had responded well and he had never felt fitter, "I knew that eventually my knee would fail me, but in the meantime I was doing everything possible to strengthen it and extend my career," he explains. "Our run of success helped take my mind off it. I was enjoying myself too much to worry about it. Even though at 31 I was the oldest player in the squad, by the end of the season I was definitely one of the fittest, which was a huge improvement from when I had arrived at the club." Bob and Paul Stancliffe were the only two players left who had been born in the 1950s, giving away over 12 years to Dane Whitehouse, the youngest member of the first team squad, who was born in 1970.

Bob returned to pre-season training refreshed and invigorated, and a little apprehensive at the prospect of playing Second Division football for the first time. Throwing himself into the training regime, he knew he would need to reach the peak of his fitness against better quality players. "There was a set pattern to the week's training. Monday and Tuesday were hard days and Harry pushed us until many of the players were physically ill. We often did a cross-country run through Graves Park, which I invariably won. Wednesday was a day off, and on Thursday and Friday we concentrated on pattern of play. The week always ended up with a no-holds-barred North v South match. It was hard but fun and I really felt the benefit."

"I looked at the fixture list and did a double take when I saw huge clubs like Leeds United, West Bromwich Albion, Newcastle United, Sunderland and West Ham. It wasn't so long ago when I had Aldershot, Chesterfield, Bury, Southend and Wigan to look forward to. Now I would have the chance to test myself against some of the most famous teams in English football. The previous season, we had outplayed Division One Norwich City in the FA Cup, and I felt that we had the team, players, management and system to do well. We were a totally unknown quantity as very few games were televised in those days. Dave Bassett described us as 'A bunch of thugs.' Most of our opponents didn't have a clue about us or what they were letting themselves in for when they came up against the Blades."

Despite top clubs sniffing around the likes of Agana and Deane – hardly surprising given their 61 goals the previous season – there were, surprisingly, no firm offers for either of them. Bassett was able to hold on to his key men, strengthening his defence with the signings of Mark Morris, Colin Hill and David Barnes for a total expenditure of £312,000 – big money in those days.

Bob was pleased to see them arrive. Morris was "A good, solid centre-half who had played for Bassett at Wimbledon and Watford. He struggled at first, just as I had, but he came through his problems and did very well for us. Barnes came from Aldershot. Harry always loved a quick full-back. He was a complete nutcase and fitted right in with the rest of us." Colin Hill was an experienced and versatile defender who could play at either full-back or centre-half. His arrival threatened the place of Bob's friend Chris Wilder. "That is football," Bob philosophically says. "Eventually everyone's time comes."

Midfielder Julian Winter, signed for £50,000 from Huddersfield but left after a chronic, long-term cruciate ligament injury restricted him to a sole appearance in the Yorkshire and Humberside Cup. Bizarrely, he was eventually to return to the club for two spells as Chief Executive Officer. Experienced defender Steve Thompson, his job done, was allowed to rejoin Lincoln City.

As injuries to Agana, Duffield, Bryson, Stancliffe, Hill, Barnes, Deane and Wilder began to bite, Bassett was allowed to wheel and deal. Extra money was found to reinforce the squad.

Experienced left-back/midfielder Wilf Rostron made the short journey from Hillsborough to cover for Barnes, who was recovering from a hernia operation, and the suspended Martin Pike. Bob admired the way he settled in. "It's tough to move across town and not many did it. Wilf was a hard man and got stuck in from the start. Soon after he arrived he scored a crucial goal away at Wolves that really helped the fans take to him. He became a true Blade and his versatility proved invaluable to us." Rostron subsequently joined Brentford as player and assistant manager, reuniting eventually with Bob, "Maybe he had put in a good word for me with the manager, Phil Holder?"

Carl Bradshaw – another local boy and a former Owl – arrived on loan from Manchester City before signing permanently for £50,000. Paul Wood replaced Alan Roberts on the right wing – "Tricky, good in front of goal with a great delivery," according to Bob. Mike Lake arrived from Macclesfield for £40,000 but never really recovered after breaking his leg, and £30,000 was paid for Billy Whitehurst, who provided experienced cover for Agana and Deane, more than living up to his unflattering mention in the matchday programme after he had played against the Blades earlier in the season for Hull City. It described, "The usual irritating presence of the aggressive Billy Whitehurst."

Like Alan Hansen, who in his autobiography, *A Matter Of Opinion*, described him as "One of the opposing strikers who frightened me the most – and I do mean frightened," Bob was a great admirer of Whitehurst. "It was far better to have him on your side than playing against you," he points out. "What he did for us was priceless. He came mainly to sit on the bench and to come on if we needed a late goal. He was the best header of a ball I ever played with. He had no pace but he was so strong and you could never get the ball off him. Defenders were terrified of him and he was a perfect target man. He so nearly scored a winning goal in the penultimate match at Blackburn, which would have seen us promoted a week early, when he put everything and everybody into the back of the net – except the football."

Above all, Bob admired his manager's "uncanny knack for finding just the right man. He always managed to pick people who would fit right into our madcap dressing room. There was no room for prima donnas and thankfully we never signed any. Slowly but surely he was bringing in a better calibre of player."

As newcomers arrived, it was time for some of the old guard to depart. Bassett bought low, sold high – a trait greatly appreciated by Managing Director Derek Dooley. Roberts left for Lincoln City for £63,000, Pike to Fulham for £60,000, Gannon to Stockport for the same amount. Francis needed regular first team football at his age (26), joining Burnley for a handy £90,000. (That season, BBC2 screened a fascinating, groundbreaking behind-the-scenes look at life at Bramall Lane, and the six-episode series, banally called *United*, provided an insiders' through the keyhole insight into all aspects of the club. In one memorable scene, Bassett was shown bidding farewell to Francis, treating the departing player with great dignity, thanking him for everything he had done for the club and wishing him well at Burnley, while making it clear that it was time for him to leave. "And don't nick anything before you go," he finished).

The team's pre-season tour was to Germany this time, winning one out of three but still managing to score nine times. A week before the season, Wednesday visited Bramall Lane for a "Centenary Celebration Match." Bassett made it clear in the souvenir programme that "Though today's match is classed as a friendly, everybody will be trying to win. After all, there's a lot of pride at stake." Wednesday's manager, Ron Atkinson, acknowledged that "There's always that bit of extra tension in these fixtures." This was not going to be the usual pre-season friendly.

In a disappointing goalless draw in front of a packed Bramall Lane, an encounter between Bob Booker and Carlton Palmer, Wednesday's combative midfielder who played 18 times for England, helped to secure Bob's place as a United legend.

"I was really psyched up for my first local derby," says Bob. "It might only have been a pre-season friendly but it was deadly serious to everyone involved, especially the thousands of fans supporting both teams. Major bragging rights were at stake as the teams would not be facing each other in the Football League."

"Carlton Palmer was in their midfield and I knew that our paths were bound to cross. Frankly, I relished the prospect. We were not friends; on the contrary, I thought that he was an annoying and arrogant so-and-so who flaunted himself around town. As soon as the game started he seemed determined to wind me up. He kicked me, I got up; he abused my family and myself, and I just ignored him." The flashpoint came in the 35th minute, Palmer's frustration finally getting the better of him. "He growled 'I'm going to do you, Booker.' My only response was 'Don't talk about it, Pin Head (his nickname), just do it!' That was like a red rag to a bull. He sprinted after me, screaming and shouting, and then kicked me hard down the back of my Achilles tendon. This all took place off the ball, and out of sight of the referee, Keith Hackett, but not the Blades fans, who saw what had happened. It wasn't really too painful, but I went down in a heap and I decided to feign injury. The crowd went berserk and luckily the linesman had seen what Palmer had done and started desperately waving his flag in order to attract the ref's attention. The game stopped and players jostled as I lay on the ground. Derek French ran on and said, 'All right son, where are you hurt?' I just looked up and winked at him and replied, 'Nowhere, you idiot. Just get your sponge out, do your stuff and look busy.' I milked it for all it was worth and the next thing I hear is Derek gleefully telling me that Palmer has been sent off. I then gingerly got back to my feet, shook myself down and walked away." Palmer's red card meant he missed the first three games of the season. "It served him right and he got exactly what he deserved."

What happened next would irrevocably change Bob's relationship with the United supporters. "The next thing I hear from the Kop End is the Blades fans singing 'We've got Bobby Booker, he's a dirty fooker, he's six foot tall and he cost fook all.' The chant just seemed to come out of nowhere, but I was stunned and delighted. I had earned my own song at Brentford, but it had taken me years and I always felt in the back of my mind that it was somewhat sarcastic in tone. This time it was totally different as I thought it showed the growing love and respect that I shared with every Blade. Whenever I heard the chant it made me feel – not six feet, but nearer ten feet tall."

If one chant wasn't enough, the United fans soon came up with another, the catchy and immortal "OOH-AAH BOB BOOKAH," which is still heard even now on the Bramall Lane terraces, or whenever Bob returns to Sheffield. In Nick Johnson's excellent, *Match of My Life*, Bob made it abundantly clear who was the original and who was the plagiarist. "Everybody thought it was Eric Cantona's chant, but it was definitely mine. The Leeds fans heard the Blades supporters chanting my name when we played them the following year, and only then did they start singing 'OOH-AAH CANTONA.' Never let a Leeds fan tell you otherwise. They stole it from us."

Even favourites, though, are not immune from criticism, a misplaced pass or wild shot still ensuring a groan of frustration. But the crowd was behind him now. After a tough struggle that could have gone either way, Bob had finally been accepted, considered one of them. He fully recognised the fans' part in his success. "The more they cheered me, the better I played."

Any fears that Bob may have had about coping with the demands of a higher division were dispelled when United totally outplayed and overpowered an unsuspecting West Bromwich Albion team at the Hawthorns, winning comfortably by three clear goals. The United programme subsequently paid Bob a fulsome compliment when it described his performance. "In midfield, Bob Booker – who has sometimes been accused of 'not jumping his height' – silenced most of his critics by dominating the aerial part of the midfield battle, while still finding time to distribute the ball accurately and well." United wore their new, distinctive luminous yellow away kit for the first time that afternoon. It soon caught on and became a bestseller for Umbro. Bob loved it. "But the following season we stopped wearing it as apparently it clashed with the stewards – and that's my excuse for putting the ball out of play all the time!"

United took the Second Division by storm, victorious in ten of their first 15 fixtures. They lost at home to West Ham in a game they had totally dominated, winning 28 corners but unable to beat the veteran Phil Parkes in goal. By the end of October, United were looking down on the rest of the division. Bob was not surprised by their exceptional start. "Nothing had changed. We just did exactly the same as we had been doing for the last year or so, and the opposition could not cope with our fitness and firepower. Personally, I was on a roll, full of confidence and was even scoring a few goals. I was playing the best football of my life, my hunger was totally restored and I was far more disciplined in my lifestyle. At nearly 32 years of age I was obviously beyond my prime, but despite being the oldest in the team I was far fitter than I had been in my mid-20s. Looking back, I now realise that I had merely been going through the motions at Brentford, but now every game really mattered. Trying to be objective, I was still the same player as I had always been, as I wasn't coached or taught anything new or different, but what had changed was that I was performing every week in a different structure alongside better players." He knew how to do his job. "I was playing in a system that was ideal for me and made me look a far better player. My touch had not really improved but I was encouraged to make late runs from midfield, and could have scored even more goals than I did."

His first goal of the season came in a rollercoaster 5-4 victory over Brighton in September – at one point, United had been leading by three goals. "Bob Booker, well positioned beyond the far post, made it look easy – although it decidedly wasn't, but his well-struck shot flashed across John Keeley into the net," described Pritchett in the *Sheffield Star*. Bob then scored against Swindon, according to the report in the programme, by "flicking his header in a looping arch over keeper Fraser Digby and his defenders," followed by another header that proved to be the winning goal against Stoke City.

Despite his improved performances and undoubted value to the team, Bob took nothing for granted. Most home programmes contained the *Frenchie's File* injury update column, constantly reminding him that Simon

Webster was slowly but surely regaining fitness. "Booker, given an uncertain reception on arrival, is now hugely popular because of his honest commitment, and he has settled into central midfield," summarised Pritchett. "But he, more than anyone else, will be aware of Simon Webster's shadow."

Bob welcomed the competition. "I was full of admiration for Simon and accepted that his bad luck had given me my opportunity. I was delighted that he was on the way back, but it was now my shirt and it was up to him to try and take it from me." Bassett, like most managers, wanted as many options as possible for every position. He felt that Webster was the more physical of the two, but Bob's attacking prowess gave him the edge. As befitting a former striker, Bob provided a real goal threat, particularly with his head. In Bassett's perhaps overwrought imagination, Bob reminded him of England World Cup winner and former United player/coach and manager Martin Peters, who "ghosted in unseen and always found time and space in the penalty area." Webster himself acknowledged that it would not be easy to get back into the team, managing a creditable 20 appearances for the first team before the end of the season, playing alongside and occasionally replacing Bob.

One of the most notable victories was at Watford, where a United team led by Bassett, Taylor and French, with three more former Hornets on the pitch in Agana, Morris and Rostron, comfortably won 3-1. This was Bob's first league game at the club closest to his home since his Brentford debut, and he made the most of the opportunity, assisting on the final goal for Francis. "All my Watford mates were there and barracked me, good-naturedly I hope, throughout the match. To go back there, win, and for me to play well in front of my family and friends meant so much to me. I got totally carried away at the final whistle and celebrated at the Watford end where my dad and friends were standing. In retrospect this was not very clever, and I received a lot of bemused looks and abuse from Watford fans who did not have a clue who I was."

The promotion campaign took a temporary back seat when the reward for a narrow win over Wolves in the Zenith Data Systems Cup was a local derby against Sheffield Wednesday at Hillsborough. A secondary tournament, but neither manager insulted the intelligence of their respective supporters by trying to play down the importance of what was destined to become a tussle for footballing supremacy in the city. United were flying high, Wednesday were desperately attempting to keep their head above water in the First Division.

Played in front of a fanatical 30,464 crowd, the game, for once, lived up to expectation. United trailed 2-1 as injury time approached before Booker deflected a shot from Deane ("It simply hit me and went in"), for a last-gasp equaliser. "Deane hammered the ball in from the left and it flew off Bob Booker to send Unitedites wild," concurred Paul Thompson in the *Sheffield Star*. A fluke goal, perhaps, but it did not prevent Bob from jumping on the railings and pointing towards the United fans packed in the Leppings Lane End. There was to be no happy ending; in extra time, a tiring United team allowed John Sheridan to run half the length of the field unchallenged, finding enough space in a packed penalty area to score the winning goal.

Back to the bread and butter business of the league; mid-table West Bromwich Albion travelled to Bramall Lane in December seeking revenge for their opening day defeat, but were sent packing with a 3-1 scoreline in which Bob, described subsequently in the match day programme as "The hero of the hour," struck twice from John Gannon corners. "BOOKER PRIZE!" screamed the headline in the *Sheffield Star*, followed by "United Booker-ed their place at the top." With his tongue at least halfway in his cheek, Bob unequivocally labelled himself "The danger man. They could not cope with me at the back post as I scored with two textbook headers from Brian Deane's near post flicks."

Swindon Town's programme for their match against the Blades the following week was the first publication to air the implausible thought that was already beginning to take root inside Bob's head. "There could be a Bob Booker prize as the player most surprised to be in the First Division," it suggested. "Bob spent ten years at Brentford and he will be 32 in January, but if it's OK for Butch Wilkins and Peter Reid, why not Bob Booker?" Why not indeed? The prospect became a great motivator.

United's promotion credentials would be put to the test by Leeds United on Boxing Day. The *News Of The World* previewed the clash with an article memorably titled "MACHO OF THE DAY," subheaded "Vinnie v Booker tops the big Christmas bill." Fleet Street stalwart Reg Drury's piece focused on the potential midfield tussle between Bob and Vinnie Jones, his former neighbour from Bedmond, eagerly anticipating "this reunion of Southern softies in the crunch meeting of Northern hard men." "They are still great mates, but this is the first time they've been on opposing sides," said Bassett, doing his best to fan the flames. "You can be sure the sparks will fly. I came up here to get away from Vinnie, and now he's coming to haunt me on Tuesday like the ghost of Christmas past."

The media hype meant it was no surprise that the two of them locked horns. "Our friendship counted for nothing that day," recalled Bob. "We just kicked lumps out of each other and the referee, Trevor Simpson, let us get on with it. Vinnie tried to unsettle me with a few well-chosen words such as the 'I've shagged your sister' line, but to no effect, as I knew that Tina had far too much taste to have consorted with the likes of him. I didn't react, and my only reply was, 'Let's see who gets the man of the match award.' That touched a nerve and when the referee wasn't looking he ran up and booted me up the backside, but I got the last laugh as the match ended 2-2 and the *Sheffield Star* headline read, 'BOOKER MAKES THE DIFFERENCE IN BATTLE OF THE GIANTS.' It also mentioned in passing that the man of the match was a certain Bob Booker. 1-0 to Booker, but perhaps I should have kept *shtum*."

The return match at Elland Road came five games before the end of the season – a vital promotion clash as Leeds, Sheffield United and Newcastle United vied for two automatic promotion places. "Vinnie's revenge took place even before we made it onto the pitch. I stupidly let my guard down and was caught totally unawares. Our kit was waiting for us, laid out as normal in the away dressing room with both long and short-sleeved shirts hanging on the peg for me to choose from. As soon as I picked up both number four shirts I saw that someone had tampered with them. The short-sleeved one was in one big knot and both sleeves of the long-sleeved shirt had been tied in so many knots that the kitman had to cut them off, so now I just had two short-sleeved shirts. Thinking that was that, I ruefully put my short-sleeved shirt on followed by my shorts, which unfortunately had been smeared with Deep Heat and my pre-match preparations were severely restricted. And just to rub salt – or something else – in the wound, we were totally outplayed and lost 4-0. Booker 1 Jones 2."

Bob did not miss a league match until the New Year, his consistency recognised with a one-year contract extension in January. "Heading for his 32nd birthday, the big ex-Brentford man, an unknown until Bassett drafted him to Bramall Lane 14 months ago, has been a revelation," summarised Pritchett. "A Bramall Lane audience, initially suspicious, have no reservations left about his commitment, contribution and enthusiasm. But now he must be hoping beyond hope that he might, even now, have a crack at the First Division before he retires. No one deserves it more."

Bassett also paid generous tribute. "Bob is a great pro. He has done really well for Sheffield United. Remember he was a free transfer, but he came here and went straight into the team. He has played in midfield and scored six or seven goals. He has played at the back when we had a crisis and done a good job up front. When I look back at the transfer deals that I have done, I suppose Bob is as good as any of them. He is now with us for the rest of this season and next. Bob is one of those players who go through their careers doing a first-class job without getting noticed. I really appreciate what he has done."

From being washed up and barely clinging to the vestiges of his career, the transformed Bob became a regular starter in a team threatening to make a meteoric rise from the Third to the First Division in consecutive seasons. No wonder he sometimes found his change in fortune hard to believe. "Sometimes I really had to stop and check if this was all really happening to me and that it wasn't a figment of my imagination. It was also the first time in my career that somebody had offered me an extended contract in the middle of the season. It was wonderful that my contribution had been recognised by the club. On a practical basis I was now earning the, to me, unheard of sum of £425 per week, with the prospect of a further increase to £500 if we were promoted to the First Division. For the first time in my life I did not have to worry about money."

After signing his new contract, Bob confirmed just how confident he was feeling about the club's prospects. "I think we shall win promotion. For me, it's been a great year. Who could ask for more? Well, one thing, perhaps. A chance to play in the First Division next season. That would be something special."

United also fought their way to the last eight of the FA Cup – "fought" being the operative word, having taken six matches to get there, including a replay victory over Watford and the local derby with Barnsley going to a third match before United finally prevailed. Their reward was a plum home tie against Manchester United, played before 34,344 fans at a packed Bramall Lane. Bob was tasked with nullifying Mark Hughes, a man at the peak of his powers and one of the best strikers in Europe.

Bob had easily got the better of the likes of Trevor Senior during previous appearances at the back, and had been voted man of the match by the travelling supporters at Bradford City a week previously. His defensive performance that day was described in the United programme as "Cool, calm and collected – he didn't put a foot wrong all afternoon." Hughes, though, was a totally different proposition. Bob spent the days before the match worrying about his chances of coping with his threat.

Match day dawned. As was his wont, Bob went out early to warm-up, stretching his knee in a rare sight during the days when players were not often seen on the pitch until just before kick-off. "I came off the pitch by the tunnel area all psyched up for what was, without doubt, the biggest game of my life, where I was greeted by my sister Tina and her partner, Ian Bolton, and Christine, who had all sneaked past the stewards," says Bob. "Tina said, 'Come on Bob, you can do this,' while Ian somewhat tactlessly reminded me of what was in store for me. 'Mark Hughes will try and distract you and do everything he can to put you off your game. He will stamp on your toes, dig you in the ribs and then try and turn you. Stick close to him and don't lose your concentration even for a split second.' Finally, I turned to Chris, who just looked at me and asked 'Do you like my new dress?' Her comment made me laugh and totally relaxed me."

"Unfortunately we never really got started and lost 1-0 in a tight game in which we did not really do ourselves justice. We conceded a soft goal from a corner that shouldn't have been given and Hughes lived up to his reputation, but I did not let myself down."

Out of the cup, promotion was all that mattered. Bob scored a crucial equaliser at Brighton – his 50th league goal – followed by what Pritchett described as "intelligent covering," playing a key part in the subsequent 3-0 win over Wolves. Then came a setback. United came away from West Ham smarting after an unexpected 5-0 thrashing.

Bob played alongside Morris that evening. "Paul Stancliffe was lucky enough to miss the game through injury. Stuart Slater tore us apart and my direct opponent, Jimmy Quinn, scored a hat trick. The manager went crazy afterwards and called us both 'a couple of donkeys' and I did not feature at centre-half very often for the rest of the season."

Bassett did not repeat his mistake of selecting Bob on plastic, sitting Bob out of the 2-0 win at Oldham Athletic, most notable for Simon Tracey's penalty save from Ian Marshall. Bob played second fiddle for a few matches, Webster and Todd partnering Gannon in midfield.

With the promotion challenge faltering after crucial defeats by Sunderland and Portsmouth in early April, Bob was recalled to the team and made an immediate impact, scoring in consecutive home wins. He struck with what the local press described as a "majestic header" against Watford, matching it with a similar effort against Oxford United, a game which went to the wire, the three points only gained through a fortunate last-minute own goal by Oxford's Mike Ford. Michael Morgan's report in the *Sunday Express* succinctly summarised what Bob brought to his team, "MoM: Bob Booker. Battler."

Bob loved scoring goals. The one against Oxford was his ninth of the season, matching his best ever tally at Brentford back in 1984/85, when he performed chiefly as a striker. He had helped cement the team's position in second place, feeling confident about the *denouement*. "We were on a roll and now thought promotion was in our grasp." However the Blades were hammered 4-0 at Elland Road by Leeds before coming out on top in two out of their next three games. So it all came down to the final match of the season, in which United had to travel to mid-table Leicester City, level on points with Leeds who had a superior goal difference. A win would ensure their return to the First Division after 14 years.

As Bob prepared for a game that could take his career to unforeseen heights, he was taken aback by a totally unexpected surprise. "Our skipper, Paul Stancliffe, had been injured for the last couple of matches and would also miss out against Leicester. Dave Bassett came up to me in the hotel on the evening before the game and said, 'You deserve to take this team up and I am giving you the captain's armband.' I was flabbergasted and it was the proudest moment of my life. There were a few others who could just as easily have been given the honour: Chrissie Wilder, a local Sheffield lad who was passionate about his club, Mark Morris, who always led by example, and Wilf Rostron, who was vastly experienced. Why did Harry choose me? I would like to think that he saw in me qualities that a captain needed, particularly having the respect of his teammates and the fans, but most of all being determined to lead by example."

"I had captained Brentford a few times, and having played under so many different skippers, I had an inkling of what was required. Standing in the tunnel with my teammates lined up behind me and thousands of fans waiting anxiously for the arrival of the players, gave me an incredible buzz and is something that I can still remember today. There was so much at stake. Our fate and the outcome of the entire season depended on this one game." He didn't need to say anything. "Everyone knew exactly what they had to do. They were a bunch of seasoned professionals who would do whatever it took to ensure that we received the reward that we felt we fully deserved after months of monumental effort. We were, as always, well prepared and totally confident that we would win the game and achieve promotion."

Bob was in midfield, with Colin Hill partnering Mark Morris in central defence. Leicester's previous biggest attendance that season was around

18,000, but on 5th May 1990, over 21,000 packed into Filbert Street. "It seemed that at least half of them had come from Sheffield," recalls Bob, "And we knew we could not let our supporters down. The noise was deafening and it felt like we were playing at home. The police and stewards could not cope with them and there were exuberant and triumphant pitch invasions after every goal we scored. The plaintive requests from the PA announcer of 'Would the Sheffield United fans please go back to your seats and keep off the pitch' were totally ignored. Many had come in fancy dress and it felt quite surreal to have United fans cavorting in front of me dressed as Pluto, Mickey Mouse and Donald Duck!"

"We went a goal down very early on when Gary Mills scored and a few harsh words were exchanged. We went up a gear and proceeded to take Leicester apart. Agana and Deane scored three between them and we were 4-2 up at the interval – aided, it has to be said, by an injury to their goalkeeper, Martin Hodge, who eventually had to go off."

A steely-eyed and determined Bob sat quietly in the dressing room at half-time, totally ignoring a protracted argument between Bassett and his assistant, Taylor, about defensive organisation at corners. The Blades comfortably saw the game out, scoring again, to win by 5-2 and finish runners-up to Leeds United. The title was lost on goal difference but, most importantly, they were back in the First Division.

A talking point afterwards was the confrontation between Bob and Leicester's star midfielder, Gary McAllister. "I brought him down and he screamed, 'Who the hell are you?' The United fans were all singing, 'OOH-AAH BOB BOOKAH,' so I just looked down at him and said, 'I'm OOH-AAH BOB BOOKAH, can't you hear them?' He just gazed at me like I was totally mad, got up and walked off shaking his head."

One of the finest days in the club's recent history heralded long, loud and pronounced celebrations, particularly when news broke that Wednesday had been relegated. The headline in the *Sheffield Star*, "BLADES GLORY – OWLS DOWN," underlined the balance of power reversal in Sheffield football.

The team returned to Sheffield to continue their celebrations, but Bob opted to go straight home to Watford. "I went to my car with Tina and my dad, and a fan came up to me and asked me for my shirt, but I had already promised it to Mick Rooker. I was caught up in the moment and instinctively gave him my captain's armband, and have regretted doing so ever since. This was the one and only time that I captained the team, and what a day it was. I still have my shorts from that day but I really wish that

I had kept hold of the armband. Hopefully the fan still has it and cherishes it as much as I did, but if he is reading this book, then I would really like to have it back, please."

"I might have missed the celebrations in Sheffield, but when I arrived home, Chris and our neighbours had decorated the street with banners and bunting and I was given a wonderfully warm welcome, so I didn't really miss out too much."

Chris Wilder later revealed that the players found a life-sized cardboard cutout of Bob, taking it with them when they went celebrating in Sheffield that night. He was with them in spirit.

Bob rejoined his teammates for a post-season celebratory trip to Magaluf. "We all met up at the airport and were split up into two groups for the journey. Mine consisted of Billy Whitehurst, Mitch Ward, David Barnes, Mark Todd, Paul Stancliffe and myself, with Derek French in charge – a major error as he behaved just like one of the lads. The other group had Harry and Derek Dooley in charge."

"Celebrations started straight away. We had just finished a long, hard and successful season, so we all wanted to let our hair down and escape from the pressures of football. After two hours of non-stop drinking, Derek French called for some order and attempted to board the flight. Derek, Stan and I, being the elder statesmen, headed for the departure gate, leaving the stragglers behind. Suddenly we could hear Billy Whitehurst and David Barnes, both well worse for wear, making their way up the steps ready to board the plane. As they appeared at the front of the plane they were in good spirits, to say the least."

"Eventually the rest of our group boarded and things calmed down a bit. We were signing autographs with a marker pen. Unfortunately, Barnsey decided to stand up in front of a screen that was used for showing movies, and started mimicking a Harry Bassett team talk. He was using the marker pen to write tactical instructions for Billy Whitehurst on the screen. All seemed fine until I felt a tap on my shoulder and heard a voice say, 'I work for the airline and you should know that those screens cost about £10,000 each.' I passed this information onto Derek French. His response was, 'Keep your head down, son, they're on their own!' We slid down in our seats and we were both giggling like a couple of schoolkids."

"The stewardesses had by now approached Billy and Barnsey and were not amused at what was going on. Billy was trying to apologise and defuse the situation by asking for a cloth to clean the screen, but it was a permanent marker pen, so the harder he rubbed the worse it got." Airport police made their way onto the plane. "They got into conversation with Billy, who was a hothead, and he started arguing with them. The captain then appeared, as he was concerned about the plane losing its take-off slot, and he and the police decided to remove the group of players who had boarded late – Billy, Barnsey, Chris Wilder, Dane Whitehouse and Mitch Ward. So off they went and we hoped we'd see them later on if they could get on another flight."

"Once we arrived at Palma, I phoned Chris Wilder and he said that the press had got hold of the story and photographers had chased him and the rest of the lads through the airport. Later that night I received a call from Chris saying that the incident had just been featured on ITV's *News At Ten*. The following day, *The Sun* gave the story front-page coverage."

Bob was tickled pink and knew it meant a lot when, at the end of the season, *Flashing Blade* awarded him an A- grade in its popular *End Of Term Report* column. "Robert has proved the staff here totally wrong," it remarked. "We all believed he was a sure-fire candidate for the D stream but his performances have resulted in his elevation to the A stream. He is a loveable rogue who has become a cult figure amongst pupils young and old alike."

Fan support and encouragement transformed Bob, contributing towards an incredible, unforgettable season. The journey from apprentice upholsterer to potential First Division footballer, a state of affairs that was totally beyond anything he had ever contemplated when he started out at Brentford all those years ago, was complete.

He now had a decision to make. "It did cross my mind for a split-second to retire there and then," admits Bob. "I wondered if anything could surpass last season, but I soon dismissed the thought. I had never been a quitter and I wanted to see if I could cope with the First Division. After all, I had worked so long and hard to be given the opportunity."

As 10,000 Blades had sung throughout that glorious afternoon at Leicester – "The Blades Are Going Up!" Bob desperately wanted to be a part of it.

# CHAPTER 21
# SETTLING DOWN

Bob had always lived in the south, treasuring being surrounded by a close-knit family and good friends. Upon moving to Sheffield, he found himself alone in an alien city, making a new life for himself while adjusting to a new manager, team and style of play. Supporters sometimes forget that the more settled footballers are off the field, the better their performances are likely to be on it.

Bob knew the first few months were going to be strange, difficult and unsettling. "Being transferred to the Blades brought about a massive change in my life from every perspective, with a new stadium, new fans, new city, new teammates and hopefully a new collection of friends. Probably the last thing on my mind was where I was going to live. I was very naïve and just took it for granted that something would be sorted out for me. Much of what was said in the initial contract talks with Dave Bassett passed me by as I was in a daze and totally overwhelmed. I remember him saying that initially the club would put me up in the Moat House, a decent hotel on the outskirts of town, but this was only a short-term solution, and after that it was up to me to sort myself out, although they gave me a generous travelling and accommodation allowance for the first six months and contributed towards my eventual moving costs."

Initially enjoying his time at the Moat House, Bob found everything was done for him – life was "a bit of a novelty." He returned to Watford as often as he could, either on his midweek day off or after Saturday's match, but his change of circumstances put an unavoidable strain on his relationship with Christine. "Everything happened so quickly and there was barely time to think, let alone make reasoned decisions about important life issues," he says.

Christine also had to make a tough choice, particularly as she came from a similar background to Bob's, "I'd just got a promotion at work and I did not want to give up my job, so Bob spent the first year in Sheffield on his own. Eventually, though, we got fed up with being apart, and although I was very apprehensive, as I've got a big family in Watford and I'd never lived away from the town before, I also moved to Sheffield."

# SETTLING DOWN

Bob made the best of a difficult situation. "Living apart wasn't ideal, but we didn't really have any choice in the matter. Christine came up whenever she could. We also had Bruno to consider, as it was difficult asking anyone to look after a ten-stone Rottweiler. Dad ended up as his primary carer and was great with him, but Bruno was so strong and we had to ensure he could cope."

Bob managed about six weeks at the hotel before it started to wear a bit thin. "I like my own company but there is only so much television you can watch. I was not playing very well and finding it hard to settle into the team. Being on my own meant that I started to brood, stare at the walls and worry about everything, and the more I worried, the worse I seemed to play. I really needed to get out and breathe some fresh air. There was a park within walking distance of the hotel. On the afternoons when I wasn't working with Derek French, I would stroll over to Graves Park to do some bird-watching. This was a wonderful way of switching off and later on, when Bruno came up to join me, it was even better."

Bob might have been finding it hard to establish himself on the pitch, but it was a different matter in the dressing room, where he quickly became accepted and extremely popular thanks to his bubbly personality and wicked sense of humour. "Thankfully there were quite a few southerners in the squad who were able to understand what I was saying, but the others just laughed along anyway and made fun of me. We all mucked in together and the atmosphere was the best that I ever experienced in my career."

However well they got on with each other for a few hours every day, Bob was really worried about how best to find more permanent accommodation. His fears were unfounded, soon finding himself inundated with offers from his teammates.

"I was not looking forward to searching for somewhere to live as I was still trying to find my way around the city, but it all turned out perfectly. Derek French was in digs with Geoff Taylor, Ian Bryson and his wife Kirsty, in a large old house in Upperthorpe, a suburb of Sheffield, and a strong Blade area, not far from the city centre."

"I was stretched out on the treatment table one afternoon while Frenchie was working on my knee and I started complaining that I was getting fed up with living in the Moat House. He said, 'We can't have that. You need to be happy. Come and live with us. Kirsty is a wonderful cook, you get on fine with Jock and there's plenty of room as Geoff is hardly ever there. It will be great.' I also had the offer to live with Chris Wilder but Derek twisted my arm and I decided to give it a go."

"This was a completely different world to the luxury of the Moat House. The nearest we got to a Jacuzzi was when Geoff Taylor farted in the bath. I shared a room with Derek at the very top of the house. Geoff's room was situated right below us, which wasn't ideal, as every time he went to the toilet the water cistern took ages to refill which would get on my nerves and stop me from sleeping."

"The house could well have come right out of the film, 'Psycho.' It was on a hill, very isolated and surrounded by loads of trees. It felt a bit spooky, and one night when Derek and I were asleep I suddenly felt the presence of something in the room. Derek must have had the same sensation as we woke up simultaneously and we both started screaming and ended up clutching hold of each other on the same bed. 'Put the light on,' said Derek. 'Did you see that?' I nodded my head, 'Yes.' We had both seen the ghostly figure of an old lady sitting on the end of the bed. We finally calmed down and got back to sleep, but to this day we still talk about that moment. I have no idea about the history of the house but I am certain that it was haunted."

"I was also spooked a few weeks later when I was in the house alone late one afternoon. It was pitch black outside. I was washing up some dishes when I bent down to get something, and as I got back up a face was staring balefully at me through the window. I screamed and jumped backwards. Once I recovered, the man put his thumb up and in a strong northern accent said, 'Now then, I've come to read the gas meter.' It was definitely time for me to leave."

After training the very next morning, Bob asked Chris Wilder, on bended knee, if his previous offer was still open. Bob moved in with Chris and Tony Agana, who already lived with him in a lovely house on the outskirts of town, in Gleadless. "The three of us got on famously and I stayed there for around nine months until Chris's parents sold the house. Most Friday nights before a home game we would visit the local pasta house to engage in some serious carbo-loading, something the club encouraged us to do. We always ate early and resisted the temptation to have a drink with our meal, as being seen out on the town on a Friday evening could easily have been misinterpreted. After the meal it was back to the house to watch a video, and then it was off to bed to rest up for the game."

"Tony Agana often spent hours alone in his room practicing his saxophone but despite all the time he spent, his repertoire only extended to one song. He must have been a slow learner. The real reason that they loved having me around was that I was a bit of a neat freak and they knew that I would always keep the kitchen spotless and tidy up their mess. I didn't mind as I quite enjoyed it, and actually found that washing up helped keep me calm. I was a lot older than both of them but we were all on the same wavelength and I had a great time living there."

"Tony and Chris loved it when I went back to Watford after games – not, I hope, because they were delighted to see the back of me, but because they knew my mum would be busy baking and that I would return on the Sunday night laden with bread pudding and her special chocolate and mint cake, which they would devour. The last thing I would hear as I left the dressing room after a match was never a warm and friendly 'Have a good weekend, Bob,' but a growled reminder from the pair of them, 'Don't forget the cakes.' It was nice to know that I was needed."

Trips back to Watford depended upon the vagaries of the fixture list and the whim of his manager. "I remember once when I had not been able to go home for a while. I was desperate to see Christine and my friends and promised them that I would be on my way straight after Saturday's final whistle. Disaster struck as we lost and left the pitch to the sound of boos from an angry home crowd. That was nothing compared to what awaited us in the dressing room. Dave Bassett laid into us all, nobody escaped his wrath, and eventually it was my turn. 'Bob, what were you doing out there? I've seen milk turn quicker. You never won a tackle or header all afternoon and when you did get the ball you gave it straight back to them. You were rubbish.' We were all cowed into silence, with every player looking down at the floor. The manager's parting shot before he slammed the dressing room door was 'You let yourselves and the fans down so I will see you all on Sunday morning at eight o'clock. None of you ran around today so you can do it in the morning instead.' There goes the rest of my weekend, I thought, and I wasn't looking forward to the telephone call I would now have to make to Christine cancelling my trip."

"As I came out of the shower, Dave came up to me and whispered in my ear. 'Never mind what I just said, get yourself back to Watford, and I will see you on Monday.' In the heat of the moment, he'd forgotten how long it had been since I had been home. I thought about it for a few moments, then made that call to Christine. I wasn't going to let my teammates suffer without me, and it was another fortnight before I was able to go home."

# OOH-AAH: THE BOB BOOKER STORY

Once describing himself in an interview in the *Oxford Mail* as being "Honest, loyal, selfish, obsessive and a bit of a nutter," Chris Wilder remained close friends with Bob. "I was often tasked by Harry Bassett with looking after the new signings and talking to them about the city and the club," says Wilder, remembering those days with fondness. "Perhaps that's the reason he kept me around for so long. Christine was back in Watford and Bob stayed up here during the week and he went home as often as he could. We worked hard and played hard and we burnt the candle at both ends. We would come back home to a bombshell every Monday morning and spent the whole week tidying up. There were pictures of Bruno all around the house and there certainly weren't nearly as many photographs of Christine as there were of the dog. We called Bob 'Wildlife' as he was always looking out of the window at foxes, birds and rabbits and he would reel off the names of the breeds of every creature that he saw. Happy days indeed."

Christine would visit as often as she could, splurging out on a hotel with Bob, allowing them peace and quiet together. The team and partners would sometimes socialise together, generally when the team had won. Bassett thought that young players found it easier to forget the pressure when they let off steam, but warned them to be careful, well before the era of camera phones and social media exposed any and all outings. "Find somewhere nice and quiet to spend time with your families," he told the players, who generally adhered to his advice. "And be sensible." Bob tended to stay in. He had already been on the receiving end of the fans' ire and frustration, and he had no intention of giving them any additional ammunition.

Circumstances dictated that Bob had to move again after Chris Wilder's parents decided to sell their house, buying a beautiful property in Norton, situated down a private road, surrounded by a seven-foot-high stone wall.

"Chris and his parents wanted me to see their new home and when I arrived they pointed me towards a staircase just off the lounge and told me to go up and then go through the door at the top," Bob says of his visit. "I had no idea what to expect, but I needn't have worried as the door opened up to reveal a fantastic self-contained one-bedroom flat. It still didn't click until they said, 'This is for you, if you'd like to live here.' I was totally amazed and could barely get the words out to accept their generous and totally unexpected offer. My flat was perfect as Christine could come up and stay whenever she could, and they also had two gorgeous Labradors, Santi and Bobby – one black and the other golden – so most afternoons I could take them for long walks in the park. I was totally in my element and very happy. The entire Wilder family was so good to me and I will be forever grateful to them, as their kindness played such an important part in my eventual success at the club. I really think that there is a massive correlation between off-field contentment and playing well on the pitch, and as soon as I sorted out my accommodation, everything seemed to improve for me."

"I really missed Christine and we often discussed her coming up to Sheffield on a permanent basis, or at least for her to stay up for longer periods if her work commitments allowed. I also really wanted Bruno with me, which would give my dad a break from looking after him. Financially, things were finally much easier for us. We had done up our house in Watford from top to bottom and built an extension at the back for Bruno. Much as I missed him, I knew I could not have Bruno living with me in my small flat, so it was time to move again."

"Once again, in December 1989, it was my teammates to the rescue, as Martin Pike was looking to rent out his two-bedroom terraced house at Mitchell Road, as he wanted to move in with his girlfriend. He was happy for Bruno to live there too, and once I had put up some fencing it was perfect for him – we were finally reunited. My next-door neighbour, Frank, was a Sheffield Wednesday fan – but despite that we got on very well and soon became friends."

Bob also made friends with Keith Palmer, a builder who, before he moved out, Martin Pike had hired to build a fireplace, without mentioning the fact to Bob, who was surprised to find him working downstairs on his first morning in Mitchell Road. Keith hit it off straight away with Bob, becoming a regular visitor to his bungalow. Bob loved spending time with Keith and his wonderful family, Josie, Gemma and Jo, and remained in touch despite their move to Saudi Arabia.

"All that I needed now to make my family situation complete was for Christine to join us, but before that happened we decided to look to the future and buy a new house together. Despite how well things were going for me now in Sheffield, I was under no illusions. I knew that sometime in the not-too-distant future it would all have to end and I would just be another unemployed ex-footballer, so I needed to put down permanent roots while I could afford to do so. Dave Bassett also gave me some good advice and suggested that despite how much I had grown to love Sheffield, it made far more sense for me to settle in Watford. Christine had seen a lovely detached house in Sheepcote Lane in Garston, just around the corner from where we lived. We sold the house in Briar Lane for £185,000 and paid £197,000 for the new one, as it was rundown and needed a lot of work. Christine oversaw most of the work and her brothers were also a great help as we renovated and redecorated the house. Having had to count the pennies ever since I became a professional footballer, it was wonderful, finally, to be in a position to afford to buy a proper family home, and the proceeds of my contract extension and signing-on fee certainly came in helpful to pay for all the necessary work. I really felt that I had arrived."

With his future accommodation sorted in Garston, Bob could finally relax. Having Bruno with him in Mitchell Road also provide a great fillip. Bob had the back of his Ford Sierra Estate – no flash sports car for him – fitted out with a special cage, allowing him to leave Bruno in the car with the tailgate open while he trained, taking him for a run around the training ground later on. Bob refuses to admit whether Bruno bettered his owner's running ability.

Christine also decided that it was time to take the big step. "I'd imagined it to be all chimneys and smoke but it wasn't like that and I noticed a big difference in the people there. They would say 'Good morning' to you in the street and I was a bit sad to come back."

Christine and Bob were very happy together, loving their time in Mitchell Road. In early 1990, they got engaged after nearly six years together. Christine decided not to work in Sheffield. "We had a chat about it and decided that I'd stay at home particularly as Bob finished at lunchtime every day and we'd go out and have a good time."

Christine was never a massive football fan. "If Bob really wanted me to go, I would, but he knew that I preferred not to, he was quite happy that I stayed at home with the radio and Ceefax on."

Christine knew exactly where she stood in the pecking order with Bruno. "We had a big photograph at home of Bob and me and an even bigger one of Bruno. Bob absolutely worshipped him and when he was on his own one New Year's Eve in Sheffield with some of the other lads, at midnight they all asked each other who they were missing most. Bob's answer was Bruno!"

Mitchell Road was to be Bob's last home in Sheffield. "My time there was unbelievable and I made some fantastic friends. I will always cherish my memories of the time I spent in this wonderful city."

The crowning glory for Bob was marrying Christine on 8th June 1991 at All Saints Church, Leavesden, just north of Watford, with the reception held at the Conservative Club. After long and careful thought, Ian Bolton narrowly beat off the challenge of Bruno to become Bob's best man.

Bruno was, in Bob's opinion, far better looking than Bolton, but as he was married to his sister, Bob took pity, listening yet again on his wedding day to the story of Bolton having put Bob "in his pocket" on his league debut at Watford back in 1978.

Most of the United team came to support him, as did his friend and Blades supporter Joe Elliott, the lead singer of Def Leppard. Elliott was a great admirer of Bob and would always, to Bob's great embarrassment, get him to stand up and take a bow whenever the band played in Sheffield, once even bringing Bob on stage with them. Much to everyone's delight, Joe provided an impromptu performance on the piano at his hotel the night before the ceremony.

"It was a really happy day. We went back home at the end of the evening because we didn't want to stay at the hotel with the players, as we knew that our room would have been trashed. The night before the wedding I had a meal with Joe Elliott and his girlfriend, Karla, and he presented me with my wedding present, a platinum disc of their multi-million selling album, 'Hysteria.' Bruno missed out on the day as he was in kennels and Christine and I went off for an incredible honeymoon in Mauritius."

"It had been a long journey for us both," reflects Bob. "But we got there in the end."

# CHAPTER 22
# COMMUNITY SERVICE

Dave Bassett is not the only person to whom Bob Booker owes so much for his eventual success at Sheffield United. Mick Rooker helped Bob come out of his shell when he was struggling to establish himself and show Blades fans exactly who he was and what he could offer the team and city. Bob took his advice about always showing total commitment; his game was based around it, and as his performances improved, he acknowledged the Kop End after every match. The fans eventually took him to their hearts, but that was only half the story. Bob became Rooker's secret weapon and worked tirelessly to forge closer links between the club and the city it served and represented.

Bubbly, effervescent and positive, Rooker is the unsung hero every football club needs – a man whose incredible impact and enormous contribution to the marketing, sales and community relations efforts of Sheffield United will only fully be recognised when he is no longer involved with the club.

A torrent of words explode from his mouth when he explains his story at the club – impossible to exactly decipher through his impenetrable accent and machine gun, staccato delivery, exuding an enthusiasm to share his thoughts.

"I joined Sheffield United Football Club in September 1987 as the pools office representative," he says. "I did leave for a short time in 1999, when I joined Andy Daykin at Hull City, but when there was a change at boardroom level, and Derek Dooley became chairman, he brought us both back – and I am still here. I was made redundant in 2012 for two hours until Kevin McCabe intervened, and I was back at work the next day. When I first joined the club I called at pubs and retailers and contacted many of our supporters to sell our scratch cards. My other main responsibility, because of my news trade background, was to promote and increase the membership of the Red Ribbon Daily Draw. I was promoted to pools office manager by Andy Daykin and took on extra responsibilities, including selling the kit sponsorships and looking after the mascots and match sponsorship packages. My main responsibilities now are promoting the Super Draw Lotto, programme sales and running the Away Blade coach travel scheme."

"I am always on the lookout for players who are willing to help me and spare some time and a bit of themselves in giving something back to the local community. Footballers sometimes forget that they are seen as role models and the fans really appreciate meeting them. Some give their time grudgingly, but Bob Booker was undoubtedly one of the best players I have ever worked with. He had a lot of time on his hands as initially he was living up here on his own without Christine or Bruno. He needed something to do to fill his spare time rather than sit in his digs and brood. It also helped that Bob is one of the most down-to-earth men that I have ever met. He never put on any airs and graces – he was simply a pleasant working class lad who had been fortunate to have the talent to become a footballer. He never lost his enthusiasm for the game and was always happy to engage with the supporters. We hit it off right from the start, particularly once he finally began to understand what I said to him."

Bob enjoyed spending time with Mick. "Most afternoons, when training was finished, I would end up in Mick's office having a chat and getting to know the lingo. I loved his passion for the club and he was very well known all around the city. He promoted the club nonstop and was very good at it. He soon invited me to join him on his rounds. I had plenty of time and nothing much else to do once I had finished my gym sessions, so I decided to take him up on his invitation. Initially, I was a bit nervous and unsure how the fans would react to me. The attention I got really surprised me. The contrast between Sheffield and Brentford was amazing; I could have walked down Brentford High Street without being noticed or recognised by anyone, but here it was totally different. After a few weeks I was getting stopped regularly in the street for my autograph or a picture. It was bizarre – I felt more like a film star than a journeyman footballer."

Mick once described his main hobby as "Taking Bob Booker to Do's." Christenings, shop openings, pubs, clubs, quiz nights, fishing matches and garden fêtes all received a look-in. He particularly enjoyed visiting Norfolk Park Fisheries, the fish and chip restaurant on Park Grange Drive which sponsored his home kit.

Mick especially remembers one outing they made together. "Bob met a young lad at a club event and signed his programme. The boy said, 'Do you want to come to our house one night for your tea?' Bob did not bat an eyelid, 'Yes, of course I would.' 'When would you like to come?' asked the boy. 'What night do you have meat and potato pie and chips?'

'Monday.' That was settled then – we would both be there if his parents were willing to cook. The next day his mother phoned me up and said she thought her son had been telling fibs. He'd gone home and claimed that Bob Booker was coming round to their house on Monday for tea. She was gobsmacked when I told her that it was the truth. We arrived bright and early the following Monday to find about 20 kids waiting outside the house for autographs. It took quite a while to get through the front door. Apparently the dad usually sat with a tray on his lap watching the television at teatime, but when we arrived he was all dressed up in a suit, shirt and tie, sitting at the dinner table. We spent a couple of hours there eating a delicious meal and chatting. We all had a great time."

"Within a week, Bob was deluged with around 40 similar requests. He would have been as big as a house if he had gone to them all so he wrote a lovely letter with a personal message to each child, politely declining the invitation. 'Dave Bassett has put me on a strict diet, so many thanks, but I'm afraid that I can't come.' Each letter was individually written and signed by Bob and included a signed photo of him." Bob laughs at the memory. "Meat and potato pie became one of my favourite meals. I really had to watch my weight because I became a bit too fond of them."

"I just felt comfortable meeting the fans as we had so much in common in terms of our shared background. I never forgot that they are the ones who pay your wages, so it is crucial to put something back and reward them for all their loyalty. What I loved most of all was seeing the look of joy and delight on their faces when you arrived. United used to hold Open Days at the club and I couldn't believe the number of fans who would turn up. You could be pinned in a corner signing autographs for up to four hours, but I enjoyed every minute."

Bob also felt it did him some good. "Doing these things really helped me integrate into the city and settle down. I still go back to Sheffield whenever I can, although I do not want to outstay my welcome. Last year I was invited to do a Q & A in Sheffield. Despite having left well over 20 years ago, the response was unbelievable. Derek French joined me on stage for the evening and after an hour of storytelling I sat and signed autographs for half an hour. A lad appeared in front of me and said, 'You don't recognise me, do you?' He then showed me a photograph of him, Mick Rooker and me at the table at his house eating meat and potato pie. What a great moment – I will always treasure that."

"It also felt a bit weird that I was signing autographs for young kids or teenagers who were not even born when I played." They were brought up on DVDs of Bob playing, hearing their dads singing 'OOH-AAH BOB BOOKAH!' Crazy but wonderful times.

"I remember watching a film at the Crystal Peaks cinema complex. I was sitting in the middle of a row when I could sense that some people had recognised me. Little did I realise that they would make their way towards me in the middle of the film, causing people to stand up. It was really embarrassing but there was not a lot I could do about it. I just signed all the autographs as quickly as possible."

"All the attention was very flattering and really enjoyable. It was so much better on the pitch, too. The fans were singing my name and I was feeling part of something special. There was a real correlation between the support I received and the improvement in my performances."

"Mick was really thoughtful, too. At most away games he would drive my car to the stadium where we were playing so that if we got a good result I could shoot straight off back to Watford to see my family. Mick helped put me on the map in Sheffield and I owe him so much. I was only at the club for three years, but it seemed like a lifetime. The city and the club made an indelible impression on me."

"When the new stand was built, it contained 31 Executive Boxes. The fans had to choose from a list of around 500 players whose names they'd like to see commemorated on the front of each box with a brass plaque. I was honoured and surprised to have one named after me. The fact that mine was placed between Tony Currie and Brian Deane was the icing on the cake. There is a statue of the great Derek Dooley outside the ground with the names of some ex-players engraved below him. What a privilege to be included among all the great players that have represented this wonderful club."

"Blades fans are incredibly loyal. I could not believe it when a couple of coachloads supported me at my testimonial match. After the team was relegated from the Premier League on the last day of the 1993/94 season, I was having a dinner party at home in Watford when I suddenly heard cries of 'OOH-AAH BOB BOOKAH!' coming from outside. At first I thought I must be hallucinating, but the sound persisted. When I opened the front door I found a group of United fans on my doorstep who had all made a detour on their way home from the match in London. I invited them all in and they stayed for a couple of hours and drank the house dry." Bob was delighted to help them drown their sorrows.

He still visits the club whenever he can, making guest appearances at pubs and clubs. "It's great talking about all those special times and how much we achieved so quickly. I can hardly believe that people still remember me after all these years. I will never forget how much they mean to me. They took me to their hearts and helped make my three years in Sheffield so unforgettable."

I asked the Sheffield United supporters who frequent the *S24SU* Sheffield United fans forum for their verdict on Bob Booker the man, and I can do no better than end this chapter with a few of their comments.

Sheffielder stated, "Players like Bob epitomise what being a Blade means to us. Bob was the sort of bloke you would want at your side, at a football match, in a fight, at war, in a pub." Blade for Sale was also lucky to have Bob come round to visit his home. "Bob Booker is beyond legendary. He is everything we need more of in the game – a humble, hard-working hero with time for everyone, even an 11-year-old kid he didn't know from Adam. He is a brilliant, brilliant man." Grappler felt that "Bob connected with the fans who loved him, and in return, he loved the fans and the club." Finally, georgebernardshaw summed Bob up. "A Blades legend because he became one of us."

# CHAPTER 23
# STAYING UP

You might well imagine Bob Booker, full of fear and trepidation at the prospect of facing the best players in the country, seriously doubting his ability to cope with the demands of the First Division. This would be incorrect; a changed man, he relished the challenge awaiting him and his teammates.

Sometimes he still found it hard to believe where he was, less than two years after being on the football scrapheap and the verge of retirement, but he had finally reached the top through good old-fashioned virtues of hard work, dedication and self-belief. His good fortune was being part of a team made to measure for his skill set.

"I did my best to rest up throughout the summer and get as fit as I could," he says. "I knew that I would have a lot more chasing around to do, as I would be attempting to close down far better players. I could not wait to see the fixture list." When he did, it finally began to sink in that the former upholsterer would be taking on the biggest teams in the country. "Our first few opponents included Liverpool, Derby County, Manchester City, Leeds United, Chelsea and Spurs. I wasn't overawed or wondering where our first point might be coming from, I just felt invigorated and excited at what lay ahead. We fully deserved to be there, and we also had the advantage of being a team of unknowns who would be underestimated by everyone we played against. I knew that we would take a lot of the bigger names by surprise."

"My knee was as good as it would ever be, I felt fit enough to play in Division One, and the prospect certainly did not frighten me. That's what came of playing for someone like Dave Bassett, who was a wonderful motivator and man manager. He helped me believe in myself, probably for the first and only time in my entire career." He had been far more concerned before the start of the previous season, never anticipating hurtling straight through the Second Division in his best ever season. "I was very satisfied with my final tally of nine goals from midfield and, even though I was 32, I still thought there was a lot left in the tank. We had fully earned the right to play at the top level and I deserved the opportunity and fully intended to make the most of it, even though it was something that was far beyond my wildest dreams. Harry had instilled a bit of a swagger in all of us. We were confident in our own ability and it was us against the world. We had absolutely nothing to be scared of; we would not change the way we played, either, and our opponents would not relish what was coming from us if we got it right. We would just play our normal system and let the other teams worry about us."

Martin Tyler gave his considered verdict on United's style of play. "It's certainly not kick and rush," he commentated on the Sheffield United end of season compilation video, "There's a lot of thought as to where the long passes are to be played."

Consecutive promotions were probably more than even the eternal optimist Dave Bassett could have expected, knowing he would need to strengthen his squad if they were to survive in the top flight. He was happy with his attacking options of Deane, Agana, Bryson, Whitehurst and Bradshaw, but a defence which had conceded 58 goals the previous season would be severely tested in the First Division.

Full-back John Pemberton arrived from Crystal Palace for £300,000. Bob thought he was a little bit different from the norm, "He was a good lad who initially struggled to mix in with the rest of the squad, and was a bit distant. John was a fashion icon who really loved his clothes and I spent a lot of time with him. On the pitch he had a lot of pace and was a great crosser of the ball."

Paul Beesley cost £375,000 from Leyton Orient. "He was a typical Scouser and a left-footed centre-half who complemented Mark Morris and gave us a better balance. This meant that Paul Stancliffe was now on his way out after giving the club such wonderful service."

Jamie Hoyland took the initial expenditure up to the £1 million pound mark. Signed from Bury, the midfielder was the son of a former United player who now ran a pub near the ground. "He was promising and good on the ball, but he took time to get used to how we played and struggled to cope with the demands of the First Division."

Phil Kite also arrived from Bournemouth, replacing Benstead as reserve goalkeeper. There was also plenty of defensive cover with the likes of Colin Hill, David Barnes, Wilf Rostron and Chris Wilder all challenging for a start. Bob finally saw off the challenge of Simon Webster, who was transferred to Charlton Athletic, probably still ruing his misfortune.

As the season progressed, further experienced recruits arrived in the shape of Brian Marwood and Vinnie Jones. The presence of Anders Limpar meant that, at 30 years of age, Marwood was expendable at

Arsenal. With a reputation made at Sheffield Wednesday, his £300,000 capture seemed a sensible move, but his best days had gone, although Bob found him impressive at set plays and corners.

Jones signed in September from Leeds United for a club record £650,000 fee. Bob fully recognised that his arrival had huge personal implications. "Vinnie and I had grown up together and he had played for the reserves and youth team at Bedmond when I was in the first team. I knew that the writing was on the wall for me when he arrived and that he was going to take my place because he wore the number four shirt, played in the centre of midfield and basically did what I did. He had a lot of top level experience, had played for Dave Bassett before at Wimbledon, was nearly seven years younger than me and also possessed a long throw, which suited the way that we played. He was also far more aggressive than me. You don't pay that amount of money for a player without playing him, but I was determined to fight as hard as I could to hold onto my place."

Already firm friends, the pair had enjoyed their previous tussles, feeling no animosity. "We both knew that it was just the way it was; everyone was replaceable and the manager would always be looking to strengthen the squad. We ended up as roommates and drove to training together. At least if Harry was trying to replace me he had to spend a lot of money to do so, which I took as a backhanded compliment. Vinnie cost nearly 20 times more than the £35,000 Brentford paid for Wayne Turner when I was out injured."

Goals were far harder to come by for the Blades in the First Division, with a miserable final tally of 36 – less than a goal a game – representing 42 less than they had managed the previous season, albeit in a lower division. Deane was as reliable as ever despite lacking support, and Bryson, as usual, weighed in with some crucial goals. Injuries took their toll on Agana, who failed to score until the final game of the season, and Whitehurst was no longer a threat at this level. In the New Year, Bassett attempted to fill the gap by turning once again to a known and trusted figure in Glyn Hodges, a gifted but enigmatic winger who had been a member of his "Crazy Gang" at Wimbledon. Bob welcomed his arrival, "The crowd loved him straight away and he became our flair player. He was probably the only member of the squad that you had to carry as he was neither a runner nor a tackler, but we were happy to do his donkey work because whenever you gave him the ball he would make something happen. He provided quality, goals, and a bit of flamboyance and he was the nearest we had to a Tony Currie."

# STAYING UP

Despite the boost of scoring 22 times in four matches on a pre-season tour to Finland, including two from Bob against a Medskogs-Timra XI (strangely enough, Bob has no memory of his feat), the team struggled from the start with no wins and only four points from their first 16 league games. Bob looks back on "The run from hell," with mixed feelings. "We were really struggling, but for some reason I was not too worried and was certain that our luck would change. Most of our losses were in tightly-fought matches, and only Spurs and Norwich beat us heavily. It would just be that extra bit of quality that beat us. I knew we were short of options up front and I even resurrected my role as centre forward at Southampton, put myself about and got booked for my trouble."

"I made my First Division debut on the opening day of the season against Liverpool, who I had last played against for Brentford in 1983." Only 9,092 people had gone to an eerily deserted Anfield in a meaningless Milk Cup second leg tie, (Liverpool's lowest ever League Cup attendance) but 27,009 fans, including Bob's dad, squeezed into Bramall Lane, creating an incredible atmosphere. "This is what dreams are made of. Given different circumstances I could well have been out cleaning windows rather than playing against the current league champions at the age of 32. I never thought that something as incredible as this could ever happen to me. At one point that afternoon there was a break in play, the fans were singing my name, and I just looked up at them and my dad with my face wreathed in smiles – it does not get any better than this. How could this have ever happened to me?"

Bob was never *blasé* or complacent, resolving to absorb everything, enjoying it for as long as it lasted. "I knew that, subject to form and injury, I was going to be playing against the likes of Liverpool week in, week out. I was just going to try and grab everything I could, as I knew the clock was ticking and that I was at the back end of my career."

Bob clearly describes the major differences between the top three divisions. "Quite simply, the quality of the players, their first touch and the speed of the game. Divisions Two and Three were fairly similar apart from the odd exceptional player such as Strachan and McAllister. Division One was a massive step up in every conceivable way, in particular fitness, sheer talent, squad depth, the stadia we played in and the size of the crowds. The hardest thing I found to cope with was the speed of thought, as top players knew what they were going to do with the ball before they received it. In the lower leagues you wait until you get it and then decide."

When Simon Tracey was stretchered off against Liverpool, Bob finally had the chance to wear the only shirt missing from his near-full set. He wasn't keen, John Pemberton instead volunteering as, "He used to muck around in goal in training, I was relieved it was him and not me." Bob was certainly not overawed by the quality of the opposition; the *Sheffield Star* notes that he hit a shot just over the bar "after a surging run."

Given his previous visits to Stamford Bridge as a youth, it was a "big thrill" for Bob, recovering from a toe injury, to come on as a substitute there and help the Blades recover from a two-goal deficit. Vinnie Jones scored his first goal for the club, his presence already depriving Bob of regular selection. "I was coping fine with the demands of the division but I was now in and out because of Vinnie. I was travelling with the team and Harry loved having me on the bench because I could slot in anywhere. I felt part of it when I was not playing but also a bit disappointed as I thought I could still contribute, and I played a few games in the reserves to keep my fitness levels up."

Apart from a start as an emergency right-back at Villa Park, Bob was playing a bit part role by the latter part of 1990. He came close to scoring a late equaliser against Sunderland, only foiled by a fine save by the brilliant Tony Norman.

A hamstring injury caused Bob to miss most of the December league programme, although he came on as a late substitute in an incredible Zenith Data Systems Cup win against Oldham Athletic, when the Blades scored seven times without reply after being two goals down. This proved a turning point. Finally, at the 17th time of asking, United won a First Division match, beating Nottingham Forest 3-2, yet again coming back from behind as the fans' support helped get them over the line. United won two of their next three games, against Luton and Queens Park Rangers. From being marooned at the bottom of the league with relegation looking inevitable, the great escape was on.

Bassett knew things would come right. "Despite the results, we never lost our self-belief or became negative. We knew that if we kept doing the same things then our luck would turn."

After sterling service, Rostron was allowed to move on to Brentford, but before he left he issued a rallying call which summed up how every player felt, "They have the spirit, the belief and the ability to stay up."

Bob returned to fitness in mid-January, enjoying a perfect view, from his position at right-back, of Vinnie Jones's booking after five seconds at Maine Road. "Vinnie was only following instructions," says Bob. "Harry had told him to get stuck into Peter Reid as quick as he could – something he did too literally." Referee David Elleray finally lost patience and gave

Jones a second yellow card after the break, this time for a rather soft foul, ensuring that this was one of the 12 times that Jones was sent off throughout his career.

In his tenth start of the season, in late January, Bob experienced his first victory after a last-gasp Glyn Hodges goal saw off the threat of Derby County. Bob took pride in coming out on top in his personal battle with Mick Harford, another powerful old-school striker, once described by Michael Calvin as, "A centre-forward with the instincts of a cage fighter."

Next up were Southampton. Keen to seize any edge, Bassett named Wilder as captain for the day against the team for whom he had played as a youngster. "I just wanted us to score as many goals as possible against the team that released me," he says, having told his teammates as much.

This was one of the most memorable matches in Bob's career. "Vinnie was suspended so I was given my favourite number 4 shirt. It was a cold, misty day and, given the weather, we had our lowest crowd of the season. The pitch was rock hard so I took out my metal studs and tapped in small leather ones so that I could get a better grip. They didn't work too well as I went to chest the ball down after a corner, slipped, fell over and the ball somehow got stuck between my knees, but I managed to recover and scrambled it in. A minute later, I hammered the ball in, hard and low, from another Ian Bryson corner. Both goals were scored in front of the Kop and I celebrated wildly."

"We were 4-1 up with five minutes to go when we won a penalty, and with the game already won the thought crossed my mind that I had never scored a hat trick for the club. This would be a great time to do so and it would probably be my last chance too. I jogged up from midfield but before I could grab the ball I saw Harry on the bench waving me back so I stopped, knowing that if I took it and missed he would slaughter me. My hesitation was fatal and John Gannon seized his chance, but he ballooned the ball over the bar and I never scored a hat trick for Sheffield United." Gannon tried to explain away his miss by stating that he "hit it harder than necessary because I thought the keeper was going the right way."

Wilder laughs when asked if he would have given Bob the spot kick. "Everyone knew that he couldn't take a penalty." Bob remains unconvinced. "I still lie in bed at night imagining what would have happened. I had never taken a penalty before, even at Bedmond, but did manage to score past Vinnie Jones in my testimonial match, so I have a perfect record. I would have run up, probably shut my eyes, and blasted the ball as hard as I could. Who knows if I'd have scored past Tim

Flowers? As far as I am concerned I scored a moral hat trick and the lads must have felt the same as they gave me the signed match ball, which I still have in my shed together with the tankard I won for being voted man of the match."

Bassett puts the blame totally on Bob. "It was his fault, he behaved like a shrinking violet," he scorns. "He should have been more assertive and just grabbed the ball."

Pritchett also found it hard to believe how far Bob had come, remarking in the *Sheffield Star*, "A career which looked to be drifting quickly to a close at Brentford three seasons ago reached a new peak against Southampton with the first two Division One goals of his career."

This was the second in an incredible run of seven consecutive wins, but as far as Bob was concerned nothing had changed apart from the fact that the ball had finally started to run for the team, "The system was still the same, but everything clicked and it all started to come together."

Wilder, too, was unsurprised when the team started winning. "Dave Bassett's recruitment was brilliant and we now had better players in a system that worked and had remained unchanged since the Third Division days. We were so well organised and had great desire and the fans stayed with us and gave us great support. No wonder we started to pick up points – and the more we won, the more confident we felt."

United marked Booker's achievement by extending his contract until the end of the 1991/92 season, so his future was assured for another 15 months, by which time he would be 34. But there was a double-edged sword as, despite his two-goal performance, Bob found himself relegated to the bench for the next match against Everton.

"I was really disappointed to be dropped and I went to speak to the manager, which was something that I never normally did. He said, 'I know you played well but Vinnie's back from suspension and he is going to play. Don't worry, you're an important part of the squad, you will get a lot more games this season and renewing your contract should tell you how much we appreciate you.' He made it clear where I stood and I had no option but to accept his verdict. I was still pretty frustrated but, looking back, I played in 29 out of our 38 league games and started 19 of them, which was a pretty good record and one that I was content with."

On as a substitute against Everton and Manchester United, Bob arrived just in time to admire Brian Marwood's late winner against Everton and lay on Carl Bradshaw's clincher against United with a perfect near post header from a Jones long throw.

"We missed Glyn Hodges after his six-match ban for head-butting an opponent, and he also had to deal with Harry Bassett, who was furious and fined him two weeks' wages, but we managed to cope without him."

Even though United had won seven games in a row, and then eight out of nine, their appalling start to the season mean that they were still not safe from the drop, particularly when they lost their next two matches against Nottingham Forest and Arsenal, when Booker was outmuscled by Kevin Campbell for Arsenal's first goal. The next game, away at Queens Park Rangers, was crucial – the Blades still needed another win in order to guarantee their First Division survival.

This match was to prove perhaps the most important in Bob's career. "It will go down in folklore as the day I helped keep the Blades up, which hopefully ensures that I will never be forgotten at Bramall Lane."

Bob was playing at centre-half that day, "My dad, Tina, Ian and a lot of my friends all came to cheer us on and were watching the match high up behind the goal we were attacking in the second half. We soon went a goal up and dominated the match but QPR equalised against the run of play, which meant that we desperately needed another goal in order to be safe, and with five minutes to go my big moment arrived. We won a throw in down by the right corner flag and all their defenders backed off because they were expecting the usual long throw from Vinnie. We had spoken at half-time about mixing things up and now it was time to try the unexpected. He threw it short to John Pemberton who whipped in a perfect cross and I managed to get on the end of it, beat Danny Maddix and Darren Peacock in the air and score with a glancing header in at the far post, right in front of my family and friends. I will never forget that moment and the celebrations that followed both then and at the final whistle. Andy Daykin hugged me and said, 'Well done Bob, you've just saved the club £1 million.' I replied, 'Just make sure I get some of it in my bonuses,' but I am still waiting. We were dead and buried at Christmas but the way we recovered just typified the spirit in the team, the football club itself and amongst the fans. That incredible day in West London matched the promotion-clinching win at Leicester the previous season for its excitement and its importance to myself and everyone involved with Sheffield United." In the euphoria surrounding Bob's winning goal, not many people remember that, shortly beforehand, Bob's valiant blocking of a point-blank header from Roy Wegerle, seemingly bound for the net, saved United from going behind – so he was a double hero on the day.

Pritchett paid full tribute to Bob and his "glorious header" in the *Sheffield Star*. "There is seemingly no end to the romantic story of Bob Booker. In the shadows at Brentford, never able to make an impact on the game, on the brink of going part-time and buying into a window cleaning business, he wrote another chapter in one of the game's most remarkable stories at QPR on Saturday. His romance with football seems destined to run and run." The national press also highlighted Bob's performance; he is named as man of the match in every report I have read.

"To keep Sheffield United in the First Division after a start like that has given me more pleasure than anything else I have done in football," Bassett acknowledged. "And it's nice to do it with a goal from somebody like Bob, who cost us nothing."

Bob won another man of the match award against Spurs in the next match, earning "A real cheer from the crowd for a fancy back heel." He can surely be forgiven for his appalling back pass that was played without looking and intercepted by Carl Shutt, who scored the winner for Leeds United at Elland Road. Bob came on to a hero's reception as a substitute in the final game of the season at home to Norwich, Pritchett describing his "tremendous welcome from the crowd." United finished in 13th place, 12 points clear of the drop that for so long seemed inevitable.

Bob could be well satisfied with his season's work, proving all his critics wrong to show that he belonged in the top flight. The *Flashing Blade* gave him another A- ranking in its *End Of Term Report*. "Robert continues to surprise us all," read its effusive verdict. "Everyone thought he would struggle in the higher grade. He took to it like a duck to water. One of the most popular pupils in the school."

Bob felt he still had much to give. "I hope I can continue next season. I play in a few different positions so I hope I can fill in. I think there's a year or so left in me yet." Before that, he had another important event to look forward to, capping a wonderful season with his marriage to Christine.

# CHAPTER 24
# GOODBYE TO SHEFFIELD

Refreshed from his honeymoon, Bob eagerly awaited his second season in the First Division. The fairy tale showed no signs of ending, exceeding expectations with his regular appearances in 1990/91, scoring the goal that ensured the Blades remained in the division and not looking out of place in a team that finally found its feet when all seemed lost.

"I was 33 years old, coming into the final year of my contract and had few illusions about earning another one. I had no wish to leave the club – why should I? I was now a First Division footballer, earning more than I had ever done, and I was quite happy to be part of the squad. My knee felt good, or as good as it could be, given the circumstances, and it hardly bothered me except in cold weather. Having a rest in the summer and playing less also helped, and I still worked hard with Derek French."

"I certainly didn't feel like I was a veteran and the oldest player at the club, but my body was gradually telling me I was nearing the end, as it took me longer to recover after each game, particularly given how I was expected to play and the energy I had to expend in every match."

Perhaps he received a warning sign during the pre-season training camp at Arborfield Garrison. Bob was accustomed to being one of the fittest players in the squad and was disappointed to finish sixth in the overall fitness table out of the 24 players present – a more than decent result, but not as good as he expected given his natural fitness and running ability.

Unlike the situation at Hillsborough, where newly-promoted Sheffield Wednesday were rewarded with a third place finish in return for lavishing over £3 million on Chris Woods, Paul Warhurst, Nigel Jemson and Chris Bart-Williams, Dave Bassett was, as normal, forced to shop in the bargain basement. Everything was done on a shoestring, with no marquee signings or major strengthening during the close season. Clive Mendonca, Tom Cowan, Adrian Littlejohn and Nathan Peel arrived, offset by the departures of Mark Morris and Paul Wood to Bournemouth. Vinnie Jones joined Chelsea early in the season for £575,000, followed by Tony Agana, who cost Notts County £750,000.

Bob fully understood United's financial constraints but knew they had the massive advantage of their team spirit. "Without exception everybody fitted in. It was a ruthless dressing room, which was its strength, as anyone getting above himself would have been found out very quickly and would not have lasted very long. I was one of the jokers and also liked getting behind the microphone on a night out. I kept telling the same old stories but my teammates seemed to like them and still laughed – or groaned. Perhaps they improved with the telling?"

Bob was sad to see his friend, Jones, leave the club, who he felt had been a positive influence. "Vinnie was a big name who cost a large fee but, surprisingly, he was very insecure. We used to share a room before away games and he would always be looking for some reassurance from me about how he had been playing. Despite all his efforts, he did not do quite as well as we had perhaps needed or expected."

Bassett recognised Bob's popularity and leadership qualities by naming him club captain after the sudden departure of Vinnie Jones.

Not all the fans were happy. Paul Wilkinson wrote to the *Sheffield Star* bemoaning the lack of quality in the squad. "Week after week we have to watch players of the calibre of Vinnie Jones and Bob Booker, whose only contributions seem to be a wave to the crowd at the end of the match." Harsh words, perhaps explained and exacerbated by poor early season results which saw the Blades win only once in August and September, plummeting to the bottom of the league.

Bob played in all of the opening 12 matches, filling in at the back, up front and in midfield. "Nothing changed. I travelled with every squad and even if I did not start I still felt fully involved. It was my football club and I did not feel at all out of it. Whenever I came on or off the pitch I received an incredible response from the crowd. Their support made me feel ten feet tall and filled me with confidence – what an incredible transformation and turnaround there had been since my arrival and the early dark days."

"I was named at right-back against Leeds United and, although we lost 4-3, I played really well and won my personal battle against Gary Speed. What I remember most about this game was wrestling the linesman. I bundled Lee Chapman out of the way to get the ball after it went out for a throw and, without looking to see who it was, I pulled the linesman over my shoulder. He hit the ground and I got booked for it." Peter Fitton in *The Sun* described Bob as "appearing to manhandle a linesman," thinking it was "so close to a wrestling bout that the baying crowd did not know whether to call for two falls or a submission."

Bob's left knee began to play up. A small arthroscopic procedure cleaned it out, but he did not play again for the first team after 5th October. "Despite my injury, it never crossed my mind that it was time to leave – that would have been terribly difficult for me given how much I loved Sheffield, and anyway, footballers always think that they are immortal. But Harry Bassett took the decision out of my hands."

"We were due to play Sheffield Wednesday at Bramall Lane on 17th November, a game that everyone in the city was looking forward to, and I was fit again and hoping to get back into the squad when Harry called me into his office not long before the kick off. 'Phil Holder of Brentford has been on the phone asking about you.' His words took me totally by surprise. I thought I would finish my career at United at the end of the season, but in football you never know what is around the corner. I hardly even took in the fact that it was my former club, Brentford, who were interested in me, and I had no idea how they were doing. I was so immersed in what was happening here."

"Harry broke the silence and said, 'I think you should consider it.' I managed to blurt out 'Really, Harry, I am very happy and don't want to leave.' He then laid it on the line very bluntly. 'You've got the rest of this season here but I'd be very surprised if you'll get another contract. You need to look after yourself. The way Brentford are talking they will offer you a contract for the rest of this season plus another two years, which will take you up to 36 years of age. You'll also get a signing on fee. You live nearby in Watford and you aren't going to stay here forever. It's going to come to an end soon.' My stomach lurched. This wasn't what I wanted or even expected to hear, although deep down I knew it was coming at some point, but you never really think it will happen to you."

"Harry kept on at me. 'I think you should talk to Phil and see what he is offering. It would be a good move for you and you can go back to Brentford on your own terms as a First Division player. You must consider this carefully.' I always listened to Harry as I knew that he was a straight talker who told it exactly as it was, and he was basically telling me that my time was up. I said that I would speak to Brentford and I did it, there and then, in his office. Phil Holder offered me a fantastic deal and I agreed to join them without even speaking to Christine."

"Bassett said, 'You've made the right decision and now I want you to go out onto the pitch and say goodbye to the fans. You've been fantastic for me and the club and you deserve a proper send-off.' It all happened so quickly, I was in a daze, and I put on a tracksuit top and almost had to be helped out onto the pitch. Dave Kilner announced the news of my departure as I came down the tunnel in front of a full house." 31,832 rabid supporters were asked to show their appreciation for the man they had just been informed had signed for Brentford. "The Wednesday fans jeered and sang, 'Who are you?' I expected nothing more from them, whereas the Blades gave me a rousing reception and an incredible send-off with a chorus of 'OOH-AAH BOB BOOKAH!' that seemed to go on forever. I stood in front of the Kop with my arms raised and tears streaming down my face. I completed my lap of honour and could barely drag myself off the pitch. I was emotionally drained. I could not have asked for a better way to say 'goodbye' and then, to cap it all, United put on a fantastic performance and won the local derby 2-0."

"I really did not want to leave, but later that day, when I was finally able to think straight, I knew that it was the right thing to do. I had to go as my time had come, and at least somebody else wanted to give me a job. Harry was doing me a favour – he was looking after me and helping to secure my future. It has to be said that I received an incredible contract from Brentford which gave me security for another two-and-a-half seasons on the same money that I had been earning at United."

It was ironic that having previously been taken for granted by Brentford, and paid so poorly, Bob was now returning triumphantly to the club with a £36,300 signing on fee as a First Division regular. Almost exactly three years after leaving them, seemingly on the road to nowhere, he was now one of their top earners – an incredible change in fortunes. Bassett felt that Bob got exactly what he deserved. "He had proved himself at a far higher level with Sheffield United and that's what persuaded Brentford to give him that contract. It did not turn out to be the wisest decision that they ever made, but it certainly made up for all the previous years when Bob played there for peanuts."

Bassett found releasing players or telling them that it was time to leave to be the worst part of his job. "It was never easy and I really didn't enjoy it, but honesty was always the best policy. I knew how horrible it felt, as I had also been bombed out of Chelsea as a kid. Your instincts tell you when a player's time is up. It can come very quickly and you just know that he can't cope any longer. You have to be honest and ruthless and tell him how you feel. For example, I really liked Chris Wilder but Kevin Gage was quicker and had more top-level experience, so I signed Kevin to replace him. With Bob it reached a point when I just felt that he wasn't going to be in the first team any longer and there was no point in him hanging around if he wasn't going to play."

Bob reflects on his time at Bramall Lane and his relationship with the supporters. "I felt humble and honoured to be part of them. Like them, I was from a working class background and they could all relate to me; the boy from the factory who had come to play for their football club. What I experienced there was something far beyond my wildest dreams. But the opportunity was there for me and I took it, against all the odds. My dad summed it up perfectly just before I signed when he said, 'You've earned this,' and he was right – I had. My move to Sheffield United was my reward for all my efforts in the lower divisions. When I signed, I never imagined the incredible journey we would be going on, and doubted that I would last three months, let alone three years. I suspect that I probably surprised Dave Bassett, who thought that I was just a short-term solution when Simon Webster was injured."

"Deep down, I never thought I was capable of achieving as much as I did there and I certainly surprised myself, but unless you try you will never find out. When I signed I thought that it could all go horribly wrong, and it nearly did, but Harry Bassett, Geoff Taylor, Derek French and all the players were so supportive from the start and eventually the fans got behind me too. That made me feel even stronger."

"I will be forever grateful to Dave Bassett, as he put me on the map as a player and believed in me. I always had guts and energy in abundance but he helped me make the most of my ability and saw things in me that I never suspected I possessed. I would have run through a brick wall for him, despite him calling me a donkey at West Ham. There are countless players out there with more ability than me but I doubt if any of them possess the same level of passion and determination. I really believe it came from those early years in the furniture factory, looking after my workmates, learning a trade and being in the real world. That's what got me through and stood me in good stead, whereas the modern day footballer goes straight from school into professional football without knowing or experiencing anything different. Once I became a footballer I was never going to let it go without a fight, as I knew what life would be like without it and I didn't want to go back to my former life."

Bassett remembers Bob with great fondness. "Bob stepped up the leagues with us and proved that he could cope with everything that was thrown at him. I wasn't sure at first if he could play in the First Division but he rose to the challenge, as he always did, adapted well to the level and did some excellent work there. He fitted into the team like a glove and it was an ideal move for both parties. He was always a good footballer with an exemplary character. He was a great professional, always willing to do anything for the team and the club. He became an icon and a legend in the city – the fans really took to him, they loved him for who he was."

Bob received many tributes from United fans. The December 1991 edition of the *Flashing Blade* was practically a valedictory issue, acknowledging his contribution and affinity with the supporters.

The Mole on Bob Booker's Cheek wrote: "Sir Bob was one of the most popular players at the club and he scored some of the most important goals of last season. Not bad for someone who was thinking about quitting football and starting a cleaning business until he was picked up and became a megastar at Bramall Lane. I am sad, like many others, to see him go. Not only was he a good player, he was one of the nicest people you could wish to meet. 'OOH-AAH!' became a cult figure complete with his own chant and I believe he is sad to leave but he really enjoyed his time here and so did we. Good luck at Brentford, Bob, you may be gone but you'll never be forgotten. 'OOH-AAH!' will live on."

*Flashing Blade's* Editor, Matthew Bell, paid similar tribute to him in an affectionate and perceptive review of Bob's time at the club. "Whoever said that modern day football lacks characters never came across Bob Booker. Perhaps if it came down to pure footballing ability Booker would never have made a career as a professional, but he has always possessed other qualities in abundance, such as commitment, enthusiasm and determination, that have kept him going when other more talented individuals have fallen by the wayside."

"Everybody had expected Dave Bassett to replace Booker during the close season but… as the season progressed it became clear that Booker was a crucial member of the team and rather than expecting him to be replaced, he was becoming irreplaceable… and Booker was quickly developing into a cult figure with the supporters."

Bob "let nobody down," in the First Division, he wrote, and it was "fitting that Booker should be the man to score" the goal that secured First Division survival at Queens Park Rangers.

"Bob received a deserved send-off just before the start of the Wednesday game. His reception as he took the cheers and applause brought tears to the eyes. He shook hands with all the other players and shared a hug with Brian Deane, a visible demonstration of what his teammates thought of him." Bell ended his eulogy with the heartfelt words, "Bob Booker, we love you" – a sentiment he shared with most other Blades.

The official programme allocated a full page expressing the club's gratitude for his service, a tribute that is rare in its heartfelt and lyrical nature. "There have been more exciting or contentious deals at Bramall Lane in the past but few that could have provoked such goodwill and warmth at both ends of the deal," it reads. "Quite simply Bob is an anomaly, a one-off whose relatively modest talents have belied his appeal to the fans. In an age where money talks and many players betray their loyalty, he has selflessly earned a reputation built on values too easily forgotten or discarded."

"Bob's contribution has been well documented and needs little repeating here, but it took nerve to uproot at his stage of career and move north in the first place. To cope with the initial barracking and win the fans over was even more impressive, especially as his then-girlfriend and relatives were still 150 miles away – times can be hard and lonely in a big city when things aren't going too well."

"Bob's off-field contribution was immense, partly as a means of filling his time but basically out of his sheer humility and pleasure in being a soccer player. The trick was to be like that and yet still enjoy the respect of his fellow players. He certainly did."

"Almost exactly three years in Sheffield brought Bob moments of achievement and joy the likes of which he couldn't possibly have envisaged – the Second Division, the First, goals, captaincy and his very own chant. In all honesty, 'Roy of the Rovers' almost pales into insignificance when you consider Bob was just about washed up and 30 when he came here."

"Bob, the pleasure has been all ours and we wish you all the very best. On second thoughts, you probably don't need our help. With the way your career has taken off you'll probably sign for Liverpool for £5 million in about three years' time. 'OOH-AAH!' wouldn't sound right in Scouse, though."

Pritchett also bade farewell to Bob in an article in the *Sheffield Star* headlined, "HOW BOB WAS JUST THE JOB." Bob "was not, nor would he claim to be, one of the most gifted players in United's recent history. But somehow, through his sheer love of the place, he established a bond with the fans that many better players have never equalled... Booker had only one way to play – with enthusiasm, commitment and scrupulous sportsmanship. He was, in some ways, one of Bassett's best signings, and Bramall Lane will be a less cheerful place without him."

Derek Dooley was appreciative of Bob's achievements at the club, feeling that he "epitomised everything that is good in football. A team-man through and through, his positive attitude rubbed off on the rest of the team. He was willing to play anywhere in the interests of the team... on top of this, he was always a great ambassador for the club, ever willing to do more than his fair share of public relations jobs. A man anybody would be proud to know."

Perhaps the tribute that Bob enjoyed the most was hearing himself described as his friend Joe Elliott's football hero, alongside Tony Currie.

Bob has a folder containing many letters sent to him by United fans, thanking him for his efforts at the club. They remain very precious to him, highlighting the bond that developed between him and the fans.

Despite his fitness problems on arrival, Bob was either a starter or substitute in 109 of the 127 league games that United played throughout his stay, wearing every shirt except for the numbers 1, 5, 7 and 11.

Bob left Sheffield reluctantly, with so many fond memories. He had been exceptionally good for the club and the fans; they and the city itself had been wonderful for him. It was a partnership and mutual love affair made in heaven, giving him three of the best years of his life when he performed like Superman, growing as a person. It remained to be seen if he had any more miracles left in his locker when he returned to his first love – Brentford.

# CHAPTER 25
# NEVER GO BACK!

Bob's feet never touched the ground after he agreed to rejoin Brentford. "I went straight back to Mitchell Road after the Sheffield Wednesday match, threw as many of my things as I could into a couple of bags, grabbed Bruno and set off the following day for Watford, where Christine was waiting. Like me, she was stunned and bemused by the speed of recent events," he remembers. "There was no time to say goodbye to anyone and I went back to Sheffield later on for a leaving party that the club kindly arranged for me. There were massive similarities to my move to Sheffield three years earlier, which also happened so quickly that I barely had time to think or draw breath."

"I used the journey to reflect and the overriding thought going through my mind was, 'What on earth have I done?' In truth, I was really conflicted and concerned about going back. Dave Bassett had made it clear that he wanted me to leave, but I did feel that I had been pressured into making a quick decision and hadn't checked if there were other opportunities for me. Maybe this was a time when it would have been helpful to have had an agent working on my behalf?"

Chris and Bob's return to their roots would allow them to set up home close to their families. "I knew Brentford and how the club operated and felt honoured that they wanted to bring me back. I would also have some security and a guaranteed wage for the best part of three seasons and could postpone the inevitable worry about what I was going to do when my football career was over. On the other hand, I was pretty apprehensive about going back as a senior player to the club where I had started my career scrimping and saving on £60 per week. I realised that, yet again, there would be massive expectations on me as I would now be one of their best-paid players and judged as a former First Division footballer. I just hoped that the fans, who had always been very mixed in their reaction towards me, would not expect miracles, as I hadn't changed and was the same Bob Booker doing what I had always done, although I was fitter and more confident now. I let my heart rule my head and hoped that everything would turn out for the best."

"I went into the ground on the Monday and it did feel good signing such an amazing contract, and I had made it clear to the manager, Phil Holder, that I was only coming back on my terms and wasn't going to sign for anything less than I had been earning at Sheffield United."

Phil Holder told the *Middlesex Chronicle* why he had signed Bob. "He is a fantastic pro who has gone through the leagues with Sheffield United. He's learned a lot from that which he can pass on to our younger players. He is very versatile which is important at this level. He scores goals, tackles and will be an asset to the squad."

Holder now confesses that his chairman, Martin Lange, had not been keen on signing Bob, thinking that he was too old and would struggle to maintain his fitness levels. Holder persuaded Lange that he needed the experience of a model professional who was worth his weight in gold in and around the dressing room, even when he was not fit.

Bob was encouraged by what he heard from Holder. "He saw me as a leader and as first choice in his midfield playing with Simon Ratcliffe, who I knew was a good player. I had kept myself fit and looked forward to playing every week but, at my age, I told Phil that I'd have to manage myself and could not go flat out in training every day, and he was happy with that. Holder didn't mention my knee and the physio Roy Clare gave it a cursory examination but there really wasn't much of a medical."

"All I knew about Brentford was that they were top of their league and going for promotion, which was a totally new experience for me there, and that they saw me as an experienced head who would help get them over the finish line. I had no idea how they played and thought I would be joining a team that played more of a passing game than I had been used to. That worried me too, although as I was shortly to learn as soon as I saw them play that I did not need to have any fears on that score!"

Brentford supporters knew that something was up; the *ClubCall* premium rate telephone information service was buzzing with rumour, hype and innuendo. Like many others, I dialled 0898 121108 – a number indelibly fixed in my memory banks – several times every day, ideally from work, listening impatiently as Peter Gilham prattled on and spouted interminable and irrelevant nonsense as the cost of the call racked up before the meat was finally revealed – in this case, "Brentford to sign First Division star." It has to be said that it was a real anti-climax when Bob's identity was finally revealed.

Bob was none too amused when he heard about this. "The club wanted to make the most of my arrival but all they did was pile more pressure on me and their actions were totally unnecessary and unhelpful. I wasn't a 'First Division star' and would never have claimed to be one. The fans were probably expecting someone like Graham Rix to arrive. I'm sure that there was a palpable sense of disappointment when they heard it was me, as I probably wasn't the favourite player for many Bees fans." The inimitable Gilham says he had neither wanted nor intended to mislead the Brentford fans, but had been instructed to use the words that he did on the *ClubCall* bulletins.

Bob trained for the first time on the Wednesday at the London Transport ground at Osterley. "It was lovely to see so many familiar faces in Terry Evans, Jamie Bates, Keith Millen, Gary Blissett and Neil Smillie. They gave me a warm welcome and were full of questions about life up north under Harry Bassett. I felt that they now all looked up to me because I had been playing in the First Division so recently."

Phil Holder, who had taken over from Steve Perryman in 1990, has a legacy that should never be diminished or forgotten, becoming the first Brentford manager since Harry Curtis to lead the team to promotion to the second tier of English football – a feat later matched by Mark Warburton. Holder changed the image of the club and its playing style. Brentford were no longer a soft touch. He inherited a wonderful platform from his former Spurs colleague, moulding the team into one that was the antithesis of the diminutive manager, a ball-playing midfielder during his own career at Spurs and Crystal Palace. Brentford were big, tough, hard to beat and, in Dean Holdsworth, Gary Blissett, Marcus Gayle and Neil Smillie, had a front four to fear.

Holder adapted Perryman's passing approach with the help of his assistant manager, Wilf Rostron, introducing a far less cultured and more pragmatic, direct style of football, which brought results. He instructed the team to get the ball forward as quickly as possible, bypassing the midfield, where the skilful Allan Cockram was swiftly jettisoned. Brentford were often not very pretty to watch, relying extensively on set pieces and long balls, with the midfield often ignored. But they could also play, particularly in the opponents' final third.

Former Bees winger Andy Driscoll neatly sums up the difference between the two managers' approaches. "Phil was long ball and got experienced players in, whereas Steve wanted to play." Neil Smillie also admitted, "We were pretty direct and had the players to do it."

Brentford were reinvigorated by the return to full fitness of Holdsworth, who scored a hat trick on the opening day of the season. He formed a lethal partnership with Blissett, scoring a combined 56 goals in all competitions that season.

Bob could see that Holder had built a strong team taking no prisoners and playing very similarly to Sheffield United – so much for the tippy-tappy football he had been concerned about. "My job was to win the ball, get it wide to Marcus Gayle or Neil Smillie and get into the box and support Dean Holdsworth and Gary Blissett. There was a good group of players at the club and there were no cliques, but the dressing room was far less intense than had been the case at Bramall Lane. I thought that although there were some strong voices and leaders, like Terry Evans, they were not used to winning and their recent success seemed to take some of them by surprise, but confidence grew as the team gelled."

Bob had joined a happy, well-run club with an excellent relationship between the squad and its manager. Millen thought the secret of the team's success was its spirit. "We were so close and would run through brick walls for each other… as a group we were focused on trying to achieve something special. That's what drove us forward." Evans had, "loads of time for Phil. He's a great bloke, honest, open, tells you how it is, which I think everyone wants. The dressing room ran itself. I thought his man management was good." Blissett also, "got on with the manager OK. He said it how it was. The players that didn't get along with Phil were the ones that didn't like his style of play." Smillie had played with Holder at Crystal Palace and thought he was, "fantastic for the club."

Bob looked forward to his second debut for the club. "My first game was on the Friday night away at AFC Bournemouth and, given how the team played, I thought that I would fit in quite easily and fill the gap left by the recent sale of Keith Jones. I was a bit worried because of my age, although Neil Smillie was only about six months younger than me. I really wanted to contribute and help the team achieve something. I had improved as a player since the fans had last seen me, as I was more confident, and being wanted really helped. My touch was better, although I was never encouraged to linger on the ball, but as you get more experienced you realise that you always have a bit more time than you think. I certainly felt that I was now a far better footballer."

Bob was surprised to see Paul Wood and Mark Morris, two of his recent teammates from Sheffield United, playing for Bournemouth. Jim Levack, in the *Middlesex Chronicle*, described Bob as the "prodigal son" who "won an ovation from the fans." He played well, was "straight back into his stride" and was "more than a match for the irrepressible former Liverpool star, Jimmy Case." The match ended 0-0. Bob felt relieved to have contributed to a result in his first game. The evening of 22nd November 1991 was to prove the high spot of Bob's ill-fated return to Griffin Park – it was to be all downhill from there.

Returning home in the early hours of the morning, Bob's knee felt typically stiff. "But when I woke up I felt a painful crumbling and grating sensation in my knee whenever I moved. I immediately feared the worst. I dreaded ringing the manager but eventually I summoned up the courage to call him. 'My knee is swollen, boss and I'm in terrible pain.'"

"There was a silence down the other end of the telephone as Phil took in what I had said, before he replied, 'Don't worry, go and see the doctor and just get back playing as soon as you can.' I appreciated his concern, saw the specialist and was told to rest up. Eventually the swelling went down and the pain became more bearable."

Bob was devastated. A frustrating and debilitating regime of rest and treatment, interspersed with the odd day of training and the occasional game, continued throughout the next season and a half. His face falls as he struggles to describe these dark days. The normally articulate and cheerful Bob becomes more hesitant and despondent, finding it desperately hard to express his thoughts. Long silences interspersed with distant and faraway looks emerge in a struggle to resurrect dark memories that he has repressed for so long.

"I wanted to do my bit for the team and the fans, but I was in constant pain from my knee with bone rubbing on bone. I was told that it was just wear and tear and there was nothing that could be done. I know everyone did their best for me but I really missed having Derek French around, as I felt that he really understood my situation and had worked tirelessly with me to build up my knee and keep me fit. I did manage to play a few matches, but I was not able to do myself justice because of the pain. I was not really involved with what was going on and, because I was generally getting treatment on my own, I did not see too much of my teammates. I really do not have too many clear memories of what happened that season, or indeed the next one."

Facing a crisis over Christmas with players out through injury, suspension and illness, Bob came in against Hartlepool on New Year's Day with a day's training under his belt, helping the team to a hard-fought 1-0 victory. Holder was full of admiration for Bob. "It is a tribute to him that he battled on for so long," he said, watching him hobble off after 81 minutes. Despite the pain, Bob gritted his teeth, continuing as best he could, managing to play in almost every match until the end of March. But he knew that his lack of mobility made him a shadow of the player he had been. Holder praised him and Ratcliffe for their efforts in a vital win over title challengers Stoke, and Bob scored his first goal since his return with a 20-yarder at Chester. Bob contributed to a win over Preston in a game that was not easy on the eye. Preston manager Les Chapman expressed what many felt. "Brentford are a hard side to beat. They have got to be one of the biggest and most physical sides in the league." Bob's goal against Torquay helped earn a narrow 3-2 victory when, according to Levack, he was "industrious" and "silenced his critics, including myself, when he opened the scoring with a deftly-placed header from a Neil Smillie cross."

The fans did not understand the problems Bob faced, beginning to boo him mercilessly. His manager came to his defence, telling the boo boys "Don't bother, because he loves it. Bob is the sort of bloke who revels in it. He loves to prove people wrong and none of us are in any doubt that he will. He is also a calming influence and a great leader." Playing in constant pain, Bob eventually had to admit defeat and tell his manager that he was unable to continue; he was replaced by loanee Detzi Kruszynski for the promotion run-in. The Bees timed their late run perfectly, won their last six games and came up on the rails to take the title on an unforgettable final day of the season at Peterborough in front of 4,100 exuberant travelling supporters. The celebrations were wild and raucous and Bob played little part in them. There is a photograph of the team celebrating in the away dressing room at the end of the match. Bob is tucked away in the back row, there in body rather than spirit.

"I went to Peterborough and celebrated after the match with the lads, but my heart wasn't in it and I just did not feel a part of things," he admits. "Deep down I knew that I had not really contributed much to the team's success and I didn't even go back to Griffin Park to celebrate with the rest of the squad. I did receive a Championship medal but it really means nothing to me, as I did not feel that I had earned it. It's really ironic that I did not get a medal when I played a large part in helping Sheffield United to consecutive promotions, yet I was given one for doing very little for Brentford." Holder felt that Bob's sentiments simply emphasised what an honourable man he was.

I can still taste the horrendously expensive bottle of Perrier-Jouet champagne that my wife and I contentedly glugged down to celebrate the title win. But I might not have bothered had I known then what was to happen the following season.

Bob says the Brentford and Sheffield United teams that both won promotion from Division Three were "Not a million miles apart." "But in my opinion Sheffield United had the edge because of the strength of the Agana/Deane dual spearhead and the fervour of their fans."

"Graham Benstead was a fantastic shot stopper in goal and we were very strong in defence. Brian Statham came in at right-back. He was good on the ball and a tough tackler. I liked him and always felt that he was a bit too bright to be a footballer. Jamie Bates was brave, put his head in and was Brentford through and through. His mind would wander and he was prone to losing concentration. He liked a cigarette and I think that football was just a job for him. Terry Evans was one of my best friends. He wasn't quick but he had a massive presence and was lethal in the air. He's the only player I have ever seen head the ball over the Brook Road Stand. He was so aggressive and powerful and created havoc at corners at the far post where he was looking for a near post flick on from Marcus Gayle. Keith Millen had really improved since I last saw him. He read the game well and was excellent in the air. Keith is totally dedicated to the game and I am not surprised that he has gone on to enjoy a long career as a coach and manager. Billy 'Pitbull' Manuel lived up to his nickname at left-back. He was small and tough and a real scrapper but he lacked mobility and Chris Hughton, an inspired signing whose experience was priceless, replaced him for the promotion run-in."

"Simon Ratcliffe was solid in midfield. He was a bit dour and went about his business quietly. He broke play up well and had a decent shot on him too. Neil Smillie was pure quality and a great pro who gave everything. Despite his age, he was very fit and was still very quick in short bursts. He was a wonderful crosser of the ball and very dangerous when cutting inside on his left foot. Marcus Gayle was still learning the game but was strong, quick and hard to knock off the ball. He could play down the centre but I preferred him as a winger. He probably had the hardest shot at the club."

"Gary Blissett and Dean Holdsworth were not a bad pairing up front. Bliss was an excellent target man who was two-footed with a decent first touch. He was a good finisher and although he was a really talented player he could have had an even more successful career. He lacked self-discipline, drank and smoked, and I was like a Dutch uncle to him, but he was never going to change. Deano was only 23 at the time but was a very confident young man who was a bit full of himself and someone who knew he was going onto bigger and better things. He and Bliss did not mix much off the field but they had an excellent understanding on it. Dean would pull off the far post and Bliss would come short and, if you gave him a chance, Dean was deadly and very cool in front of goal. I thought Deane and Agana just had the edge, as they were both so quick and had a real hunger for goals. They were also friends off the pitch which I think helped."

"Richard Cadette had started off the season in the team but he and Phil Holder never saw eye to eye and were always rowing over our style of play. Richard was never a Holder type of player and it was best for everyone when he left for Falkirk. Kevin Godfrey was a good, unassuming squad member who could fill in anywhere up front. Another who started off well was Lee Luscombe, a young winger from Guernsey who arrived from Southampton. We called him 'The Lizard' as his tongue was always flicking in and out. He had a good left foot and did things totally instinctively. He was uncoachable, as he would never listen to what he was told or take anything in. He would just take people on and either lose the ball or put in a cross. He was a bit like Paul Brooker at Brighton later on, a confidence player who if he started well would be fine, but if not, you'd do well to take him off after 20 minutes. He had no football intelligence and I never thought that he would make it – and he didn't."

A season that ended so well for Brentford was a total damp squib for Bob, who now had a tough decision to make about his future, "I had two seasons left on my contract and I really felt that I still had something left to prove. With some rest over the summer I hoped that my knee would recover sufficiently to allow me to play some part. The manager also thought that my previous experience in the First Division, as the second tier had just been renamed, would come in handy."

Bob rested and iced his knee, concentrating on building up his quad muscles. He came back as ready as he could for pre-season training, even playing in a few friendly matches. But he was obviously struggling and he realised that his days as a first choice player were over.

"I could still feel the pain of bone grinding on bone. I had the knee lasered a couple of times which helped smoothen it for a while, but the relief was only temporary as the pain would always return. I was frustrated and depressed as I was not able to do my job properly, and I got by from day to day as well as I could. The money was good but I was embarrassed and wanted to feel that I had earned it."

Holder had to cope with a far higher standard of football without the services of his top scorer Dean Holdsworth, who was sold to Wimbledon in an appallingly bad deal that brought in £720,000 plus two players, Detzi Kruszynski and Mickey Bennett, neither of whom proved good enough.

So naïve were Brentford in their negotiations that they failed to include a sell-on clause in the deal, which came back to haunt them when Deano joined Bolton Wanderers for £3.5 million in 1997. It's Brentford, innit.

There was massive interest in who would attempt to replace Holdsworth and his 38 goals from the previous season, creating a feeling of total bemusement when the unknown and unheralded Murray Jones eventually arrived from Grimsby Town for £75,000 – a man with no previous track record of scoring goals. He was a total disaster; tall, lean, awkward and gawky, with shorts hitched up high. After flattering to deceive with a well-taken goal against David Seaman in a behind closed doors friendly against Arsenal, he repeated the feat with a mishit cross against the might of Merthyr Tydfil, but never scored in 20 first team appearances, very rarely looking like doing so. Bob was none too impressed. "Apart from Keith Millen, who was a mate of his, none of the other players had heard of him. The one thing he had going for him was his confidence. He was very full of himself – too confident, in fact. He thought that he was Alan Shearer and was sure that he would be a success. He was deluding himself, as even in training he showed us nothing and rarely managed to put the ball in the net. For a man of his size he showed no physicality and he could barely control the ball. Initially the crowd hated him and then, perhaps even worse for him, they started to feel sorry for him as he was so obviously out of his depth. We knew that we were in trouble if we had to rely on him for goals."

Holder holds his hands up. "Quite simply, he was a bad buy. He was a Londoner who I'd seen a fair bit of playing for Crystal Palace reserves and he had always looked decent. Initially I lost trace of him when he went up north but when I caught up with him he was keen to come back to London and looked to be up for it. I thought he could do a decent job for a fee that I could just about afford, but he never produced. I was only given around £60,000 to replace a top-class striker in Dean Holdsworth, which was a totally false economy."

Attempting to replace Holdsworth on the cheap proved to be a massive own-goal by the club. Eventually a club record £275,000 was spent on the larger-than-life Joe Allon from Chelsea, but he did not score enough goals. Holder felt that Allon neither justified his fee nor set a good example with his refuelling habits off the pitch, helping lead other players astray. Bob used to travel into training with Allon and Blissett, "Joe was an utter nutcase and he and Bliss always wanted to stop off for a drink when all I wanted to do was get home. He was a decent player and an enormous improvement on Murray Jones, but still not quite good enough, although he did cheer me up when I was at a low ebb." Despite stories to the contrary, Holder said the club was never in a financial position to sign Stan Collymore from Crystal Palace – someone who might have made all the difference, as his goals kept Southend United in the division.

Bob bemoans the inactivity. "Phil Holder was unable to bring in the quality of player that we needed. We were also ravaged by injuries. Terry Evans damaged his medial ligaments on the opening day of the season and was irreplaceable. Shane Westley was nowhere near as good as him. Benno also missed quite a few games although Gerry Peyton did well. Unfortunately, young Ashley Bayes also had to play a few games in goal. He was a lovely lad but was really nervous and lacked confidence. He was a bag of nerves whenever he played and made some awful errors, which totally deflated everyone. Neil Smillie and Simon Ratcliffe also missed a lot of games, Chris Hughton was forced to retire because of his knee and I hardly managed to play at all. Detzi and Mickey Bennett were both in and out and Kenny Sansom and Alan Dickens were well past their best. Paul Stephenson was a good signing and Grant Chalmers really impressed me as a skilful young midfield player, but he was in the right place at the wrong time as Phil Holder did not believe in him and he drifted away – a waste of a good talent."

Statham could see the writing on the wall. "When players suffered long-term injuries, we couldn't afford to replace them adequately. I think that's why we struggled. It was a reasonably sized squad but there was a lot of inexperience there and we just didn't have sufficient quality."

Ratcliffe agreed. "I don't think the players we were bringing in were better than those we had," he said, feeling that newcomers coming in on higher wages without necessarily improving the squad had a negative effect on team spirit. Billy Manuel gave his opinion on *getwestlondon.co.uk*, "Relegation was terrible, the worst moment of my life. With the players we had we were unlucky to go down. I think the trouble was we tried to bully teams, which may have worked at the level below, but you can't do that at the new level we were at. The players we were coming up against were so much better – you have to find a different angle."

Holder is very open and honest about his constant battles against the odds and lack of financial support. "We went into bat with a team of very aggressive, tall, strong players, but we needed to change our style in order to adapt to the demands of the new division and the better players we faced. We just could not afford to bring in good enough players. I had to make do with what I could find. Recruitment was down to me and my judgement was poor in several cases. The injuries did not help and we had quite a few things go against us. I remember having to play Marcus Gayle at left-back where initially he did very well. What capped it all was Notts County equalising in the 98th minute at Griffin Park, and I still don't know where the referee found all that extra time. In the end, that was the difference between us staying up and going down."

Ever since that fateful Easter Monday, Brentford fans have vilified the referee, Ray Bigger. He is now working in Singapore as managing director of an architectural practice, and is happy to talk. He is totally unrepentant about his actions, which he thought were fully justified. "The irony of it was when I was driving home from the game I was listening to a Brentford supporter who called in to a radio phone-in show in order to have a rant about my timekeeping. The talk show host told him, 'I was at the match and I thought that the referee was absolutely correct as Brentford were slowing the game down.' Brentford employed a lot of timewasting tactics as soon as they went ahead. I made it very clear to their players during the remainder of the second half by tapping my watch whenever I thought they were timewasting, so they knew that if they kept this up we would be out here all night. I also remember that there were some injuries in the second half. Referees cannot win and are criticised if they do add on time and equally so when they don't. As we left the ground, for the first time ever in my refereeing career a home fan got a bit bolshie and he started mouthing off at me, so one of my linesmen, who was extremely tall, stepped in and said 'Do you have a problem?' and he quickly backed off. I had also refereed a friendly match a few years previously when Phil Holder was playing for Crystal Palace against Croydon Amateurs and sent him off, so I am sure that he does not have happy memories of me, although at the time I did not have a clue that he was the Brentford manager. Ironically, before the end of normal time I stopped play for an injury and a home fan started shouting at me and saying that he could have done a better job than me and, stupidly, I held out my whistle and offered it to him. Maybe Brentford fans wish that he had taken up my invitation."

Bob had no complaints about how he was treated. "Phil Holder was very sympathetic and told me to do my best to get fit. He didn't put me under any pressure, but it was obvious that I was drifting out of contention. The trouble was I never knew how I would feel from day to day. I could have three days when I could get around reasonably well and then I would struggle for a week, which was no good for anybody. My knee had just deteriorated beyond repair and there was nothing that could be done about it. I did manage to complete three games in a week in late August, and I scored against Fulham at Craven Cottage, which gave me a real boost. That was my last goal, as it turned out. The knee then flared up again and I was forced to rest. I came on as a late substitute at Leicester and barely touched the ball and was then named as a sub for the Coca-Cola Cup tie away at Spurs."

Levack reported that Bob had "a storming game in midfield" against Fulham, scoring with a "sweet left-footed shot." Holder was well aware of what a fit Bob could bring to his team, delighted by his goal at Fulham and claiming Bob, "Looked like he did in his Sheffield United days. Bob has done a good job in the last two games and it will be difficult to drop him," he said a few days later. Unfortunately, injury did the job for him.

The *Middlesex Chronicle* reported that Bob suffered a "serious knee injury" at Spurs and "The rejuvenated utility man hobbled off following a seemingly innocuous incident with Spurs keeper Walker." Roy Clare was reasonably positive about Bob's prognosis, "He has just aggravated the old injury – it is not as bad as it looked."

Bob knew just how serious this latest injury was. "My studs stuck in the grass and I over-extended my left knee. I was stretchered off with a strained patella. It felt as bad as when I did my cruciate in 1986. I had it scanned but the only answer was rest and physiotherapy. Roy Clare treated it every day but otherwise I was left to my own devices, and would go jogging and lift weights. Roy did everything he could with the limited resources that he had, but I certainly missed having Derek French around to look after my knee."

"This was a miserable time for me and I was like a bear with a sore head. Terry Evans knew exactly what I was going through, suffering similar problems, and we would try and cheer each other up and take Bruno and Terry's German Shepherd, Satan, out for long walks. Chris Hughton also had a bad knee and bravely tried to play through the pain barrier, but eventually he had to admit defeat and give up. I thought that I might not be far behind him. I did go and watch most of our home games but the results were getting worse as relegation threatened and I have blanked out most of my memories of what was an awful time for me."

Marcus Gayle, then still an inexperienced player trying to make his way in the game, retains fond memories of Bob. "He was down in the dumps about his knee and I remember seeing him in the dressing room almost in tears as he realised that his career was probably coming to an end. Despite his problems, he made an excellent impression on me. He helped me and all the other young players and set a good example for us to follow and we all respected him."

Bob managed to play in a 5-4 Capital League win over Orient on 28th October but it was one step forward and ten back. It was 18th February before he was able to play again in a 5-0 reserve team victory at Reading. On 23rd March, Bob made his final Football League appearance as an 85th minute substitute for Paul Stephenson at Grimsby, celebrating a win as a Blissett goal gave the Bees their first victory in eight games. Holder paid tribute to his contribution. "Bob Booker did OK in his short spell. Having Terry (Evans), Bob, Keith (Millen) and Jamie (Bates) out there was like having the old guard back."

Bob's final game as a professional came on 8th April when he helped the reserves to a 3-0 win against Reading. The progress of his rollercoaster playing career could best be described by the word "bouncebackability," first used by the then-Crystal Palace manager Iain Dowie in 2004. But for all Bob's persistence, determination and sheer bloody-mindedness, there was no coming back for him this time.

The season went down to the wire; Brentford were relegated by a single point, throwing away their hard-earned elevated status after a catastrophic season of cock-ups on the pitch, in the dugout and in the boardroom, culminating in a final day capitulation at Bristol City. Everybody was to blame. The memories are still painful; the club had the ammunition but not the vision or foresight to remain and consolidate in that division. This was a massive opportunity thrown away. On the ill-fated final day of the season, the Bees could still stay up if Birmingham City failed to beat Charlton Athletic.

There is an intriguing story from a Charlton Athletic player who was in their team that day; Birmingham needed to win to escape the drop, while Charlton had nothing to play for. Brentford had long since raised the white flag at Ashton Gate, relying upon their fellow Londoners to do them a favour. No such luck. The Charlton team, who had dominated a scoreless first half at St Andrew's, were allegedly warned by a very senior policeman, who entered their dressing room uninvited at the interval, that their safety could not be guaranteed if they won the match. It is not known if he had a strong Brummie accent! Understandably, they downed tools. A late, dubious, blatantly offside goal from Paul Moulden, allowed by officials perhaps intimidated by the vociferous crowd, sent Brentford down. This was a typically farcical end to a farcical season – one the club took years to recover from.

I asked journalist Jim Levack, who saw most of Bob's games throughout his time at Brentford, to write his verdict on him, "From the moment he returned, the writing was on the wall for Bob. The fans had revered him for years for his commitment, loyalty and never-say-die approach to each game in a red and white shirt."

"He was one of us, a bloke who'd worked hard to get where he had. And that was why we loved him. But, in the days long before the invention of the internet, the club issued a statement just before his arrival, to whet fans' appetites. We would shortly be announcing the capture of a 'First Division star.' Of course, that was true – he'd become a cult hero at Sheffield United with a series of swashbuckling, endeavour-filled displays that took the Blades to the top flight – but it was unfair in equal measures. The anti-climax of re-signing a by now ageing midfielder with a dodgy knee was palpable. He never really recovered from that appalling PR blunder."

"Bob managed just 19 league games and two goals in a second spell that was always going to end in frustrating disappointment for all parties. I would rather remember 'Sir Bob' for his wonderful first stint at the club and the Sand Dance song, as I'm sure every other Brentford fan does. And that, as with any club legend, is just as it should be."

Holder thought very highly of Bob, "He was a perfect professional who trained and worked hard, gave you everything you asked of him and always wanted to better himself. I am not surprised that he did well in Division One, playing in a system that was ideal for him. A fit Bob Booker would help any team and if he had been able to play regularly for me we would have stood a far better chance of staying up."

Bob's second period at Brentford was a disaster through no fault of his own. His suspect knee finally decided to give way, leaving him crippled and totally unable to do himself justice. At Sheffield United, Bob and the crowd fed off each other with remarkable results. Now the rapport had gone. There was no real connection or spark with the Brentford fans owing to his injury; Bob faded into the background despite his best intentions and endeavours. This was not the return he had wanted or envisaged. As an appalling season came to a close, where would his future now lie?

# CHAPTER 26
# BACK IN THE GAME

The immediate aftermath of Brentford's relegation was the harsh sacking of Phil Holder, who described his team's abject final day of the season surrender at Bristol City as a "slur on my managerial ability." Phil had done his utmost to keep the team up against almost insuperable odds. "It took me a long time for my wounds to heal," he later said. "I had never experienced the disappointment of the sack and it was the most hurtful thing that ever happened to me." A desperately sad and cruel end to his managerial career.

Eight players received free transfers, including the experienced Kevin Godfrey, Alan Dickens, Kenny Sansom and Wilf Rostron. Bob was left twisting in the wind, spending the early part of the summer prevaricating, trying to decide what he wanted to do next. With a year left on his contract, in his heart he still thought he could make a contribution to a concerted promotion push from Division Two, but his head – and the rest of his body – was telling him it was time to call it a day.

"I had been playing professionally for 15 years now, and at 35 I had certainly had a good innings. My left knee, as was generally the case, improved with rest, strengthening exercises and the healing effects of the sun on it, but it was never going to be strong enough to allow me to play every week. David Webb, who I had watched play at Chelsea back in the 70s when he had been one of my heroes, was appointed as Brentford's new manager and I thought that I would simply wait and see what plans he might have in store for me."

"I spoke to my brother-in-law, Ian Bolton, who got straight to the point and gave me some excellent advice. 'You'll have to be very careful as you've got a year's money and the last instalment of your signing-on fee to protect, with no guarantee of any money coming in after you stop playing. Look at it from David Webb's perspective; he's almost certainly been asked to cut costs and what do you think he sees when he looks at you? A 35-year-old with a bad knee who is never fully fit. Someone he can't rely on, who has barely played for the club over the last couple of seasons. What's more, you are also one of the top earners. It doesn't take a genius to realise what he will want to do. He will be targeting you.' What

Ian told me was a real eye-opener and shook me out of my complacency. It helped prepare me for a bumpy ride when Webb finally got round to speaking to me."

"Eventually the call I was dreading came from the club secretary, Polly Kates, 'David Webb would like to see you.' I thought that our meeting would be about as pleasant as having root canal treatment, and I wasn't far wrong. This was the first time I had ever met Webb and he soon dispensed with any pleasantries. He shook hands with me, lounged back in his chair, looked me in the eye and then let fly. 'Well, you're not fit, I don't think you'll ever be able to play for me. You've got all this money coming to you and we need to sort it out, come to an agreement and get you off the wage bill.' I was taken aback by his bluntness and I found him very intimidating, a really nasty piece of work, and I felt that he was trying to bully me. I finally blurted out, 'I have still got a year left on my contract here,' but he wasn't interested in what I had to say. 'We will give you £18,000 in full and final settlement of everything that you are owed. Oh, and if you decide to stay I will make it as difficult as I can for you. You will find yourself running around the track on your own every day. Your life will be hell here. Now go home and think about it.' Although I suspected what was coming, and knew that it was just business as he was simply doing his job, the way Webb handled the meeting still shocked me. I contrasted his attitude and approach with that of Harry Bassett who, even when he was releasing a player, always managed to get his desired message over loud and clear yet still treated him with dignity and respect. Here I'd been made to feel that I was a piece of garbage being disposed of, and none too gently at that."

"I was talking things over at home with Christine when Webb rang me that very same afternoon. 'Have you made your mind up yet?' I lost it with him. 'We only spoke this morning and I told you I would have to go away and think about it and talk to my wife. This is the end of my career that I am talking about and now you are pressing me for an instant decision!' Webb, again, didn't listen to me. 'Come in tomorrow and take the money that I offered you.' I felt as if I had been beaten up, as perhaps, verbally, I had. I was owed about £25,000 on my contract as well as the final third of my signing-on fee, or around £37,000 in total, and three post-dated cheques totalling £18,000 did not appear to be a particularly attractive offer, but the fight had gone out of me and what else could I do? I still felt a bit embarrassed at having been paid so well for playing so little and I think that this also clouded my judgement. I saw little point in haggling with Webb, who obviously did not want me at the club, and the prospect of training on my own was horrendous."

"Webb did the same a few years later to Paul Davis," an experienced player whose much-heralded move from Arsenal turned sour very quickly. "He too was eventually forced out by Webb. As I saw him trudging around the track on his own, a pleasant, unassuming man and a good professional, I thought to myself that he was being treated outrageously and he should just take the money on offer and go, like I did. I accepted the offer, put the phone down and burst into tears."

"Christine and I drove in together to Griffin Park the next morning as we had arranged a weekend in Portsmouth, and that was probably the worst day of my career. Everything I had achieved seemed so distant and a million miles away from where I was now. My envelope had been left for me at the ground with three post-dated cheques inside. That was it; that was my farewell to professional football after 15 years and over 450 appearances. No-one to greet me, no handshakes, no speeches, no thanks, no goodbyes, no messages of appreciation, no applause, no rousing choruses of 'OOH-AAH BOB BOOKAH!' It all ended with a whimper. What a let-down and total anti-climax. It was not what I had envisaged whenever I had thought about how my career would end, and I could not help contrasting it with my farewell at Bramall Lane. That is the reality of football when your time is up. You just have to try and get over it as well as you can and get on with your life, which is far easier said than done."

On the long and mostly silent drive to the south coast, Bob thought about Ian Bolton and reflected upon the similarities when their careers came to a shuddering halt. Nothing had gone right for Bolton at Griffin Park after joining in 1983; he never looked like fulfilling the fans' high expectations for a player with such a successful track record. His spell turned into a nightmare.

Bolton recalls that difficult time. "Fred Callaghan was sacked soon after I arrived and his replacement, Frank McLintock, one of my heroes from his time at Leicester, didn't fancy me as a player. I stayed until the end of the 1983/84 season and they offered to pay up my contract. That was a huge decision for me and I can remember driving back down the M1 to Watford after picking up my final cheque from Martin Lange, and it suddenly hit me, 'What the hell am I going to do now? Nobody is going to pay me to be Ian Bolton the ex-footballer, I am now in the real world.' I really struggled initially but managed to combine playing football part-time with finding a new career outside the game, which was tough, as I had left school at 15 years of age without any qualifications. Thank God I had my wife, Tina, behind me. She worked in a bank, was very level-headed and was earning far more than me. She was a wonderful support to me. It took me four years to learn how to cope with no longer playing football. I got a job selling Ford motor cars but was made redundant after nine months. Then I became an assistant site manager on a building site and I also worked in football on the commercial side before I saw a salesman's job in Bedfordshire, which I fancied. It went well and three years later I was made sales manager and then moved to a sales job selling industrial doors in Watford. The owner was a huge Watford supporter and I had been his favourite player. It took me a while but eventually I fell on my feet. One minute you are top of the world and next, you have gone from the limelight and returned to obscurity. It was a very tough transition and it isn't something you think about when you are a teenager setting out in the world of football. At least I was able to empathise with Bob, give him support, and be the sounding board he so desperately needed, as I had gone through an identical situation and experienced the same feelings of loss, confusion, emptiness and despair that he did."

While he was playing, nobody ever spoke to Bob about how tough life might be once he had retired from football. Like so many of his contemporaries, he was pretty much left to fend for himself. He is grateful to have had Christine and Ian to help him cope with the situation he now faced. Many others in a similar position were not so fortunate.

*The Football League Paper's Where Are They Now* column features a grainy black and white team photograph dating back up to 40 years or so each week, providing an update on what the players have been getting up to since they retired. Some – a very small minority – remain household names, predominantly as managers and coaches, but the overwhelming majority have faded away into relative obscurity, their glory days long passed, working in a variety of humdrum or mundane jobs.

A worrying number have also passed away. I find it hard to realise or accept that a gnarled veteran, in his early 30s when I first started watching the game 50 years ago, is now in his dotage – or worse.

How do retired footballers cope with being out of the spotlight, no longer a global, national or local hero? They have to adapt to the dull and prosaic reality of managing their own affairs, making their own travel arrangements, finding alternative employment, adjusting to a massive reduction in their earnings and even looking after their passport, rather than having it held for safe keeping by their club.

# OOH-AAH: THE BOB BOOKER STORY

Retired footballers have on average, around 16,000 days to fill from the time of their retirement until their death – and it is not surprising that many of them find this transition difficult, if not impossible to manage. Many fall upon hard times. The loss of their former fame, glory, stature, even sense of purpose can be drastic and catastrophic: over 150 ex-footballers have ended up in prison, predominately for drug offences. Others suffer from mental health issues and bankruptcy. Divorce is rife, with a third of all footballers ending their marriage within a year of hanging up their boots. Tragically, suicide is all too common.

An exceptional book by writer and stand-up comedian Alan Gernon, *Retired*, is certainly not a barrel of laughs, providing a disturbing analysis of the never-ending variety of troubles and problems that footballers can face once they stop playing. It details what can and does happen to them, and what support and help is available to them when things begin to go wrong as they struggle to readjust to normal life.

Some of the statistics are mind blowing. Research by XPRO, a charity set up to help, support and advise former professional footballers, highlights the following:

- There are 60,000 former players living in the UK and Ireland
- Two out of every five Premier League players, who earn an average of £42,000 per week, face the threat of bankruptcy within five years of ending their career
- Eighty percent of retired players will suffer from osteoarthritis

World players' union FIFPro revealed that 35% of former players faced problems with depression and anxiety, particularly if they had suffered serious injuries during their playing career, more than double the figure for the general population.

Ian Bolton and Bob found it extremely hard to emerge relatively unscathed from what Niall Quinn has so memorably described as "an adults' playground," when adapting to the real world.

Bob felt lost without the daily routine of training, quickly sinking into depression. Initially, he spent much time lying on his bed staring at the walls, and became difficult to live with. The only respite he had was when he took Bruno out for long walks. "There were some dark days ahead. The first Monday without football hit me like a thunderbolt. Christine had gone to work and I was left on my own with nothing to do and nowhere to go and I stayed in bed until lunchtime. Having been a professional footballer since 1978, I now had to face the fact that I was out of work and I must admit there were many days when I felt really down."

"I was also worried about how we were going to cope financially. I had been given three post-dated cheques totalling £18,000 – a tidy amount – but that wasn't going to last forever, particularly when we had a £90,000 mortgage. I needed to keep busy and try and find something to occupy myself with and, thankfully, something turned up fairly quickly. After a few weeks, a good friend of mine, Alan McKane, turned up at the front door. He owned a small cleaning business, which was doing well, and he asked if I wanted to go out for the day and do some work with him. I had nothing else to do and it got me out of the house, so I accepted his offer. It was good to keep busy and get back into a regular working routine and the £50 per day I earned also came in useful."

"The work involved cleaning windows and newly built houses after the builders had finished. I had to be up at the crack of dawn but I was used to that from working in the factory. I was happy to get my hands dirty and I threw myself into the work. I often came across people who recognised me and that was somewhat difficult at times as I saw them giving me a double take. This made me feel uncomfortable and self-conscious, as I worried that they were thinking 'What a comedown,' as I had gone from playing football to being on my hands and knees cleaning floors. I simply understood that I was unemployed and needed to work both for the money and, just as importantly, to keep my sanity."

Bob's knee began to improve. He put out some feelers about playing some local football, soon receiving a call from Harry Manoe, the manager of Harrow Borough, a locally-based Isthmian League team who had just won the Middlesex Senior and Charity cup competitions.

"I knew Harry as he ran a double glazing company. I was sorely tempted to try and play again as I missed football, as well as the dressing room banter, and I thought that my knee could stand up to a few hours of exercise every week. Harry was great and put no pressure on me. He made it quite clear he would love to sign me and that I could train and play whenever I was fit enough. I didn't want to just turn up on a Saturday when players who had been training twice a week were not getting picked because of me, but I said that I would give it a go and see how I coped. Like Brentford and Sheffield United, Harrow Borough also played in red and white stripes, which I took as a good omen, so I said to Harry 'I will play for you as long as you give me a short-sleeved number 4 shirt and a pair of Puma Kings, size 11,' and they were waiting for me when I turned up for training for the first time."

# OOH-AAH: THE BOB BOOKER STORY

"I really enjoyed the football, it reminded me of my Barnet days. I played in midfield and at the back. The standard was good. It was very physical, but I didn't mind that. I didn't manage to train as much as the rest of the squad but I always tried to be there every Tuesday and Thursday night. The players seemed to look up to me and made me feel welcome. It was good to be back playing and that also contributed to my more positive state of mind."

Money was still a problem. Bob took an ex gratia one-off payment of £30,000 from the PFA instead of a pension, using it to pay off some of his mortgage. Harrow paid him about £200 per week, decent money which came in very useful. Combined with Chris's salary and his earnings with McKane, he kept ticking over.

"Alan knew I was a hard worker and he soon approached me with a proposition to become his partner in return for a £10,000 investment into the business. This sounded interesting and I was tempted. I discussed it with Christine but she wasn't sure and told me to be careful. She encouraged me to keep things as they were because something else might come up. We had some very heated discussions as Alan was pressing me for an answer and I was feeling a bit overwhelmed. Christine was adamant about me not parting with the money so eventually I turned the offer down. Alan was not happy and our friendship ended, which was tough as we had known each other for 25 years, but I learned the hard way never to mix business and pleasure."

Bob was now at a loose end, filling some of his time by working for his old friend Russell Hansard for £60 per day. He also decided to see if he could stay in football by using his knowledge and experience to become a coach, obtaining his FA Preliminary Coaching Badge via a 30-hour course spent entirely on the training pitch, apart from a basic examination on the laws of the game. The syllabus was fairly rudimentary and outdated in its scope, failing to include areas such as nutrition, physiology, sports medicine, warm-ups or warm-downs. It was soon to be replaced by the FA Coaching Certificate, but Bob passed, earning the right to coach players without further supervision.

At the end of the 1993/94 season, with Harrow Borough having finished in a solid ninth position, Bob finally decided to hang up his boots, but this time it was on his terms and totally his own decision, making him feel so much better and providing some closure. Soon afterwards, before he had time to consider what his employment options were, football's freemasonry came to his rescue. Bob received a surprise telephone call from Polly Kates at Brentford. "David Webb would like you to come in for a chat." That was more than enough for Bob's antennae to go up, given how his previous conversations with the Brentford manager had gone. This time the discussion would be about the job as youth team manager, which had just become vacant after the departure of Peter Nicholas to a similar role at Crystal Palace. Bob went in for an interview and the job was his. He was back in the game.

# CHAPTER 27
# LEARNING MY TRADE

"I was really surprised to hear that David Webb wanted to meet me as I had not expected to find my way back into the game so quickly," reflects Bob. "I had no formal coaching experience and didn't think that anyone at Brentford even knew that I had obtained my FA Preliminary Coaching Badge, but obviously the news had got around."

Bob later discovered that he had been recommended to Webb by Barry Quin, another of the unsung heroes of the game who spent over two decades working in a variety of roles at the club, predominantly running the Centre of Excellence on a shoestring, even becoming caretaker manager for a brief spell in 2007.

"When I had played at Brentford I had always tried to spare some time after training to pass on my knowledge and offer some tips and practical advice to the youngsters, and perhaps my efforts had been noticed," said Bob. "I also felt that having been a utility player would help me as a coach, as I had a unique insight into the requirements for every position. I spoke to Ian Bolton before I met Webb and he had really encouraged me and filled me with confidence that I could do the job, 'It's a great opportunity for you and you will do just fine. You have excellent organisational skills, you are passionate about the game and can talk to players and deal with their problems and emotions.'" He was right. "I also thought back to my factory days when I had a team of workers to look after and I had to ensure that all their needs were met. It gave me a great grounding and I learned my trade that way. I could see parallels with the task I would face at Brentford if I was offered the job."

The timing of the call was perfect, just as Bob had begun to contemplate what a life without football would mean for him. "Football had dominated my life for over 15 years and initially I would have found it hard to cope without it, but my priority was to provide for my family and I think I would have found work in the building trade. I loved being outdoors and could never have worked in an office. I had a good work ethic and was not driven by money. I would have looked for something which made me happy and was not too stressful, and my unrequited ambition was to work in a zoo." Thankfully, perhaps, for the animals, football came knocking and Bob could not resist its siren call.

"The meeting with David Webb went very well and neither of us mentioned our last uncomfortable encounter. He was friendly and talked as if it was a foregone conclusion that I would take the job, and it really didn't feel like an interview. He did not say a lot. 'I have heard good things about you and know that you have always been a loyal club servant. I want you to start right away and we will pay you £300 per week. You will be the youth team manager, and I will let you get on with the job without interfering, and my assistant manager, Kevin Lock, will help you whenever you need some advice.'" Bob would be in sole charge, under no pressure to win games. "Your remit is to help develop and bring through some kids who will eventually be good enough to play for my first team," continued Webb. "It all sounded very simple and straightforward," says Bob. "I accepted on the spot."

This appointment was made in 1994, when different attitudes prevailed. From today's perspective, it seems horrifying to think how anybody could be given sole charge of a large group of impressionable teenagers in such a cavalier fashion on the basis of a brief, unstructured conversation, without references being taken, positive vetting, Disclosure and Barring Service (DBS) checks and verification. Quite rightly, the situation is totally different today.

As soon as he took over, Bob realised the scope of his role was far broader than he had envisaged. "I worked almost every hour in the day from Monday to Saturday. I would leave home at 5.30 every morning and arrive at Griffin Park within the hour. I then picked up the club transit van, which I am certain was still the same Sherpa Van we had been given for reaching the Freight Rover Trophy Final way back in 1985. I would then drive over Kew Bridge and pick up the first team training kit from the laundry by 7 o'clock. I would bring it back to the ground, sort it out into piles for each player, roll it up and pack it all away into a kit bag together with all the boots which had been cleaned by the YTS players, who arrived at about 8.45am. They would help me load all the kit, boots, footballs, bibs and cones into the van and they would all pile in with me and we would drive to the London Transport Training Ground, which was nearby at Osterley. When we arrived there at 9.45am some of them would then clean the dressing rooms and the van, and the rest would lay out the training kit in the main dressing room, ready for the full-time professionals before they turned up for training at 10am."

"I would then take my lads training, which I generally did on my own, although Barry Quin sometimes came to help me out. Occasionally, first teamers such as Nicky Forster, Bob Taylor and Kevin Dearden would come over after they had finished training and join in with our shooting practice. We would train for a couple of hours and then pick up all the dirty training kit which the first team players had left in their dressing room before they all drove off as quickly as they could at midday. I did leave them bins for their discarded kit but they would generally ignore them and leave everything strewn around the floor. I would supervise the kit and boots being packed into laundry bags and I would then drive back with my squad to Griffin Park. There was no lunch laid on and no thought was given to providing the YTS squad with any nutritional advice, so I can only imagine what they ate." Bob would leave them to clean the boots, driving back to the laundry with all the dirty kit. "The trainees did a thorough job, as they would all receive tips at Christmas from the couple of professional players that they each looked after. Brian Statham was the best tipper and would often give his boot boy £100. Others were not so generous and were the subject of bitter complaints from the YTS boys, who were only earning about £60 per week themselves and needed the tips to help keep their heads above water."

"Once I dropped off the kit I would come back to Griffin Park and check on the youngsters. I would then take them for a 12-minute run around the track surrounding the pitch or make them run up and down the terrace steps. They would all finish for the day at about 3pm. I then did my paperwork in a cubbyhole I shared with Kevin Lock under the main stand and I would not leave until the manager had gone home. David Webb would generally coach the first team once Kevin had done the warm-ups and a few passing drills. He would then go back to Griffin Park before leaving for his home in Southend at about 3.30pm. I would try and leave by 4pm and always got stuck in traffic at Hanger Lane before getting onto the M1, and it was generally around 6pm when I got home, absolutely shattered. I did not receive any expenses or a petrol allowance, so sometimes I would drive the club van home in order to save money."

"The YTS boys trained every day except Thursday, when they were supposed to go to college in Kings Cross in order to take courses in business studies and sports science. Most of them hated going and would do almost anything to avoid doing so as they didn't think that they needed to study. They were all so naïve and were certain that they would make the grade, which really upset me as I knew how few of them would ever make a living out of football. Outstanding prospects such as Marcus Bent were offered professional terms at 17 but they were few and far between, and the majority had a couple of seasons between the ages of 16-18 to prove that they deserved a professional contract. Each year generally no more than a couple of them would be rewarded, and of those, only a mere handful ever played a single game in the Football League. The odds were stacked against them."

Bob did his best to keep their feet firmly on the ground, managing their expectations. Many thought that they had made it when they signed their initial YTS contract, not realising that this was merely the first step on a ladder that the overwhelming majority would fall off long before they reached the summit. "Terry Mitchell was someone that I found particularly frustrating, as he had lots of ability but none of the discipline and dedication needed to make a career for himself. Others seemed to reach a certain level then plateau and stop progressing. Ryan Denys and Dean Clark were both very talented but never trained on, which was a shame. I know that I am old-school but I felt that all the cleaning work they had to do was a necessary part of their education. I thought that it was valuable and toughened them up, helped teach them to respect the senior professionals and not to take anything for granted. I remember that when I was an apprentice in the upholstery factory I had to clean up and make sure that my team had all their tools and equipment. I was a skivvy but it helped me learn my trade and taught me some discipline. Colin Ducass arrived late for his first day on the YTS scheme and walked in as if he owned the place, so I sent him straight back home. I tried to be tough but fair and to teach them values and manners so that even if they never became footballers, ideally they would develop as people."

Each year, Bob inherited a squad of about 15 players, predominantly locally based and living at home. A South Londoner would have been classed as a foreigner; overseas players were unheard of. Brentford's better placed neighbours, Chelsea and Queens Park Rangers, generally picked off the best players. The players ranged in ability. Some, such as Bent and Kevin Rapley and, later in Bob's reign, Michael Dobson and Kevin O'Connor, always looked odds-on to earn a professional contract. They stood out by possessing more natural talent, but also worked hard, demonstrating their hunger to improve throughout their apprenticeship. Others stayed at the same level or could not cope with the standards demanded both on and off the pitch.

Incredibly, Bob was never asked to ensure his youth team played in the same way and shape as the first team, as would surely be the case nowadays. Pattern of play was left entirely to him, generally deploying a 4-

4-2 system, given its success at Sheffield United. It was also the easiest system for his players to learn.

"I also had to deal with all the necessary paperwork and I found this hard as it was something that I had never had to do before. I had to write a log on each player which summarised his progress, and this was discussed and signed off with him every month. I would meet all the parents together at the start of the season and inform them of their son's weekly schedule and ask for their help in keeping the boys on the straight and narrow. I was always available to meet them on an individual basis when required."

Bob made the final decision regarding the future of every YTS player, using Lock as a sounding board before giving the thumbs up or thumbs down. "It was something I always found really hard to do, as in the overwhelming majority of cases it was bad news that I had to impart," he says. "I just tried to be as honest as possible, reinforce their strengths as a footballer but tell them why and where I felt they had fallen short. I would emphasise that I was not infallible and that they should now go out and prove me wrong, although I do not think that anyone ever did. Some were surprised, others accepted it, and many cried when they heard that they were being released. I would always do my utmost to try and fix them up with a local non-league team if they wanted to carry on playing senior football."

The hardest thing for Bob was the sense of isolation, picking things up for himself, with Quin and Lock sparing as much time as their jobs allowed. Bob obtained the services of Neil Mason as his physio, a former YTS goalkeeper who failed to make the grade but returned to the club with the probably unique title of assistant physio/youth team physio/reserve goalkeeper, even sitting on the bench as substitute goalkeeper for the first team early in the 1994/95 season. Mason now runs a successful private practice with his twin brother, Bradley. "We had some goalkeeping problems at the time with Kevin Dearden suspended and Tamer Fernandes suffering from appendicitis," he says. "I came within a whisker of playing on the opening day of the season at Plymouth, but Tamer recovered just in time. Bob Booker was a legend at the club and the young players all responded to him and he gained their instant respect. He was a great character who knew exactly what it took to become a professional footballer and also play for Brentford. He always had a smile on his face but he knew when to flick that competitive switch. He was a joy to be around and I have never heard a bad word about him. Bob was an enormous help to me as a young physio and the YTS boys all learned so much from him."

Always prepared to help and muck in when required, Bob inherited a number of other jobs that nobody else seemed to want to do. A multitasker, he became kitman for every team at the club. He would pack all the first team playing kit and boots on a Friday, laying it out ready in the dressing room at Griffin Park for home games. If they were playing away, he would prepare everything for the physio, Roy Johnson, who would act as kitman on the day. The youth team would kick off at 11am every Saturday. Afterwards, if there was a first team game at Griffin Park, Bob would take over as kitman if he could get there in time.

Bob was never asked for his input on first team affairs. But he picked up many tips from watching Webb and Lock, learning that the key requirement of an assistant manager is to demonstrate loyalty and support to his boss, but also act as a sounding board and query his judgement when necessary. He noted that Webb and Lock worked well together, even if they never socialised. Bob also packed the kit for the reserve team, run by Lock, and whenever possible Bob would go to the matches, which were held in midweek, to provide an extra voice on the bench.

Bob was on a standard contract with a three-month notice period. Nothing was said to him at the end of his first season, nor was there any sort of formal evaluation. He assumed he was still required for the following season, turning up for the first day of pre-season training.

Bob loved his job, but it took a lot out of him. "This was the hardest work I had ever done and the hours and workload were brutal. Sometimes I would even go and watch Barry Quin's centre of excellence teams on a Sunday as I would be inheriting their best players. I did not ask for a pay rise as I was so happy to be working in football. Chris was still working and between us we could get by on our joint salaries but, understandably, she was concerned about the limited amount of time we were spending with each other. We started to drift apart. We would visit her family for lunch most Sundays and I tried to do some bird-watching and see my friends, but I had so little free time."

Continuing in his position throughout Webb's spell as manager of the club, Bob tasted some success at the beginning of the 1996/97 season, when his youth team won the prestigious Royal Mail Cup in Portsmouth. Winning four games in a hectic week-long competition, they beat Bournemouth in the final with a 5-3 win, including two goals from Rapley. Garry Duffy, another promising youngster who never made the grade, was named player of the tournament. "The lads loved it and it gave them all some confidence. The worst thing about the week was driving the squad from London to Portsmouth and back seemingly every day for a week, as we could not afford overnight stays. Even I drew the line at the players sleeping in the transit van."

When Mason moved on, Bob recommended an old friend of his, Kevin Burke, who, in inimitable Brentford style, was hired as groundsman and assistant physiotherapist. All went well for Kevin until a home match against Swansea City in March 1996, when Webb signalled down from the director's box for Paul Abrahams to replace Forster. Burke misunderstood his instruction, taking Lee Harvey off instead. Another substitution was made a few minutes later, with David McGhee coming on for Forster. Webb was furious, sacking Burke immediately after the game, but was forced to eat humble pie and reinstate him when nobody could get into the training ground the next day, as Burke had the only set of keys. Bob, Burke and Lock soon became known as "The Three Amigos."

After narrowly missing out on promotion in 1995 and 1997, everything turned sour the following season with the rump of the Brentford squad being broken up. Martin Lange sold the club to a consortium led by Webb, who became chief executive. He appointed the relatively unknown Eddie May as manager, who brought in the former Chelsea winger Clive Walker as his assistant. Lock became football coordinator, with Bob remaining as youth team manager.

Bob was unsettled by the change in regime. "May and Walker hardly spoke to me in their short stay and never asked me anything. I had very little to do with them. Kevin Lock was also sidelined and he, Kevin Burke and I spent more time working together and often slept at the ground after midweek home games, as by the time we had cleaned the dressing room and packed up the kit it was hardly worth going home."

May and Walker lasted only 15 games before being sacked and replaced by Micky Adams, who had just walked out on Swansea City after a mere 13-day stay, having previously led Fulham to promotion. Bob's ears pricked up at the news, as he remembered Adams playing for Southampton when he had scored twice for Sheffield United in 1991. He wanted to make a good impression on his new boss.

"On his first day he came into the dressing room and introduced himself. 'Hi, I'm the new gaffer and this is Glenn Cockerill, who's my assistant manager. All I want from you is hard work and we will talk properly soon. I don't know you, so just be loyal and we will see how it goes.' I knew that I was on trial as he wanted to check me out and see whether I could be trusted. As he was about to leave, he saw the two camp beds in the corner where Kevin Burke and I intended to sleep that night. 'What are they there for?' 'Well,' I answered, 'you are asking for loyalty and hard work so we will be sleeping over tonight.' From that moment we just hit it off and struck up a good relationship. Every Friday after training I would go to his office and discuss the week's work over a beer."

"I learned so much from Micky. He was a wonderful man manager who inspired loyalty. In a short period of time he revolutionised the club from top to bottom and introduced more discipline. He knew everything that was going on around the football club and was first in and last out every day. I continued to act as kitman at as many first team games as I could, and the big difference was that Micky started to ask me for my opinion, and I felt more wanted and involved. He inherited a mess and eventually we were relegated on the last day of the season, but at least we had a go. He was also far more interested in the youngsters than his predecessors, as he knew that they represented the future of the club, and he accepted the responsibility of informing the YTS players of their fate, which took some of the weight off me."

"By now I had been youth team manager for several years and finally I was beginning to feel that I knew what I was doing. Hopefully I understood when it was time to be stern and when we could all have a laugh together. I would not stand for any bullying or hazing and, thankfully, I was never aware of any abuse or unacceptable behaviour. Although there was the time when Kevin Burke and I came into the dressing room one day after training and told the youth squad that they all needed to have a flu jab. We each had a sterilised needle and we bent them over the table and injected them all in the buttock and then put a plaster on them. Once we had finished we, came clean and, thankfully, they all seemed to find it amusing. But I am not proud of what we did and it is something you would not even contemplate doing today – and rightly so."

"I did not go on any coaching courses while I was working at Brentford, nor did I apply for any jobs as, initially, I was happy where I was. I was trying to teach my charges to become better footballers and men and ideally improve them through my personal example. They all seemed to respond and I never heard any complaints. I also received lots of letters from parents thanking me for what I had done for their son even if he had been released. I tried to be as approachable as possible and help them with their problems. Some boys needed an arm around them, others needed to be pushed – the key was realising who needed what."

Relegation was followed by another sale of the club, this time to Ron Noades, who paid £750,000 for Webb's shares. Adams was sacked unceremoniously, with Lock and Cockerill also leaving the club. Noades became owner, chairman and manager, bringing in his coaching "Dream Team" of Ray Lewington, Terry Bullivant and Brian Sparrow.

"I was really sorry to see Micky Adams go as he had done an excellent job in difficult circumstances," says Bob. "He left with his mini fridge under his arm and his head held high, and he spoke to me on his way out, 'You are totally dedicated to your job and are really good to have around the place. I am going to keep my eye on you, as I like the way you work.' That made me feel very good about myself and also gave me some food for thought, as I knew that most jobs in football are given to friends and previous work contacts."

Bob thought that he would also be on the way out but his situation was helped by an act of kindness by Webb who, just before he sold out to Noades, put Bob on a one-year rolling contract, offering a semblance of security. Bob's salary had by now crept up to £350 per week, and Adams had also arranged for him to receive 50% of the first team bonus, which came in extremely handy, particularly when the results started to improve in the new season.

As quickly as things had improved for Bob under Micky Adams, they deteriorated under Noades, who eased him out of any first team responsibilities apart from handling the kit. He now had to report to Geoff Taylor, his former assistant manager at Sheffield United, who became director of youth football.

"I was still called youth team manager but in reality Geoff ran things, picked the team and took the training. Geoff was an excellent coach and I learned a lot from him. He treated me very well and kept encouraging me, but after four seasons in sole charge, it felt like a demotion to me. I just did the running around. It was a difficult situation for both of us but given the strength of our relationship, we handled it as professionally as we could. All the other coaches had company cars apart from me. Ron Noades barely talked to me and I wonder if he even knew who I was. Brentford won the Division Three title at the first time of asking and I went to our last game at Cambridge, but I was just a gofer and did not feel the slightest part of it."

"I know that they wanted to get rid of me but I was protected by my rolling contract and decided to sit tight. I had a couple of years in limbo and really did not enjoy myself, as I was well down the pecking order and pretty much treading water. Finally, my luck changed and at the beginning of October 2000, I received a totally unexpected telephone call that was to change my life. 'Hi, Bob, it's Micky Adams. How do you feel about coming to join me at Brighton?' 'What, as youth team manager?' 'No, as my assistant manager. Alan Cork has decided to join Bobby Gould at Cardiff City and I want you to replace him.' I almost asked him to repeat what he had just said as I really couldn't believe what I had heard." Bob considered it a huge step up. "We had kept in touch since he had left Brentford and I was delighted for him when he had become Brighton's manager in April 1999. This came as a real surprise to me, particularly as I knew how close Micky was to Alan Cork. 'When do you want me to start?' 'Can you leave straight away as we need to talk about your contract and I want to introduce you to the chairman?' was his response. I was delighted that someone believed in me and was willing to offer me such an incredible opportunity. I told him I would have to sort things out with Brentford, but I would come down as quickly as possible."

"I told Geoff Taylor straight away and he was delighted for me. I then took huge delight in telling Brentford's managing director, Gary Hargraves, what had happened: 'I've just been approached by Brighton.' 'As youth team manager?' 'No, as assistant manager to Micky Adams.' He looked surprised when he heard this. 'You won't mind if I leave today as I need to go down there in order to sort out my company car, company credit card, company mobile phone and my expense allowance?' It gave me great pleasure to say those words to him given how much I had been forced to struggle in order to make ends meet at Brentford. Gary had the good grace to wish me luck, and that was that; I was on my way to Brighton after six years coaching at Griffin Park."

"Christine was pleased as she knew that I was in a rut, but she was worried about all the extra travelling. I went down to Brighton on the Monday and met Micky Adams and Dick Knight at Topolino's restaurant in Hove, which I renamed Sackolino's after Dick fired me there several years later."

Topolino's was a Brighton institution which finally closed in 2014 after 28 years. It managed to outlast even Bob. Local newspaper *The Argus* remarked, "It was said that if Mr Knight invited you for dinner at the Hove restaurant, it was not worth ordering dessert – you would be out of a job and out the door before long." Bob can attest to that sentiment.

"I was offered a one-year rolling contract for £500 per week, a company car, a company credit card (which used to bounce) and a full share of the first team bonus. This was an enormous increase on what I had been earning at Brentford, and I was delighted to accept. The only problem at this meeting was trying to get a word in, as Dick Knight dominated the conversation, wreathed in a cloud of cigarette smoke. He was so knowledgeable and enthusiastic and totally sold me on his vision for the club, with the expectation of a new stadium to be opened in Falmer within a couple of years, at which point Micky Adams, who knew far more than me, visibly rolled his eyes. Dick asked me about my background and my footballing philosophy, which was the first time I had ever heard that word used in a footballing context. We seemed to get on, it was a good meeting and everything was agreed."

The youth team manager was now an assistant manager – unsure whether to be excited or terrified at the prospect.

# CHAPTER 28
# THE SEAGULLS

Bob's knowledge of Brighton & Hove Albion prior to his appointment was sketchy in the extreme.

"I knew hardly anything about the club and it was not really on my radar," he admits. "The phone call from Micky Adams offering me the Brighton job came completely out of the blue, like so many of the opportunities I received throughout my career. Beyond knowing that Brighton were in the Third Division, I was totally ignorant about their recent traumatic history and the trials and tribulations they had gone through in order to survive. At that time I wasn't a great one for watching football apart from *Match of the Day*, and had little knowledge of other teams and players, but I knew that this would have to change to meet the demands of my new job. My ignorance was commonplace within the game as there wasn't much television and media coverage in those days of the lower divisions, and footballers are notorious for remaining within their own little bubble and not bothering with anything that does not directly concern them. I was soon to learn that Micky Adams had signed several players I knew very well from their Brentford days, but again, that was news to me at the time, as footballers never stay in touch. At the end of the season they invariably say 'See you soon' to all their teammates, but the next time they meet up is generally at the start of pre-season training. When someone is transferred they always promise to keep in touch, but again, it almost never happens. I had remained in contact with very few players from either my Brentford or Sheffield United days, so I had no idea who was at Brighton at the time I joined."

"The last time I had played against Brighton was way back in the 1989/90 season when I was at Sheffield United. I recall scoring in both games, a seesaw 5-4 early season win at Bramall Lane and then a vital equaliser in the return match. The Goldstone was a proper old-school, traditional stadium, and my main memory of playing there was of the away dressing room and having to go gingerly down the steps into what was probably the biggest and deepest plunge bath I had ever encountered. You had to be very careful not to slip and fall in. I used to warn Mark Todd, the smallest player in our team, that he needed to wear a rubber ring and tread water or run the risk of disappearing into the murky waters and never being seen again."

"In the days before the Health and Safety lobby oversaw the demise of the plunge bath, there would be lots of farting, drinking and smoking going on and you would all happily lie there together, excitedly chatting and luxuriating after a good result and letting the stresses, aches and strains of the afternoon's exertions wash off you. Or, conversely, there would initially be a complete silence after a defeat beyond the lapping of the water, and you would just be waiting for someone to start bitching and moaning and allocating blame. Somehow things never seemed the same after the move towards single baths and showers."

Dick Knight – and, to a lesser extent, Micky Adams – gave Bob an instant update and history lesson regarding the club during their initial lunch meeting at Topolino's in October 2000, making Bob realise just how tenuous the club's situation was; how close they had come to oblivion.

Brighton & Hove Albion FC were slowly coming off life support after barely surviving a horrendous few years which saw the incomprehensible and widely condemned sale of its beloved Goldstone Ground come about thanks to a fifth column from within the club, led by the chairman, Bill Archer. Albion only stayed in the Football League thanks to Robbie Reinelt's second half equaliser in a winner (or, fortunately for the Seagulls, non-loser) takes all final day relegation clash at Hereford on 3rd May 1997.

The influence of newly appointed manager Steve Gritt, who accepted the poisoned chalice, in conjunction with the positivity engendered by the passion and organisation of a supporter base that would not allow the rug to be pulled out from underneath their beloved Seagulls, heralded the start of an unbeaten run of 12 home matches which, ironically, turned the soon-to-be-abandoned Goldstone Ground into a fortress. But despite their eventual survival, this also represented the lowest ebb of a club with a rich and proud history.

Much of their existence since the Second World War had seen Albion languish in the third tier of the Football League, with the fans enjoying the talent of the odd star player on his way up such as Johnny McNichol, later to win the First Division Championship with Chelsea, and future England international Jimmy Langley. The goals of Adrian Thorne finally saw Second Division football achieved in 1958, but Albion's eventual Division Three South Championship triumph, by a narrow two-point margin over their nearest challengers, Brentford, was a tainted one, with rumours of match fixing and of Watford lying down before the crucial final game of the season which saw Albion triumph 6-0. Their progress could not be sustained and, despite the efforts of prolific goalscorer Bill Curry, Albion fell into the bottom division in 1963. The arrival the following year of former Spurs double winner and England international centre-forward Bobby Smith, perhaps the biggest name ever to sign for the club, came out of the blue, and his 19 goals, aided and abetted by the likes of Jack Smith, Jimmy Collins, Dave Turner and Jack Bertolini, saw the Fourth Division Championship won and the start of better times for the club, culminating in promotion to the First Division in 1979.

Albion remained in the top division for four years, buttressed and inspired as they were by the talent of two of the club's greatest ever players – Mark Lawrenson, who left for Liverpool in 1981, and goal machine Peter Ward, who Bob had encountered in his initial trial for Brentford. FA Cup glory was so nearly theirs in 1983, but Gordon Smith's last-gasp miss let Manchester United off the hook and manager Jimmy Melia was denied a Wembley victory jig in his famous white shoes. Smith has been mocked and vilified for nearly 35 years, but it is often forgotten that it was his perfectly-placed header that gave Albion the lead. The season would end with a relegation and cup final defeat double.

"Some Albion fans see that defeat and relegation as the beginning of a decline – or at least a malaise – which directly led to the sorry state the club found itself in by the mid-1990s," says journalist and Albion fan Ben Miller. "Two years after a 3-1 playoff final defeat against Notts County denied the club a return to Division One, only the last-gasp sale of goalkeeper Mark Beeney to Leeds United staved off a winding up order. But the saga was about to worsen beyond belief, as the club fell into the clutches of northern DIY mogul Bill Archer. Dick Knight, the advertising guru and lifelong Albion fan who had to sit through years of poisonous negotiations in order to eventually wrestle the club away from him, succinctly described Archer as 'a chancer,' emphasised by the princely sum of £56.25 which he paid to become the chairman of a club in dire straits. His henchman and acolyte, local politician David Bellotti, swiftly became despised by the fans for his petty-minded banning orders and seemingly endless stream of inventions about the way the club was being run and its future. Paul Samrah, a staunch Albion fan, fortuitously noticed that the club's Articles of Association had been brazenly altered so that any profit from the sale of the ground could legally go into the pockets of the owners. When Bellotti was confronted in his office by fanzine editor and undertaker Ian Hart about this amendment, his complexion is said to have gone as white as a goalpost, even if, typically, he denied the change had anything to do with the sale of the Goldstone Ground, which Archer and Bellotti had insisted was the only way to clear the club's considerable debts."

They had, predictably, exaggerated the club's predicament, continues Miller. "While it owed considerable sums to debtors, the decision to sell the ground – a move clearly being made for the benefit of the club's predatory owners, rather than the books – was a horrific idea which would bring almost a century of football opposite Hove Park to an abrupt, unnecessary and heart-breaking end. The Goldstone was part of Sussex's fabric, a fabulous old place, which had witnessed the Albion as champions of England in 1910 when as Southern League Champions they then beat Football League winners Aston Villa in the Charity Shield, England Under-21 matches, David Beckham's debut and even a performance by Slade. It had a magnificent terrace in the North Stand, which reverberated and throbbed with passion on match days, as well as the old Chicken Run, scene of many a run-in with visiting fans throughout the decades."

This was a club and ground loved by its local community, and the suggestion that the Goldstone would be demolished for reasons which could at best be described as dubious caused uproar, protests and, the season after a last-minute decision by the board to stay for one more year, an incredible Fans United event. 14,000 supporters from around the world converged on a home game against Hartlepool to show solidarity with Albion supporters and spur the team on to a 5-0 win – a vital result given that the team was languishing several points from safety at the bottom of Division Three.

Some clubs can withstand the trauma of relegation from the Football League, licking their wounds, cutting their cloth, regenerating and eventually coming back even stronger, as has been the case with Lincoln City in the 2016/17 season. At worst, stabilisation within the non-league pyramid is usually possible. Brighton's situation was entirely different and it is more than likely that Albion would have gone out of existence had journeyman striker Robbie Reinelt not carved his name in Sussex folklore by equalising at Hereford on the final day of the 1996/97 season, thus condemning the home team to the relegation trapdoor and oblivion. The club was on its last legs, penniless, holed below the waterline, and would surely have had little or no hope of either survival or recovery.

Miller outlines how the fans responded, "The NIMBY brigade had their moments in the torrent of council meetings and letter-writing campaigns that followed, but Albion fans always faced the battle and responded persuasively and with good humour. Characteristically determined and witty, supporters had to continuously use both of those qualities to orchestrate protests and drag the club out of the hands of the businessmen who shamelessly sought to destroy it. Once Knight had control of the club, bright green t-shirts were a signature of the campaign to bring the club back to a temporary home in Brighton, and John Prescott, the then-deputy prime minister who was ultimately responsible for a decision over the club's proposed permanent home at Falmer, received sacks full of Valentine's Day cards from Albion fans at his constituency office in Hull."

The club even survived a dreadful two-year exile to Gillingham and a traumatic 23rd place finish in 1998, with relegation only averted by the fortunate presence of a quite appalling Doncaster Rovers team that lost 34 times that season and were somehow even worse than Brighton. The second season in Kent saw a slight improvement under former Brighton legend Brian Horton, but his departure to Port Vale presaged a slump, which his successor, Jeff Wood, was unable to reverse. A disastrous run of nine defeats in ten games again placed Albion's Football League status in jeopardy and Dick Knight was forced into yet another managerial change, which this time paid dividends.

Micky Adams was an unpolished managerial gem. He was his own man who had fallen out with a couple of egotistical chairmen at Fulham and Brentford and walked out of a job at Swansea after a mere 13 days when the goalposts were changed over promised transfer funds. He needed and deserved a chairman who would believe in him, and found one in Knight. The boost of his arrival ensured that survival was achieved with a 17th place finish.

Money was tight with what little income there was, given the meagre gate receipts from playing at Priestfield Stadium for two seasons, channelled into the ongoing and seemingly never-ending political struggle to obtain a new stadium within the city. The club relied upon the generosity of its directors, fan donations, the begging bowl and, later, even the proceeds of a Coca-Cola fans' competition to subsidise the signing of a player in Colin Kazim-Richards, an unpredictable and temperamental striker who became known as the "Coca-Cola Kid." Gary Hart was a rare cash purchase from Stansted who cost the vast sum of £1,000 plus a set of tracksuits (just as Bob had done back in 1978), repaying that sum many times over with 13 years of dedicated service.

The summer of 1999 finally saw good news for the club, with the tireless efforts of the supporters rewarded with the granting of planning permission for a temporary home ground at Withdean Stadium, an athletics venue which was, with great difficulty, converted into a rickety football stadium that was barely fit for purpose. Crowds were likely to increase significantly over the minuscule numbers of heroes who had braved the ridiculous three hour and 150 mile *schlep* to Gillingham and back, although much of the increased revenue would have to be earmarked for the significant transportation and infrastructure costs required to meet the stringent conditions imposed upon the club in order for it to be allowed to return to the city.

Adams was given some funds to strengthen a squad that was patently unfit for purpose. He generally relied upon the tried and tested – experienced players who he knew well and could rely upon and trust, and he spent wisely on the likes of Paul Watson, Charlie Oatway and Paul Rogers. The revamped squad celebrated its long-overdue return to Brighton with a confidence-boosting 6-0 mauling of Mansfield Town. The team took time to gel, needing the goals of Bobby Zamora, an inspired loan signing from Bristol Rovers, to galvanise the Seagulls to an unbeaten run of 14 matches and an eventual 11th place finish.

Most fans were just happy to be able to watch their team play in their own city again, even in such cramped and uncomfortable surroundings, but expectations were rising and it was hoped that the 2000/2001 season would see Adams and his sidekick, Alan Cork, lead the team to promotion, particularly as even more players arrived, including the skilful but woefully inconsistent Paul Brooker. The talismanic Zamora was signed for an eye-watering £100,000 fee. Adams favoured an aggressive brand of high-tempo and often direct football, which did not always find favour with either the chairman or some of the supporters, who preferred a more measured approach. But the early signs and results were promising. The unexpected departure of Adams's close friend and confidant, Cork to Cardiff, where he eventually took over as manager from Bobby Gould, threatened to derail the promotion bid, and it was crucial that Micky Adams found an immediate replacement who was on the same wavelength as him and could act as his sounding board. Luckily, he knew just where to look.

# CHAPTER 29
# MICKY ADAMS (PART 1)

Managers tend to surround themselves with coaches that they know they can trust and rely on. Given his recent experiences, Brighton's Micky Adams was understandably more determined than most to work with someone who could watch his back. Mohamed Al-Fayed had peremptorily dismissed him at Fulham just four months into a new five-year contract in favour of the higher profile Kevin Keegan, shortly after Adams had won both promotion and the Third Division manager of the season award. He then lasted less than a fortnight at Swansea City, "I had 13 days there which was pretty controversial at the time," he explained to the *Daily Telegraph*. "I got promised 'x' amount of pounds for the squad but the money never materialised and I told them they could look for another manager. I walked out on principle."

In 1959, Ian Fleming wrote in *Goldfinger*, "Once is happenstance. Twice is coincidence. The third time it's enemy action." Adams must have nodded his head in appreciation at the astuteness of this aphorism when his next managerial job, at Brentford, also ended quickly and badly. He inherited a squad that had been denuded of its best players, and now largely comprised of low quality, cut-price nonentities. Assisted by his former Southampton teammate, Rod Stewart lookalike Glenn Cockerill, who at 38 was comfortably the best player in the team, he brought in a series of experienced campaigners. But for all his energy and enthusiasm, the Bees were relegated on the final day of the season.

Adams felt that he had done a good job in difficult circumstances. "I signed loyal players who I knew and trusted and I took them around with me. We did not lose too many games but we could not score and it was the draws that killed us." David Webb then sold the club to Ron Noades, who immediately sacked Adams and appointed himself manager. Thus ended a turbulent year in which he had lost three jobs. No wonder he had trust issues and valued loyalty above all other virtues.

Adams took a temporary backseat, becoming assistant manager at Nottingham Forest before finding himself at a loose end following the dismissal of Dave Bassett in January 1999. Adams had impressed Dick

Knight with his knowledge and passion for the game when they met at a reserve match. He was Knight's only candidate to replace Jeff Wood.

Adams brought his friend Alan Cork with him as his assistant, building a tough, gritty and experienced squad together in the image of their manager, perfectly equipped to compete and win the physical battles of the Third Division, but also containing some creative players. Most importantly, most of them were known quantities: Paul Watson, Charlie Oatway, Danny Cullip, Darren Freeman, Warren Aspinall and Paul Brooker had played for Adams at either Fulham or Brentford – three of them had played for both clubs. Adams had built up an extensive knowledge of players and recruited other strong characters in Richard Carpenter, Paul Rogers, Michel Kuipers, Nathan Jones and Andy Crosby, who would all play significant roles over the coming seasons.

It is all very well sharing goals throughout the team, but any successful side needs a regular goalscorer. Lee Steele was a poacher with little physical presence, but Bobby Zamora was the real deal; skilful, quick, elegant and deadly. Adams recalls how he arrived at the club, "We were going through an indifferent spell and struggling for a big centre forward. David Cameron wasn't up to it and we had been outbid by Brentford for Lorenzo Pinamonte, so I called Ian Holloway at Bristol Rovers, who told me, 'I have got a young lad who's been on loan at Bath City. He's only 19 and totally raw, but he has scored a few goals for them.' I was not totally convinced but we were desperate and the clincher was when Ian told me he was only earning £140 per week, so I said 'Send him down.' The rest is history."

By the time of Cork's departure in September 2000, it was clear that Brighton were mounting a serious promotion challenge. Maintaining momentum was crucial. Cork felt that the opportunity to manage Cardiff City was too good to pass up. Having been Adams's assistant at three clubs, it was time for him to become a manager in his own right.

Adams had inherited Bob as his youth team manager when he had taken over at Brentford in 1997. Bob was quick to remind him of the two goals he had scored for Sheffield United against Adams's Southampton back in 1991, but his new boss purported to have no memory of that feat. Adams recalls that first conversation, "I looked him straight in the eye and told him that I didn't know him but I would give him a chance and see if he was hard working and loyal, and if so we would be fine. He pointed out the camp bed in the corner of the dressing room and told me he was so committed that he would be sleeping there that night. I burst out laughing and we soon became great friends. I knew that we would work well together."

Adams had promised to keep his eye on Bob when he left Brentford, knowing exactly who he wanted as Cork's replacement at Brighton, "Corky's departure surprised me as he had always seemed happy as a number two. I was disappointed, but Bob Booker was my immediate choice to replace him. We had stayed in touch and I knew he was unhappy at Brentford. He jumped at the chance to join me at Brighton and it was the best decision I ever made."

Dick Knight interviewed Bob, who accepted the job before he had seen Withdean Stadium or the training ground at the University of Sussex. Smiling at the memory, Bob recalls that he was always instructed to take potential new signings for a cup of tea at The Grand Hotel, where they could see Brighton at its best. Under no circumstances was he to show them the stadium before their signature was safely on the contract.

Dick Knight had vaguely heard of Bob from his time at Sheffield United. "Alan Cork was a good coach and would be hard to replace and when Micky made it clear that he wanted to hire Bob I backed his judgement. He made an excellent impression on me when we met at Topolino's. Bob was very intelligent and had a lovely sense of humour and it was clear that he and Micky were on the same wavelength."

Bob visited the training ground after lunch, which he greeted with a rueful smile, "Dick Knight loved the sound of his own voice but he was a fantastic chairman who knew his stuff. He made it clear to me that the club was being run on a shoestring and initially I was horrified when I saw the training ground. The facilities were awful, the players were spread over a number of small dressing rooms, the pitches were bumpy and we could only train whenever the university allowed us. Sometimes we had to train on rugby pitches, which made shooting practice interesting, or we would use the AstroTurf pitch, which took its toll on players' knees. At least they had to clean their own kit and boots, so that would not be my responsibility, as it had been at Brentford. Micky did his best to create an 'us against the world' atmosphere and ensured that the players made the best of things. I had seen far worse so I just got on with my job."

"Next we were off to Withdean Stadium, which was a total shambles. It was a small, decrepit athletics stadium with a football pitch surrounded by a running track. There were two uncovered stands, one holding 1,800 fans and the South Stand which contained 4,500 temporary seats installed on a grass bank. It held less than 7,000 fans overall, and there was no real atmosphere there, but we turned it into a fortress. The dressing room was a portakabin with a crooked floor and a leaking roof. There was a tiny office in the home dressing room, separated from the players, where Micky and I would go at half-time if the players were arguing with each other and we would let them sort things out for themselves."

"Steve Winterburn, the groundsman, worked on his own with only a lawnmower, tractor, fork and a rake. No wonder the pitch was awful. There were no sprinklers or sheets to protect the pitch, which was either flooded or too dry. If a match was in doubt there would be a general SOS and everyone would turn up with mops and try to get the pitch into playable condition."

This was turning into a long first day, ending with Bob getting his first sight of some of the players in a reserve game at Worthing against Oxford United.

Bob returned home very late that night, exhausted but exhilarated at the challenge he faced. Initially, he commuted every day from Watford, leaving at around 5.30am and arriving at Adams's rented house in Burgess Hill before 7 o'clock to bring his new boss a cup of tea and the newspapers. Bob would get to the training ground at about 9 o'clock, an hour before the players.

The physio, Malcolm Stuart, introduced himself to Bob by covering his telephone with cling film on his first full day. When he finally managed to remove it he received a mysterious call purporting to come from the Samaritans, "You're going to need us in this job."

"The long-serving kitman, Jock Riddell, had just left and was soon replaced by John Keeley, who acted as kitman and goalkeeping coach – it was just like being back at Brentford. Dear old Jock used to sell antique furniture at car boot sales and the first time I went into the kit room at the training ground the playing strip was buried under a pile of his unsold stock. He died in 2002 and we all went to his funeral at the Downs Crematorium. Just as we carried the coffin inside, a seagull landed on the roof and we all burst into tears."

Bob shared an office at the training ground with Micky; Malcolm Hinshelwood, Dean Wilkins and Vic Bragg from the youth section all crowded in next door. Dean White also arrived at the same time as Bob as reserve team coach and chief scout.

Bob fretted all the way to Brighton. Despite all the frenzied activity of the previous day, neither Knight nor Adams had outlined his responsibilities, but he had no time to think as he was thrown in at the deep end on his first day with the players. Adams told him to run the session, starting with a warm-up, followed by some ball work and passing drills. He said he would come out and join him afterwards. Bob knew that he was being tested and wondered if Adams knew that this was the first time he had ever taken a session for professionals rather than the youth team.

"I was worried about how the players would take to me and whether they would make my life difficult. I already knew some of them from their time at Brentford and had played with Darren Carr at Sheffield United, but I wasn't particularly close to any of them."

Bob had particular concerns about one player. "I had clashed with Warren Aspinall several times in his Wigan days and he had developed a reputation for being difficult and upsetting people. How would a wily old pro like him react to me telling him what to do? I was his assistant manager now and I needed to earn his respect. Micky introduced me to the players and I could see Warren looking at me with an enigmatic grin on his face. I had no idea what he was thinking. I tried to put him out of my mind and I got them into a circle and said, 'Right lads, I'm Bob Booker and I'm taking over from Alan Cork' and went straight into the session, which was quite nerve-racking as I was winging it. The players tested me straight away and tried to wind me up with comments like, 'That's not how Corky did it,' but I gave it right back to them: 'He's gone, I'm here now and I am not Corky! I'm doing it my way!' Thankfully the players responded and seemed to enjoy the session. That was a crucial milestone for me as if things had gone differently I could have lost control of the squad and been finished before I had even started. I learned that it isn't necessary for every player to like you as long as they respect you."

Former teammate Darren Carr that week told Andy Naylor in *The Argus* just what Bob Booker would bring to the Albion. "He was well liked (at Sheffield United) and I cannot see any reason why he won't fit in with the lads. He is very bubbly and has a good sense of humour, so he will take over from Corky in that respect."

Bob was a quick learner and realised that he was fortunate enough to be working with an experienced and committed group of players who largely policed themselves.

"There were several leaders. Danny Cullip, Charlie Oatway and Richard Carpenter were the loudest and ensured that nobody coasted. If Bobby Zamora was not producing then Cullip would have him up against the dressing room wall and tell him to 'Start running around as you're costing me my bonus.' The players would point fingers and sort things out, which is exactly what you wanted. Everyone was encouraged to speak up and it was a very vocal dressing room, but there were no cliques, no bullying, nobody went too far and everyone accepted criticism. They reminded me of the Sheffield United squad in the way they looked out for each other."

Adams understood how difficult it was for Bob at first. "He knew nothing about the club and had to prove himself to a strong group of fiercely competitive and opinionated players and take over from an established number two in Corky. I kept my distance and Bob became the link between the players and myself, and he ensured that they knew what I wanted. If I was not happy with them then training would mainly consist of running, and sometimes the players would take their frustration and high spirits out on Bob and he would be ragged and stripped naked. He always took it well – maybe he enjoyed being manhandled by Charlie Oatway."

Bob soon worked out what was required. "I decided to create my own job description and get involved in everything. It was up to me to take the weight off Micky, provide my opinions and make myself indispensable. I understood that trust was paramount as Micky only tolerated people that he could rely on. He had no time for yes men and wanted someone with opinions about players, tactics and substitutions who could help him make good decisions under pressure."

Bob became the link between Micky and the players. "I had to earn their trust and deal with all their problems, ideally on my own, but also know when I had to involve the manager. Apart from Danny Cullip, who would always go straight to Micky, they would come to me with their problems and complaints. Maybe they were a bit wary of what Micky would tell them and preferred to hear it from me. Gary Hart was always the first to ask me why he had been dropped and I would try and tell him Micky's reasons. Micky kept his distance and largely ruled by fear. He knew how to press their buttons, and he told them exactly how it was. The players responded and never crossed him – instead, they would take it out on me and call him 'Mein Führer' and 'Little Legs,' which was fine, as I knew that it was only frustration and high spirits and I made sure that things never went too far."

"I remember a spineless performance at Scunthorpe in the FA Cup in December 2000. The defeat was partially my fault as, when Micky finished his team talk, I sent them out onto the pitch to a resounding cry of 'Unleash hell,' as I had just seen *Gladiator*. That worked well. Micky was seething all the way home and when we arrived in the early hours of the morning I had to tell the players to be at the training ground at 8am. He ran them around the nearby pond remorselessly for 45 minutes shouting: 'You didn't run around yesterday for the supporters so you can make up for it now.'"

"My job was to pick them up after he had criticised them. Micky would keep his distance so I could go in and calm everybody down. I kept it light, enjoyed joking with them, and as assistant manager I had to be one of them, but also ensure that they did not see me as a spy. They knew what would and would not get back to the manager, such as when someone refused to pay a fine, and sometimes they would use me as a conduit to Micky, particularly when they wanted permission for a team night out."

"I was a voice for Micky to get into the players and also a vehicle for the players to communicate with the manager."

"Sometimes I had to assert myself, challenge them and make it clear who was in charge – or the inmates would be running the asylum. I knew that Micky would always back me up but I could tell that the players trusted and respected me. That was the key."

Paul Brooker was one of the stars of the team, an enigmatic and maddeningly inconsistent winger who mixed days of brilliance with others where he was hardly seen. He also enjoyed working with Bob. "He was always happy and joking around but was also firm when he needed to be," he says. "Bob was very approachable and easy to talk to when you had a problem. He worked well with Micky Adams, who was more of the bad cop, and they were an excellent partnership."

Bob recalls, "We tried to mix things up and sometimes as we were walking off the pitch at half-time Micky would say 'You can be bad cop today' and I would go in and hammer them, which took them by surprise as that was normally Micky's role. He would then interrupt me and say 'I think you're being a bit harsh, Bob,' and pick them up. Reverse psychology like that always seemed to work."

"I helped Micky with the coaching and some days I would take all the training and on others we shared it. Micky was an excellent coach and I learned how he ran his sessions and I used many of them for the rest of my career. He was always very structured and organised and the players enjoyed training as he varied things, and they were never left standing around. His team was extremely fit and there were lots of timed pitch runs."

Bob loved coaching, "Particularly when something you worked on in the week came off in a match. We spent hours practicing near post flick-ons by Cullip for Zamora to score, as well as a well-rehearsed free kick when Zamora would jog towards Paul Watson and they would pretend to have a chat before Bobby sprinted off just as Paul bent the ball in. He would invariably be unmarked and have a strike at goal."

"I kept an eye on the young players coming through and I scouted players and future opposition, either alone or with Micky. I also liaised with the secretary, Derek Allan, regarding accommodation, pick-up points and training arrangements for away games."

"It was almost like being married to another man – after all, I already made Micky a cup of tea and brought him his newspapers most mornings. I was at his beck and call but I seemed to know instinctively what he wanted, learned quickly and I made it up as we went along. We were already friends from our time together at Brentford but I could not take anything for granted and it was clear that you had to be on your toes with him. If you made a mistake he would come down hard on you. I completely messed up all the pick-up arrangements and caused chaos on the way to a northern away game and he went ballistic with me and I never repeated my error. I totally respected and learned so much from him."

Knight was rarely at the training ground but he soon learned that Bob had settled in well. "There was a discernible gap between Micky Adams and the players. He did not want to get close to them and Bob was the perfect bridge and ensured that the lines of communication were maintained. He was very easy-going and the players responded to him, but Bob made it clear that they could not take any liberties."

Adams was also delighted with his new assistant. "Bob has an infectious nature and gets on with everyone, which is a rare skill. Sometimes when you go into a club you wonder about peoples' ulterior motives, but Bob was so loyal and he also made me laugh, and I like people who do that. But there was far more to him as he was a deep thinker who really knew the game. He was not afraid to voice his opinions firmly, both to the players and me, and he was a good coach."

"Most importantly, he built a rapport with the players, who liked and respected him, which was crucial, particularly as nowadays you have to be more of a babysitter and if you don't keep players happy you are finished. I knew that I could drip-feed things into them through Bob and that he would pass on my instructions and keep the dressing room happy and in check."

Bob was relieved that his arrival did not see an end to the team's success, continuing on their winning ways before clinching promotion after a 2-0 victory at Plymouth in April 2001. A narrow win over promotion rivals Chesterfield, who had been fined £20,000 and deducted nine points after a series of financial shenanigans, ensured the championship was won. Albion eventually finished 10 points ahead of Cardiff City; Adams was voted manager of the year and Albion only lost seven times after Bob's appointment in October.

Bob did not enjoy the initial celebration, "I went to Micky's house for a drink after the Chesterfield match and he put on all his favourite Billy Joel albums, which he knew I detested. He sat back in his chair, glass in hand and with a contented look on his face, told me, 'That's it, the job's done and I am going to leave things up to you now, Bob,' and I made the majority of the decisions for the final couple of matches."

Knight took the players to The Westin La Quinta in Marbella to celebrate, noticing with surprise an initial absentee, "Micky Adams came out later as he did not want to socialise with the players. Bob and Paul Rogers were in charge and we left Marbella reasonably intact." Bob laughed, as the chairman had either given an extremely sanitised version of events or was not fully aware of what had gone on.

"Warren Aspinall came in late on the first night and cut his hand when he knocked over an expensive vase in the lobby. There was a tell-tale trail of blood leading to his door. Despite the damning evidence he was adamant it was nothing to do with him and he asked for a DNA test. Eventually we clubbed together and paid for the damage. He further disgraced himself by chatting up the chairman's wife, not the best idea if you are trying to get a job on the backroom staff! Another afternoon, a group of players wearing pillow cases with eye slits came in and trashed Micky's room. I knew who the culprits were as they were stupid enough to stand outside my door afterwards and laugh about what they had done, but I took it in good spirits and Messrs Mayo, Cullip, Oatway, Rogers, Hart, Jones and Carpenter escaped without punishment. I came out to the swimming pool one afternoon wearing a white bathrobe and a Michael Jackson mask, peeled off my robe, which revealed my striped bathing trunks with a false backside and dived into the swimming pool, swam a length and walked off. The players all seemed to enjoy my impersonations and I felt accepted and part of the group."

Bob spent as much time as he could exploring Brighton, soon falling in love with the city. Initially, he commuted from Watford but the driving soon began to take its toll on him, particularly when he and Adams had been out scouting the night before. Increasingly often he would sofa surf with Adams, Malcolm Stuart and his wife Lorraine, or Matt Hicks, the football liaison manager, who became a particular friend.

"I became a bit of a nomad and by the end of the season I was generally only going back to Watford every Sunday. I knew that I would have to move down permanently, which would put further strain on my relationship with Christine."

"I was doing well financially and I received a £10,000 promotion bonus, which I used to pay for an extension on the house in Watford."

Bob had enjoyed an exceptional first season at the club, culminating in his first promotion as a staff member. He had felt under pressure following the success of the previous partnership between Adams and Cork, but he had been his own man and put his stamp on the job. The friendship he shared with Micky Adams had grown deeper, and they developed an exceptional working relationship based on mutual trust and respect.

Bob recalls one incident that brought them even closer together. "We were sitting in his conservatory late one night and wanted a drink. Micky thought there was a keg of beer in the utility room, so we started drinking it, but it was a bit warm so he told me to get some ice out of the freezer. I put the ice into the glasses and it started frothing up as we drank the beer. It tasted a bit odd but we finished it and went to bed. We were sharing a bed so Claire, who had just given birth to their son, Mitchel, could get some uninterrupted sleep – it's a manager/assistant manager thing! In the morning we both felt awful and Claire burst into the room and asked, 'Where is all the ice?' 'We used it in the beer,' replied Micky. 'That was my frozen breast milk.' We looked at each other and he said 'That's the closest you will ever get to her breasts,' and we laughed our heads off. Claire eventually saw the funny side."

"We were confident about our prospects in Division Two in 2001/02, particularly as Micky had signed a new contract and brought in another of his old boys, Simon Morgan from Fulham. His knees were worse than mine and he barely trained, but he was another leader who read the game brilliantly."

"Micky took us to Ballygar, a village in County Galway, for a pre-season tour. He loved going there although there was only one sloping training pitch at the back of a pub. The trip was great for team bonding and some of our party stole a life-sized horse which was kept outside the pub, and tried unsuccessfully to bring it upstairs to Micky's bedroom before leaving it in the training field."

# OOH-AAH: THE BOB BOOKER STORY

After losing to Sligo, Albion took part in the "Battle of Longford." It all started badly when Longford Town scored an early goal that never crossed the line. A number of unsavoury incidents followed, including an elbow on Crosby, a falling-out between Wicks and Carpenter, a red card for Oatway, and a brawl following an appalling tackle by Steve Melton. Not surprisingly, the game was abandoned at half-time. Bob did not help to defuse the situation when he popped his head around Longford's dressing room door and said, "Thanks a lot for the game lads," before beating a hasty retreat. Adams apparently gathered his team together once they had made their escape, with bottles and cans pinging against the side of their coach. Instead of giving them the expected bollocking, he simply said, "You'll do for me, lads."

Adams and Bob's partnership continued to flourish as Albion set the early pace in the Second Division, with Adams winning the September manager of the month award following a run of four wins and two draws.

There was an early setback in October with an unexpected home defeat by Brentford. The following day, Bob received another shock when Adams told him that he was leaving to join Leicester City as assistant manager to Dave Bassett, with the expectation of taking over as manager at the end of the season.

"I knew that Micky was very ambitious and wanted to manage in the Premier League. He felt frustrated at the lack of progress regarding a new stadium for the club and knew that the higher we took Brighton, the harder it would be to sustain success, given the constraints of Withdean and the limited budget available. But I did not have a clue that he was about to leave."

"I was devastated and while I totally understood his reasons, I felt that I had been left in the lurch. We had struck up a great relationship which was ending prematurely and I felt that we had unfinished business. I knew that there was nothing for me at Leicester as Micky was going there initially as assistant manager. But just as when he left Brentford, he said that he would try and take me with him as soon as the opportunity arose. He kept his word at the end of the season. I knew I had done a good job but I was unsure of what would happen to me now as I had only been at the club for a year and I felt very vulnerable, as most managers would want to bring their own staff with them."

Adams explains his decision. "I was very ambitious and, given the problems we faced, I just could not see Brighton progressing at the pace I wanted. The higher we progressed the more difficult it would be to maintain our success. Dick Knight was always telling me how close we were to getting permission for a new stadium in the city, but Bob and I would have a drink every Friday after training and our toast was always, 'Falmer, My Arse.' We knew just how far away it was, despite Dick's words."

"Like most chairmen, Dick Knight was strong-willed and opinionated, but he also talked a lot of sense. He never went behind my back and would speak plainly whenever something was on his mind. I was happy to listen to him, although the lunches at Topolino's were hard work as I used to come out stinking of tobacco, but we had good chats and I am extremely grateful to him for his support."

"I was sorry to leave Bob behind as we got on so well both socially and professionally, and it is not every manager who is willing to share his wife's breast milk with his assistant."

"In retrospect, I was a little bit eager and hurried in my decision to leave. I wanted to progress as quickly as possible but maybe I should have stayed another year and seen out the next title win – two in a row would have been incredible for me, but that's life."

# CHAPTER 30
# PETER TAYLOR

Micky Adams's resignation left Bob in a potentially difficult and vulnerable position. "Without any warning I had lost my friend and mentor and felt like I was a dead man walking," he says of the news. "Micky had given me my opportunity and taught me everything I knew, and we had developed a close relationship. I knew how he thought and instinctively understood what he wanted from me, and I was concerned that I would be unable to build up as effective a partnership with anybody else. I was still learning my trade and didn't have much confidence in my ability to find another job. In fact, I had never applied for a management job in football and had no idea how to do so, as I had been approached by David Webb and Micky Adams before I joined Brentford and Brighton."

Dick Knight then did something that guaranteed him Bob's eternal gratitude, "I was at the training ground on the Wednesday morning trying to raise the player's spirits, and indeed, mine too, after a home defeat and the loss of the manager when the chairman turned up unexpectedly. I had not seen too much of him over the previous year but I sometimes accompanied Micky on his weekly lunch with him and I respected him for his exceptional juggling act in managing to keep so many balls in the air. He took me to one side and this was our first-ever private conversation. He said, 'I know exactly how you're feeling at the moment, so I want to assure you that you're staying and whoever becomes manager will have you as his assistant. He will be fortunate too, as you've done a great job over the past year and will remain as his link with the players.'" Bob felt valued and wanted, his job secure. "This fantastic gesture calmed me down, set my mind at rest and reinvigorated me. But there was even more, 'I'm working as quickly as I can to hire a new manager but I would like you and Martin Hinshelwood to take charge of the team at Huddersfield on Saturday, and probably Swansea too, next Tuesday in the LDV Trophy game.' I was stunned, as it had never crossed my mind that I would become the caretaker manager. Dick then spoke briefly to the players and left, leaving me totally surprised and elated."

Reflecting on the conversation, Bob realised that neither of them had discussed whether he should apply for Adams's job. He gave some cursory thought to throwing his hat into the ring, quickly concluding that he was happy and fulfilled in his current position.

"I have never wanted to be a manager," he confirms. "Being an assistant was a specialist role which I grew into, thrived in and really enjoyed. I was well aware of my strengths and weaknesses and being an assistant manager suited me. I think I could have done the number one job but I really would not have enjoyed it or have been true to myself. I was temperamentally unsuited to the role and knew that I did not possess the confidence, drive and inner strength to make tough decisions about dropping and releasing players. Maybe I was just a bit too nice and lacked the ruthlessness that managers require. I did not know enough about other teams and players. I was an organisation man and was happy helping and advising the boss, but I just did not want the pressure of taking the ultimate responsibility myself. I also loved bantering with the players and this would have had to stop if I became a manager."

"Some assistants, and Nathan Jones is an excellent example, make it clear from the outset that they are highly ambitious and want to move up one day, and that is quite understandable. I was very loyal and never wanted to take the job of any manager I worked for, whereas I was well aware of some assistants who actively plotted to do so, and I had no respect for any of them."

Adams knew Bob inside out – Bob, perhaps, opened up more to him than to some of the other managers he worked for. His verdict was totally clear and unambiguous, "I never saw Bob as a manager because the job requires a totally different set of skills and he was far too nice a guy, which is meant as praise rather than criticism. Bob would have struggled with some of the unpleasant tasks he would have faced, such as releasing players. With his personality, the manager's job might well have tipped him over the edge." Adams is spot on in his assessment, proving how well he knew Bob and what made him tick.

Knight is also extremely forthright. "I thought that management was a step too far for Bob and would not have suited his personality. He'd have found it very stressful and I did not think he wanted to take on that much responsibility. I saw him as a vital part of the jigsaw, as he was an exceptional assistant manager who was quite brilliant at his job. Even if Bob had asked me, I wouldn't have appointed him as manager – he was far too valuable where he was."

"It can't have been easy for him to adapt to the personalities and needs of the six different managers for whom he worked," Knight observes. "Micky Adams, Peter Taylor, Martin Hinshelwood, Steve Coppell, Mark McGhee and Russell Slade were all totally different in their make-up and approach. Four of them had been top players, they were all strongly opinionated, confident and knowledgeable, and yet he managed to win the friendship, trust and respect of all of them, which was no mean achievement and testimony to his ability."

Hinshelwood had an inkling that Bob was more interested in the job when Coppell left in 2003. Bob took over for a five-game spell before the arrival of Mark McGhee, but denied any interest, insisting it was just newspaper talk and his name had been added to the shortlist purely for cosmetic purposes. A 4-0 loss at Brentford ended his chances anyway.

Perhaps Bob lacked the self-confidence to push himself forward; maybe he could have adapted to the requirements of the job, just as he had successfully met every previous challenge he had faced? I believe that Bob was extremely astute and recognised exactly what he did best and, crucially, also enjoyed doing, taking the morally courageous decision to concentrate on making himself the best possible assistant manager rather than seeking to progress further. Bob was well aware of the consequences of failure as a manager – the sack was inevitable. Why put himself in that position, risking unhappiness at the same time? Instead, Bob served six managers impeccably for nearly eight years, building a new life for himself in Brighton, loving a job that he excelled at and was well rewarded for. Who can say that he was mistaken in his judgement?

Bob's first spell as caretaker manager produced a 100% record, with 2-1 victories at Huddersfield and then Swansea in the LDV Trophy. Bob dropped skipper Rogers for the Huddersfield game, switching to a more attacking 4-4-2 formation, with Steele playing alongside Zamora.

Hinshelwood laughs when recalling this match. "Bob was taller than me, so he was in charge. He drove me mad as when we took the lead he kept turning round saying, 'It doesn't get any better than this.' After about the eighth time I finally said, 'Bob, please shut up,' but when we went two goals up, he started up again, 'I told you, it doesn't get any better than this.' Then Huddersfield scored and I never heard another peep out of him for the last few minutes as we desperately held on."

Dirk Lehmann's only goal for the club ("Perhaps the weight of his earrings prevented him from jumping higher?" remarked Bob), helped

Albion to a victory at Swansea on the following Tuesday, but Bob's short spell in charge ended before he could get a taste for the job.

Despite the ongoing problems with the stadium and finance, Dick Knight managed to attract a number of impressive and high profile managers to the club. His next appointee, Peter Taylor, was no exception. A former international footballer, he had managed the England team on one occasion as a caretaker and had also been in charge of the England Under-21 team, Gillingham and Leicester City, who had sacked him a couple of weeks previously and replaced him with a combination of Dave Bassett and Adams. Everyone in football seems to be linked; these coincidences are the rule rather than the exception.

Knight had been impressed with Taylor's coaching ability as well his knowledge of the Second Division from his spell at Gillingham. The interview went well, as Knight recalls, "I told him 'This is a fantastic opportunity – normally a new manager has to pick up the pieces after someone else has failed, but you're inheriting a really strong and successful squad chasing promotion, and you really just need to keep things ticking over and not change anything. There is also an excellent man in place as your assistant manager who knows the club and the players extremely well. You will quickly learn just how good he is as he will adapt to your way of working and act as your link to the players. See how things go, and if after a couple of months you find you cannot work with him then we will sit down and resolve matters.' He was happy to accept the job on those terms."

"I had the choice of Brighton or Southend, which was really convenient for me, and I was tempted, but it was an easy decision on footballing grounds as I wanted to get Brighton promoted and back into the First Division," remembers Taylor. "I am delighted I did as it was a wonderful year. Dick made it clear that I would have to work with the existing staff and that was fine as, unlike most managers, I have rarely been one to bring people with me. Once Dick mentioned Bob to me I spoke to Steve Perryman about him, and he set my mind at rest. I was happy to see how things went with him."

Bob was simply pleased that he still had a job, aware that he would have to prove himself once again – a tough task given Taylor's reputation as a coach. "I was on trial and had to be at the top of my game, but I was organised and had a good relationship with the players and could be Peter's link to them. I met him for the first time on the Thursday before the Oldham game and, using the same approach as I had previously at Brentford with Micky Adams, I broke the ice by saying, 'I hear you do a good Norman Wisdom impersonation, and I do a few myself.' He laughed and we discussed the squad and he already knew a lot about the players. He said, 'Just do your normal training routine and I will watch and maybe step in.' He reassured me that he wasn't going to make any dramatic changes and wanted me to carry on as normal and act as his eyes and ears."

"I took the players out, told them that the new gaffer seemed fine, and set up a small-sided game. As normal the tackles flew in. Charlie Oatway kicked Nathan Jones up in the air and then Danny Cullip went straight through Gary Hart. I could tell that Peter Taylor was getting extremely agitated. He stepped in and frantically blew his whistle. 'What's going on?' 'We are just doing what we always do.' He looked horrified. 'From now on there will be no tackling on a Thursday or Friday.' He reined in all their aggression and introduced shadow play without the opposition, which they found boring. It was his way and it worked, but it was totally different to Micky's approach. I did what he wanted and took some players for extra running after training to get rid of their excess energy."

Taylor had his own insecurities, seeking to re-establish himself after losing his job at Leicester. He quickly came to realise just how great an asset he had inherited in Bob, "I could see straight away that I was going to be very happy with him, not only in his work but also as a person. He totally respected my position and I trusted him, which was crucial to me. The team spirit was fantastic and Bob contributed hugely to that. He was a lovely man who did a great job and was never afraid to disagree with me and provide his own opinion."

"I did more of the coaching, particularly later in the week when I think it is important for the manager to get closer to the team and let them know what he expects from them. Bob was very organised and before matches he briefed the players about our set pieces and the oppositions' strengths and weaknesses. I had always done this previously, but he wanted to do it and was good at it so I let him have his head. He was honest with players and could get angry when it was necessary. He was always good company whenever we spent time together watching games, at the training ground, during games and socially."

"In my time I have taken over from lots of successful managers such as Tony Pulis, Martin O'Neill and, indeed, Micky Adams, so I understood that I would be stupid to change things too much. We generally played 4-5-1 or 4-3-3 away from home but also switched to 4-4-2 with Lee Steele coming in. I signed Junior Lewis on loan, who was a big influence and made the team play, as he always wanted the ball and never hid. He took the ball off the defenders, ensured we kept possession and we provided

Bobby Zamora with better service – and if you gave him the ball you were guaranteed goals in that division."

Bob thought that Junior Lewis was "A very unorthodox player. He wasn't up with the pace at first and was pigeon-toed with an awkward gangly style of running, but he grew on the lads. He did well and kept Charlie Oatway out of the team."

Taylor mostly left well alone but Bob did disagree with his plan to move the left-footed right-back Paul Watson to the left-hand side, an experiment that did not work; he was a potent attacking threat cutting inside onto his natural foot.

Bob did less coaching, taking the warm-ups and small sessions with players not involved in the first team, sensing that Peter made more decisions on his own than had been the case with Micky Adams.

There was only one slight misunderstanding when, in late October, Taylor told Bob that he was going to play either Andy Crosby or Matt Wicks against Colchester, instead of the injured Danny Cullip, "I thought that Crosby would be the better choice as he was bigger and stronger, and Peter agreed with me. I made a mistake and told Andy on Friday to prepare himself for the following day, but just before kick off Peter Taylor read out the team and named Wicks instead. I felt Andy's eyes boring into me and I lost credibility with him."

Bob was impressed with Taylor's style and approach, "The players took to him and he had a good sense of humour. He was far more laid back than Micky but would scream at them if necessary, and he totally lost his head at both half and full-time at Brentford, where we were battered. But that did not happen too often. It was more of a working than a social relationship but we got on fine and would share a few drinks together on a Friday night before away games."

Despite the change of manager, Brighton kept winning, engaging in a three-way tussle with Reading and Brentford for the two automatic promotion places. A Zamora winner against Peterborough United in April, allied with Reading's failure to win at Tranmere the following day, guaranteed promotion. The championship was won after a 0-0 draw against Swindon Town before an ecstatic Withdean crowd.

Knight praised his management team, past and present, in the matchday programme, "My heartfelt thanks to Peter Taylor and Bob Booker, the coaching and backroom staff and of course the players – they have all worked tremendously hard over two enthralling seasons and will rightfully take their place in the Albion's all-time hall of fame. One man who is not here today, but who has played a big part in the Albion renaissance, is Micky Adams. He may have departed for Leicester in October (and I take nothing away from what Peter has achieved since), but Micky not only led us to the Third Division Championship last season, but also laid the solid foundations on which Peter was able to build so well."

Albion held a victory parade which ended up at King's House, the city council headquarters in Hove. Bob had something special planned which has now gone down in Albion folklore.

"I spoke to Dick Knight and told him that I wanted to dress up as Freddie Mercury and go out onto the balcony and lead the crowd in a resounding chorus of 'We Are The Champions,' and he guffawed and said, 'I love the idea, Bob, it is so Brighton.' I hired the outfit of yellow jacket, white trousers and wig and practiced at home with Christine for a week. On the big day, the PA played 'We Will Rock You' and the fans all joined in before I came out in full costume, and without boasting I think I stole the show as I swung from the balcony. Southern FM's Nicky Keig-Shevlin was standing in the crowd with former player John Byrne, and she asked him 'Who's that idiot?' 'That's Bob Booker,' he replied. That was the first time she ever saw me and little did she know that she would be marrying 'that idiot' a few years later."

The euphoria did not last long. Taylor rang Bob the following day and said he was leaving, disappointed about next year's budget and the far-off promise of a new stadium. Bob noticed that Taylor had left the Hove celebrations early and missed his party piece, but this was a case of *déjà vu* – just as with Adams, he was taken totally by surprise.

"Dick Knight told me in my interview that the new stadium in Falmer would be ready in about a year and a half, but that was obviously not the case," says Taylor, explaining his decision. "I just felt that it should not have been said to me. At my request, I managed without a contract and said, 'Let's see where we are at the end of the season.' I knew that playing at Withdean made things really difficult and that the budget would not be great. I felt that it would be really difficult to stay up if we were still playing there. Maybe a combination of our momentum, the quality of the squad and keeping hold of Bobby Zamora would keep us up for the first year, but it would get progressively harder for the club to sustain success. Unfortunately, I was proved correct when, despite having Steve Coppell in charge, they were relegated at the end of the following season. I would never have left if the new stadium had been on the horizon and my relationship with Dick Knight was fine, but the interview did not make it clear about the stadium situation and I was a bit disappointed. I didn't have a job to go to and it took me until November before I took over at Hull City."

Taylor is quick to pay tribute to Bob. "I really enjoyed my time at Brighton. A football season is a marathon and you have to be able to enjoy spending time with the people you work with. I was comfortable with Bob in every way as we worked and played hard and we always laughed together. We stayed in touch and I often asked his opinion about players. I did think about hiring him when I was appointed at Wycombe in May 2008, but I went with Junior Lewis as he lived nearby."

Bob also enjoyed working with Peter, "He was an excellent coach and a pleasant man with a good sense of humour. He liked to make decisions by himself and was less inclusive and more aloof than Micky Adams. I got to know him reasonably well but he left before we developed a close relationship. I enjoyed my spell with him, but preferred working with Micky, as I felt more involved. Most importantly, I proved to myself that I could work well from scratch with a stranger. I must have been doing something right as he kept me on – and my Norman Wisdom impression was better than his."

# CHAPTER 31
# HINSH

The players returned to Marbella in May 2002, their celebrations slightly muted by the uncertainty over the managerial position, with Bob among those feeling the pressure. "I was surprised The Westin La Quinta allowed us to return after the previous year's high jinks. My priority was to relax with the players after a long and exhausting season, but instead I spent most of the trip talking to Dick Knight about contracts and potential signings. He was paying me a compliment by picking my brains and using me as a sounding board, but I found our chats uncomfortable and stressful. I realised that he knew far more about players than I did."

These difficult conversations confirmed Bob's instincts to remain in his current role and resist any managerial aspirations. Knight reiterated his importance to the club, offering him a new, improved contract.

Bob's happiness and fulfilment would normally have led him to sign the contract straight away. "I was delighted that Dick wanted to keep me on," he says. "But he didn't seem to have any idea who the new manager would be, which really unsettled me. I had managed to establish a good working relationship with both Micky Adams and Peter Taylor, but the thought of having to do it again concerned me. What would happen if the new man did not take to me?"

"Money has never been a massive priority but I had just earned my second successive £10,000 promotion bonus, so I had no worries on that score. What was upsetting me was my relationship with Christine." They had drifted apart, rarely seeing each other and had all but separated.

"Considering how long we had been together I felt sad and guilty about our situation. The club had understandably been pushing me to relocate to the Brighton area and offered me a generous moving allowance, but Chris did not want to leave Watford. Eventually I rented a terraced house in Payton Drive in Burgess Hill, where Watson and Zamora lived."

Bob had been speaking regularly to Adams, receiving much-needed support about his marital situation from the new Leicester City manager. Adams had just taken over from Dave Bassett, beginning the process of assembling his coaching staff in a bid to return the club to the Premier

League at the first opportunity. "That May, I tried hard to get Bob to join me at Leicester," he says. "He and Alan Cork would have worked together. I wanted them both on my coaching staff as they were different characters who would have complemented each other."

Bob was sorely tempted. "It is all about timing and Micky approached me when I was feeling very low and insecure. I knew that we would work well together and Leicester were also about to move into a brand new stadium and had the backing to challenge for promotion. I contrasted their situation with ours at Brighton, where we were going into the unknown as the poor relations stuck at Withdean, with no manager in place." This "hard decision" took Bob several days. "Micky was my friend and had given me my opportunity, but I also felt a great deal of loyalty towards Brighton, given what the club and Dick Knight had done for me. I spoke to the chairman and he put a lot of pressure on me to stay. In the end I told Micky that I was very flattered and extremely tempted by his offer, but it just did not feel right to leave the club in the lurch." Micky was disappointed but phlegmatic. "I understood his reasons. He was trying to establish roots in Brighton and it would have been a wrench for him to leave. I had to wait until my second spell at the club before we were reunited."

Bob answers without hesitation when asked if he regrets staying at the club. "My life has panned out extremely well. I liked the area, I was comfortable there and I had made some good friends. I was very unsettled at the time because of the problems with Chris and I really needed some stability in my life. If I had left then I would never have married Nicky. I have no regrets at all, even though I could have shared in three successive promotions (and probably bonuses too) given that Leicester City went up at the end of the next season."

New contract signed, Bob's salary rose to £650 per week, sharing in the players' bonuses and leasing a Mercedes from Vince Pemberton, owner of Rivervale Cars, in Portslade – a "fantastic bloke," according to Bob.

Knight issued a statement declaring that he was "delighted" Bob had "Responded to our faith in him. He is an excellent coach and assistant manager and he has played a crucial role in the Albion's success – helping to bond the unique team spirit that has led us to the back-to-back championships and facilitated the smooth transition from one manager to another at a critical time in last season's campaign. His contribution has been tremendous and he has gained invaluable experience from two excellent managers."

Knight was not finding it easy to replace Taylor. Some potential candidates were concerned that Albion would find it hard to cope with the step up in status, particularly given the budget available, and did not want to be associated with a struggle to remain in Division One. Others were hard to pin down or not quite what he wanted.

Knight knew that despite their success, Brighton was not the easiest sell. "I had to make every candidate aware of the financial realities, as most of our income went into infrastructure. The price of playing at Withdean was high, as we had to subsidise the Park and Ride scheme and pay for 90 stewards every game who protected the interests of the local residents by maintaining a one-mile exclusion zone. In the 2002/03 season, the average attendance in the First Division was around 18,000 – ours was 6,651. About half of our gate receipts went on those additional costs, and we therefore had one-sixth of the average income of our competitors. We also spent money on new contracts for some of our best players, such as Zamora, Kuipers and Cullip."

Knight approached Steve Coppell, who had just left Brentford, but he was incommunicado on holiday in the Far East. Cameroon manager Winfried Schäfer was an interesting candidate, but did not speak much English. Bob, who was aware of the club's interest in Schäfer, told Knight that he had been practising his German – or at least an unconvincing German accent. It wasn't enough to persuade the chairman to take a chance.

There was one internal candidate: director of youth Martin Hinshelwood, known to everyone at the club as "Hinsh." He was a youth development coach who had built an excellent reputation since seeing his playing career at Crystal Palace cruelly cut short by injury at the age of 24. He had enjoyed a spell as Barry Lloyd's assistant manager and acted as caretaker before the arrivals of Liam Brady and Adams, as well as assisting Bob in the role in 2001.

Hinsh was considered a safe pair of hands – loyal and highly skilled at his job, with extensive experience of bringing through talented youngsters. Most importantly, he also harboured managerial ambitions, making it clear to Knight that, after serving a 25-year apprenticeship, he was ready and willing to take over. "The frustration of packing up so early as a player made me even more determined to progress as far as I could in coaching and management," he recalls. "I had a lot of experience and I believed I was ready to become a manager. Dick Knight interviewed me but I didn't hear anything and I thought that was that. I knew he was looking at other people."

Hinsh swallowed his disappointment and made plans for the running of his youth section. The first team squad reported back leaderless for pre-season training on 3rd July, little more than five weeks away from their opening league game. The clock was ticking, preparations for the new season were long overdue and, after an unsuccessful attempt to pry former Brighton captain Danny Wilson away from Bristol City and an inconclusive meeting with a jet-lagged Coppell, the chairman decided to delay no longer. With Bob out of the frame and "not interested," the last man standing, Hinshelwood, was named as manager on 15th July, signing a two-year contract 11 long weeks after the resignation of Taylor.

At a press conference at The Grand Hotel, Knight praised his new appointee for his "stability, continuity, hard work, dedication and long-term loyalty." Hinshelwood wittily stated that he was "not a big name, just a long one." He thought the team could cope with the higher division, but asked the supporters to be patient.

Hinsh told me that despite his outward show of confidence, he privately held serious misgivings about the task he had taken on, "To be honest I let my heart rule my head and I should not have accepted the job. It was a poisoned chalice, and I was setting myself up to fail. This was totally the wrong time to take over as I was inheriting a squad that was used to success but had little or no experience of playing at this level. I wanted to give an opportunity to the players who had won promotion, but I knew we needed to bolster the squad with four or five new players with experience of the First Division. I did not have sufficient time or budget to build a squad that was strong enough to compete. That being said, as a coach you can't turn down an opportunity to manage, as they do not come around too often, and if it happened again tomorrow I would do exactly the same – but this time I'd try to win a few more games."

Bob recalls that Dean Wilkins and Dean White also helped with the coaching. "Like Micky Adams, Hinsh was a little bit old-school. He preferred to play 4-4-2 and was exceptionally good with the young players, many of whom were thrown in at the deep end in light of the number of injuries we suffered. Some, like his nephew, Adam, and Dean Hammond, swam; others were out of their depth and sank without trace, which was totally unfair on them as they were simply not ready to play first team football. We did everything we could to support Hinsh but it was clear that the squad was neither deep nor strong enough."

The players welcomed Hinshelwood's appointment, but early warning bells should have rung when, at the AGM of the Albion Supporters' Club, the new manager stated that the players were so used to calling him "Hinsh" that he had to fine them when they didn't call him "gaffer."

Hinsh appreciated Bob's support. "I had first met Bob at youth team matches when he was at Brentford, but I only got to know him properly after he joined Brighton. He was a funny lad and really should have been a comedian, but he took the game seriously. The players loved him but also respected him, and nobody ever answered him back. He was a great help to me when I was in charge. He helped me keep my spirits up at a time when nothing seemed to be going right."

Hinsh did what he could in the limited time available, bringing in a series of trialists who disappeared without trace. Despite the problems, the opening match saw an unexpected and convincing victory at Burnley by a side containing no new faces. This led to an awkward encounter between Bob and Nicky Keig-Shevlin, as she explains, "The first time I spoke to Bob was memorable, but for all the wrong reasons. I interviewed him on the club's internet TV channel, *Seagulls World*. I had been reliably informed that he was amusing and easy to talk to, but I found him to be monosyllabic and very hard work. I did consider cutting the interview short but decided that one of us needed to be professional. The next day Bob called to apologise. He explained that he'd heard me on the radio saying the players were flying to the first game of the season at Burnley and I'd commented 'How big time is that' which I'd meant as a compliment and testimony to the club's ambition. Unfortunately he had taken it the wrong way."

The win at Turf Moor papered over the cracks, raising expectations ahead of a dreary goalless draw against Coventry in the first home game of the season, highlighting Albion's lack of penetration. The loss of their only goal threat, Zamora, to a serious knee injury was a mortal blow to Albion's hopes of establishing themselves in the First Division.

Hinsh did manage to sign experienced striker Paul Kitson from West Ham, but he was over the hill and rarely fit, making little or no impact. Guy Butters needed time to regain match fitness. To Knight's *chagrin*, his new manager raised immediate question marks about his judgement when he rejected the opportunity to sign Steve Sidwell and Kolo Toure on loan from Arsenal, convinced that he already possessed better youngsters at the club. Toure was a total unknown at that point, but Sidwell was a youngster of immense promise who had impressed at Brentford the previous season, scoring against Albion.

He did sign one loanee, Arsenal striker Graham Barrett, although he seemed to spend more time suspended or on international duty than playing for the Albion. As is often the case with struggling teams, the treatment room filled up: Hart, Kuipers, Melton, Pethick, Brooker and Jones joined Zamora on the injured list.

Hinsh could see the way things were going. "After the Burnley game I wasn't altogether joking when I said that 'I should pack up now because it wouldn't get any better.' It was all downhill from there. We needed some luck and received absolutely none, and we could not recover from losing Zamora. I could have signed Sidwell, and maybe in retrospect I should I have done, but I thought Dean Hammond deserved a chance, and he went on to have a long and successful career. Given our lack of resources I had no option but to play the likes of Shaun Wilkinson and Danny Marney, who gave me everything but weren't good enough. I wanted to bring our youngsters through but maybe I was a bit naïve."

Results and performances went from bad to worse as confidence levels plummeted. "Losing becomes a habit," laments Hinshelwood. "But we suffered lots of narrow defeats that, given some luck, could have gone the other way. We were never battered and the injuries killed us."

Knight was asked about his manager's future in an interview on BBC Southern Counties Radio following Albion's defeat by Gillingham in mid-September, replying in ominous, prophetic style. "If a team went ten matches losing every one, then you've got to do something about it."

He was true to his word. After Watford inflicted Albion's tenth consecutive defeat, Hinshelwood was sacked. Albion were in freefall, six points from safety and running the risk of being cut adrift.

Hinsh's first instinct was to leave the club, but after a few days' thought and the encouragement of Bob and the two Deans, Wilkins and White, he decided to remain, becoming director of football while performing his previous duties as director of youth.

Managing the club did not work out for Hinsh, largely due to all the extenuating – perhaps even insurmountable – circumstances when he took over. He was to become caretaker manager again in 2009, after Russell Slade's departure, providing the club with 14 years of excellent loyal service, fully deserving Bob's description of him as a "great club man."

# CHAPTER 32
# STEVE COPPELL

Dick Knight's next managerial appointment also did not disappoint as he had an exceptional reputation and track record. Steve Coppell had been his first choice when Peter Taylor resigned but the experienced former Crystal Palace, Manchester City and Brentford manager was holidaying in the Far East, proving elusive and hard to pin down. When they did finally meet on his return, he was bleary-eyed and almost comatose.

When Hinsh did not work out, Knight tried again – this time finding Coppell bright-eyed and bushy-tailed, eager and available to take on the challenge of saving Albion from an immediate return to Division Two. Brighton fans, willing to ignore or forgive him his Crystal Palace background in light of his track record, generally welcomed his arrival on a one-year contract. The previous season he had led an excellent Brentford team to a double over Albion and a place in the playoff final.

Knight recalls briefing his new manager. "I sat Steve down when he arrived and told him that this club was in a unique situation as it had been saved by the efforts of its supporters, but was still in a desperate battle for a new stadium. I gave him the full background and he fully understood our position and that we currently had to play in a stadium that was not fit for purpose."

Coppell was unfazed when Knight told him of Bob's capabilities. "Steve was perhaps more experienced than his predecessors and did not insist upon bringing in his own man."

As for Bob, it was *déjà vu*. He was getting used to continually having to prove himself. "I was in awe of Steve's reputation as a manager and a deep thinker and worried that he would want to work with someone a bit more cerebral than me. I desperately wanted to make a good impression, so on his first day I made sure I arrived at training even earlier than normal, at about 8 o'clock, only to find that he had beaten me in." A Croydon resident, Coppell would get in at 7am to beat the traffic. "I took him to Withdean that afternoon and he asked me to have the away dressing room repainted in the drabbest colour possible and to ensure that on matchdays the radiators in there were turned up to the maximum and not adjustable.

He also made sure that the warm-up balls given to the opposition were slightly deflated and in poor condition. Every little edge helps."

Bob had nothing to worry about – Coppell accepted him straight away. "From my point of view, inheriting Bob was not a problem. Throughout my managerial career I must have had a dozen or more assistants and I never insisted on having the same person with me. Obviously there were some I worked with better than others, but I was stimulated by the input of new people. I enjoyed picking up their ideas and learning from them rather than hearing the same voice every day."

Steve had a more pressing problem to solve. "It was a funny situation as I was taking over from Hinsh but he hadn't left the club, which had the potential to be awkward. I met with Hinsh and said I was quite happy for him to stay. He was highly regarded and I valued his input."

Hinsh explains what happened next. "Dick Knight offered me a job as director of football without defining the role, so I asked Steve what he thought it meant. His response was to hand me a blank sheet of paper and say, 'It's up to you to do what you want.' He was as confused as I was, so eventually I went back to looking after the kids but still did some work with the first team." Coppell was grateful that a potentially difficult situation had been averted. "I did not know Bob but when I met him and Dean White they both seemed very capable," he says. "Bob did most of the daily work and Dean was an excellent sounding board who told you how it was."

"I had done my research and knew that we had some strong personalities in the dressing room who needed careful handling, and I quickly realised that Bob was a marvellous diplomat and a good communicator. He was able to keep things verbally light and funny and still get unpalatable messages over to the players that might otherwise have been problematic or unpopular with them."

Coppell inherited a team that had gone 11 matches without a win, losing ten of them. With only nine goals scored and 21 conceded it was clear that there were serious issues at both ends of the pitch.

"Something wasn't right. In my first game we were two up against Sheffield United and looking comfortable, but we somehow contrived to lose. We then lost 5-0 at Crystal Palace, which was humiliating and embarrassing." Four of the goals were from set pieces, highlighting the problem. "Einstein defined insanity as doing the same thing over and over again and expecting different results, so I knew that I had to change things very quickly or it would be impossible to arrest our slide."

# OOH-AAH: THE BOB BOOKER STORY

"I had to change a few things and bring in fresh faces, and, like most managers, I went for tried and tested players who I knew could do a job for me. I was delighted that Arsenal were still willing to loan us Steve Sidwell. I had known Siddy since he was a young boy of 11, playing with my son at Chipstead. I had taken him to Brentford the previous season and, at 19, he had already demonstrated that he was going to develop into an exceptional box-to-box midfielder who could defend, pass accurately and score goals. I had also worked with Ívar Ingimarsson at Brentford and he had played an entire season at centre-back without getting a single booking. He and Dean Blackwell, who came in from Wimbledon, were calm and solid defenders. I also rescued my former Palace midfielder Simon Rodger from Woking. He and Sidwell strengthened the midfield and we started to gather a bit of momentum."

"I had no idea – and I really did not want to know – how things had been done before my arrival. I had my own way of working which Bob quickly grasped. He was the link between the players and me and also did a lot of the coaching. Training was very structured and everything was geared to the team being ready and fully prepared to win Saturday's game. At the beginning of the week you are like a pianist practising your scales, concentrating on the basics such as defensive and attacking principles, with lots of repetition drills covering finishing, passing, heading and crossing. On Thursday and Friday we got game-specific and concentrated on the opposition. I was one of the pioneers of video analysis at Crystal Palace and introduced it at Brighton. Then it was seen as a novelty – now it is commonplace. I would give the players dossiers and show them footage that highlighted our opponents' style of play, strengths and weaknesses and, most importantly, how we would go about trying to win the game. I also concentrated on our strengths and tried never to frighten my team by making the opposition appear as supermen. I hated full-on practice matches – we played sharp short-sided games, but they were never allowed to get out of hand, with tackling kept to a minimum. I was amused when Bob told me about my predecessors' differing approach to them."

Coppell kept "a professional distance" from his squad, making Bob's role key. "The players knew they could trust and rely on him. Bob loved his job, particularly the daily banter with the players, and I cannot think of a single day when he did not have a smile on his face. His enthusiasm was infectious. He kept everyone happy even if the atmosphere was awful after a defeat. He was great company, easy to work with, loyal and trustworthy. I could tell him anything, knowing it would not go any further. He would always give me his opinion and if I decided not to go along with him he would still support me totally. It is a wise man who is content with his lot. His role suited his personality and Bob seemed happier being part of a team rather than leading it."

"I don't know of anyone who has a bad word to say about him, which does not mean that he was simply a yes man or a joker. I am not a ranter or raver but if points needed to be made then I would do so. Bob very rarely did the same, so when he did it lent more weight and gravitas to what he said, and the players really listened and took his criticism on board."

"The players worshipped and respected him and would even ask him for permission if they wanted to go to the toilet during training. Nobody went without asking, which was something that I had never seen before and always made me laugh. It reminded me of the film *Cool Hand Luke*, with the prisoners asking the guards for permission to have a drink."

"He is a unique character; how many people in football go twitching? Bob was the perfect assistant manager as far as I am concerned and it was a pleasure, privilege and delight to work with him."

Bob, too, learned much from his boss. "Steve restored confidence and brought the best out of a set of players who, when he arrived, did not know where their next win was coming from. He was very calm with them, almost never raised his voice or had a go at them, but he always got his point over and the players really respected him. Training was simple and straightforward and focused on pattern of play, and Steve allowed me to take most of it. He was well ahead of his time in terms of his dependence on video analysis and the use of a sports psychologist in Robert Forzoni. We used to play tapes of the opposition in the coach on the way to away games, which certainly made a change from a ghetto blaster. Steve was a loner but maybe opposites attract; we got on well and would socialise together on the night before most away games."

"Steve was the most demanding manager I ever worked with," says Knight, who was impressed by Coppell's quiet, studious and professional approach – thoughtful, painstaking, reserved and analytical. "He was a great student of the game who spent most afternoons poring over videos. He was punctilious in ensuring that the players were all fully prepared and knew their instructions and Bob adapted to his approach. Like Micky Adams, Steve was very distant from the players. He knew their strengths and weaknesses but used Bob to communicate with them."

Zamora's return to fitness in late October gave the team a focal point up front, responding with 14 goals, but no-one else came close to double figures, although Sidwell, who scored five times in 11 games before Arsenal sold him to Reading in January 2003, might have done if Brighton had been able to persuade him to join them instead. This would not be the last time Albion lost a valuable asset to a club boasting a chairman just as ambitious as Knight but, crucially, possessing something that Albion lacked. The Madejski Stadium, a modern, state-of-the-art arena, was a major source of revenue to Sidwell's suitors.

A victory over Millwall in February saw Albion climb out of the bottom three for the first time since the end of August, raising hopes that, after three consecutive wins, the tide had turned. But results remained up and down. Despite a glorious win at Reading – Sidwell and all – a listless home defeat to Preston left them marooned in the bottom three, never to recover.

The club could have done without Zamora's ill-judged comments in the *Daily Telegraph*, made at the wrong time, diverting focus from the relegation battle, "I'd obviously love to play in the Premiership. It is frustrating. I could break my leg next week and never get the chance to play in the Premiership. I've worked hard for three years with Brighton. I don't really talk to fans about moving because they seem to get a bit annoyed. They can get a bit aggressive." Knight felt he had to respond in *The Argus*. "We've not received an offer for him and if we do he will be kept informed at all stages, as it states in his contract," he assured fans. "He is obviously one of the finest players ever to grace an Albion shirt and we want him to stay. Bobby clearly feels he deserves his chance of playing in the Premiership and that's fair enough, but the article was untimely and, in that sense, disappointing to the club. We were going into a tight relegation weekend with four games to go. I want Bobby to do his talking on the pitch and not in the newspapers. There are still two games to go."

Albion went into the final game at Grimsby three points from safety, knowing a win might not be enough to save them. A 2-2 draw meant they finished 23rd in the table, six points from safety.

The team had responded to Coppell's influence and quiet professionalism, performing more like a mid-table team with 41 points in his 34 games in charge, but unable to make up for their appalling start to the season. "We took it to the last game of the season and the fans were grateful for that," he believes. "It restored a little bit of credibility, and also created some level of optimism for the future, which was very important given the situation the club was in."

Coppell made his feelings clear in *The Argus*. "I feel there's just got to be some investment in the team," he implored. "The original investment has carried them through from the Third Division to the First and there has been no reinvestment in that time. That original investment just showed that if you hand-pick the players you want, you can get some rock-solid players who can carry you for a couple of years."

Knight certainly got the message but might well have had something to say back, given the club's never-ending financial problems.

As for Bob, "I was completely devastated. This was my first relegation as a coach and it was hard to take. Steve Coppell did everything he could, but the gap was just too great to make up. This was also my first year without earning a bonus, and I made sure I kept out of the chairman's way in case he decided to dock me some money instead."

Coppell decided to stay at the club and signed a one-year deal, leaving Bob relieved and delighted to start off a new season with the same manager who had ended the previous one.

To nobody's surprise, Zamora finally got his wish in July 2003, signing for Tottenham Hotspur for a club record fee of £1.5million plus a sell-on clause – the only offer on the table, requiring great perseverance from the chairman, who remorselessly inched Daniel Levy up from his initial derisory £750,000 bid. £420,000, or 30% of the profit, went to his former club Bristol Rovers, whose initial £100,000 price for Zamora seemed laughable.

Club captain Paul Rogers retired and Paul Brooker opted to join Micky Adams at Leicester, a move he regrets. "I turned Brighton down but I would have played a lot more if I had stayed," he tells me. "But the lure of the Premier League was too much for me to resist."

The diminutive Leon Knight came in from Chelsea, initially on loan before signing for £100,000. For all his ability in front of goal, he was extremely high-maintenance off the field, with a poor attitude preventing him from the stellar career his talent promised. Brighton – and, eventually, everyone else – ran out of patience with him.

Darius Henderson, on loan from Reading, got off to a poor start with his new strike partner when he insisted on taking a penalty at Oldham on the opening day of the season, much to Knight's loudly expressed disapproval, exacerbated when he scored twice later in the game.

Coppell was confident that his team would challenge for promotion from the Second Division. But as a supporter rightly pointed out at a pre-season Fans' Forum, he had lost Zamora, Brooker, Rougier, Ingimarsson, Barrett, Rogers and Kitson from the wage bill, replacing them with Knight, Henderson (both loanees, although Knight would sign a permanent deal) and the only permanent new signing, goalkeeper Ben Roberts. Money was still extremely tight at the club – particularly so since relegation – a situation that would not change for several years.

Establishing themselves in the top two, the season started well for Albion. The only cloud on the horizon was another expression of frustration from the manager in *The Argus*. "This should be a club who should be looking at the (transfer) market seriously as buyers," he argued. "There has been negative investment in the team for probably three or four years now. We've been losing players, losing income. There has been nothing put back in the side and that's because of the unique situation and demands of the new stadium. I will be delighted when a decision is made on the new stadium because then we have got a direction. Hopefully that direction is positive and we can start investing in the team again, rather than wasting it on lawyers and public inquiries."

Matters were not going to die down. Coppell takes up the story, "We played at Middlesbrough in the Carling Cup on the Wednesday and stayed up north for a few days as we were playing at Hartlepool on the Saturday. We were second in the table, I was really enjoying it and we had a really good team. Everything about the job was good; I enjoyed the drive from home. I was even one of the few people who liked being at Withdean. After a difficult first season I thought we had a real chance of going up."

"While we were away I received a phone call from Dick Knight saying, 'John Madejski has been on the phone now that Alan Pardew has gone to West Ham, and he would like to speak to you about the Reading job.' 'Listen Dick,' I replied, 'I am really enjoying my time here, I like Brighton, we are almost top of the table, I am quite comfortable here and if you don't want me to speak to them that is fine with me. Joining Reading is not a huge ambition of mine.' To my surprise, Dick was very insistent. 'No, no, no. I understand how the football world works, you should go and speak to them.' I tried again to dissuade him, 'If you say, chairman, that you don't want me to go I am quite happy to stay here, and I will never bring this conversation up again in the future.' He seemed determined for me to talk to Reading. 'No I think it is only right and courteous that you go and speak to them.' So I went to speak to them and initially I turned them down. But a few days later they came back and I agreed to join them – but I left reluctantly."

# STEVE COPPELL

"It was not that Dick Knight wanted me to go but I later found out that there was a compensation payment of around £200,000 made, which was very important to the club given their circumstances. Dick was great with me and we had our regular Friday lunch where I did a lot of listening and nodding. He is a unique character and he always ordered a 'DK Special,' which made me laugh. All's well that ends well – I went from one terrific club to another and worked for two chairmen who I had a lot of respect and affection for. Brighton went up at the end of the season too and I was very pleased about that – perhaps I should have asked for half my bonus?"

Knight has a slightly different memory of what happened, mentioning in his autobiography the offer of a ten-year deal to Coppell to become director of football. As soon as Madejski called, he knew Coppell would be unable to resist the opportunity of managing a club likely to challenge for promotion to the Premier League, enjoying far greater resources than Brighton. On 9th October 2003, he joined Steve Sidwell at Reading – the third Brighton manager to resign in two years.

Coppell's departure also took Bob by surprise, "Steve seemed very happy, relaxed and in control, and I did not expect him to leave," he says. "Now I knew I would have to prove myself once again."

# CHAPTER 33
# MARK MCGHEE

Bob's main challenge now was to keep the team on track while the chairman hired yet another new manager, "Initially things went well. We beat Grimsby and Forest Green Rovers. But we lost my last three games in temporary charge, and were thrashed by Brentford. Steve Hunt, a player Steve Coppell had wanted to sign, tore us to shreds."

This humiliation proved too much for Bob. "I was embarrassed by our surrender on my return to Griffin Park. I totally lost the plot at halftime, sending the teacups flying, which was so unlike me. I finally began to understand just how lonely and exposed you are as a manager, and found this spell as a caretaker soul-destroying and very stressful."

It was a chastening experience for him, giving him more empathy with managers who he now realised had to confront hugely complex and delicate situations every single day. "The players did their best for me, and continued to call me 'Bob' rather than 'gaffer,' which was fine with me, as I knew I wasn't going to be in charge for long. I couldn't wait to hand over to the new man. I thought to myself 'Never again!'"

Dick Knight had to sift through more than 50 applications, but two good candidates appeared on his final shortlist – Leroy Rosenior and Mark McGhee. Rosenior had impressed while making bricks with no straw at Torquay. But his former club would be due compensation, whereas McGhee was available, having just been sacked by Millwall. Given his greater experience, Knight felt that he was better equipped to spearhead a promotion challenge.

McGhee recalled meeting Dick Knight in a London hotel. "We got on famously and I was offered the job shortly afterwards." He was immediately enthused by the Brighton project. "I liked what the chairman said about the fight for a new stadium. I realised straight away what a wonderful asset it would be for the community, and I was proved to be correct. My only concern was how long it would take to come to fruition, and how the team could be funded in the meantime, particularly if we were promoted that season."

"A manager is only as good as his chairman, and I was very fortunate in that respect. John Madjeski and Theo Paphitis were both hard acts to follow. Dick Knight was much more laidback. He had the blood of the club running through his veins and we got on brilliantly. I was used to being left to get on with things and he did not interfere. I met him for lunch every week at Topolino's, where we would talk things through."

As far as Bob was concerned, McGhee was happy for continuity, "Dick spoke to me about Bob, his role and his importance. After leaving Wolves I had decided not to take staff around with me. I told Dick that I was happy to give Bob an opportunity. It was refreshing for me to hear fresh voices and learn from others, so I was very open to the idea."

For his part, Bob was cautiously optimistic, "I had played against Mark when he was at Newcastle, and was well aware of his track record. Naturally, I was glad still to be in a job, but I had to prove myself yet again, knowing the likely consequences if we did not get on together."

McGhee put Bob at ease as soon as they met at his initial press conference at The Grand Hotel. "I walked in and shook his hand, and he said something to me in his broad Scottish accent, which I found hard to understand. He was then asked a question about me, and replied, 'If you are going to have an assistant, then at least have a big one who can look after you.' We talked afterwards about the players. I was relieved and delighted at how well we got on. He called me 'Big Man' and, because of his protruding bottom teeth, we all called him 'Piranha Teeth.'"

Mark, too, was happy with his first impression of Bob. "We both had a similar sense of humour and thought the same way about the game. I had no doubts that we could form a good partnership, but I think he had his concerns about me after my first training session with the players."

McGhee was clearly keen to make a strong impression on his players, "Initially I was just watching and listening as Bob took them through their paces, and all I could hear was players shouting and screaming at each other whenever someone made a mistake or misplaced a pass."

He waited for the right time to make his point. "At the end of the session, I gathered them all together and fixed my attention upon the nearest player, who happened to be John Piercy, and gave him a verbal volley. 'I don't know who you are or what you are doing here, but you are not training with me again if you behave like that. You are a total disgrace.' He was completely nonplussed. Then I turned to Dan Harding, 'I have watched you train today and your attitude has been excellent.' He could not hide the smile on his face. I turned back to the first player and said,

'How did that make you feel?' 'Terrible.' 'Well, I didn't actually think that your attitude was awful. Look how much better you all feel when you are encouraged by your teammates. There is a time and place for criticism, but it will come from me and not from all of you.' Getting rid of all that negativity really helped as I could see that Dan felt he was king of the jungle when he was praised. I did feel a bit sorry for John, who was the innocent stooge I needed in order to make my point."

"I could see Bob looking at me as if I was crazy," said McGhee, "but he quickly grasped what I had done, and we soon became firm friends. I loved that he was such a positive person who always tried to see the best in everyone. I did most of the coaching, with Bob taking the warm-ups and passing drills, and I always encouraged Bob and Dean White to chip in with ideas. I was not concerned with how things had been done before my arrival, I just got on with things and ensured that we were always attacking, aggressive, and on the front foot."

Meanwhile, Bob was happy with Mark's approach and the division of labour between them. "Mark liked to work with the strikers, while I looked after the midfielders and defenders, and we shared the work between us. I was his link to the players, but he also developed a good relationship with them. He gave them a lot of leeway but came down hard if the tempo was not right or if players pushed him too far, which did not happen very often as he had a presence about him. He would join in the training games and the players would line up for the privilege of kicking the pair of us. He did not go in for all the video analysis that Steve Coppell had introduced but otherwise made few changes. The players raised their game, as is generally the case when a new manager arrives, and we soon recovered the ground lost from my spell in charge."

Leon Knight scored 27 goals that season, and was a vital part of the team, but he proved to be one of the most difficult players that Bob ever had to deal with. "Leon was disruptive and his shoulders would drop if he was not enjoying a training session, or if he felt that it did not suit him. He was selfish, self-obsessed and did not work hard enough. Everything had to revolve around him, and if he was not the centre of attention he would switch off. He had no interest in being part of a team. If things got too bad then I would lose it with him and send him in. The players also got fed up with him and wouldn't let him get away with his lack of effort. There was some rowing on the pitch and pushing and barging in training, and Danny Cullip, in particular, was not slow to tell him how he felt about his attitude."

Recognising Knight's importance, Booker brought things to a head. "I could see that the situation was deteriorating and we had to find a way to sort things out before Leon became totally alienated from the group. He had so much ability, provided that extra something, and we really needed his goals. One day, after he misbehaved again, I sat him down. 'Leon, come on, what's it all about, you know it's a team game?' 'Well, I want to practice my shooting.' 'We do that at the end of training, it is not just about you, everyone else has to be involved too.' He did not take that very well, so I said, 'I will tell you what, I will come into training at 9 o'clock tomorrow. I will get 20 footballs and a goalkeeper and we will have an hour's one-to-one, just you and me against the keeper, shooting and finishing, which is exactly what you want.' 'Would you do that for me, Bob?' 'Yes, but we can't do it every day.' He calmed down straight away, got in early with a smile on his face, and we had a great time with me serving balls for him to turn and shoot past the keeper. That's all he ever wanted to do. It didn't really change anything about the way he behaved though. He was a loveable rogue and high maintenance, but he could have been another Jermaine Defoe and played for England. He was so frustrating."

Bob may have used the carrot with Knight, but his manager preferred the stick. "Leon had eased off towards the end of the season and had gone five games without scoring when Mark took him to one side as we prepared for the playoff final and warned him, 'I'm not sure if you will be starting on Sunday.' He left him to simmer for a couple of days. Leon responded and trained brilliantly for the few days before the match. He was totally focused upon the task in hand – and, of course, he ended up winning the game for us. That was great man management."

Knight wasn't the only one to get on the wrong side of McGhee. "He also dealt firmly with Mark McCammon when he challenged his authority at Burnley," says Bob. "McCammon answered him back at half-time after he had been criticised, claimed he was being discriminated against and stormed out of the dressing room. I tried to calm him down, but he refused to come back. McGhee ordered him off the team coach and McCammon made his own way home by train, which ensured headlines in the national press."

McGhee was a strong character, marching to the beat of his own drum and asserting his authority. "We were thrashed by Bristol City in Mark's first home game in charge," says Bob. "As I was about to slink off home I heard him calling me, 'Hey, Big Man, we are going out for a beer tonight.' 'Don't be daft,' I replied, 'we can't be seen out in Brighton after such a heavy defeat.' 'Why not? I am the manager and if I say we are going out for a beer, we are going out for a beer.' So we went out to drown our sorrows. Everyone was in for training on the Sunday, and John Keeley came up to us and asked, 'Good night last night? One of my mates saw you and it looked like you were having a great time.' Mark turned round to him and replied, 'Keel-o, you just tell your mate to wait until we win a game, and then he will really see us out enjoying ourselves.' That put him in his place and I spent many convivial evenings with Mark, who rented a flat in The French Apartments on the seafront."

The new manager soon put his stamp on team matters, overseeing a 4th place finish, six points shy of automatic promotion. Swindon Town were beaten on penalty kicks on an epic night at Withdean. This was perhaps unsurprising given the time and thought the manager had spent on preparing for a penalty shootout, and Bristol City awaited Albion in the final at the Millennium Stadium.

"Mark McGhee came into his element, hyped up the players and made them believe that we would win. We travelled down a couple of days before the final and stayed at St David's Hotel on the Cardiff waterfront. I remember Mark discussing the arrangements with Derek Allan, and saying to him, 'I'm not sure, should we have white wine the first night and red the next?' which Derek found very droll. We trained well and there was an excellent atmosphere and a feeling of great confidence."

"As we left the hotel, Mark gave me a CD and told me to play it at maximum volume just before we arrived at the stadium. I put it on and it was David Bowie's 'Heroes' with its stirring lyrics. Everyone on the coach was singing at the top of his voice and we were all so pumped up. I knew at that moment that we were going to win."

The McGhee magic continued right until the first whistle. "Mark was very calm and composed in the dressing room. He simply named the team and told Leon Knight that he was playing, which was another masterstroke. When we got back from the warm-up he asked me to fetch a flipchart. He stood it up for all the players to see. On one side he had written the names of every team in Division Two and on the other he had listed the sides in the First Division, and as they filed out he simply looked at the players and said, 'What do you want? Who do you want to play next season? It is up to you.' His team talk was done in three sentences with not a single mention of the opposition."

On a stiflingly hot day, a poor match was settled by Knight's calmly-taken penalty kick near the end after Chris Iwelumo was tripped. McGhee never missed a trick, telling the unused substitutes to jog down the touchline to where the Albion fans were seated, whipping them up into a frenzy to help the team over the line. Nothing was left to chance –a managerial masterclass by McGhee.

"We had a wonderful journey home that night," says Bob, recalling the celebrations. "The players' wives and families joined us on the coach and Mark gave me £500 to buy drinks and champagne for everyone. We all crowded into the Sportsman Pub in Withdean, and it was a long night."

Dick Knight summed up Albion's achievement in *The Argus*, "We all worked really hard and I think we can be very satisfied that we pulled it off. It wasn't pretty at times, but it was effective. From a managerial and coaching point of view I feel satisfied I made the right decisions that got us the results in the only way we could get them. I am well pleased with the performance, albeit I would like us to look better. Hopefully in the future we will."

Bob could look back with pride on a job well done, rewarded with a £12,500 promotion bonus – his third in four seasons.

Soon it was time to plan for the new season as founder members of the newly renamed Coca-Cola Championship.

As normal, budgets were tight. Money was poured into the fight for Falmer, forcing the club to launch the "Alive & Kicking" fund. McGhee, noticeably, appeared to be more sanguine and pragmatic about the situation he faced that his immediate predecessor. "The future and survival of this football club has to go before any other decision," he accepted, avoiding public comment about his problems in building a team strong enough to survive in the Championship. Journalist and Brighton fan Nick Szczepanik describes him as "a grown-up, unlike some of the overgrown children in the game."

Dick Knight told *The Argus* that he and Mark had been "burning the midnight oil," trying to bring in fresh blood, but finding it next to impossible to sign Championship-hardened players, despite the playing budget rising by almost £1 million.

Iwelumo decided to play in Germany – a big loss – and Leon Knight also missed the first three matches of the season through suspension.

A ragtag and bobtail of foreign forwards joined on trial. Swiss-born Maheta Molango survived the cut, scoring five goals in pre-season, albeit against weak opposition, to convince McGhee to offer the former SV Wacker Burghausen striker a three-year contract. He started off like a whirlwind, scoring after 12 seconds of his debut at Reading and almost earning a penalty immediately afterwards, but found it hard to cope with the physicality of English football, fading away despite scoring five times against Sidley United in the Sussex Senior Cup.

Bob was not too impressed. "Dick thought that he would become the next Bobby Zamora, but he proved to be a better lawyer than footballer, and is now chief executive of Real Mallorca."

Darren Currie was an exceptional capture on a free transfer from Wycombe, proof that there are bargains still to be found if you know where to look. "He had no pace but was tricky and a beautiful crosser of the ball with either foot," says Bob. "I have seen a lot of naked flesh in dressing rooms, and he had more tattoos than anyone else."

Currie settled in well – too well, perhaps – before the chairman eventually persuaded Ipswich to increase their original £75,000 bid to £250,000. It was a figure too good to turn down – particularly for a 30-year-old free transfer. His stay at the club had been short.

Danny Cullip was another departure, joining Sheffield United for a similar fee having provided exceptional service both on and off the field. After playing 242 times for the club, he wanted to move on, making a poor choice to sign for Neil Warnock, with whom he rapidly fell out. Cullip did not last long at Bramall Lane, with McGhee unsuccessfully trying to bring him back on loan.

£500,000 for two players was far too much to ignore given the funding demands of the public inquiry into Falmer. Not for the first or last time, footballing needs took a back seat to ensuring survival.

With Knight struggling and goals in short supply, McGhee struck gold when he switched defender Adam Virgo to attack, something he had tried occasionally the previous season, when Virgo had come off the bench.

Bob had discussed this option with McGhee, totally agreeing with his manager's decision. "Mark had to make the most of what we had; we desperately lacked firepower. Adam was big, strong and mobile, chased everything and proved to be an excellent target man. He really looked the part and he did a great job, scoring nine times. He was our best player, and without him we would have gone down."

"Mark was tactically very astute and switched us to three at the back at White Hart Lane, in the FA Cup, when we only lost to an extremely dubious late goal. One of the few highlights of a desperate season was winning at Sheffield United. Leon scored a last-minute winner for us, and

I received a magnificent welcome, which I milked for all it was worth. We won an award for the performance of the week from the League Managers' Association, and Mark gave me the prize of an engraved vase, which I still have at home."

"We fought hard to stay up and needed a point from our last game at home to Ipswich, who were still challenging for automatic promotion. Mark was a good friend of their manager, Joe Royle, but he was distinctly unamused, and used some extremely ripe language, when Royle brought on wave after wave of strikers, trying to force a late winner. But we clung on to a 1-1 draw."

It was a close-run thing. Brighton finished 20th, surviving by a point after scoring just 40 goals all season.

Bob did not want to go through such an experience again. "I was emotionally drained and cried my eyes out when the final whistle went. The whole season was hard work and totally exhausting."

McGhee was in no doubt about the feat. "Staying up in our first season in the Championship was as good as any other achievement in my managerial career, including reaching the playoffs with Wolves and Millwall," he smiled. "I had to play young lads who were not ready or good enough when we lost key members of the promotion team."

Brighton & Hove City Council leader Ken Bodfish agreed with him when he commented in *The Argus*, "The Albion's achievement in staying up this year ranks with any in the club's history. How Mark McGhee has managed it on the shoestring budget at his disposal I will never know." McGhee was named BBC TV South-East's coach of the year.

He had a tough decision to make, realising that the following season would be no different – a case of pushing water uphill in pursuit of yet another miracle while Dick Knight jokingly craved a season of "mid-table anonymity."

"I have often thought that I should have resigned after that first Championship season," confesses McGhee. "I was in demand at that time, and would probably have found a less difficult managerial job. I spoke to Bob and Dick but, after a lot of thought, I decided to stay on, even though I knew that it would be more of the same."

Bob remembers the conversations they shared. "Mark wasn't sure what to do, and I thought that he made the correct decision. To his credit, he was also concerned about the job security of the backroom staff had he left the club."

The squad was strengthened with a windfall, the "Coca-Cola Kid," Colin Kazim-Richards, arrived after Brighton fan, Aaron Berry, won £250,000 for his club to spend on new players. Knight had been tipped off about a young striker at Bury, signing him for an initial £55,000.

Incomings were more than offset by outgoings. Dan Harding, who had established himself as a quick and aggressive left-back, rejected a new contract to join Leeds for a tribunal-set fee of up to £850,000, of which Albion eventually received around 50%.

Virgo's performances the previous season had attracted some interest, and in July 2005 Knight's negotiating skill ensured that was he was able to extract £1.5 million from Celtic for his best player – very much more than the chairman thought he was worth.

McGhee knew the score, but at a stroke had lost two of his most valuable players, knowing full well that all available funds would be poured into the Falmer black hole. He would be expected to source replacements from the bargain basement. It was getting harder for him to continue to pull rabbits out of hats; the signing of Argentinian striker Federico Turienzo, proved as disastrous as that of Molango.

Turienzo came to the club following a recommendation to Liam Brady from his former Juventus teammate Zbigniew Boniek. Bob tried his best with him. "I gave him lots of extra shooting and heading practice, but to no avail. He tried hard and was a delight to work with, but he spoke no English and was unable to adapt. That was £150,000 down the drain, and Mark and I knew that we would be unlikely to see that kind of money again."

"We were forced to play Leon Knight and Colin Kazim-Richards up front, but other teams found it easy to defend against us, given our lack of physicality, and we were never able to hold the ball up."

Leon Knight was up to all his old tricks, eventually leaving for Swansea for £125,000 in January. Typically, he began with a first half hat trick on his debut against MK Dons, but Kenny Jackett found him as difficult to manage as Mark McGhee, selling him 12 months later. Perhaps the best clue to his character comes from his outrageous comments in the *South Wales Evening Post* in late April. "It was terrific to see Brighton go down," he sneered. "I was absolutely delighted that they got relegated. You cannot understand how happy I was."

There was no respite for Bob, finding his hands full looking after Kazim-Richards. "Colin was another one who was full of himself, swaggered around and thought he had made it," he says. "He was frustrating, as he had so much ability, but he was totally uncoachable. Whatever you asked him to do he simply did the opposite. He did everything his way, and listened to nobody."

I reminded Bob of what he had said about him at the Fans' Forum in August 2005, "Colin has a great attitude and he wants to learn." He laughs ruefully. "Well, I got that one wrong, didn't I? I think Colin was still in the honeymoon period and on best behaviour when I said that."

"We tried everything we could, but nothing seemed to go right. Only one team scored less goals than us and only one conceded more, so it was patently obvious that we were going to struggle to stay up."

"The players never gave up and loanee Paul McShane set a great example, but we lost Carpenter and Oatway to injury. We were never out of the bottom three after January and finished up exactly where we deserved, bottom of the table, 12 points from safety. Losing 5-1 at home to Stoke on the final day of the season summed the season up perfectly."

In his autobiography, Knight suggested that McGhee and Booker were not as effective as they had been, taking their eye off the ball. He was particularly upset that neither bothered to arrive on time at London Colney for a friendly match arranged for Albion to watch a potential loan target, Arsenal winger Quincy Owusu-Abeyie. Bob accepts they made a mistake. "Dick was pushing for us to sign the player, but Mark was not so keen. We had trained in the morning, but there was no excuse for turning up late."

"Mark and I were a tight unit and we sparked off each other, but we were unable to turn things around. We knew that the season had been a disaster, even though there were lots of mitigating circumstances. The crowd also turned on us, and I got some abuse from behind the dugout, which I sometimes reacted to. I found it hard to keep my customary smile on my face when I tried to raise the players' spirits, and there were times when I could have done with somebody to pick me up too. Many of the fans were ready for a change and wanted Mark to go, and if he went, I was pretty certain that I would be leaving with him."

With the board split, Knight used his casting vote to keep McGhee – and therefore Bob – in his job, but it was a close-run thing. Their previous experience in winning promotion from Division One helped, but Knight freshened things up by promoting Dean Wilkins to first team coach.

Bob understood the rationale for the move. "Dean was a good coach with lots of experience of working with young players and our financial situation meant we would be relying increasingly on youth. He also provided the players with a different voice. Mark thought that he would probably have been sacked if he had not agreed to work with Dean. The three of us worked together during pre-season. I took a backwards step as Dean did more of the coaching."

Despite the vote of confidence, Bob felt they were on thin ice and borrowed time, particularly as Tony Bloom, who had invested heavily in the club and was becoming increasingly influential, made it clear that he was in favour of a change of manager. Wilkins was also an obvious successor. "I had been the great survivor, working for five different managers, but my time was running out."

Strenuous efforts were made to strengthen the squad without much success. Non-league striker Alex Revell, was the only major arrival. Winger Sebastien Carole left for Leeds United and Kazim-Richards, who had made clear his desire to leave, joined Sheffield United on transfer deadline day for an initial £150,000, plus a later payment of £280,000 when he moved on to join Fenerbahçe in June 2007.

The first two matches were won but a run of four winless games saw the fans restless, and the axe fell in early September. McGhee was sacked – this time Bob went with him.

Knight told *Seagulls World* that McGhee had "lost the fans" and that the club was "not moving forward on the playing side." He also felt it necessary to "make a complete change." Bob had to go too, leaving Wilkins in temporary charge.

Bob recalls how Knight sacked him. "As soon as Mark learned his fate he called me and said that I would also be hearing from the chairman. In truth, it was not too much of a shock, but this would be the first time I had ever been fired as a coach. I was having a nap when Dick called and said, 'Are you OK, are you *compos mentis*?' I had no idea what he meant, so I said, 'Yes, I have got my shorts on.' Dick laughed. 'Can you come down and meet me now at Topolino's?' I knew what was coming."

"Dick was there with Martin Perry and he offered me a beer. I said, 'I am not really in the mood for a drink, can we just get on with it?' 'Do you want something to eat, Bob?' I could see that this was not easy for him as we had always got on well together, but eventually he managed to get the words out: 'This is difficult for me, but it is time for me to make some wholesale changes. You have had a good run as assistant manager, but I need to make a clean sweep. You have been great for us and done a fantastic job and I want to thank you for everything. We will make sure you are looked after properly, and I wish you all the best.' Short and sharp – just like the drop. Topolino's had now become Sackolino's."

Dick Knight is forthright in explaining his reasons for sacking Bob after six years of exceptional service and achievement. "Bob had to go when Mark did," he declares. "They had become friends, but they got too close and I did not feel that Bob was his own man any longer. He was not doing the job as well as he had been before. He had problems in his personal life that affected him and he was not as upbeat as normal. I felt that they had both lost the dressing room and that Bob wasn't enjoying the same relationship with the players as before. Bob did a wonderful job and I am so grateful for everything he did for the club. I made sure that we honoured his contract and he left with a year's money. As for Mark – I had protected him for a long time, but I thought that the time had come."

Bob read these words with great interest, pausing to gather his thoughts before responding to his former chairman's comments. "There is some truth in what Dick said. My eye was off the ball at work, but I disagree that I was under Mark's influence, as it was a similar relationship to the one with Micky Adams. I treated Mark with the same respect as I had every manager I had worked with. I certainly wasn't his lapdog, there just to agree with him and do his bidding. He asked for, and took, my advice all the time. I also do not accept that we lost the dressing room or that my relationship ever changed with the players. I would certainly have noticed if it had. In retrospect, I should have told Mark to be at Arsenal for that friendly match."

"Christine and I had divorced and I'd bought a house in The Hornbeams in Burgess Hill. I was also in a serious relationship with Nicky Keig-Shevlin. She'd left her husband in early 2005 and moved in with me soon afterwards. We were blissfully happy together, but I was conscious that I had lost one marriage due to the demands of football, and was determined not to jeopardise this relationship. So yes, my priorities did change and I was distracted and less focused on my job. I did leave training a bit earlier and sometimes didn't go on scouting trips when I might have done."

Nicky was equally content, "I ended up leaving my husband to be with Bob. This was not a decision either of us took lightly but we were just drawn together and it felt right. To this day I regret the hurt I caused Richard but know it was totally the right decision as Robert and I are soulmates."

Bob left Topolino's feeling shaken and distraught. "I found it hard to take in that after six years of total involvement with the club, everything had come to an end, and I would have to find something else to do. I had loved my time at Brighton, the job was a massive part of me, and I had no idea how I would cope without it."

How would Bob face the future without football?

# CHAPTER 34
# RESPITE

Bob Booker felt "devastated" and "a broken man" when Dick Knight fired him after six years of loyal and unblemished service. "What made it even harder was the fact that I really loved that football club – so much so that I had not followed Micky Adams to Leicester when I had the chance," he says. "I loved my job as well as all the people I worked with. Albion meant everything to me and my role helped define me as a person. And suddenly everything had been taken away from me."

"Reality hit home when I cleared my desk the following morning and dropped my company car off to Dean Wilkins. That really upset me, and, irrationally, I felt angry and disappointed that I had gone and he was still there. My departure was so sudden and there was no party or send off. In a way it reminded me of leaving Brentford in 1993, but at least this time I was treated impeccably by Brighton."

"On reflection, I thought that the decision to get rid of me was reasonable. I had enjoyed a long spell there and it was becoming harder and more exhausting to keep proving myself to so many new managers who all presented me with different challenges. The job was tough and stressful but, with rare exceptions, I thrived on it. I felt as if I had been knocked down a few pegs and my confidence took a real blow. What made things even worse is that I suddenly felt like I was a non-person. Nobody in the game offered me anything. Micky Adams, Steve Coppell and some of the players called to commiserate, but most of the people I considered to be friends ignored me and seemed to disappear."

He soon realised that he could not sit by the telephone, willing it to ring. "I had to try and make something happen. I wanted to get back into football and Chris Wilder asked if I would come and work with him if he got the Cambridge United job, but he was unsuccessful. I eventually scouted for Micky Adams, but I did not push myself – mainly because I lacked self-belief and did not think that I was high-profile enough. Who was I going to call? Who had ever heard of me? I knew that most jobs in football went to friends and cronies and I did not think that anybody would be interested in hiring me."

Such negativity demonstrates that Bob had lost confidence in his own ability. But he did not have too much brooding time, as an immediate opportunity opened up.

"The week before I was fired, a friend of mine, Bob Laundon, who managed Pease Pottage, asked me to help him out and take a training session. I enjoyed myself, but looked upon it simply as a one-off until fate intervened. I had time on my hands and Bob suggested that I work with the club on a more regular basis. Their Finches Field ground wasn't far from home and I jumped at the opportunity. I took training with Bob every Tuesday and Thursday, stayed for the entire season, and the players responded by finishing second in Division Three of the Sussex County League and also won three cup competitions. I tried to make them a bit more professional in their attitude and approach and we even borrowed the Brighton team coach to travel to the cup finals."

"Unfortunately we became victims of our own success as seven of our best players were poached at the end of the season, and we both decided to step down. I loved every minute of my time with the club. It was wonderful to stay involved in football, even at this level, and put something back without there being any real pressure on me."

Bob helped off the pitch, too. "Bob Laundon ran a company that fitted kitchens and bathrooms and offered me work whenever I wanted it, and I was delighted to earn £50 a day. I didn't care if people recognised me and thought that this was a bit of a comedown. I needed to keep busy and not mope around the house. I was used to getting my hands dirty. I started off cleaning up and making the tea but I watched how Bob worked and soon learned how to assemble cupboards. I was tickled pink, as I had no idea how to knock a nail in a wall. I worked with him for a couple of years and it was a good distraction and highly therapeutic. I am so grateful to him for helping me get through such a tough time."

Nicky was proud of how well Bob adapted to his new situation. "It was a totally different timetable for him," she says. "He'd start early and never know what time he'd finish. Many a time I had dinner ready for him, which ended up in the bin as he was back so late."

In 2007, the couple found a beautiful two-bedroom apartment in Puerto Pollensa in Northern Majorca, a location Nicky's family had been visiting since she was a child and, in Bob's view, "The best thing we ever did."

"It became our escape and we went out there every few weeks. It is our second home and the plan is that one day we will retire and spend half the year out there."

Life settled into a comfortable routine, spending as much time as they could in Majorca. "Occasionally we would book cheap flights and fly out for the day," says Nicky. "We'd get the early flight that arrived in Palma at 8.45, go to the apartment, meet friends for lunch, go to the pool or beach in the afternoon, meet more friends for dinner then get the 11 o'clock flight back. The locals must have thought we were mad."

The break from football gave Bob some breathing space, beginning to realise how much his spell at Brighton had taken out of him. "Now I was out of the game I understood just how stressful it is to work in football, with the relentless pressure of having to win games and keep the players happy and motivated."

Bob had finally taken back control of his life, thoroughly enjoying choosing exactly when he wanted to work, even returning to Withdean on scouting missions. In July 2007, just after secretary of state Hazel Blears finally gave Falmer stadium the go-ahead, he played for the "Albion All Stars" in the warm-up game that preceded Kerry Mayo's testimonial match against Reading.

There was only one thing missing. Bob still hankered after a return to football – he had known little else for 30 years. But the longer he was out of the game, the less likely it was. He knew that his best and perhaps only chance depended on one of his former managers giving him the call.

His prayers seemed to have been answered when Knight lost patience with Dean Wilkins. Despite a seventh place finish in 2007/08, narrowly missing out on the playoffs, Knight felt the team had underperformed, particularly given the presence of potent new strikers in Nicky Forster and Glenn Murray. All was not well behind the scenes, with stories of player discontent and questions over Wilkins's man management skills. Knight had lost confidence in his managerial ability; with the prospect of Falmer now a reality rather than a mere chimera, he decided he needed a more experienced manager who could lead the team back to the Championship. He knew exactly who he wanted to hire.

Micky Adams was available after leaving his post as assistant manager of Colchester. In May 2008, he was a surprise appointment as Brighton manager, with Wilkins demoted and offered a role as first team coach.

After a gap of six-and-a-half years, Adams's decision to return was risky – and the future of his former assistant was unclear.

# CHAPTER 35
# MICKY ADAMS (PART 2)

Bob was surprised by the news of Micky Adams's return to Brighton. He had not spoken to his friend for a while, nor stayed in contact with Dick Knight. Maybe, just maybe, there would be an opportunity for him to resume his partnership with his former boss.

At the press conference announcing his arrival in May 2008, Adams admitted he had "grey hair" and was "fatter" but also pointed out he was a "wiser and more experienced" manager. The move happened very quickly, coinciding with Adams seeking a new challenge. Following his departure from Brighton in 2001 because of his ambition to manage at the top level, he had, in his own words, an "eventful time" at Leicester, leading them to promotion in 2003 but failing to keep them in the Premier League the following season. A difficult spell at Coventry saw him lead the Sky Blues to eighth place in the Championship, but he did not enjoy a healthy relationship with the board. Brighton, he felt, was a case of unfinished business, setting Championship football as a realistic target within the three-year duration of his contract.

Knight was delighted to have convinced Adams to return. "Nine years ago, when I first met Micky, I said, 'We'll be in our new stadium in two years,'" he wisecracked. "The other day when I saw him, I said, 'We'll be in our new stadium in two years!'" Adams dead-batted when asked specifically about the prospects of either Bob or Alan Cork joining him, confirming that he did not envisage the established coaching set-up at the club changing. Despite reiterating that message to Bob when they eventually spoke, Adams made it clear that the door was not closed, promising to make contact if the situation changed.

Dean Wilkins had been given time to overcome his disappointment at losing the manager's job and decide whether he would remain as first team coach. Adams was happy to work with Wilkins, reiterating his respect for his predecessor's coaching ability. Bob was left in limbo while the drama played out.

The first chink of light came shortly afterwards, when Ian Chapman resigned from his position as first team coach and reserve team manager. "Dean Wilkins sold me something to come to the club, and when that was removed it didn't feel the same to me," he told *The Argus*. "I just felt it wasn't right, so I have decided to move on." A week later, Adams announced his intention to appoint a development coach to work with the club's young professionals. Bob's ears must have pricked up when he heard those words, but no firm decisions about staff changes could be made until Wilkins made up his mind.

The summer dragged on with no word from Wilkins, forcing Knight to impose a deadline in a bid to end the ensuing uncertainty and prevarication. Finally, more than a month after Adams's arrival, a figurative puff of white smoke belched from Withdean. Wilkins would be leaving the club, a decision succinctly summed up by Andy Naylor in *The Argus*, "The departure of Dean Wilkins is in both his best interests and those of Albion. Remaining at the club as senior first team coach following his removal as manager would have been an accident waiting to happen."

Adams finally knew where he stood and he was left with only Dean White as assistant manager; no coach or reserve team manager was *in situ* when the players reported back for training at the end of June.

Phlegmatic but hopeful, Bob decided to go to Majorca with Nicky, who remembers what happened next. "It was a Wednesday and we were shopping at the market in the port when I saw a coin on the floor. Being superstitious, I picked it up, saying, 'See a penny pick it up, all day long you'll have good luck.' We went back to our apartment. Shortly afterwards Micky finally called Bob and offered him the job as reserve team coach." Bob laughs, remembering a very short conversation. He told Micky he "would be on the next plane," thankfully remembering despite his jubilation to mention his forthcoming marriage to Nicky, the day before the season started; a small family affair followed by a blessing in Majorca a month later.

Adams spoke of his pleasure at the appointment when it was announced on the official club website. "He worked tirelessly for the club in his first spell – and he played a huge part in the club's success," he said of Bob. "I am bringing him back in a slightly different role. One of his main strengths is his coaching ability and he will be dealing with the reserve team and the development squad that we have put together." Adams expected Bob to work closely with White, who would remain assistant manager.

Knight was unsurprised by Bob's return. "Bob was just Bob – always upbeat, back to his normal self, and he fitted in seamlessly," he says. "He did not bear any grudges – it was the obvious solution and I was happy about it as I knew how well they had worked together."

Bob was back in his element on the training ground, taking up a fairly fluid role. "Micky told me, 'Officially you're not going to be my coach and your job title will be reserve team coach, but I want you back here next to me as we trust each other.' I happily accepted the £350 weekly salary. The money was not important to me as I was back, and it was like coming home again. We went straight off to a training camp in Ballygar on my first day, but there were no riots this time."

Pre-season training went well, but playing resources were so stretched that Bob was named as a substitute for a game at Stansted alongside Matt Hicks. Much to his relief, at the age of 50 he was not needed. The two friends remained safely on the bench, telling each other tall stories of what they would have accomplished had their services been required.

Bob soon noticed a change in Micky. "He worked as hard as ever and was totally focused on his job. He had always struggled to trust people but he opened up a bit and was more approachable, relaxed and laid back in his approach. He was more tolerant of what was going on and did not lose his temper as much. He still kept his distance from the players, but no longer ruled by fear."

"My role was similar to before, but I was now officially number three and was careful not to usurp my authority and step on Dean White's toes. He mainly concentrated on the off-field organisation while I helped Micky with the coaching and took the reserve games. The three of us ran things and worked well together."

Adams felt comfortable with Bob. "He was just the same and as good as ever," he says.

One of Adams's great strengths was his knowledge of players and his acumen in the transfer market, but his touch, and maybe luck, had deserted him and his signings were spotty in the extreme, suffering numerous injury problems.

Adam Virgo, whose career had stood still since he left for Celtic, returned too, having played for Adams on loan at Coventry. New defender Colin Hawkins soon needed a hernia operation, injury-prone winger Kevin McLeod arrived from Colchester and Matt Richards returned for a third loan spell. The marquee signing was experienced utility player and former Millwall captain David Livermore, from Hull City, but he disappointed, seeing his season wrecked by poor discipline and a knee injury. Kerry Mayo and Gary Hart, who had been released by Wilkins, were handed reprieves.

"Our recruitment was poor," concedes Bob. "Money was tight. None of the new signings did very much. We were crying out for another Charlie Oatway, Danny Cullip, 'Dodge' Rogers or Richard Carpenter – a winner with a killer instinct who could inspire and lead by example. Injuries bit deep and we also lost Nicky Forster and Glenn Murray for spells, which we could ill afford."

Adams was shortlisted for League One manager of the month for August following a bright start, but results soon declined and Albion failed to win their first six home games, including a desperate loss to a Walsall team down to nine men.

Just when the fans were beginning to murmur, Albion responded brilliantly, beating Premier League giants Manchester City on penalties in the Carling Cup. Knight describes the battle between the haves and the have-nots as "One of the most memorable games we played at Withdean." After a late equaliser forced extra time, Bob remembers City manager Mark Hughes striding onto the pitch in the interval, his face like thunder, screaming at his players, "You'd better not lose this game."

Veteran Robbie Savage arrived on loan from Derby – an attempt to shore up the midfield and provide some leadership – and became the victim of perhaps Bob's greatest ever prank.

The new signing arrived for training at 9.30am driving his splendid black Mercedes, to be greeted by a shifty and dubious-looking character who, according to Miles Godfrey in *The Argus*, "was dressed up in a car parking attendant's fluorescent jacket, complete with goofy teeth and Robbie Savage-esque long blonde wig." Savage was directed to a parking spot before being asked by the attendant if he would sign an Albion shirt. He obliged and was told, "I think you're great. Can I sit in your car?"

The whole team watched in hysterics. Savage was bemused by the whole episode, only seeing the joke when Bob revealed his true identity. "I met Bob Booker this morning – he's a real character," he said in an understatement. "We wanted to give him a real Albion welcome and I did him hook, line and sinker," smiles Bob. "But he was a lovely lad who took it in the spirit it was meant."

For all his effort and influence, Savage was past his best. Bradley Johnson, borrowed from Leeds, made more impact, scoring two goals on his debut to inspire a 3-2 win over eventual champions Leicester City.

The pattern was set for a stream of loanees to help plug the massive gaps caused by a seemingly never-ending injury list.

# OOH-AAH: THE BOB BOOKER STORY

More gloom, when Hartlepool knocked Albion out of the FA Cup, and a successful run in the Johnstone's Paint Trophy distracted attention from a series of defeats which saw Albion far nearer the bottom than the top of the table.

Adams recognised the seriousness of the situation. "At the moment I am not doing the job that I was brought in for," he told *The Argus*. "Given time, I am confident I'm the man to turn it around."

Only a Luton Town team facing certain relegation from the Football League after a savage 30-point deduction for financial irregularities stood between Albion and a lucrative visit to Wembley in the final of the Johnstone's Paint Trophy, but two dire performances culminated in defeat on penalties. The season was over, and only a relegation struggle remained. Adams knew the importance of winning. "I feel like I'm in a Wild West movie and the undertaker is measuring me up for a coffin," he admitted to *The Argus* before the second leg. He was not far wrong.

Bob saw the warning signs, "The fans got behind Micky at first, as it was the return of the prodigal son, but they soon became disillusioned with results and you could feel the tide turning."

Influential Brighton fan John Baine, the club poet-in-residence and PA announcer, summarised the plight of the season while venting his spleen on BBC Southern Counties Radio. "I thought it was spineless, inept, clueless garbage, an absolute disgrace – the absolute opposite of everything we hoped to get from Micky Adams," he ranted, presciently adding, "He didn't sound like the Adams of old, he didn't sound like the guy of thunder and fire that we loved and who did so well for us before. He isn't the man he was, he's not there anymore."

Commenting in *The Argus*, Albion reporter Andy Naylor called this criticism "a ridiculous overreaction," noting the problems Adams faced given his depleted squad. Knight supported him in the January transfer window, bringing in six players.

Bob was concerned for his friend. "His heart told him to come back but his head should have said no," he thinks. "It is so hard to return to the scene of your previous success. Micky built up an incredible squad first time round and, understandably, he was unable to recreate that spark or repeat that success in the limited time he was given. Things just did not come off for him, even though we did very much the same in terms of training and preparation."

"Getting to Wembley would have been a lifesaver for him and made up for some of the poor results and performances in the league, but we were dreadful in both games against Luton and fully deserved to lose."

After the mid-February cup defeat, Adams met Knight. He called Bob immediately afterwards. "That's it," he said, "I've gone."

"Micky told me that he had met Dick Knight at the Little Chef at Hickstead, and they had mutually agreed that he would leave straight away."

"I went straight over to his house and we had a glass of wine together. He said, 'I don't know where that leaves you.' I was so sorry for Micky and just thought 'Here we go again. That's my lot.' I was certain that I would be on my way too."

"Dean White was in charge of the team at Millwall and I was on the bench with him. Micky had already picked the side, but Dean changed it and put Adam Virgo up front, and he scored the winning goal. We met up that night and Micky, as competitive as ever, was annoyed with Dean for altering the team."

"I just kept my head down and stayed in the background waiting for the axe to fall, but Dick did not speak to me, although he announced that Dean and I would be in charge for the next couple of games."

"Micky Adams did not work out and resigned after winning only six of his 29 league games in charge," explains Knight. "It was a very strange situation and we agreed to make it 'by mutual consent' as I had no intention of sacking him on the day before a game. It was not working as well as we all hoped and he had made some strange signings, which went against his normal policy of bringing in experience. None of them made much of an impression. I thought that he had lost his confidence."

"I went back, but it did not work out," Adams tells me. "I knew the club from before but I was not given enough time to allow things to gel. We did not get instant success first time round and this was no different. People just ran out of patience."

Just seven months after his return, Bob's future was again in doubt.

# CHAPTER 36
# RUSSELL SLADE

Jim Gannon, the manager of Stockport County, was Dick Knight's first choice to replace Micky Adams, having been impressed by his fluid, attacking style of football. Bob had played with Gannon at Sheffield United, but never thought his quiet, softly-spoken teammate would become a manager. Talks between Knight and Gannon went well, but he opted to remain at Stockport and was in charge when they played Albion on the last day of the season. His loyalty proved to be misplaced, suffering redundancy when the club went into administration.

Paul Ince wasn't interested and Knight decided that Nicky Forster was far more valuable scoring goals than standing on the touchline.

His third choice, Russell Slade, who had just left Yeovil Town, agreed to take the job until the end of the season, with the carrot of a £10,000 bonus if the team stayed up.

Slade is one of football's great survivors, managing 10 clubs over the past 23 years and knocking on the door of the 1,000 club, taking charge of more than 800 games. Often underestimated and taken for granted, he is a shrewd, skilled and proven operator, leading Grimsby, Yeovil and Leyton Orient to play-off finals while twice being named as League One manager of the year.

"Coaching is important but I think it was Steve Bruce who said that '80% of football management is about man management,'" says Slade. "I agree with him. The game can be very cruel but I realise that it does not owe me anything. I thrive on work and whenever I am at home for more than a couple of weeks, I fret and get stir crazy."

Slade was well aware of how difficult his task was. "They were struggling near the foot of the table with only 14 games left. Dick Knight made it clear that I was his third choice, but I was fine with that, as well as only having a contract until the end of the season. I was confident in my own ability." He told *The Argus* that he looked forward to "eight weeks of madness."

Introduced to Slade by Knight, Bob was delighted when his new boss shook his hand and remarked, "I'm sure we will get on as we are both Blades!" Slade had two spells as caretaker manager at Sheffield United.

Slade was happy to work with Bob, welcoming the continuity he provided. "Generally I know what I want so it's been fine to inherit someone," he says. "I worked well with Kevin Nugent at Orient and Charlton, but generally I do not take the same assistant from club to club. I treat people on their merits and make my own mind up."

"I had heard of Bob Booker and knew of his reputation. Bob was always so happy around the training ground. He was a really positive man who possessed the ability to walk into the dressing room and make all the players laugh. But he was also perfectly capable of having a go at them when he needed to. He was a good coach who loved his job and kept morale high."

Bob saw a kindred spirit in Slade. "He was bubbly and enthusiastic and a breath of fresh air, which was just what we needed at the time. Technically he was very good too. His strengths were his man management, organisation and attention to detail. He was very meticulous in his preparation and used flip charts in his team talks to ensure that everyone knew his role."

"I was still third in the pecking order, but I soon made it clear to Russell that I was best suited to becoming assistant manager again. He and I were doing most of the coaching anyway. Dean White's strengths were his knowledge of players and his ability to be blunt and honest and tell it as it was. I was more organised in terms of preparing and setting up coaching sessions, but we were good mates, juggled responsibilities and mucked in without upsetting each other, although my actual title did not change."

Initially, results remained poor. But Slade's first victory – a 5-0 thrashing of his old club, Yeovil – was particularly pleasing given the manner in which he had left them.

Bob could see the tide had turned. "The fans loved Russell's enthusiasm – he would run down the touchline whenever we scored and the players also responded to him. Gary Hart was rejuvenated, loanee Gary Dicker was excellent in midfield and Lloyd Owusu was magnificent – a real handful who scored some crucial goals."

"It was a hell of a fight and we won five of our last seven games before beating Stockport to stay up on the last day of the season. I had thrown myself back into my job and was pleased with my contribution."

# OOH-AAH: THE BOB BOOKER STORY

What Bob kept quiet at the time was a horrific and terrifying incident with long-term repercussions that took place in April when he and Nicky managed to take a few days off in Majorca.

"I fell asleep on the terrace after a boozy night out and eventually went to bed. I woke up at 4am feeling very strange. I went to the bathroom, looked in the mirror and my whole neck was swollen, my eyes were puffy, my airway blocked and I was struggling to breathe. I managed to wake Nicky up and pointed to my throat, which had closed up. I could now barely talk and I was going blue."

"She called the emergency number as I slumped to the floor and luckily there was a doctor nearby who gave me an injection of adrenalin and immediately called an ambulance. I was rushed to hospital and in my semi-conscious state when they wheeled me into intensive care I thought that I was dying. My whole life was flashing through my mind and I never thought that I would see my family and friends again."

Bob was in intensive care for two days. "The doctors had no real explanation but thought that a spider had crawled down my throat while I was asleep on the terrace and bitten my windpipe. Had the initial doctor not acted so speedily I might not have survived. I was in an awful state and didn't want to go back to the apartment. We came straight home but I broke down at the airport. I was very depressed and was off work for a few weeks. I spent most of my time crying in bed. I started taking an antidepressant, Mirtazapine, that helped, and Nicky's love and support kept me going. Everyone at the club, particularly Russell, was very sympathetic and understanding and eventually I managed to get back to work."

Nicky was worried that he wouldn't be able to cope, "I was concerned that all the football banter would be too much for him, but I think the players had been warned about his fragile state and were gentle with him. It was a terrible time. Sometimes I thought he was getting over it and then suddenly he'd just start crying again or refuse to go out. This was so unlike Bob that it made it even harder to bear. I just didn't know what to do to help him."

"The first time we returned to Majorca was horrendous. When we walked into the apartment, Bob screamed as if he was being murdered, which was terrifying to hear. We'd go out for dinner and he'd suddenly start crying in the middle of the restaurant. Once when we were in the supermarket I thought he was having a heart attack as he said his chest was hurting and he was sweating profusely. In fact it was a panic attack. It was like living with a time bomb. By the end of the stay I was so worried that I persuaded him to go to the doctor who diagnosed him with Post Traumatic Stress Disorder. His near death experience had really made him aware of his mortality and of those he loved. It was a terrible time but, because we're a strong couple, we got through it. Bob still has issues with mortality but I think he's got his head round it a bit more now, thank goodness."

Bob acknowledged, "I am normally upbeat and bubbly, but to this day I have anxiety attacks, sleep badly and get worried. I am still taking the pills."

Slade had impressed Knight, who enthused in *The Argus*, "He is very modern in his thinking, but retains the absolute fundamental quality of management which is the ability to motivate and get more out of a player than the individual perhaps even realises. The fans have embraced him and love him because he is human."

A massive change at the end of the season saw Knight step down and become life president after 12 years as chairman, making way for Tony Bloom, the major club benefactor who would be responsible for funding much of the cost of the new stadium. Knight's contribution cannot be overstated; without his passion, persistence, dedication, skill and sheer bloody-mindedness, the club would likely have folded.

He fully understood that Bloom would put his own stamp on things, moving quickly to offer Slade a new contract. "He had kept us up, so one of the last things I did before I stood down was to give Russell a two-year contract, as he deserved it. I also thought that he would probably not last too long under the new regime, which I felt wanted a higher-profile name in charge. He had done good work and it helped protect him."

Slade had developed an excellent relationship with Knight. He found Bloom "more distant and stats-based, but he treated me well."

Bob looked forward eagerly to the new season. "The money still wasn't very good but at least I was given a car allowance and share of player bonuses," he says, finding Bloom "pleasant, with a dry sense of humour."

Slade was allowed to recruit new players. On the recommendation of White and chief scout and former Brighton manager Barry Lloyd, he assembled excellent talent in Andrew Crofts, Elliott Bennett and Gary Dicker, pushing hard for the signature of striker Liam Dickinson, against Lloyd's advice. "He waddles around the pitch, he can't jump, his first touch is crap, can't head the ball," Lloyd said in Michael Calvin's *The Nowhere Men*. "The only thing he didn't do was put his hands in his pockets." The damning verdict proved correct for a striker who scored only four times in 27 league appearances – a total waste of £450,000.

The new arrivals and appointment of Bloom raised expectations, but Albion got off to a sluggish start. "Falmer was finally on the horizon," says Slade. "There was a change of approach and I feared that Tony Bloom wanted to hire a bigger name. I brought in some new players but we also lost 17 from the previous season. It takes a while for players to settle, and I was not given sufficient time."

Albion were in 20th place by the end of October, winning just three of their first 15 games, including a 7-1 mauling at Huddersfield. Six players had been sent off, 27 goals conceded. "Russell played a high tempo game and the players were pumped up," says Bob.

The fans were becoming increasingly vocal in their disapproval. Loud boos rang out at half-time of a 3-3 draw with Hartlepool at Withdean, heralding Bloom's decision to make a change. Slade, White and Bob were duly summoned to the Gatwick Hilton.

"Russell told me that his teams generally got off to a slow start and then built up steam as the season progressed," says Bob, discussing the firing squad. "There had been very few rumblings and the crowd still supported him, so I did not see this coming. I was very surprised when he rang to tell me that he had been sacked and that I would shortly be hearing from the managing director, Ken Brown."

"The dreaded call eventually came and I met Tony and Ken at the hotel. The chairman handled the situation himself, which I appreciated as he could have left it for his managing director. He said, 'It is time for a change, Bob. We are moving to the new stadium soon and we are going to make a clean sweep.' I said 'I would really like to have been there when we moved in, chairman, that was my goal.' He looked at me, shook his head and replied, 'I'm sorry about that, but this is simply a football decision. I have to make changes, shake things up and move this club on.' He shook my hand and said, 'I want to thank you for all the years you have been here. You have played a huge part in our success and been a great club servant.' I wished him and the club all the best, as he did me, and he told me that Ken would sort out my payoff, which he did."

"My departure was handled properly and with dignity. As far as I was concerned Tony Bloom was fully entitled to do whatever he felt was best for the club and I had no problems with him. I was upset that I would not help see the club into Falmer but I had to smile at the memory of a conversation I had had with Micky Adams the previous season. We had visited the site of the new stadium with the players and he turned round to me and whispered, *sotto voce*, 'Neither of us will be here to see it' – and he was right. As for Russell, I helped him move back to Grimsby and we have stayed friends ever since."

Bob had enjoyed his second spell at the club and felt as good as ever. "The players responded to me and I was just sad that it had been cut short before we arrived at Falmer – and after almost 16 months I was unemployed again."

# CHAPTER 37
# CODA

Bob analysed his strengths and weaknesses in the hope of staying in football and obtaining another coaching position outside of his immediate network of contacts.

"I passed my UEFA B Licence in 2001 but I thought that practical experience was far more valuable than theoretical, and that badges meant very little," he says. "I could organise and put on a decent session, keep control and improvise when I needed to. I could keep players interested and they respected me. My main strength was in demonstrating skills and techniques. Given my versatility as a player I had a good knowledge of every position. If I did a defending session I knew how they should react. I could show midfielders how to open their body up or look over their shoulder before they got the ball and from my experience up-front, I knew how to teach strikers how to receive the ball, turn and find space. I demanded high standards but knew when to crack the whip and when to ease off."

"I was also good at developing a rapport with referees, their assistants and fourth officials. Just as I had done as a player, I always called them by their first name and maybe it helped us from time to time. My main job on the bench was to control my manager and make sure he was not sent to the stands. Micky Adams and Steve Coppell were both very verbal. Peter Taylor would rant at the officials and Russell Slade would get in their faces. At Withdean, I always stood outside in the rain as the fans were not under cover and it was only fair that I got wet too."

Describing Bob's qualities, Dick Knight calls him, "The quiet assassin. He was very strong underneath that jovial, warm and likeable exterior. He was sharp and shrewd and one of the nicest people I ever met in football. I love people who combine professionalism, enthusiasm and a sense of humour and Bob Booker gets full marks in every category."

"He was a very good coach who understood how to get the best out of players, whatever their personality. Bob played a big part in the revival of Albion."

# CODA

Encouraged by Nicky, Bob took a proactive approach, writing to every club in the country offering his services, to no avail. He treasures a sensitive, kind and thoughtful handwritten reply from Sir Alex Ferguson, bolstering his spirits at a difficult time.

"Micky Adams did ask me to join him at Port Vale, Tranmere, and Sligo Rovers, but none of them sounded particularly attractive and the money offered was awful."

It was a different matter when Adams was appointed manager at his hometown club, Sheffield United, in December 2010. "That was the dream job for both of us and Micky asked me if I would be interested in joining him. I said 'Of course,' and was very excited at the prospect, but he decided to hire Alan Cork instead because of his recent experience coaching young players. I was disappointed, but it did not work out for Micky and he was sacked at the end of the season. In hindsight it was lucky I was not offered the job – it would probably have jeopardised my relationship with the club and fans when it all ended badly."

"I mentored Charlie Oatway and he had been gaining experience helping me look after the reserves at Brighton. He stayed on when Gus Poyet replaced Russell Slade and did a similar job to me, acting as his link to the players. Charlie called me the season after I left, asking if I would be interested in becoming the kitman. I jumped at the chance and was interviewed by Gus in my old office, which felt a bit weird. He described the role and I said, 'I know this club and how players work and have a lot of relevant experience.' He then asked, 'How would you feel if you're downstairs packing kit and we are outside training?' 'That would not bother me as my job would be doing the kit. I would not be coming in as a coach.' I was hopeful, but it all went quiet and I heard nothing for a long time until Charlie eventually let me know that Gus had decided to hire a younger lad in Chris Leppard."

"I also had the potential opportunity to join Southampton as kitman under Alan Pardew, but the job fell through and I was a victim of office politics."

"I reconciled myself to the fact that I was never going to get back into football and initially mourned my loss. But then I realised that I didn't need the pressure and hassle of being away so much and travelling up and down motorways. I wanted to be with Nicky and also visit Majorca more often. My time in football had come and gone and I was happy that was the case."

"It is not until you leave football and emerge from its bubble that you understand what else life can offer. I spent over 30 years working for Brentford, Sheffield United and Brighton and I could not have had a better time. I will never forget the amazing experiences that I had. But even if the phone rang tomorrow I would never go back."

"I worked as often as I wanted fitting kitchens for Bob Laundon, and my wages went up to £60 per day, but I was not getting any younger and did not want to do this for the rest of my life. Nicky had stopped working as a radio presenter and also had to make a difficult adjustment. She was now working in a doctors' surgery and we had to budget carefully as our joint incomes were massively reduced."

"We were sitting on the terrace in Majorca one day when Nicky said, 'Why don't you become a driving instructor? You'd be your own boss, you have brilliant people skills and it is a form of one-to-one coaching. It would really suit you.' This was a 'Eureka' moment and I am so grateful to my trainer Maggie Jakins, Mark Nicholson and Sue Blinco; without their support I would never have qualified. Eventually I earned my coveted green badge and I have been running my own business for the last 15 months and love every minute of it."

"I am still involved in football and I did get to Falmer after all for its opening day in 2011, as I was asked by Paul Rogers to work in the hospitality lounges. I now host the Rivervale Lounge and also do the match commentaries with Tim Humphrey on *Seagulls TV*. I work at every game and am so excited at how far the club has progressed." He calls Tony Bloom's chairmanship "astute," and Bob eagerly looks forward to the start of the new Premier League season.

"I am delighted with how well my two other former clubs are doing. I was honoured to be inducted into the Brentford hall of fame in November 2014 and am always made so very welcome whenever I return to Griffin Park. It is still the friendly club it always was and I will be forever grateful to them for giving me my start in football."

"I am so pleased for my friend Chris Wilder who has led Sheffield United to so much success. I go up there as often as possible for Q&A's in pubs and clubs and get a wonderful ovation when I go out onto the pitch. I still find it hard to believe that I have my name on a hospitality box as well as on the wall of fame and the statue of Derek Dooley – I am sandwiched between Joe Elliott and Brian Deane."

"I am blessed because I now have total contentment in my life. Nicky is my soulmate and we live in the beautiful Royal Oak Country Park in

Wineham which is a perfect setting for bird-watching. Its owners, Gordon, Sandra and Ollie, and his wonderful girlfriend, Ingrid have all become very special friends and we enjoy spending time with them."

"We spend increasing amounts of time in Majorca where we have made so many wonderful friends. Jaime Romero Galera's advice when we were buying our place made the process so easy. Billy and Irene Dipple have changed our lives. They may be a few years older than us but they have so much energy and enthusiasm that they put us to shame. Their friendship has enhanced our lives. When the four of us get together, we are constantly laughing plus eating and drinking far too much. They are retired so are fortunate enough to stay in Majorca from April to October each year, something that we aspire to when the time is right."

"Another family who have embraced us are the Orejuela Romeros who have a small restaurant in Cala San Vincente. It is owned and run by Poli and his beautiful wife, Francisca – both of whom are wonderful chefs. They have three boys who also help out in the restaurant – Dani, Poli Jnr and Alberto. We have enjoyed many a raucous night at their restaurant. At the end of the evening we always ask them to ring for a taxi, but they never will as one of them always drives us back. How thoughtful is that – although I suspect they use it as an excuse to get out of clearing up the restaurant at the end of the night!"

"We have a saying that we use with all of our friends in Majorca which is 'Amigo Para Siempre' and that means 'Friends For Life.' That is so true of all of these people. We love them all and they are a huge part of our lives."

"I am fortunate in that I can earn as much as I need, working as often as I want, doing something that I love which also fulfils me."

"I lost my beloved dad a couple of years ago, but my mum, Brenda, is still around, as is my mother-in-law."

"I am so happy with how things are now. My life has had its ups and downs but I have always tried to embrace things, take them in my stride and show enthusiasm, however menial the task."

"I really believe that some higher force has mapped out my life for me, given the strange manner in which so many things have occurred – and yet they always seem to turn out for the best."

"My ambition now is simply to carry on as I am and enjoy life with Nicky and our beloved Bichon Frise, Alfie."

The apprentice from the factory has come a long way.

Let's end with Nicky and her thoughts. "I feel like the luckiest woman alive to call myself Bob Booker's wife. He is the most thoughtful, kind, funny, loving person I have ever met. We went through a tough time to be together, but it was well worth it and I wouldn't change a thing."

# BIBLIOGRAPHY

Armstrong, Gary. *Blade Runners: Lives in Football*, Hallamshire Publications Ltd, 1998

Armstrong, Gary & Garrett, John. *Sheffield United FC – The Biography*, The Hallamshire Press, 2008

Barton, Joey. *No Nonsense: The Autobiography*, Simon & Schuster, 2016

Bassett, Dave. *Harry's Game*, Breedon Books, 1997

Bennett, Dean, Hazlewood, Paul & Levenson, Simon. *We Are Brighton!* Pitch Publishing, 2002

Calvin, Michael. *Family: Life, Death and Football: A Year on the Frontline with a Proper Club*, Corinthian, 2012

Calvin, Michael. *The Nowhere Men*, Century, 2013

Calvin, Michael. *Living on the Volcano: The Secrets of Surviving as a Football Manager*, Century, 2015

Camillin, Paul & Weir, Stewart. *Albion The first 100 years*, Pavilion Publishing, 2001

Clarebrough, Denis & Kirkham, Andrew. *Sheffield United: The Complete Record*, DB Publishing, 2012

Coumbe, Frank & Haynes, Graham. *Timeless Bees: Brentford F.C. Who's Who 1920-2006*, Yore Publications, 2006

Croxford, Mark, Lane, David & Waterman, Greville. *The Big Brentford Book of the Seventies*, Legends Publishing, 2011

Croxford, Mark, Lane, David & Waterman, Greville. *The Big Brentford Book of the Eighties*, Legends Publishing, 2011

Croxford, Mark, Lane, David & Waterman, Greville. *The Big Brentford Book of the Nineties*, Legends Publishing, 2013

Dooley Derek & Farnsworth, Keith. *Dooley! The Autobiography of a Soccer Legend*, Hallamshire Publications, 2000

Dunphy, Eamon. *Only a Game? Diary of a Professional Footballer*, Kestrel Books, 1976

Dunphy, Eamon. *The Rocky Road*, Penguin Ireland, 2013

# BIBLIOGRAPHY

Gernon, Alan. *Retired: What Happens to Footballers When* the *Game's Up*, Pitch Publishing, 2016

Hansen, Alan. *A Matter of Opinion*, Partridge Press, 1999

Haynes, Graham & Twydell, Dave. *Brentford F.C.: The Complete History 1889 – 2008*, Yore Publications, 2008

Johnson, Nick. *Sheffield United. Match of My Life*, Pitch Publishing, 2012

Knight, Dick. *Mad Man*, Vision Sports Publishing, 2013

Lane, David. *Cult Bees & Legends. Volume 1*, Legends Publishing, 2005

Lane, David. *Cult Bees & Legends. Volume 11*, Legends Publishing, 2005

McVay, David. *Steak... Diana Ross: Diary of a Football Nobody*, Reid Publishing, 2012

McVay, David. *Steak... Diana Ross 11: Further Diaries of a Football Nobody*, Reid Publishing, 2016

Nelson, Garry. *Left Foot Forward. A Year in the Life of a Journeyman Footballer*, Headline, 1995

Rosenior, Leroy. *"It's Only Banter,"* Pitch Publishing, 2017

Ward, Andrew & Williams, John. *Football Nation: Sixty Years of the Beautiful Game*, Bloomsbury Publishing, 2009

Woodhouse, Curtis. *Box to Box: From the Premier League to British Boxing Champion*, Simon & Schuster, 2016


**Newspapers, Newsletters, Magazines & Fans Forums**

Carder, Tim. *Albion Almanack*, 2000-2009

Beesotted

Brentford FC Matchday Programme

Evening Mail

Ealing Gazette

Flashing Blade Fanzine

FourFourTwo Magazine

Griffin Park Grapevine

Middlesex Chronicle

North Stand Chat

S24SU Forum

# BIBLIOGRAPHY

Sheffield Star & Green 'Un

Sheffield United Matchday Programme

The Argus

The Daily Telegraph

The Times

# ACKNOWLEDGMENTS

It really was not too difficult to get people to open up and talk about Bob Booker. In fact, the problem was generally getting them to stop, so well regarded is he. I interviewed the following people and I would like to thank them all for sparing the time to share their memories of Bob with me:

Micky Adams, Tommy Baldwin, Dave Bassett, Graham Benstead, Ray Bigger, Ian Bolton, Fred Callaghan, Steve Coppell, Terry Evans, Derek French, Barry Fry, Marcus Gayle, John Griffin, Ron Harris, Martin Hinshelwood, Phil Holder, Lee Holmes, Dick Knight, Pat Kruse, Neil Mason, Andy McCulloch, Mark McGhee, Frank McLintock, Gary Phillips, Gary Roberts, Mick Rooker, Andy Sinton, Russell Slade, Peter Taylor, Keith Tonge, Chris Wilder

Thank you to Bradley Walsh for writing such a warm and thoughtful foreword. Ben Miller worked so hard and so speedily and his editing suggestions immeasurably improved the text. The following were also extremely helpful to me in terms of providing general encouragement and advice, exchanging information and opinions, allowing me the use of their photographs, checking and confirming dates, facts and memories, reading chapters and making extremely helpful editing and proof reading suggestions.

Gary Armstrong, David Bolchover, Paul Briers, Matthew Bell, Nick Bruzon, Paul Camillin, Tim Carder, Mark Chapman, Mark Croxford, Simon Dack, Alex Fynn, John Garrett, David Lane, Jim Levack, Andy McWhirter, Andy Naylor, Tim Street, Nick Szczepanik, Paul Vernon, Ian Westbrook, Stewart Weir, Mick Wright

Thanks to all of you. Lastly, and most importantly, my thanks to Bob Booker and Nicky Keig-Shevlin without whom there would not be a book.

Bob and his dad playing football on the beach at Porthcawl, circa 1965

Rotherham v Brentford 17th October 1978. The first time Bob's name appeared in a first team programme – look at the spelling

● BUSY BEE . . . Bob Booker cracks his first goal past the despairing tackle of Hull defender Gordon Nisbet on the way to a sensational hat-trick at Griffin Park on Saturday.

● AT THE DOUBLE . . . Steve Phillips fires home his and Brentford's second goal.

● NOT THIS TIME . . . Booker gets in a brave header but Hull 'keeper Eddie Blackburn saved.

Bob's home debut and scoring a hat trick v Hull City,
8th December 1979

Challenging for the ball v Fulham, 29th August 1981

# Booker prize for versatility

BOB Booker, Brentford's "Mr. Versatility", is the Supporters Player of the Year for 1982/83, while tireless midfielder Terry Hurlock is the players' choice.

They received their awards at the annual Supporters Association dinner at the Winning Post in Whitton, on Friday night.

Hurlock was runner-up in the supporters' awards, and was also voted best player by the association's away travel coach section.

Top scorer Francis Joseph took third place with his 26 goals, teenager Terry Rowe was fourth after his first full season in league football, and Paddy Roche's penalty saves helped him to fifth place.

Rowe was just pipped by Hurlock for the players' award.

Utility man Booker is now a firm favourite with the Griffin Park crowd, although he was once a target for a section of "boo-boys". This season he wore every shirt except one and 11, and brought the same whole-hearted approach to whatever position he was asked to fill.

A delighted Bob told the Chronicle the award more than made up for the criticism to which he had been subjected in the past.

"It was hard at the time of the barracking," he said, "but I've put that behind me now. I'm just hoping to get a regular place in the side. My favourite position is midfield, but I'm willing to play anywhere."

Booker was a striker when he arrived at Brentford, but, despite scoring a hat-trick against Hull soon after his debut, he had an unhappy time as the Bees struggled to get goals. The turning point was when he came on as a substitute to play in midfield at Swindon in November 1981. Since then he has become a vital member of the squad, and has grown in confidence and composure.

## Servant

The Players' Player of the Year award is the George Weaver Memorial Trophy, set up in 1969/70 in memory of a man who was a great servant to the club on the social side. Mr. Weaver's widow, Elsie, presented the trophy to Hurlock.

Supporter of the Year was George Moore, who attended every match and social function throughout the season.

Association secretary Pat Brown received a special award from the away travel coach section.

Club chairman Martin Lange said there was a very good relationship between Brentford's players and supporters, and nobody had done more to communicate with the fans than Stan Bowles.

Lange recalled that he had only been in the chair for a few days when manager Fred Callaghan told him that he wanted to sign Bowles.

"I nearly had a fit," said Lange. "When we met Stan at the Hilton in West London, Fred's opening remark was to say jokingly, 'tell us what you want and then we'll order the double scotches to recover'. But Stan said he just wanted to play for Brentford."

Wishing Bowles good luck wherever he plays next season, Lange said: "It has been an absolute pleasure to have him at the club. He is still one hell of a footballer and one hell of an entertainer."

Lange said that this season's squad had been the strongest for many years, and it could be further strengthened when Callaghan signed the four or five new players he wants for next season.

Association chairman Peter Gilham said it had been "an exceptional year" in terms of support, and the behaviour of the fans had been "beyond reproach".

SUPPORTERS' choice—Bob Booker.

A proud moment. Bob voted Brentford player of the year 1982/83

In where it hurts. Bob scoring v Lincoln, 10th November 1984

Bob on the ball v Wigan, 8th September 1984

After the Freight Rover Trophy Final at Wembley, 1st June 1985

Bob celebrating Ian Bryson's winner for Sheffield United against
Chelsea, 16th March 1991

Bob captaining Sheffield United to promotion at Leicester, 5th May 1990

6th Round of the FA Cup, versus Manchester United, 11th March 1990

[Cover Image] Bob smiling at his dad on his First Division debut
versus Liverpool, 25th August 1990

Bob saying farewell to the United fans before the derby against
Sheffield Wednesday, 17th November 1991

Bob with Phil Holder. Re-signing for Brentford, November 1991

Bob's Testimonial programme v Sheffield United, 11th May 1990

Micky Adams and Bob with the Division 3 Championship Trophy,
6th May 2001. Photo courtesy of Stewart Weir

Bob celebrating Brighton's promotion from Division 2, in April 2002.
Photo courtesy of Mick Wright

Bob celebrating at the Millennium Stadium after they beat Bristol City in
the Second Division Playoff Final on 30th May 2004
Photo courtesy of The Argus

Robbie Savage and Bob (Head of Parking), 1st October 2008
Photo courtesy of Simon Dack

Bob, in full Freddie Mercury mode, entertaining the Brighton fans
Photo courtesy of The Argus

Bob and his first love, Bruno

Bob, with his mum and dad, 2001

Bob & Nicky

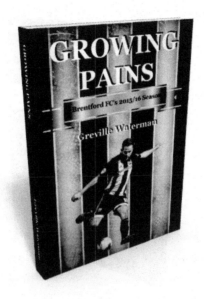
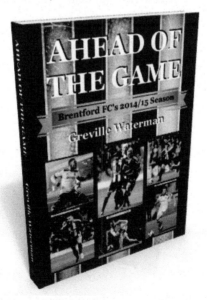

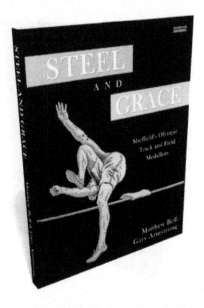
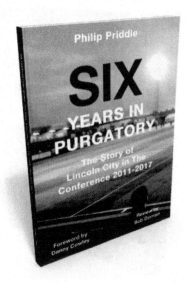